The Chicago American Giants

The Chicago American Giants

PAUL DEBONO

McFarland & Company, Inc., Publishers
Jefferson, North Carolina, and London

LIBRARY OF CONGRESS CATALOGUING-IN-PUBLICATION DATA

Debono, Paul.
The Chicago American Giants / Paul Debono.
p.   cm.
Includes bibliographic references and index.

ISBN-13: 978-0-7864-2590-7
ISBN-10: 0-7864-2590-3
(illustrated case binding : 50# alkaline paper) ∞

1. Chicago American Giants (Baseball team)
2. Negro American League.
3. Foster, Rube, 1879–1930.
I. Title.
GV875.C55D43 2007   796.357'640977311—dc22   2006026884

British Library cataloguing data are available

On the cover : Rube Foster (in suit) and his 1919 Chicago American Giants
(courtesy NoirTech Research, Inc.)

Manufactured in the United States of America

McFarland & Company, Inc., Publishers
Box 611, Jefferson, North Carolina 28640
www.mcfarlandpub.com

For Donita

Acknowledgments

I am grateful to the many who in some way had a hand in the writing of this book. My wife had extreme grace for me as I spent a good many evenings and weekends working on this text. I am thankful to the interlibrary loan department at the Cincinnati Public Library, the University of Cincinnati Library, the Chicago Public Library, the Chicago Historical Society, the Illinois State Archives, the National Baseball Hall of Fame, the Cook County Clerk of Courts and other institutions that provided access to the historical record. This work could not exist without the *Chicago Defender* newspaper.

I am indebted to fellow Negro League historians who laid much of the groundwork, including Richard Bak, Janet Bruce-Campbell, Dick Clark, Robert Cottrell, Roberto Gonzalez Echevarria, Leslie Heaphy, John Holway, Neil Lanctot, Larry Lester, Jerry Malloy, Kyle McNeary, Robert Peterson, James Riley, Donald Rogosin, Jules Tygiel, Charles Whitehead and others.

It is a foregone conclusion that most baseball historians are members of a very good organization called SABR (Society for American Baseball Research). I am grateful, not only that such a well run grassroots organization exists, but that it continually improves. This book is light on what some have typically called SABRmetrics; fortunately, SABR is much, much more than a guild of statisticians. I would like to thank all of the fellow SABR members who have given moral support over the years. There is no way to measure the value of encouragement, camaraderie, feedback and the spirit of cooperation.

In the late 1980s I met a passionate baseball researcher from Chicago named Jerry Malloy. Jerry helped me out with the early stages of this book. I was planning to lean on Jerry for more assistance finishing the book, but sadly I received an email in September 2000 that Jerry Malloy had died suddenly of a brain aneurysm. News of Jerry's death sent a shock wave through our little baseball research community. I was lucky enough to attend a memorial for Jerry, and there I was amazed to learn how many lives he had touched. Jerry had a lot to say about Negro League baseball history in Chicago. I wish he could have looked over this work as he had generously offered. We miss Jerry very much.

Lastly I am thankful to the many veterans of the Negro Leagues I have been privileged to meet over the years. I have met some in a group setting, some up close and personal. Former Memphis Red Sox pitcher Charlie Davis is a neighbor of mine and always has time to share a story from the Negro Leagues. Bobby Robinson and William Owens (who both at one time played for the American Giants) sat down with me and shared their memories in depth. Both gentlemen have since passed. I met with the King, Theodore "Double Duty" Radcliffe, on a few occasions. On one occasion "Duty" hosted my wife and me for an impromptu visit in his South Side Chicago apartment. Duty had a fantastic memory and shared with me little details, like the exact location of the hotel he stayed at in Cincinnati in 1936. Just days before the completion of this manuscript Theodore Radcliffe died at the age of 103.

Table of Contents

Introduction: Giants of American Sport

The story of the Chicago American Giants is a grand chapter in the history of American sport. With all that has been written, filmed, recorded and digitally stored about baseball, it is a wonder that the story of the Chicago American Giants hasn't been more widely circulated. The history of the Chicago American Giants is as vital to the subject of baseball history as, say, biology is to science. Just as no survey of American history would neglect Abraham Lincoln, no survey of baseball history can neglect Andrew "Rube" Foster. No less than iconic teams like the New York Yankees, the Chicago American Giants are part of American culture; yet although one can find countless books about the Yankees, or the Green Bay Packers or the Boston Celtics, books about the Giants are rare.

That is not to say that the story of the Chicago American Giants and their leader Rube Foster is unknown. Every serious work on the history of baseball makes mention of Rube Foster and the American Giants. Andrew "Rube" Foster was enshrined in the National Baseball Hall of Fame for his service to the game. You will find bits and pieces of the American Giants' history whenever the subject of Negro League baseball comes up. When you hear that *whole story* about how major league legends like Jackie Robinson, Willie Mays or Hank Aaron got their start, there will always be a connection to a mentor behind their career who played with or against the American Giants. The wrongs of omission are similar to the wrongs of commission: both denigrate the accomplishment of athletic greatness. The body of work about Negro League history has expanded a great deal in recent years, yet it is slight in comparison to the volumes on major league ball weighing down library shelves for the last century. Negro league achievements have been recollected largely through oral history passed down from grandfathers and fathers who played in or attended the games.

A goal of this book is to collect in one place the important facts about the Chicago American Giants and to chronicle the life of the organization from its roots in the late nineteenth century until its gradual demise in the 1950s. Much of the work here is collecting the various pieces and putting them together. It is impossible to be comprehensive in approaching this subject. Sadly, a great deal of the American Giants' history either was never recorded or has been lost. Even so, the Chicago American Giants was black baseball's busiest team and there is simply too much history for one volume. This book is not a comprehensive history, nor is it intended to be. I apologize in advance for the omission of certain people and events that were part of the American Giants' history not given mention in this work. I also apologize for the inevitable errors that occur when undertaking work of this sort, including misspellings and errors of fact that sometimes find their way into retelling of history. As every journey begins with a small step, this history is intended as a small and simple step toward paying just due to one of baseball's greatest teams. My deepest hope is that this work will lead to a fuller telling of the story of the American Giants, and that meanwhile it will be useful to casual reader and entrenched researcher alike.

The Chicago American Giants got their start at the end of the nineteenth century. The seeds of organized baseball found fertile ground in Chicago. A black semi-pro team known as the Unions Baseball Club was formed in 1886. The Unions became established and played in the local semi-pro league otherwise made up of white teams. Under the leadership of Frank Leland, the Unions went to the top of Chicago's semi-pro city league. After the color line was officially drawn in organized baseball, Chicago was a magnet for top black players and teams.

In 1902, Frank Leland recruited a young pitcher from East Texas named Andrew Foster. Besides uncanny abilities on the mound, Andrew Foster had a knack for organization.

Eventually it came to pass that Foster seized the reins from Frank Leland and established the Chicago American Giants. Rising from the black metropolis of Chicago's South Side, the American Giants became the most prolific team in black baseball. Success for Rube and the American Giants came naturally, although not easily. In the end Rube Foster's American Giants changed America. Even the word "America" was changed by Rube Foster's American Giants, chiseled in such a way that "American" became a fitting namesake for a team of excellent professional black ball players. Along the way Rube Foster organized and guided the Negro National League, which was for all intents and purposes a black major league. The Negro National League, referred to here as the "NNL," became the model for subsequent African American professional baseball leagues.

The father of black baseball, Andrew "Rube" Foster, died in 1930 in an Illinois state mental hospital, seventeen years before Jackie Robinson joined the major leagues. To hear the story of the integration of major league baseball as it is sometimes portrayed, Jackie Robinson and Branch Rickey were the two men who came up with the idea of integrating baseball. While no one would seek to diminish the bravery of Jackie Robinson or the vision of Branch Rickey, it is simply wrong to misplace the credit for integrating baseball. Colleagues and contemporaries called Rube Foster the Father of Black Baseball, and he deserves a lion's share of credit for paving the way for blacks in baseball. Even after a renaissance in baseball history, the vast majority of fans still don't know the name Rube Foster. So, the story of the unsung Father of Black Baseball is told here once again.

Rube Foster's career and life story is intrinsically bound with the history of the American Giants, but this book is a history of the American Giants, not a biography of Rube Foster. One of the challenges here is to give shape to the figures who were overshadowed by Rube. Even as research historians have unwound the history of black baseball, there are a handful of American Giant players whose stories have not been fully told. Yet almost certainly some of these obscured players probably deserve the highest form of baseball recognition: induction into the Hall of Fame.

Rube died during the Great Depression, a time when Negro League baseball was faced with severe challenges and possible extinction. On the financial end the Chicago American Giants sometimes found themselves at the mercy of certain white rooks who tried to turn a fast buck. In the dugout one of Rube's star pupils, Dave Malarcher, became the point man in Chicago and kept the winning tradition alive. In the post–Rube Foster era it was half-brother Willie Foster who starred on the mound for the American Giants. In 1933, the first major league All-Star game and the annual Negro League All-Star classic were initiated at Comiskey Park in Chicago. From that day forward the annual East-West Negro League game became one of the biggest events in black sport.

In the late 1930s, a wily old veteran of Negro League baseball named "Candy" Jim Taylor (who had played against Rube way back in 1909) took over management of the American Giants. Candy Jim remained skipper off and on through the World War II years until his death in April 1948 just as Roy Campanella and Satchel Paige were set to join the major leagues. The American Giants continued to play ball even as their longtime South Side neighbors the Chicago White Sox finally signed their first African American players in 1951. Opportunities in organized ball had remained scarce for African Americans even after Jackie, and the Chicago American Giants remained an option for prospective players unable to sign with a big league organization.

Baseball history is not a tale with a beginning and an end. It turns out that compiling a definitive history of baseball is impossible. It was once supposed that the tale of a white boy named Abner Doubleday who invented baseball might be forced on an innocent public. Instead inquisitive baseball lovers have gone to every corner of the Earth seeking and finding pieces of the real story of baseball. There is a lot of baseball history out there. For some, baseball will always be the sport of Midwestern farm boys; for others the sport belongs to Caribbean islanders, and to others baseball is the game of tough inner-city kids.

At times baseball historians have expended a lot of hot air discussing unanswerable questions like "What if the great black ball players had played against the great major leaguers of the day?" Poor record keeping meant that the accomplishments of many Negro League players were lost, and consequently their play was disparaged or discounted. In recent years, though, most baseball scholars have come full circle to acknowledge, appreciate and even idolize these "invisible men" of baseball.

My own appreciation of Negro League history stems from a childhood fascination for Hank Aaron's pursuit of Babe Ruth's home run record. I was enlightened when a local columnist wrote about Hank's early days with the Indianapolis Clowns. I grew up in Indianapolis and like many Midwesterners, even those from far-flung towns in Iowa and Indiana, I found the city of Chicago a magnet of interest. I never witnessed a Negro League baseball game. I never lived on Chicago's South Side. While I have been fortunate to meet a number of former American Giants players over the years, my vantage point has mostly been from a library microfilm reader. I do remember seeing old Comiskey out the window of the family station wagon en route to vacation in Wisconsin — the closest I came to visiting those hallowed grounds.

One of the first Negro League baseball historians— Robert Peterson — stated in his classic work *Only the Ball Was White*: "Tracing the course of the organized Negro leagues is rather like trying to follow a single black strand through a ton of spaghetti. The footing is infirm, and the strand has a tendency to break off in one's hand and slither back into the amorphous mass." The historical terrain of Negro League baseball is slippery throughout. It is true that record keeping was incomplete or non-existent. Let us remember that no record keeping is perfect. Many of the so-called all- time records some fans hold as absolute fact are in fact debatable (influenced as they are by a lowered pitcher's mound, a diluted pool of players, a different strike zone, the designated hitter, and other variables). The ongoing effort of a few to compile the statistical records of the Negro Leagues demands the recognition of serious fans and historians.[1]

The American Giants were just that: "Giants" in the annals of baseball. Their legend was born during a time and place of great change, America in the first half of the twentieth century. The footprints of these Giants are found from Cuba to Europe (where some players served in World War I). The base-paths were especially well worn in the Midwestern United States, but also in the Deep South, Florida, New York, and Canada, and westward to California and Washington State.

What follows is a collection of American Giants history. Much of the history has been told before in bits and pieces, but here it is collected together. Most of the factual accounts are gleaned from the pages of the *Chicago Defender* although other newspaper archives were also researched. I was fortunate to meet and interview a few of the living veteran players who shared a glimpse of Negro League baseball with me. I was also aided by the work of fellow baseball history buffs like Richard Bak, Janet Bruce-Campbell, Dick Clark, Robert Cottrell, Roberto Gonzalez Echevarria, Leslie Heaphy, John Holway, Neil Lanctot, Larry Lester, Jerry Malloy, Kyle McNeary, Robert Peterson, James Riley, Donald Rogosin, Jules Tygiel, Charles Whitehead and others. It is humbling to walk in the footsteps of Giants.

✳✳✳

In the weeks after completion of the manuscript, the National Baseball Hall of Fame inducted the following Negro League players and executives: Ray Brown, Willard Brown, Andy Cooper, Frank Grant, Pete Hill, Biz Mackey, Effa Manley, José Méndez, Alex Pompez, Cum Posey, Louis Santop, Mule Suttles, Ben Taylor, Cristóbal Torriente, Sol White, J.L. Wilkinson and Jud Wilson.

Pete Hill, Cristóbal Torriente and Mule Suttles were key players with the American Giants. Preston "Pete" Hill's inclusion is expecially noteworthy as it stands too as acknowledgment of the team he captained.

1

Prelude

It was Juneteenth 1892 in Calvert, Texas. While emancipation celebrations became universal throughout black American communities, "Juneteenth" got its start in East Texas. It's called that because it was June 19, 1865, when General Gordon Granger landed in Galveston, Texas, with a regiment of Union Army troops and read the Emancipation Proclamation, two and a half years after the proclamation of January 1863.

A whole hog was roasting on the spit. A group of men basted the meat from big pots of barbecue sauce. There were banjo players, drumming and dancing. A preacher set up his podium under a small tent and praised the Lord. Yonder in a cow pasture a group of men were tossing a ball and hitting it with a slab of wood.

One of the men hit a ball far and it rolled not far from where a young boy named Andrew Foster was walking. Andrew picked up the ball, walked over to the group of men and threw the ball toward one of the men. The ball landed with a hard pop right into the player's hands.

"Hey we got a ballplayer," the man said.

"Boy you play ball?" The man asked young Andrew.

"Yes. I can play ball," Andy said.

"Okay son how 'bout you get up here on these here pitcher's mound and toss it." The husky 13-year-old, who might have passed for a young looking 16-year-old, took the mound.

The young kid showed stature on the mound, even striking out some of the full-grown men. He was just a kid, but a kid who was devoted to baseball. He played baseball almost every day. When he wasn't actually on the ball field, he was raising a team, making a baseball with pieces of twine and old rags, or scrounging lumber suitable for a baseball bat. So while some were surprised to see this boy throw the ball better than a man, those who had observed Andy growing up, whiling away the hours playing ball in the pasture, were hardly surprised.

He was born with an asthma condition, but was raised to believe that outdoor exercise would help him reach manhood. His mother worried that all that ball playing would aggravate her son Andy's asthma condition and always told him every chance she got "take care of yourself, and don't stay out too long playing baseball." Andy's mother passed and it was left to his father Andrew Sr. to raise him.[1]

Andy's ball playing had actually been a topic of conversation among the elders in the community. He had been born in Calvert, Texas, on September 17, 1879; his father, Andrew Sr., was the head of the local AME church. The townspeople were miffed at how the preacher's son could be running around playing "base ball," recruiting their children to play.

Andrew Sr. had lectured his son at great length on several occasions. Andy promised to stay out of trouble, and while he wasn't openly rebellious, his definition of "stayin' out of trouble" did not include quitting baseball. Rev. Andrew Sr. was certain his preteenage son, who was good with words, both reading and writing, would outgrow these games.

Andy did his best in school, and with chores, but day after day he found himself drawn to the baseball diamond. While his father discouraged his preoccupation, Andy Foster realized he had a gift from God. The ability to throw a sphere, the ability to strategize and organize. Andy had a vision that somehow his future as a grown-up would have something to do with baseball.

The day came when a manager of one of the grown-up teams offered Andy a chance to make a little money. "It works like this son, everyone puts in some money and the winning team splits it up. You want in Andy?" the manager said.

"I only have couple dimes," Andy said. They allowed him to play anyway, and as the pitcher no less. Andy Foster won that game, and was rewarded by the manager with 3 bits.

While Andy didn't consider playing baseball for stakes "gambling," others did; so Andy tried to hide the activity from his father and the churchgoers. He left school while in the eighth grade to try to make a living at baseball. As Andy grew into a young man there was no hiding his natural baseball abilities. Everyone in Calvert, even white folks, heard that this big kid, Andy Foster, was the best baseball pitcher around. Andy's reputation was fueled whenever a team from Waco or Houston passed through town. At the Juneteenth celebration of 1895 in Calvert there was a larger crowd gathered around the baseball diamond watching young Andy than there was under the tent listening to the Rev. Andrew Foster Sr. This infuriated the minister, who had continued to hope that his son would put his abilities as an organizer and a talker to work for God as a preacher. Andrew Foster Sr. even went so far as to try to enroll Andy Jr. in Tillotson College in Austin, Texas, to study divinity. Andy Foster's main interest at school was the Tillotson baseball team. Soon afterwards Foster left school to pitch for the Waco Yellow Jackets. He became the top right-hander for the Yellow Jackets, touring Texas and the south central states. Thus began his education in the ways of professional baseball.[2]

2

The City of Big Shoulders and Giants (1870–1900)

Hog butcher for the world,
Tool maker, stacker of wheat,
Player with railroads and the nation's freight handler;
Stormy, husky, brawling….
— Carl Sandburg, "Chicago" (1916).

The reason there were so many Giants was that many newspapers across the country refused to print pictures of black people. But there were a lot of excellent black teams around, and they were a big attraction, even in predominantly white towns. So Giants became a code word. If you saw a placard in a store window or an advertisement in the newspaper announcing that the River City Giants were coming to town to play the local semipro team, you knew right away that the visiting team was a black one. I think everybody in the Negro leagues was a Giant at least once. I was a Giant three times.
— John Buck O'Neil, *Right on Time* (1996).

1870–1900

The Chicago White Stockings, organized as challengers to the first professional team, the Cincinnati Red Stockings, became a member of the first professional baseball league — the National Association — in 1871. In October of that same year the great Chicago fire destroyed their ballpark, uniforms, business records, score books. Mrs. O'Leary's cow kept Chicago out of major league baseball until 1874.

As Chicago rose from the ashes it reinvented itself and all things human. The ruins and debris of the city after the fire were pushed into low lying flood prone areas to make way for the first modern skyscrapers, art museums, factories as well as baseball fields. Architects, industrialists, business people, and laborers worked together to build a bigger and better city. The city previously known for its shoddy housing and filth would make itself over as the "greatest city in the world" for the Columbian Exposition of 1893. Chicago reinvented baseball too.

Baseball at one time was purely a game, but professional baseball became a business. Baseball *the business* was born in Chicago. Chicago White Stockings team president

William Ambrose Hulbert, with Chicagoan Albert Goodwill Spalding at his side, founded the baseball National League in 1875. Spalding, the founder of the sporting goods company that bears his name, was a member of the set of Chicago capitalists like Pullman, Sears & Roebuck, Armour, Montgomery Ward, and Marshall Field whose names were ingrained in the American mind as name brands.

The Chicago White Stockings won the National Association pennant five times in the 1880's. The White Stockings (actually predecessors to the NL Cubs not the White Sox), backed by wealthy Chicago notables like Potter Palmer and George Pullman along with team president Albert Spalding, had an abundance of capital which allowed them to shop for the best players. Fans packed Lakeside Park (at Randolph and Michigan streets) for most games. The park could hold about 10,000 fans and was considered the finest baseball park in the land.

Some of the world's first baseball journalists reported on the fervent goings on at the ball yard. Finley Peter Dunne of the *Chicago Daily News* is credited with coining the phrase "southpaw" because left-handed pitchers at Lakeside Park threw from the south side. Hugh Fullerton and Ring Lardner later came on the scene to raise the craft of baseball writing to an art.

Chicago White Stocking manager and first baseman from 1876 to 1897, Adrian "Cap" Anson, was the greatest major league player of the nineteenth century. He was the first player ever to compile 3,000 hits in the majors, he was the prototype slugger and won five pennants as a manager. History remembers too, that Cap Anson used his influence as a star and leader to exclude African Americans from organized baseball. Anson was the instigator in an incident that has been called "the beginning of the color line in professional baseball."

A small number of African American players were in organized professional baseball from 1874 to 1888. Notable among those early black pioneers were pitcher George Stovey and catcher Moses Fleetwood Walker. Walker was regarded as the first black to play in the major leagues, as a catcher with the American Association Toledo Blue Stockings in 1884 (although recent research shows that William Edward "Bill" White, who played in one game for the NL Providence Grays in 1879, was indeed of African American ancestry).[1] George Stovey was one of the top pitchers of his era, winning 30 games for Jersey City of the International League in 1886 — a league record that stands today. In 1887, Stovey and Walker both played for the Newark Little Giants.

Cap Anson's Chicago White Stockings were scheduled to play the Newark Little Giants in a mid-season exhibition July 14, 1887. At the time the New York Giants were prospecting for pitchers in an effort to dethrone the pale hose and had hoped to enlist Stovey.

The hour of the contest was approaching and the Newark battery began warming up.

"That's the way to throw it, Stove, way to put 'er in there," said Fleet. No catcher could catch Stovey like Moses Fleetwood Walker.

Fans began to fill the park. A brass band was playing a melody, which had fans loosely clapping along. An announcer with a megaphone came onto the field to announce the start of the game.

The White Stockings had warmed up, and were sitting in the dugout, when their manager Cap Anson walked out to home plate. Anson walked up to the umpire, looked in the direction of George Stovey and Fleet Walker and instructed the umpire and said, or is purported to have said, "Get that nigger off the field."

The music from the brass band had now died. The Newark manager came out to the plate and a discussion ensued.

"We will go ahead and forfeit if need be. I don't give a damn if you pay me or not," Anson said.

The manager of the Newark Little Giants walked over to Stovey, and said, "George, give me the ball."

"Walker, you too. Sorry fellas there's nothing I can do," said the manager.

Stovey and Walker walked off the field.

Anson's racist views were known throughout baseball, dating back to a game in Toledo in 1883 when he threatened to take his team off the field if Moses Fleetwood Walker were allowed to play. On that occasion Anson's White Stockings finally played when it was made clear to him that there would be no share of the gate if he walked off. The fact that Stovey would have been highly visible in his role pitching against, and possibly defeating, the White Stockings was too much for the intolerant Anson to bear.[2]

Sol White wrote in 1906:

> Were it not for this man [Anson] there would have been a colored player in the National League in 1887. John W. Ward was anxious to secure Stovey.... [Anson's] repugnant feeling shown at every opportunity, toward colored ball players, was a source of comment through every league in the country and his opposition, with his great popularity and power in base ball circles, hastened the exclusion to the black man from the white leagues.[3]

Blame for baseball's color line was laid at the feet of Cap Anson, but clearly others shared responsibility. The dynamics of race relations that led to baseball's color line were complex. Blacks played baseball against whites in Cuba and that was considered "okay." Blacks also participated in horse racing, boxing and bicycle racing in the U.S. without the same type of objections.

From the vantage point of the Columbian Exposition of 1893 — an event to highlight "social progress" — can be seen a sample of climate of race relations at the time. The Columbian Exposition was the crowning achievement of Chicago after rising out of the ashes. Visitors came from all over the world, spending literally small fortunes to see Chicago. The exhibition that showcased the Western Hemisphere at the end of the nineteenth century ignored the contributions of blacks to the growth of the United States. Frederick Douglass was tucked away at the fair as the official representative of Haiti, in the "Haitian Pavilion." A feature of the fair was the creation of a model city called the "White City," and for black Chicagoans, that term may as well have been interpreted literally.

Frederick Douglass was offended by the exhibition and contributed to a pamphlet published by Ida B. Wells titled "The Reason Why the Colored American Is Not in the World's Columbian Exposition: The Afro-American's Contribution to Columbian Literature." The pamphlet, which was also published in French and German, spelled out for the whole world the abuses suffered by blacks in America and documented the rejection by Exposition planners of African Americans.

While the magnates of Chicago perfected the business of baseball, the people of Chicago perfected baseball "the game" in amateur leagues. Every enclave, suburb, borough, sect, parish, tavern, guild, union, school and ethnic group fielded a baseball team. These teams and leagues were known collectively as the City Leagues. The introduction of *Spalding's Chicago Amateur Baseball Guide of 1904* gives a glimpse:

> Other cities are supporting two big base ball clubs the same as Chicago, but no city has even a small proportion of the amateur leagues or as great a number of players as our city.
>
> Were all the men in Chicago thrown out of the leagues the lineup of nearly every big team would be changed and the pennant races in most of them would assume an entirely different aspect. This draft of players into the big leagues has gone on for a quarter of a century each year seeing a larger exodus of players from this city than in preceding years and it has come to be recognized by the players and magnates alike that the most profitable ground in the country to scour for new talent is the amateur diamonds of Chicago.
>
> … It would appear that the big leagues would draw away all of the really first-class talent that Chicago possesses each year, but this is far from being the case as many of the local players have declined positions with the big league for business reasons, lawyers doctors and other professional and business men preferring to play with clubs in the city than go on the road and lose the opportunity to establish themselves in business while they are still young, declining the big salaries offered them on this account. The list of men to whom this rule applies is a long one and is increasing every year.
>
> … By actual count there are one hundred and ninety four teams signed in the local leagues making ninety-seven games each week during the season. A fair estimate of the players who actually get into a base ball uniform once a week during the summer in Chicago will be easily 5000. The spectators at the games will easily run to 50,000 each week.... [4]

Among the many leagues mentioned in the baseball guide were the Bankers League, Jewelers League, Bible Class League, Presbyterian League, Catholic Order of the Foresters League, Railway Freight Clerks League, Boot and Shoe League, Streetcar Men's League.

The City Leagues were organized in the 1880's concurrent with the success of the big leagues. Interest in the City Leagues faded somewhat in the late 1890's when the Spanish-American War drew many young Chicagoans to war. Shortly after the turn of the century until the mid–1910's was the heyday of the City Leagues, but semi-pro baseball continued on in some form or fashion throughout the segregated era of baseball.

The first black baseball teams of the nineteenth century were formed by barbers, porters and Civil War veterans. Initially games were played only a few times a year by gentlemen during holiday picnics. By 1870, a black team known as the Chicago Blue Stockings had defeated another black team, the Rockfords, for the state "colored" championship. Paralleling the baseball explosion in the white community in the late 1800's, black neighborhoods, organizations and guilds formed "nines." From these early clubs came the first black professional teams.[5]

Black baseball teams participated in the City Leagues from the beginning. The inclusion of black teams in the City Leagues might reflect more the attempted efforts of white Chicago to maintain an appearance of mastery, rather than a sincere gesture of social equality. As it turned out though, the top black team in the City Leagues, laden with major league caliber talent, would eventually come to dominate and outclass the white competition of the Chicago semi-pro circuit. This upset some of the white players who were ashamed to admit defeat at the hands of black players.

Among Chicago black teams in 1886 the "Unions" emerged as the cream of the crop. The Chicago Unions took the fight for a "nation conceived in liberty and dedicated to the proposition that all men are created equal" to the baseball field. The smoke from Civil War battlefields had only recently cleared when professional baseball was born.

The Unions changed their official name from the "Union Baseball Club" to the "Chicago Unions" in 1888. The Unions were a cut above the weekend amateur clubs. They played regularly against both black and white teams in Chicago, winning most games. The Unions secured a home field on Chicago's South Side in 1891 at 67th and Langley, prior to that they played at opponents' parks or at impromptu ballparks drawn out on a field or "on the prairie" in the parlance of the day.

In 1894, the Chicago Unions moved to a park near 39th and Wentworth; known for a time as Chicago Cricket Club Grounds, this vicinity eventually became baseball head-quarters for the South Side of Chicago— near the site for Comiskey Park. The Cuban Giants (of New York, not Cuba), known as the first salaried professional black baseball team, traveled to play the Chicago Unions in 1894. While the game was billed as a championship, it was little more than an exhibition for the Cuban Giants who made short order of the Unions. The Unions continued to improve, and employed the maneuvers on and off the field: training, recruiting, promoting in order to come out on top. By 1896, they played a full schedule against Chicago teams on the weekends and toured Indiana, Illinois, Wisconsin, Michigan and Iowa to take on "all comers" during the week.

Notable among the Union ballplayers were outfielders Mike Moore and pitcher/utility man Harry Buckner. Mike Moore wowed fans with spectacular catches and clutch hitting. Harry Buckner began his career as a pitcher for the Unions in 1896. Buckner was the ace of the Unions and during his career he also played infield, outfield and catcher. Mike Moore and Harry Buckner would extend their professional baseball career beyond the Unions, both later playing for notable black teams like the Cuban X-Giants, the Philadelphia Giants, the New York Lincoln Giants, as well as the later elite professional teams of Chicago.

Among several Union ballplayers noted for off-field accomplishments were W.S. Peters, Frank Leland and Dave Wyatt. W.S. Peters and Frank Leland became part owners in the team as well as playing, managing and officiating. W.S. Peters, who played first in 1887, became the manager in 1890 and stayed in that position until the Chicago Unions split up in 1901. Peters remained a baseball manager until 1917. Playing outfield for the 1887 Unions was Fisk University graduate Frank Leland. Leland stayed with the club and eventually became co-manager for the Unions in 1889.

After the Chicago Unions split up in 1901, Frank Leland took one contingent and founded the Chicago Union Giants. Leland's team was actually the beginning of the Chicago American Giants; it was the same "franchise" that would later be known as the American Giants. Unions middle infielder Dave Wyatt, who had limited skills on the diamond, would discover his calling as a baseball journalist. Wyatt went on to become the most prolific chronicler of early professional black baseball, writing for black papers like the *Chicago Whip*, the *Indianapolis Freeman* and the *Chicago Defender*. In 1920, Wyatt was tapped to help write the charter of the Negro National League.

In 1899, the "Page Fence Giants," a traveling team formerly based in Adrian, Michigan (southeast Michigan), relocated to Chicago and changed their name to the Columbia Giants. The Page Fence Giants were among the greatest black teams of the nineteenth century. The team was founded in 1894 by Bud Fowler (real name John Jackson) and Grant

"Home Run" Johnson. Grant Johnson earned his nickname as a semi-pro player in Findlay, Ohio. It is unknown why Fowler chose his alias, but it is believed that Fowler was the first professional African American baseball player. Fowler began his career with a team from Chelsea, Massachusetts, in 1878 and played in minor league baseball into the 1890's. Fowler left the Page Fence Giants after one year, and would later have a hand in organizing a number of other barnstorming teams. Other notable Page Fence Giants included George "Chappie" Johnson (a stalwart of early black baseball), Charles Grant (who would one day be recruited by legendary skipper John McGraw) and Sol White (author of *History of Colored Baseball*).

The Page Fence Giants punctuated their existence with such flair that they were long remembered. They roamed the country in a private Pullman emblazoned with an advertisement for the sponsoring Page Fence Company. As well as being a showcase of top black players, the Page Fence Giants included some comic entertainment at their engagements. They were said to have paraded from the train to the ballpark riding bicycles. While the Indianapolis Clowns would be crowned the kings of baseball comedy in the 1940's, baseball laced with humor dated back to the previous century.

The Page Fence Giants became a refuge for the top black players, who by that time had been barred from organized baseball. The Page Fence Giants dominated their opponents; in 1897 for instance they won some 125 games. The Page Fence Giants disbanded after 1898, but they resurfaced in Chicago with new sponsorship from an elite black social club known as the Columbia Club; hence their new name "the Columbia Giants."[6]

The appearance of the Columbia Giants in Chicago upset the balance of black baseball power in Chicago. No longer could the Chicago Unions claim to be the best in town. The two teams competed for fans, playing facilities and players. Fans took notice of the virtually unbeatable Columbia Giants, but the Unions still remained a strong team.

The friction between the two teams was so intense that the Unions refused to play against the Columbia Giants during the 1898 season, or perhaps the Unions realized that the Columbia Giants had them outclassed. The two teams would play for a post-season championship series in 1899. While the Columbia Giants were favored, the outcome of the series was by no means a given. The Unions retained Harry Hyde and Mike Moore, both of whom could break a game open. Fans and players were worked up to a fervor for the championship. When bat came to ball, the Columbia Giants methodically took five games in a row from the Unions, laying claim to the Chicago championship honors, and also the lion's share of the gate receipts.

Both the Unions and the Columbia Giants rarely lost a game. They were professionals, who trained, practiced and played together; their competition were amateur or semi-professional teams—haplessly hoping to pull out an impressive win. Winning was tradition for the top Chicago black teams. Despite the fact that there may have been hometown umps for the opposition, and fans mixing in racial slurs with jeers, the Unions and the Columbia Giants found a way to win. Summing up the record of the Unions over 12 seasons and 743 games, Sol White credited them with 613 wins, 118 losses and 2 ties, or a winning percentage of .814. The winning percentages of the Page Fence/Columbia Giants were similarly impressive.[7]

The Cuban X-Giants traveled from New York to Chicago in 1899 to play the Unions in a series of fourteen games. The Cuban X-Giants won nine of the contests. A more competitive match would have been between the X-Giants and the Columbia Giants, but the X-Giants weren't interested in playing the upstarts. Sol White took over as shortstop of the Columbia Giants in 1900, while the Unions lured Grant "Home Run" Johnson away from the Columbia Giants and added snappy infielder Dangerfield "Danger" Talbert to their lineup. At the end of the 1900 season, when the Unions met their nemesis from the East, the Cuban X-Giants, they finally won. The Columbia Giants took on and defeated another New York team known as the Genuine Cuban Giants. There was enough bad blood between the Columbia Giants and the Unions to prevent the two teams from meeting for the Chicago City Championship in 1900.

Black baseball in Chicago had to overcome one other obstacle at the turn of the century. Bryan Bancroft "Ban" Johnson, headquartered in Chicago, along with Charles Comiskey founded the American League in 1901. Chicago's American League franchise called themselves the White Stockings—better known as the White Sox, the National League team having vacated the nickname, opting instead to call themselves the "Orphans" (orphans being an odd reference to the team's missing paternal figure—Cap Anson.) The White Sox moved into South Side Park at 39th and Wentworth and expanded it by adding a new grandstand. By the time the White Sox had moved in they had displaced both the Unions at 37th and Butler and the Columbia Giants who had previously called South Side Park home.[8]

Even in the early days of black professional baseball, money was all-important. Top players were free to migrate to greener pastures. When it came to team owners, handling money is what separated the men from the boys. The Unions were well served by managers Frank Leland and W.S. Peters. They enjoyed a degree of stability not found with most other black baseball teams, especially Frank Leland who was a sharp operator with political skills and ambition. He would be one of the first blacks to hold political office in Chicago, as a deputy sheriff and as a county commissioner.

Leland was the right man at the right time. He correctly saw the need to consolidate the Unions and Columbia Giants into one team, which he called the Chicago Union Giants. The Union Giants secured a home field some forty blocks south of their former grounds, Auburn Park at 79th and Wentworth. W.S. Peters formed a ball club, with players that didn't make the cut, known as Peters' Union Giants.

3

Rube's Odyssey

"I fear nobody."
— Andrew Foster, correspondence
to Frank Leland (1902).[1]

1901–1906

Before Florida and Arizona were established as the home of baseball's annual spring training, the village of Hot Springs, Arkansas, was the venue of choice for players and teams to get into shape. They came to "boil out." The therapeutic waters of the hot springs were reputed to heal many of the common ailments that beset baseball players, sore arms, legs, joints and drunkenness. It was believed "boiling out" was an absolute necessity if a team was to have any chance at all of having a good season. Cy Young, Connie Mack, John McGraw, Cap Anson to name a handful were among baseball's early stars who made the trip to Hot Springs in March to begin training. Many top black players also went to Hot Springs to prepare for the upcoming baseball season.

Some of the black men were able to work two jobs, one in the hotels and also as baseball players in the scrimmages and exhibition games in "Thermopolis." The tradition of mixing baseball and banquet serving was established in 1885 by Frank P. Thompson, head waiter at Long Island's Argyle Hotel in Babylon, New York. Thompson recruited players to work at the hotel as waiters and formed the Cuban Giants in 1885.

John McGraw, then manager of the Baltimore Orioles, was the self-appointed grand poobah in Hot Springs, where he rented a suite of rooms at the luxurious Eastman Hotel. As John McGraw swaggered through the Eastman, he was tipped off to a player who had the stuff for the big leagues — a bellman at the hotel by the name of Charles Grant. Once McGraw had a chance to actually see Grant play he was duly impressed with his sure handed fielding and steady hitting. There was only one problem, Charles Grant was an African American. During the regular season Grant in fact played professionally as an infielder with the Chicago Unions and the Columbia Giants.

It so happened that Grant had lighter skin, straight hair and even spoke some German (he grew up alongside German immigrants in Cincinnati). McGraw, in cooperation with a few trusted cohorts, worked on a scheme to bring Grant to the Orioles. While

14

examining a large wall map just off the lobby at the Eastman, he was seized with an inspiration. Calling Grant over to him, he said: "Charlie, I've been trying to think of some way to sign you for the Baltimore club and I think I've got it. On this map there's a creek called Tokahoma. That's going to be your name from now on, Charlie Tokahoma, and you're a full-blooded Cherokee."

There was a precedent for a Native American player in baseball, Louis Sockalexis had played outfield for the Cleveland Spiders from 1897 to 1899. McGraw tested the waters by announcing he was signing Tokahoma and the news made the rounds of major league baseball. However there were several obstacles to the success of the plan. Firstly Grant was (at best) a reluctant participant in the scheme. Secondly Grant was acquainted with several players in the major leagues who knew his ethnicity. Grant's "would be" Oriole teammate, George Rohe, had grown up with Grant in Cincinnati. McGraw's plan apparently went as far as to gain a vow of silence on race matters from players who knew that Grant was black, but overall the deception was very thin.

Without missing a beat the *Sporting News* used Grant's surname in a report published on March 16, 1901:

> McGraw is at home again and tells wonderful tales of the prowess of an Indian named Grant, who played with Guy Green's Nebraska Indians. He is reported as a second Jennings and Sockalexis wrapped in one, and McGraw is likely to secure him. If Grant is any sort of player it would be good business move to sign him, as he would draw many a spectator out of curiosity. Grant is said to be a full-blooded Cherokee, and lives near Ft. Smith in the Indian Territory.

Later dispatches in the *Sporting News* gave the impression that Grant was indeed working out with the Orioles and had survived a couple rounds of cuts. Apparently it was during the workout games that a conspicuous black patronage had came out of the woodwork to congratulate Charles "Tokahoma" Grant on his promotion to the big leagues.[2]

In the end it was none other than American League mogul Charles Comiskey who recognized Grant as the Chicago Union Giants' second baseman and raised objections:

> I'm not going to stand for McGraw bringing in an Indian on the Baltimore team. If Muggsy really keeps this Indian, I will get a Chinaman of my acquaintance and put him on third. Someone told me that the Cherokee of McGraw is really Grant, the crack Negro second baseman from Cincinnati, fixed up with war paint and a bunch of feathers.[3]

The story of Tokahoma has become a part of baseball folklore. At times the story has been told with a different black player identified as Tokahoma. The tale illustrates the emptiness of the "color line." Some have seen Grant as the "would be" Jackie Robinson, but white American society in 1901 wasn't ready to accept blacks as equals. The story too stands as evidence that some of the talent in black baseball at the turn of the century was major league caliber in the eyes of respected baseball men like John McGraw.

Also among those ball players making the pilgrimage to Hot Springs at the turn of the century was Andrew Foster. Foster was well known on ball fields of Texas and Arkansas; known and feared by the opposition. He had a submarine style of pitching and somehow put every ounce of his 200-pound frame into the pitch. Some observers regarded Foster as "the greatest pitcher the game had ever produced." Foster's pitching skill was more a function of psychological prowess as opposed to raw athletic talent. Regardless of how he did it, Foster was a phenom. He mesmerized fans and players, routinely striking out ten or more batters on the way to victory.

Several big league managers who had seen Andy Foster pitch were overheard wishing they could have signed him. Legend has it that John McGraw and Connie Mack at one time hired Andy Foster to teach certain pitches to their staff. In 1902 the 22-year-old Foster caught the attention of the top black teams in Chicago. William S. Peters, manager of Peters' Union Giants, offered Foster a job with his team, but that offer did not include transportation costs to the Windy City. Dave Wyatt, the Chicago Union infielder and later black baseball's top scribe, negotiated on behalf of Foster with Frank Leland, who was completing the consolidation of Columbia Giants and Union Giants. Foster was given a spot on the Chicago Union Giant roster, however Dave Wyatt had to take the additional step of guaranteeing Foster's rail fare if for some reason Foster didn't perform as advertised.

Before Andy left for Chicago, Frank Leland warned him "that he would be put to a severe test, because the Chicago Union Giants intended to play all the good white clubs."

Foster responded coyly, "I fear nobody."[4]

So Andy boarded a northbound train for Chicago, Illinois. His seasoning as a pitcher had begun when he was still a teenager, and Foster even counted as acquaintances a few big league managers. He was a young black man leaving his home in the South for the North for the first time, among his possessions a Bible, a revolver and a baseball glove, and he was certain that no matter what happened "up in Chicago" his pitching arm would take him a long way.

The Chicago Union Giants of 1902 were led by veterans Harry Hyde, Chappie Johnson and pitcher Clarence Williams. Foster was inserted into the starting rotation of Leland's team and by all accounts he pitched well. The *St. Paul Appeal*, an African American newspaper based in the Twin Cities with a broad circulation in the Midwest, said on June 14:

> Frank Leland certainly is doing all in his power to strengthen his famous baseball team — the Union Giants, his newest acquisition the pitcher from Texas has proven himself to be a phenomenal twirler — he struck out thirteen of the Spaldings last Sunday at Auburn Park. The score was 4–1 in favor of the Union Giants.

According to one account, the first game he pitched for the Chicago Union Giants was a shutout and he lost only one game in three months. Published records of the Union Giants' games in 1902 are scarce, making it difficult to document those early days of Rube's career in Chicago. Late in July of 1902, the Chicago Union Giants departed for southwest Michigan. The first leg of the trip was by passenger ferry across southern Lake Michigan. The team then went by rail to Otsego, Michigan, a small town close to Kalamazoo. On July 30, 1902, the Union Giants squared off against the all-white team in Otsego and won by a score of 8–2; Andy Foster played at first base in that game, and Harry Hyde was on the mound. While it was somewhat unusual for Foster to be positioned anywhere other than the mound, what would happen later in the day was downright unthinkable.[5]

After exchanging a few tense words with teammates and road manager John Patterson, Andrew Foster and teammate Dave Wyatt defected from the Union Giants and joined the, formerly, *all white* Otsego team. Foster and Wyatt's departure was even more sur-

Otsego baseball team 1902. In mid-summer 1902 Dave Wyatt and Andrew Foster jumped the Chicago Union Giants to join the previously all-white Otsego, Michigan, team. Dave Wyatt middle left, Andrew Foster middle right. Foster got off to a shaky start with the Otsegos, but settled down to help the Otsegos beat all the teams in the Western Michigan league — averaging ten strikeouts per game (photograph courtesy of Nick Keckik).

prising considering the rude reception the team received in Michigan. The episode was recalled years later by Dave Wyatt:

Away back in 1902 Rube Foster had just taken out his first papers as a Chicago baseball player. Of course Rube, like all persons from the South, had to endure constantly hearing the virtues of the North as it concerns the Colored people extolled. All came to bat with high ground praises for the state "Negro Heaven," the best state in the Union they don't know you're colored. Foster fresh from the supposedly hostile country of Texas was inclined to look upon this said-to-be attitude towards the Negro with the eye of a skeptic. We crossed the lake and soon arrived at a little town where we were to make our first stand Otsego, Michigan. Starting on a walk from the depot we had gone but a short distance when we caught sight of a poster, which read "Baseball — Otsego vs. Chicago Union Giants. The Giants are great big athletic coons."

Foster at once called the manager's attention to it. John Patterson (now a policeman in Battle Creek, Michigan), was road manager and had been the leading one in the praise of the state. He said he had played several years throughout the state and had never heard the appellations usually applied to our boys used. He became indignant and suggested that we cancel the game.

We continued our journey approaching a lawn upon which some small children were playing. When they caught sight of us they exclaimed, "Here come the Niggers." When Foster
loomed in view one child, smaller than the others said, "Oh Mercy—there's a great big Nigger." Whereupon Foster set down his suitcase and went into a spasmodic laugh for about five
minutes. Between convulsions he ejaculated "So this is the Negro paradise. They don't know
you're colored oh? Why even the babies know it." It turned out to be a pretty good place
after all. Before leaving Foster had come to an agreement with the owners of the club for
regular service as a pitcher, also securing a job for the writer a position as shortstop. We
finished out the season in the little burg [David Wyatt, *Indianapolis Freeman*, March 10,
1917].

Wyatt also said that Andy Foster flashed $2500 in cash, as he jumped to the Otsego
team. It is not known where Foster got the dough, it can be safely assumed that he did
not earn it playing baseball—perhaps a family inheritance?[6]

Foster was welcomed as the ace of the Otsego baseball team, however the racial attitudes in the hinterlands of rural Michigan were unchanged by the integration of the local
baseball team. After his debut appearance for Otsego, a 5–2 win with eleven strikeouts,
the local *Otsego Union* newspaper wrote:

Foster the great colored pitcher, was in the box for Otsego.... The "Coon" kept the Allegan
[opposing team] lads guessing, they getting but five hits. He has all the methods of artful
pitching at his command and can throw a ball with trip-hammer force [*Otsego Union*,
August 14, 1902].[7]

In the second half of the 1902 season Foster led Otsego to wins over their top rivals
in western Michigan, averaging around 10 strikeouts a game. The Otsego team also played
games against the Columbian Giants of Big Rapids, Michigan, about 100 miles north of
Otsego, which included some of the former Page Fence/Columbia Giants. Foster defeated
the Columbian Giants of Big Rapids on August 28, 1902, avenging an earlier loss to his
brothers. It was remembered by his teammate Dave Wyatt that "Foster would engage in
personalities while pitching; and they always took him for a ride. Foster had a reputation as a gunman and was never seen without his Texas pistol. All the colored players
formed a decided dislike for Foster and declared he couldn't pitch."[8]

While Foster did not win any popularity contests, he had the spirit of a leader and
in a short time became very well known. He had been north of Texas for only a few
months and already the bold, menacing screwball pitcher, friend of white major league
baseball managers, was making waves in the world of black professional baseball. While
some regarded Andy Foster with suspicion and found his style abrasive, he also gained
respect. Foster found a way to strike out batters and win games. After the Otsego team
closed up shop in September Andy Foster was offered a job with the Cuban X-Giants
whom he joined in central Ohio and finished out the season with, his third team of the
1902 season.

In 1903 Foster rejoined the Cuban X-Giants, who were based in Philadelphia and
comprised of defecting Cuban Giants. The X-Giants were owned and managed by E. B.
Lamar, a white promoter from Brooklyn. According to Sol White, Lamar was "one of the
early baseball men who spent his time and mind in making the game a lucrative calling
for ball players ... his efforts were in the interest of the team and he was held in highest
regards by players." Sol White must have been using the word "lucrative" in a relative
sense. Andrew Foster recalled that he pitched for $40 a month, plus 15 cents a meal eat-

ing money. Foster was joined on the Cuban X-Giants by Charles Grant, Chappie Johnson, Mike Moore and Sol White—all legends of early black baseball.[9]

The chief competition to the Cuban X-Giants were the cross-town Philadelphia Giants who were owned by a local white sportswriter, Walter Schlichter. In the fall of 1903 the X-Giants challenged the Philadelphia Giants to a "championship series." Foster hit cleanup and won the opening game 3–1 allowing only three hits. After the Philadelphia Giants tied it Rube came back and won the third game 12–3, collecting three hits including a triple. Foster won four games in the series as the X-Giants easily won the championship five games to two.

Foster's performance in 1903 made him a star. During the off season Foster went South to play ball and was rumored to have been hired by John McGraw to teach Christy Mathewson his screwball. When Foster returned to Philadelphia for the 1904 season he, along with a number of his teammates, jumped from the Cuban X-Giants to the rival Philadelphia Giants. A bidding war between the Cuban X-Giants and the Philly Giants took place and Giants' owner Walter Schlichter was willing to pay more. As a Philadelphia Giant Rube was impressive once again. He played a variety of positions, hit decently and was commanding on the mound. At the close of the 1904 season the Philadelphia Giants again played a season-ending three-game championship series versus the Cuban X-Giants. Rube Foster was the deciding factor in the series winning two games for the Philadelphia Giants.[10]

Philadelphia was home to another rising star, this one a Caucasian named George "Rube" Waddell of the Philadelphia Athletics. Hall of Famer Rube Waddell had curious habits like leaving the mound in the middle of the game to chase fire trucks, playing marbles or sandlot baseball with Philadelphia's street urchins, and boozing it up before a game. Philadelphians loved Waddell, who was known to show up at local saloons, and then get behind the bar and serve drinks. Nonetheless, Waddell led the league in strikeouts every year from 1902 to 1907. Waddell's manager Connie Mack said once of his pitcher: "The Rube has a two million dollar body and a two cent head."

It was the following season (1904) when according to legend Andrew Foster and George "Rube" Waddell hooked up in a duel in which Andy Foster came out on top. According to the tale, after winning the game Andy Foster was dubbed by his teammates "Rube" Foster. The nickname stuck, and from that day forward Andrew Foster was known as Rube Foster. There is little debate that Foster *could have* beaten Waddell (perhaps even beaten him handily, depending on what "spirits" the great Rube Waddell was into.) No box score or written account of a Foster vs. Waddell game has ever been found—confounding baseball historians. The nickname "Rube" had become an affectionate nickname for pitchers at the time. Rube Waddell started the trend, but there were several Rubes in the major leagues at the time including "Rube" (Harry) Vickers of the Cincinnati Reds, "Rube" (Edgar) Taylor of the St. Louis Cardinals and "Rube" (Charles) Kisinger of the Detroit Tigers.

While Waddell has been lumped in with the ignoramuses of the day and assumed to be a racist, on at least one occasion Waddell played alongside colored folk. In 1898, Waddell was playing with the Chatham, Ontario, baseball team (after being exiled from Fred Clarke's Louisville Pirates for drinking) and faced the Page Fence Giants. Waddell's regular catcher Fred Phelps had split his finger in the second inning, and was replaced by a local news reporter — who after one pitch asked to retreat back to the stands. A Chatham outfielder was the third catcher of the day, but he too had to leave the game. Finally in a strange twist the visiting Page Fence Giants' catcher Pete Burns took the position as Waddell's battery mate. The Page Fence Giants won the game 9–1, Waddell allowed nine hits while the Page Fences' Sherman Barton — an outfielder by trade — held the Chathams to three hits; it is worth mentioning that Waddell had two of the three hits.[11]

Ironically Rube Foster and Rube Waddell would end up having a number of things in common. Both were said to have a habit of packing pistols, both had a way of "hexing" opposing batsmen with mental toughness and "wild eyes." And in the end, both Hall of Famers had their careers cut short by mental illness.

Rube remained in Philly and was dominating in the 1905 season as well. Foster said in an interview:

> In 1905 I won fifty-one out of the fifty-five games I pitched for that season and that was doing pretty well. We played the New York Giants, the Philadelphia Athletics, the Nationals, the Brooklyns, the teams of the New England and the Tri-State leagues and cleaned 'em all up.[12]

The Philadelphia Giants, with Foster pitching, were crowned the top black team in the East again in 1906. After the 1906 season Rube Foster, along with many of his Philadelphia Giant teammates, headed south to Cuba where they played for Club Fe. Club Fe competed in the Cuban League against teams from Havana and Alemendares. Foster asserted himself once more in Cuba, leading the Fe team to a showdown for first place against Alemendares on the last game of the season. Playing alongside Rube were early black legends Charles Grant, Pete Hill, Home Run Grant Johnson and Bill Monroe. Foster lost the decisive game against Alemendares in April 1907, which turned into a patriotic battle between the native Cubanos and the visiting African Americans who represented Fe. Foster earned the respect of his teammates who came to appreciate his leadership.[13]

After Foster steamed back across the Straits of Florida he planned his next move. Baseball was becoming more and more popular as the twentieth century kicked into gear. In the Philadelphia/New York area there were several black teams who the public would pay to see. Not surprisingly whites handled the finances of top black teams. E. B. Lamar owned the Cuban X-Giants, the Philadelphia Giants were owned by Walter Schlicter and the Original Cuban Giants by John Bright.

While many of the players often got along just fine with the white team owners, to Rube, the system of white promoters lording over and taking advantage of black players was makeshift at best. Foster had been an organizer even as a youth and understood the business of baseball. He hoped to do better for both himself and his race by organizing and promoting professional black baseball. Instead of accepting the false security as the star player for the Philadelphia Giants, Foster set his sights on Chicago where, he ventured, he could at least be involved with the business end of baseball.

4

Turf Wars (1907–1910)

> The colored wonders the Leland Giants are in a class by themselves and their followers are justly entitled to be proud of them and claim whatever honors they think exist. For the greater part of the 1908 campaign the Leland played ball as good as the major leagues, and none of the white clubs were able to do more than make a good showing against them, with the exception of Callahan's Logan Squares.
> —*Spalding Guide to Chicago Baseball* (1909).

1907–1910

In the four years Foster had been away from Chicago a lot had happened baseball-wise in the city. Albert Spalding's *Amateur Baseball Guide of Chicago and Vicinity for 1904* acknowledged Frank Leland's Union Giants as among the top teams in the City League. The *Chicago Daily News* also paid tribute to the Union Giants in a series of dignified articles and photos published in the early 1900's. So even at that early date there were baseball purists in Chicago who could put race aside and appreciate good baseball.

In 1905, Frank Leland's Chicago Union Giants, who had been a product of a merger between the Unions and the Columbia Giants, officially changed their name to the Leland Giants. Frank Leland claimed the team had a 122–10 record that year and won 48 straight games. While those figures may have been slightly exaggerated (the won-loss record was later restated as 93–25–3 by shortstop James Smith) the Lelands' professional level of ball was no match for most of the semi-pros they faced.[1]

In what would be the season of the century for Chicago major league fans, the White Sox met the Cubs in the 1906 World Series. The White Sox, dubbed "Hitless Wonders" for their poor hitting, walked away with an upset victory. History was made in the Chicago City Leagues as well. White Sox player-manager Jimmy Callahan had a salary dispute with the notoriously cheap "Old Roman" Charles Comiskey. Callahan held out, electing instead to lead a local semi-pro team called the Logan Squares, named for a neighborhood at the corner of Logan Boulevard and Milwaukee Street. Furthermore Callahan recruited some of his big league buddies in the form of a major league pitching staff composed of Jimmy Ryan, "Crazy" Fred Schmidt, and "Long" Tom Hughes plus outfielder Jack McCarthy. The City League had long been the domain of promising young players and minor leaguers with diminished career possibilities. Callahan's move upped the ante and caused the other City League teams to join the bidding war for major league talent. Major league players were interested in the City League for the money.

Following the cross-town World Series of 1906 Jimmy Callahan's Logan Squares took on both the world champion White Sox and the runner-up Cubs in exhibition games. Both major league teams had retained most of their regular starters for the match and to the shock of local fans the Logan Squares defeated both teams. The Chicago City Leagues would percolate with major league talent for the remainder of the decade, including some of the top black players in the world who were with the Leland Giants.

Sol White published his book *The History of Colored Baseball: Official Baseball Guide* in the spring of 1907. The work covered the history of professional black baseball from 1885 through 1906, outlining the top teams and players. Sol's book included in an appendix to the work an essay titled "How to Pitch" by Andrew Foster. Foster, never short on words, shared some of his secrets and tricks of the trade with aspiring moundsmen:

> A pitcher should never fully let out until his arm becomes warm and limbered up. I have lost games by not being warmed up…. Try to appear jolly and unconcerned. I have smiled often with the bases full with two strikes and three balls on the batter to unnerve them…. The three great principles of pitching are good control, when to pitch certain balls, and where to pitch them[2] [Rube Foster].

Frank Leland, at that time a deputy sheriff of Cook County, realized his error in questioning Rube's abilities in 1902 and welcomed Foster back to the fold. Shortly after arriving back in the Windy City, Rube discovered that Leland's team would make only about $150 (as a team) for a July 4th double-header — usually the biggest day of the year. Foster went to Leland and demanded a role as a booking agent/business manager; to which Leland conceded, lest he lose his darling moundsman. Rube fought stubbornly until he found a way to more than double the Independence Day payout for the team at $500. Foster also convinced Frank Leland to make him player/manager of the team.[3]

The Leland Giants, already recognized as the top black team in the Midwest, were an even better team under Foster. Foster brought battery-mate Pete Booker with him from Philadelphia; and by the conclusion of the season several more of Foster's former Philadelphia mates had joined him in Chicago.

Rare was the afternoon that an opponent would luck into a napping Leland Giant team and escape with a win. The competition was sometimes relegated to the role of spectator. The Indianapolis ABCs, a budding regional semi-pro team in those days, traveled to Chicago and met with the Lelands shortly after Foster joined the team. The ABCs were defeated by the score of 6–1 in both ends of a double-header, yet counted the beatings as a moral victory. In the words of an *Indianapolis Freeman* sports writer:

> [T]he boys were defeated, they were not disgraced, because teams from … New York to El Paso have fallen before the mighty pitching of the famous Rube Foster. The ABCs did what no other team has done so far this season. They stood right up to the plate and took to Foster's pitching…. [They] failed to reach the plate until the seventh when the touched up the "Reuben" for three singles and scored.[4]

The Leland Giants faced very little serious competition from other black teams. William S. Peters' Giants, who had split off from Leland's outfit back in 1901, still played weekend games around the Chicago area. The toughest competition was against local white semi-pro teams. In late August the Leland Giants played a three game series against a local "All-Star" team headed by "Turkey" Mike Donlin. Donlin, who had batted .356 and led the New York Giants to a World Series championship two years earlier, was a salary hold-out the entire 1907 season, opting instead to play in the Chicago City Leagues. On the All-Star team along with Donlin were major league veterans Jake Stahl, Jimmie Ryan, and Jimmie Callahan.

One of the contests took place at South Side Park, the home of the White Sox. Charles Comiskey himself was in attendance and he brought along with him the defending champion White Sox. Comiskey hoped that the Sox might pick up some ideas by observing the Lelands' winning style of play. Comiskey maintained a working relationship with the black baseball teams of Chicago throughout his career. Comiskey squeezed every dime he could out of black baseball by renting out his ballpark and felt no shame in learning all he could from watching the top black teams in action. After the game "Old Roman" said publicly: "I wish I could have signed one or two of those boys to my team."

Word went out all over the South Side of Chicago about the big showdown. Leland supporters came out by the trainloads, many dressed in pressed slacks, dress shirts and straw hats. There were slightly more white fans at the game, presumably pulling for Turkey Donlin's All-Stars. For the first game an entire Elks convention numbering more than 5,000 was in attendance.

Some of the practices of racial segregation at the big league park were put aside, blacks and whites sat in all sections of the park and co-mingled. Unofficial games between major leaguers and the top black teams stood as a testament to the democratic side of baseball during the 50 long years of segregation. The games were a rebellious act against the major league baseball establishment. (Mike Donlin and Jake Stahl were later fined by the National Commission for competing outside of organized baseball.)

Many of the baseball-crazed fans were making wagers on the outcome of the games. Writer Frederick Shorey described the scene in the pages of the *Indianapolis Freeman* newspaper:

[B]efore the game had started a good deal of money had been placed, "I've got $20 that says the chocolates won't win," said a well-known ball player who was in the grand stand amidst a crowd of colored men with conspicuous striped shirts and brilliant neckties. The effect he produced was amazing.

"I'll take $5 of that money, white man," said a flashily dressed colored man hastily producing five $1 dollar bills.

"Heah gimme $2," exclaimed another.

"An' I'll take another $5.00," said a coal-black Negro on his left, and before the white man had sat down his money was distributed in a circle about him.

Over in the bleachers, $5 bets were being split up in dollars, halves and quarters.[5]

The much-anticipated moment arrived, the Lelands came out on to the field and the rooters went wild. However Rube did not come out with the rest of the team. Rube came on the field a few minutes later, like a conductor at a symphony, or a matador, and was greeted with a thunderous ovation.

The first game was close all the way. Toward the end Foster struck out Jake Stahl, and nailed a baserunner with the trick of pretending to have the ball in his mitt on the mound, while the first baseman had it in his glove. The crowd loved it and the Lelands wound up on top by a 3–2 score. Foster pitched another game against the All-Stars and held them to three hits and the Leland Giants took the game 3–1. The All-Stars later managed to defeat the Lelands who sent pitcher Arthur Hardy to the mound.

The Leland Giants proved their mettle as a professional team capable of taking down a major league outfit and they continued a pattern of dominating their opponents. Foster later claimed that the Lelands of 1907 had an astounding 103–1 record. Winning was important to Rube; it could be said that winning was perhaps *too* important. For Rube winning meant not only winning on the diamond, but winning in business, management, social equality and in life. This competitive spirit, along with his rotundness, were early visible traits that set Rube Foster apart. It was plain as day to Rube Foster that there was money to be made for blacks in baseball; the key element missing — organization.[6]

There had been several attempts at creating a black baseball league beginning as early as 1887, all of which failed. There were a number of black professional teams in the early 1900's. At the turn of the century professional black baseball was limited to the same teams in Chicago, Philadelphia, New York, or a road team playing with many of the same players. Players like Sol White, Chappie Johnson, "Home Run" Grant Johnson, Harry Hyde, and Charles Grant were among those who scratched out baseball careers between organized baseball, traveling with the Page Fence Giants or doing a stint with the early black teams in Philadelphia and Chicago.

By 1907, there were black baseball teams dotting America from Minnesota to Florida, and many good players too. Some of these teams earned money, but without an organized league the true potential of baseball in the black community could not be tapped. Baseball's color line threatened to suffocate young black ball players. A league was necessary so that young African Americans could pursue their God given talent. There was a turning point in 1907, noted by Sol White in a postscript to his fabled *History of Colored Baseball*:

> The records made in 1907 by the rejuvenated Leland Giants of Chicago, and the newly organized professional team of St. Paul Minn. [the St. Paul Colored Gophers], has thrown the west in a fever of enthusiasm that bids fair to culminate in the formation of a National League of Colored Base Ball Teams, which will greatly augment the chances for employment of colored talent so eager to obtain an opportunity to display their ability as exponents of the national game.[7]

Foster was eager to assist with the management of the Leland Giants and the formation of a Negro baseball league. In order to have a voice in the management of the Lelands, Rube first had to charm his way into the circle of black aristocrats that ran the team. Frank Leland was a graduate of Fisk University, a leader in his community and a public official, whereas Foster's formal education was limited to a couple of years of high school. The Chicago ball club had been supported by leading black socialites since the 1880's, unlike the operations back East which were run mostly by white promoters.

Foster joined a cadre of "team officers" in a plan to reorganize the already successful Leland Giants as a publicly traded corporation. It wasn't clear whether Foster was offered a seat on the board of directors or whether he seized the position. So how was this Rube from Texas able to go from baseball flannels to a three-piece suit? Foster was a keen observer and a fast learner. When baseball was spoken Rube usually had something to say, and he commanded respect. Since Rube still played the game he had a vested interest in how managerial dealings affected players and he was well liked by the players.

The officers of the ball club like Frank Leland, who had played some ball, liked to think they could talk baseball with Rube Foster. In the end Foster could talk circles around most anyone and hang them on their own words.

The plan on the table included creating an umbrella company that would oversee the operation of an amusement park, theater, and hotel as well as the baseball park. The board of directors included Frank Leland, Major R.R. Jackson, attorney Beauregard Mosely, and professor William Emanuel, a former president of the elite black Appomattox Club. The Leland Giants Baseball and Amusement Association took out advertisements in local papers to sell stock. Advertisements ran in Chicago's black newspapers:

> The public is base-ball mad, and amusement crazy. Stocks have doubled in value in a single season. Millions can be made by those who take stock in this new enterprise. Are you in favor of the race owning and operating this immense and well paying plant, where more than 1,000 persons will be employed between May and October of each year where you can come without fear and enjoy the life and freedom of a citizen unmolested or annoyed? The answer can only be effectively given by subscribing for stock in this corporation. It has been made purposely low so that all loyal members of the race can have a share and interest in this twentieth century enterprise. Think of it, shares only ten (l0.00) dollars each you squander more than this amount any holiday.[8]

The stock offering met with limited success. The more grandiose scheme was not realized; however the ball club continued, as did "Chateau Gardens," a musical and entertainment venue at 5300 South State Street under the auspices of the Leland Giants Baseball and Amusement Association which attracted a summertime picnic crowd for several years.

The ultimate goal of the Leland baseball association was the creation of a professional baseball league. There were also black baseball men in mid-western cities like Cincinnati, Cleveland, Detroit, Indianapolis, Kansas City, Louisville, Memphis, Nashville and St. Louis interested in organizing a league. Following the 1907 season representatives of black baseball from various cities met several times in efforts to create a Negro baseball league. In a back room meeting held in Indianapolis December 18, 1907, Frank Leland was elected president of the National Colored Baseball League organization. Plans were under way to draw up a constitution, and the idea of selling stock in the league was also mentioned.[9]

President Frank Leland missed a March meeting, supposedly due to illness, but other interested parties met without him and apparently cut him out of his leadership post. There were a lot of details to be worked out regarding player salaries, umpire salaries, transportation costs, whether or not games could be played on Sundays. In a firestorm meeting held in St. Louis, it was decided that the new president of the National Colored Baseball League would be a white man named Conrad Kuebler who owned a ballpark in St. Louis.

Rube Foster did not participate in these organizational efforts. While the league meetings were getting started, Foster was on his way to Cuba to play winter ball. Rube pitched for Havana in 1908; he was joined by Chicago regulars Preston Hill, Clarence Winston and Nate Harris. Walter Ball and Bruce Petway also went to Cuba but played for the Cuban League rivals Club Fe. Foster found stiff competition on the island. In partial records of games pitched by Rube in 1908 he is credited with a 3–4 record. Alemendares, with a flashy rookie pitcher named Jose Mendez, won the Cuban championship again in 1908.

When Foster got back to the states he heard the tale of how a Negro baseball league had been established and how it just as quickly had been lost. The National Colored Baseball League collapsed before it ever got started. Failed leagues and double talk from white promoters was old news. Foster thought to himself, "if there is going to be a Negro baseball league, I am going to have to be the one to organize it."

Rube Foster strengthened his grip on the Leland Giants in 1908. By this time he had released most of the players hired by Frank Leland and replaced them with handpicked recruits. Foster showed up Leland by personally guaranteeing the salaries of his players, a sharp departure from how the club operated under Leland — who paid players out of gate receipts. Foster repeatedly postured himself as head of the team and painted Frank Leland into a corner to make him look like an impotent figurehead. As the team continued to win, attracted attention and brought in money it was Foster who was given credit. The gulf between the two men had widened.

The Lelands competed in the Chicago City League in 1908 against local teams such as the Spaldings, the Logan Squares, the West Ends, the Normals, the Gunthers, Rogers Park, Artesian Park, River Forests, Riverview Park, the Felix Colts, the Arions, and perhaps most surprisingly the Anson Colts (led by Cap Anson).

The Lelands challenged black teams from outside the region such as the Brooklyn Royal Giants, the Philadelphia Giants, the Havana Stars and the Cuban Stars to games in Chicago. The challenges were accepted, furthermore, in a deal brokered by Rube Foster; the Chicago City League Association made a contract with the New York baseball promoter Nat Strong to have the highly rated East Coast black teams play a series of games in the City League. Nat Strong was a white promoter who boasted "exclusive booking rights" for a number of New York area teams. Strong had his fingers in the till of New York black baseball from 1907 until the 1930's.[10]

There was disparity in the semi-pro Chicago City League. Some of the teams had their own ballpark, while others did not. Some teams would be forced to drop out of the league before the end of the season and scheduling was worked out as the season went along. W.S. Peters' Union Giants occasionally played a game against teams in the City Leagues, but was not a regular participant.

The heart of the City League was cross-town battles between the top teams, like the Logan Squares, the West Ends, the Gunthers, the Spaldings and the Lelands. Large crowds turned out for games between the top teams, and the players on those teams received higher payouts. Some of the semi-pro players on lesser teams circulated a petition to ban the black teams from the East Coast, because the large turnouts at those games would cut into their share of pay. The games against the black teams from the East Coast went ahead as planned. The Philadelphia Giants, staffed with early black baseball notables like pitcher Dan McClellan, third baseman Bill Francis and catcher Bruce Petway, played well in the Windy City. The Philly Giants took a game from the favored Logan Squares and hooked up with a number of the Chicago white teams. The Philadelphia Giants left town in early August and the City League contracted back to its normal geographic realm.[11]

The acceptance of black teams into Chicago's semi-pro league in 1908 was extraordinary. Even more remarkable was a series of games played between Cap Anson's "Anson's

Colts" and the Leland Giants. When Cap Anson ended his major league career in 1898, he was considered the greatest player in the game. As a player/manager he had led the National League White Stockings to five pennants. He retired a hero in the Windy City. After he left baseball he was able to cash in his popularity for a political post in the Chicago city government. In 1907, Anson experienced a reversal of fortune when he was fingered in a payroll scandal in the city government and was forced to resign. To support himself Anson did the only thing he knew how to do; he started a semi-pro baseball team.

As discussed earlier, Anson was a scapegoat when it came to placing blame for the color line in baseball. Anson brought this on himself because he had made his bigoted views publicly known, without an iota of shame. One hundred years later, there were still those who felt Anson, more than anyone else, was to blame for baseball's apartheid. In the summer of 1908, the 57-year-old Anson had a slight change of heart about his convictions. Cap Anson's team the Colts, on which he occasionally played first base, squared off against Rube Foster and the Leland Giants. The Lelands got the best of Anson Colts with Walter Ball pitching a 5–0 shutout on August 22. The two teams met again on September 6, and Anson played the entire 13-inning affair. Anson was not heard publicly retracting his previous curses, but by playing the Lelands he had contradicted his early admonishments against inter-racial baseball. Nonetheless the games between the Anson Colts and the Leland Giants are worthy of more weight in the discussion of the history of the color line in professional baseball.[12]

The battle for supremacy in the City Leagues in 1908 was between the Lelands and Logan Squares. The Logan Squares, with Jimmie Callahan at the helm, maintained a roster of former major leaguers and prospects, while the Lelands under Rube were a consolidation of the best black players in the country. *The Spalding Guide of Chicago* declared after the season:

> The colored wonders the Leland Giants, are in a class by themselves and their followers are justly entitled to be proud of them and claim whatever honors they think exist. For the greater part of the 1908 campaign the Leland played ball as good as the major leagues, and none of the white clubs were able to do more than make a good showing against them, with the exception of Callahans Logan Squares.[13]

> There was no official championship played between the two teams.

The Chicago City League was a bright spot in the long saga that is the history of racial division in professional baseball. The color line was firmly instituted in major league baseball and attempts to organize the National Colored Baseball League had recently fizzled out. The baseball men and fans of Chicago had a league of their own that both blacks and whites could participate in. The Chicago City League experience has given pause to many baseball historians to ask, "why couldn't the sport have built on the successes of the Chicago City League?"

Several of the Leland Giants again retreated to Cuba for the winter season in 1909. Walter Ball helped the Havanas to defeat Alemendares (armed with sensation Jose Mendez) for the first time in six years. Bruce Petway's work behind the plate left an indelible impression on Cuban fans. Other black players with Chicago connections who played baseball on the Caribbean isle included Nathan Harris, Pete Booker, Bobby Winston, and Harry Buckner.[14]

Rube passed up Cuba to attend to personal affairs and the business end of baseball. On October 29, 1908, immediately following the regular baseball season, Rube Foster married Sarah Watts in Temple, Texas. After the wedding, Rube headed back to Chicago to lay plans for an early spring tour by the Leland Giants. The board of directors of the Chicago Leland Baseball and Amusement Company showed further signs of splintering. Rube Foster allied himself with Beauregard Mosely, chief counsel for the company, while Frank Leland and the other primary stockholders were in a different camp. Frank Leland held the title of president/booking agent yet was kept out of the loop while Foster and Mosely laid the plans for the spring tour.[15]

Foster had learned a lot from the veterans he had associated with the last six years. He was duly impressed by the accomplishments of the Page Fence Giants, who had toured the country in a private rail car. Foster planned a tour to take the Leland Giants all over the southern United States from Tennessee to Texas and back to Chicago in a first class railroad berth. Frank Leland's ownership faction was skeptical of Rube's big plans. Leland pointed out that the Page Fence Giants had one main advantage: a wealthy white owner. From a fiscal standpoint, Rube's big idea was foolhardy, no matter how well the team drew fans, the cost of transportation and player salaries was certain to put the team in the red.

Capitalizing on his team's reputation Foster contacted baseball managers from cities throughout the South who thought they "might be up to the challenge." In towns like Nashville, Chattanooga, Birmingham, and Waco a visit from the Chicago Leland Giants was an historic event, certain to bring out the fans. With the help of Beauregard Mosely and his many "connections," Foster pulled off the 1909 spring baseball tour.

The Lelands, for the most part, had no trouble beating the home teams in the South as they got in their spring training. They did however find themselves with their hands full against the Birmingham Giants. The Birmingham Giants under the leadership of Charles Isham "C. I." Taylor were a collection of the best Southern collegiate players and raw talent including Taylor's brothers Johnny "Steel Arm" Taylor and "Candy" Jim Taylor. Rube Foster and C.I. Taylor initiated one of the great coaching rivalries in the history of black baseball on April 14, 1909.

From Alabama, the Lelands went to Fort Worth, Texas, where a great homecoming party welcomed Rube Foster. The train station was packed with both white and black folks to greet Foster. The ballpark was overflowing when the Lelands took the field. Rube was something of a folk hero in that part of Texas. The same mob scene occurred in Austin, San Antonio and Houston. When the Lelands went to Houston, a large contingency from Rube's hometown of Calvert, Texas, sat as a block in the grandstand, whooping and hollering the whole game.[16]

The Lelands headed north through St. Louis where they played one more exhibition series, before heading back to Chicago. The trip was a success. They claimed a 15–0 record, the players got into shape (although most of the key players trained in Cuba) and drew nice crowds. The Lelands rolled into Chicago feeling proud and feeling like a professional baseball team. Years later, the players would boast that "we always traveled first class, when we played for Rube." Their tour was equaled only by the globetrotting Chicago White Sox, the other South Side Chicago team. The Lelands had also brought real hope to teams in the South, demonstrating that opportunities did exist for African American ball players. Foster, the chubby self-promoter, the tough competitor, the tireless organizer, was also an ambassador and a leader of his people.

The Lelands returned to Chicago to do battle in the City Leagues. The action in the Chicago City League of 1909 was interesting, with the Gunthers (candy manufacturer Charles Gunther's team) and Anson Colts inching closer to competing with the perennial champions Lelands and Logan Squares. The managers of the City League selected Harvey T. Woodruff, sports editor of the *Chicago Tribune*, to preside over the league. Woodruff officiated the league and negotiated disagreements. Woodruff's guidance gave the league previously unattained organization and stability.

For a change all of the clubs made money and league statistics for the 1909 season were published in the *Spalding Guide.* The Lelands were the undisputed winners of the City League, finishing with a 31–9 record, while Jimmie Callahan's Logan Squares took second place with a 24–16 record. The Lelands pulled off the first place finish despite a spate of injuries. Rube Foster missed half the season after breaking a leg in a game against the Cuban Stars in July. The Lelands added left-hander Pat Dougherty to fill in for Rube, and he pitched splendidly the rest of the season. The Lelands learned firsthand of Dougherty's prowess when he opposed them in a 13-inning marathon as the pitcher for the West Baden Sprudels (a small southern Indiana resort town team), in which the Lelands finally eked out a 1–0 win. Dougherty was virtually unbeatable the rest of the way in the City League. Starting left fielder Clarence "Bobby" Winston broke an ankle, but was replaced by Charles "Joe" Green who led the team with a .333 batting average, before he too was injured.[17]

The Lelands conquered the white teams in the City Leagues, but found themselves a bit surprised when they went about defending their claims as "Greatest Colored Team in the World." There was a notable five game series played in St. Paul, Minnesota, between the Lelands and the St. Paul Colored Gophers—billed in some circles as the Colored Championship. The Gophers featured "Candy Jim" Taylor and "Steel Arm" Johnny Taylor who had faced the Lelands when they had played with the Birmingham Giants earlier that spring. Rube Foster was still hobbled by a broken leg and had to sit the series out. The series went to the fifth game knotted at two games apiece. St. Paul sent Steel Arm Taylor to the mound, and the Lelands went with Pat Dougherty. The Lelands scored one run in the third inning while Dougherty took a no-hitter into the eighth inning. In the eighth the Gophers came alive, hitting three singles and a triple to take 3–1 lead, then Steel Arm Taylor held on in the ninth and the Gophers took the series.[18]

Foster later insisted the series was mere "exhibition games ... St. Paul won, only because of the injuries." Foster, and his proponents, also claimed the Leland Giants "never [legitimately] lost a series," although Rube admitted to tying a series with the Philadelphia Giants in 1908. Foster had a way of stretching the truth, and in some circles he was best known for that habit. While the Lelands were usually a cut above the competition, they dropped a series here and there in the City Leagues, and the team — which had been virtually intact in Cuba — lost on a regular basis while on the island.[19]

In September the Lelands traveled to Kansas City, Kansas, for a three game series against the Kansas City Giants. The locals had won some 40 games straight on their home field before the Lelands came to town and shut them down by a 5–0 score. In the second game however KC pitcher Robert Lindsey turned the tables on Rube's men, striking out

16 batters as it was the KC Giants who won by a 3–1 score. Crowds were literally overflowing for the rubber game, and a section of the grandstand broke at Kansas City's Riverside Park sending hundreds falling to the ground, though none were seriously hurt. The underdog Kansas City Giants prevailed against pitcher Arthur Hardy aka "Bill Norman"—himself a Kansas native and former Kansas City Giant—by a 5–4 score and the Lelands again tasted defeat.

The Lelands played in one of the biggest series in their history when they met the defending world champion Chicago Cubs for three games to cap the 1909 season. The Cubs, who had won 104 games, finished in second place behind Pittsburgh and missed the World Series for the first time in four years. The Cubbies had grown accustomed to World Series money and a victory in the intra-city contests would go part way to making up for the shortfall. The Cubs took the game seriously, evidenced by the fact they used their top pitchers. Mordecai "Three Finger" Brown started the first and third games. Ed Reulbach, 19-game winner, started the middle game and was relieved by 20-game winner Orval Overall.

The games were a tug of war, in which the Cubs just barely got the better of the Lelands in three straight, although one game finished under protest. Walter Ball pitched well in game one, but received poor support in the field. A last minute addition to the Lelands—first sacker Bobby Marshall, whom Rube had recruited as a ringer from the St. Paul Gophers—committed two crucial errors which, combined with three additional Leland errors, gave the game to the Cubs. Marshall was yanked from the game and never again played for Rube. The Lelands managed six hits against Mordecai "Three Finger" Brown, but lost by a 4–1 score.

In game two Foster took the hill for the first time since breaking his leg in early July. The Lelands took it to the defending world champs, jumping to a 5–0 lead in the third inning then coasting to a 5–2 advantage in the ninth frame. The Lelands were one out away from winning the game; manager Frank Chance had actually left the park to disassociate himself from the apparent loss. Covering the game was baseball's most loved writer Ring Lardner, who wrote the following account of the last half-inning of the showdown for the *Chicago Tribune* on October 22, 1909:

> Bugs were hastening for the exits when their steps were arrested by the singles of [Pat] Moran and [Orvie] Overall. Heine Zimmerman had been hitting the ball on the nose most of the afternoon and he didn't disappoint this time. His safe wallop filled up the bases and spectators began to realize that the Cubs were not whipped after all. James Sheckard refused to offer at the bad ones and was passed. This forced Pat [Moran] across with a tally. Frank Schulte, afterward the hero of the play sent a sharp grounder to [Felix] Wallace, whose throw home got Overall.
>
> Now there were two out, the bases full and two runs still needed to tie. Up strode brave Capt. Howard and smote one he liked against the right field boards for a clean single, clean enough to allow both Zimmerman and Sheck to count and Schulte to reach third.
>
> Rube, feeling that he was slipping started to work about as fast as a hippopotamus would run on skis. First he tossed the ball to third base, and then tossed it to third base again. Then he walked over toward the bench and conferred with pitcher Dougherty. The pair consulted about the advisability of Rube's continuing on the mound. The umpire was then asked the score. His answer did not suit and Dougherty had to answer. The Cubs objected to the delay and so did Umpire Meyer. As Dougherty came forth from the bench a second time the ump waved him back and the Cubs came out to see what it was all about. The group then was

formed and Schulte took advantage of the interest in the conversation to sneak his way home.

When Meyer ruled him safe and the Cubs started for the clubhouse and the supporters of the Giants acted as if they were about to wound the umpire. The latter was escorted from the yard by a large policeman and Special Officers.

... Capt. Foster asserted that he was not stalling at all, but merely was asking Dougherty to take his pitching job away from him. Further more he wanted to know how one Cub could be allowed to steal home when three or four others were standing on the diamond in conversation. There was no answer to this query since Meyer had made his ruling and the athletes had left the field.

In game three Pat Dougherty went up against Three Finger Brown and held the Cubbies to just one run, but the Lelands couldn't score and lost by that 1–0 score. Foster was proud of his team even in defeat and later declared:

[S]till crippled [we] played the Chicago Cubs, twice world champions, to a standstill — much harder than the American League champions played them. In playing the Chicago National League club the Lelands accomplished what no other colored club in the country ever accomplished. Their gentlemanly way and good ball playing gained so much prestige that public sentiment forced the Cubs to meet the Lelands.[20]

Foster had quietly made an important achievement by playing head to head against white teams. The Lelands were officially credited with a 31–9 record in the otherwise all-white City League, which included seven games against Cap Anson's Colts in addition to playing the Chicago Cubs. There were two stripes to baseball's color line. One that said blacks and whites should not play together on the same team; the other that blacks and whites should not even be on the same field. Foster ignored the latter and teams followed suit (even major leaguers after the regular season.) Rube had been influenced by gentlemen from the game's early days like Bud Fowler, Sol White, John McGraw, Charles Grant, and Walter Schlicter who did not abide by the color line. He had become a leader with a political following, carrying the torch from baseball's post–Civil War days into the twentieth century. Long before Jackie Robinson, it was Rube Foster who emerged as the chief bridge builder between whites and blacks enamored of the national game. Rube's temperament — pushy, mad, boisterous— stood in stark contrast to Jackie's, and draws into question the notion that "only someone of Jackie's disposition could integrate baseball."

So while the Lelands won the 1909 Chicago City League championship hands down, they also lost a series to the St. Paul Gophers, the Kansas City Giants and the Chicago Cubs. By Rube's fuzzy logic the Lelands were still "the best colored team in the world." There was really no way to prove who was the best team in the world in those days, at least not until a league was organized. Organizing a professional league for blacks remained high on Foster's agenda. Also in 1909 the second tier Chicago Union Giants under the leadership of W.S. Peters pasted the competition in the regional Lake Shore League. The Union Giants at that time were made up of older castoffs such as Harry Hyde, and young prospects like 17-year-old Jimmie Lyons— who later went on to a notable career. The Union Giants and Lelands did not meet on the diamond, as the rift between W.S. Peters and Frank Leland dating back to 1901 had not been mended.[21]

Unfortunately the nasty conflict between Chicago black baseball magnates would come to the forefront following the successful 1909 season. Foster had chipped away at

Leland's legitimacy as team president a little bit at a time. First he became the field general, then he usurped front office duties, then he pulled off a series against the defending world champion baseball team. Rube's coup d'état was nearly complete, but Frank Leland still held some of the keys to black baseball in Chicago.

Leland tried to posture himself as a "hands off" style of president. On one occasion he publicly offered a $5,000 challenge to any team who thought they could defeat the Lelands—as if he had something to do with their success. In reality Leland had nothing to do with the success of the club. Fed up with the humiliation, Frank Leland announced that he would be forming a new club known as "Leland's Chicago Giants Baseball Club." However, the Leland Giants Baseball and Amusement Association was a corporation, and even though his name was on the team, Leland's right to use the name(s) "Leland Giants" was controversial. A court battle ensued. Rube Foster and Beauregard Mosely filed suit in Cook County complaining about the use of the name "Leland Giants" by Frank Leland. Leland and another club officer, Major R.R. Jackson, filed a lawsuit charging that the corporation was a sham. They accused attorney Beauregard Mosely of charging "exorbitant rates that would make the team insolvent if paid."[22]

Rube countered with more announcements, namely that the Leland team under his command would not play in the City League—he would leave those table scraps for Frank Leland. He also disclosed that he was working on a deal with John Schorling—son-in-law of Charles Comiskey—to play in South Side Park, the longtime home of the White Sox, who would be moving to freshly built Comiskey Park in 1910.

Leland wasn't satisfied with merely rocking Rube's boat; he tried to sink him by signing players from under his nose. Frank Leland gained agreements from Clarence Winston, Nathan Harris, Charles "Joe" Green, and pitching ace Walter Ball, all key veterans of Rube's previous campaigns. Leland also signed top players from the St. Paul Colored Gophers, including George "Chappie" Johnson, "Steel Arm" Taylor, "Candy Jim" Taylor and Felix Wallace. Then in a brilliant move which showed he was still a *real* baseball man, Leland hired a heralded prospect from Texas known as "Cyclone" Joe Williams. "Cyclone"—also known as "Smokey" Joe Williams—would land in Cooperstown some 89 years later.

On paper Frank Leland's Chicago Giants arguably had a better team than Rube Foster's Leland Giants. For his part Rube held on to Charles Dougherty and signed another young thrower named Frank Wickware, who along with himself gave the team a quality pitching staff. Foster then pulled off a deal to bring catcher Bruce Petway along with shortstop John Henry Lloyd to the club from Philly. John Henry "Pops" Lloyd, like Joe Williams, was also destined for Cooperstown. The battle between Foster and Leland had the unexpected consequence of bringing even more baseball talent to Chicago.

Normally many of the top Chicago players would have gone to Cuba over the winter. However rumor had it that the directors of the Cuban Baseball League had "drawn the color line," in an attempt to "join the ranks of *organized baseball.*" So in winter (January–March) of 1910 black players stayed away from the isle. Instead Rube lined up a series of games at the Royal Poinciana Hotel in Palm Beach, Florida, beginning in January, while Frank Leland planned a spring tour of the South with his version of the "Leland Giants."[23]

Spring training began with the specter of two teams calling themselves the "Leland

Giants," representing themselves as the *"original ... champions."* It wasn't the first time that an elite professional black team had split and both factions claimed to be the "original," and it wouldn't be the last. A faction of the Kansas City, Kansas, Giants had also split off following the 1909 season and represented themselves as the original Kansas Giants team. The Cuban Giants of Babylon, New York, founded in 1879, inspired numerous imitators— all claiming to be the genuine article. The same thing would happen years later in Indianapolis which had two teams called the ABCs for a couple of years. There were teams known to prey on unsuspecting local promoters. The manager of a team calling themselves the Cuban Giants for instance would book a game down the line somewhere. The game would be promoted, tickets sold, but when the game was actually played — the real fans would spot the impostors.

Foster's club fared well in Palm Beach, where they sparred against the Royal Giants. Frank Leland's team faced little serious competition on their springtime jaunt through the American South, although they were defeated by the Houston Black Buffaloes in a 14-inning game tainted by umpiring. Leland visited many of the same cities and towns that Rube had the previous year. There is little doubt that some of the fans in Texas were expecting to see Rube Foster, only to learn that Rube was no longer with *these* Leland Giants, but with a different Leland Giants.

Back in Chicago, Foster won a round in court when a judge ruled that "hereafter no person or persons acting for the defendants [Frank Leland] shall in any fashion use the name 'Leland Giants' as the name of the defendant club or feature the name 'Leland' in connection with...." Two weeks later the City League held a giant "Flag Raising" ceremony in which the Lelands of 1909 were presented with the official City League pennant. The ceremony was replete with a parade, a military band, souvenir booklets, extra box seats installed at Auburn Park and a

Bruce Petway was considered one of the greatest catchers of the Dead Ball era. Petway could make the throw down to second base effortlessly and with deadly accuracy. Bruce Petway etched his name into baseball history when he threw out Ty Cobb three times in three attempts during the 1910 Cuban baseball season (photograph courtesy NoirTech Research, Inc.).

game against Jimmy Callahan's Logan Squares. This gesture from the otherwise all white league, while made with some reluctance, showed some warmth in race relations at a time when Chicago was deeply divided on racial/ethnic lines. Rube would have relished raising the banner of victory, but he wasn't invited as it was Frank Leland's team who was entered in the City League and received the flag. In accordance with the court ruling Frank Leland's team name was officially abbreviated to the "Chicago Giants," but the general public, and sometimes even the press, continued to refer to both teams as the "Lelands." Rube Foster was intensely proud of the 1910 Lelands, at one time he even called the team "the greatest club of all-time," and claimed they "won 126 games and lost only 3."[24]

Rube's hyperbole had a germ of truth, but omitted key facts about that 1910 season. During spring training against the formidable Philadelphia Giants, Foster's team lost four games, winning seven and tying two (Rube apparently did not count these games in his tally). They played many games against lesser teams such as the Oklahoma Giants, Pekin, IL, Giants, Roseland, IN, Eclipses, Lancaster, PA, Trenton, NJ, and other weak teams. There was no organization or set schedule as there had been in the City League of 1909 and Foster found himself barnstorming the country against any opponent for gate receipts.

Because of the bad blood with Frank Leland, Foster's team would not meet the talented cross-town rivals. There were no contests against major league teams, as there had been the previous year. The Fosterites of 1910 were a successful team, even "great" as Rube claimed; none-the-less they were also a largely untested team. Frank Leland's "Chicago Giants" finished a disappointing second behind the West Ends in the Chicago City Leagues.

Foster traveled to Cuba at the end of the 1910 season, where the rumors of a "Cuban color line" had subsided. In an abbreviated winter campaign Foster claimed six wins. (One newspaper account said that 16 games were scheduled between Rube's team and the Havanas, but there is not a complete account of the series.) According to Cuban baseball historian Roberto Echevarria, Havana hired Pete Hill, John "Pop" Lloyd, Grant Johnson and Bruce Petway to compete in the Cuban League. History was made by catcher Bruce Petway who, according to legend, threw out Ty Cobb three times in an exhibition game played in Cuba against the Detroit Tigers. From that day forward any catcher in Cuba was held to the "gold standard" of Petway's arm. The legend of Bruce Petway, passed down for generations, lives to this day in the folklore of Afro-Cuban baseball history.

As a coach Foster was justifiably proud of his team's performance on the diamond. As a businessman he was distressed that the team, which was backed primarily by Beauregard Mosely and his own money, lost some $2100 (big money in those days) for the season.[25]

5

The Birth of the American Giants (1911–1913)

This great team would cast a shadow for the remaining years of apartheid baseball in the United States. So vast was this team's impact that the inclusion of the word "American" in its title, whether due to great vision or good fortune proved apt indeed....

— Baseball historian Jerry Malloy, "Rube Foster and Black Baseball in Chicago," in *Baseball in Chicago*, SABR (Society for American Baseball Research) Convention Publication (1986).

1911

The growing pains of professional black baseball in Chicago were as riveting as the ball games themselves. The legal wrangling of 1910 solved nothing. Rube Foster obviously would not be happy managing a team that bore the name of rival Frank Leland on a permanent basis. The issue of overriding concern — forming a professional black baseball league — had been delayed by the infighting. Only attorney Beau Mosely could claim victory as he boosted his social standing and ego by winning the judgment against Frank Leland. Mosely attempted to use his sway to organize a national professional Negro baseball league.

In a smoky room on Chicago's South Side on December 28, 1910, Beauregard Mosely pounded a gavel and called to order a meeting of a hodgepodge of black baseball organizers who met with the aim of forming a professional black baseball league. In attendance were Frank Walker of New Orleans, Tobe Smith of Kansas City, Kansas, Felix Payne of Kansas City, Missouri, representatives from Louisville, Memphis, and St. Louis as well as Rube Foster; Frank Leland was not invited.

"The National Conference of Representatives interested in the formation of a Negro National Baseball League will now come to order.... The first order of business will be to elect a Conference Chairman. The floor is now open to nominations."

"I, Felix Payne, representing the Kansas City Giants, do hereby nominate Beauregard Mosely Conference Chairman."

"Are there any other further nominations? There are no further nominations. All in favor of electing Beauregard Mosely Chairman say 'Aye.'"

Mosely proclaimed himself the chairman of the conference and then took up the business of organizing the league. Each of the representatives rose and addressed the convocation as to why the time had come to form a national black baseball league. Rube said that there would be "no black baseball, unless a league was formed." Similar sentiments were expressed by the other conferees. Beau Mosely also introduced a white writer from the *Chicago Record-Herald* newspaper, H. M. Fisher, who heartily endorsed the "National Negro Baseball League."

A resolution was then submitted for approval: *Whereas the undersigned having convened ... for the purpose of forming a National League of Ball Players, and Whereas it appears the Chicago, Louisville, New Orleans, Mobile, St. Louis, Kansas City, Missouri, Kansas City, Kansas, and Memphis representing a sufficient number of clubs and cities to form a league and ... be it resolved that a Negro National Baseball League be formed. That for the purpose a committee of three members be and is hereby appointed empowered and instructed to proceed at once to the securing of a charter in the name of the Negro National Baseball Association of America and that the capital stock be not less than $2500 dollars, and the location of the home office at Chicago, Ill.*

The resolution was approved and the committee adjourned to meet at 10 o'clock Monday, February 27, 1911, in New Orleans.[1]

Unfortunately the league was doomed from the start. With teams flung from the Deep South to Kansas and Chicago, long rail trips would have been too expensive. Missing from the league were vital cities like Cleveland, Detroit, Milwaukee, Indianapolis all of which were in reasonable proximity and were cheaper to reach by rail. The league was impractical for other reasons too: lack of money, unbalanced competition and facilities. Rube Foster recognized from the start that the league was mere wishful thinking.

Formerly staunch allies, Rube Foster and Bo' Mosely quietly parted ways. Foster wanted nothing to do with the "Leland" Giants. However, Mosely stubbornly clung to the past and was determined to trot the Leland Giants back on the field for another season—even though Frank Leland himself had nothing to do with Mosely's team. Never mind that he did not have Foster, or viable contracts for most of the former players, or any hands-on professional baseball experience himself. Mosely clung to the Leland Giants franchise because of their former reputation and use of the old uniforms. Other than pitcher Frank Wickware, who Mosely had signed under a limited contract, Mosely's Leland Giants of 1911 were a weak team and would meet annihilation on the baseball ball diamond later on the season.[2]

Rube Foster dropped hints on several occasions that he was working out a deal directly with John Schorling. Foster's previous transactions with John Schorling had been as one of the Leland Giants board members. Schorling had been the landlord for the Leland Giants at Auburn Park (79th and Wentworth) since 1905. Schorling was also lessor for South Side Park, the former home of the White Sox. Dealing directly with Schorling was a signal that Foster had cut ties with business partners and would go it alone. For the most part he kept a lid on what he was doing, but rumors surfaced that Rube was issuing advance money, "$15, $25 and $50 chunks" to his players. The scheme Rube hatched with Schorling was ambitious. He envisioned a repeat of the 1909 season with large crowds in attendance for games with top notch cross-town foes, East Coast teams, Cuban teams and culminating with an epic battle against either the National League Cubs or American League White Sox. Foster saw no reason why his team shouldn't play before large crowds every day—like Chicago's other major league teams.[3]

Foster gathered his troops at a Palm Beach, Florida, resort to launch the season. The late winter workout in Palm Beach was becoming an annual tradition. Rube's team represented the Breakers Hotel, and teams or players from various black teams represented the Royal Poinciana Hotel. The clientele at the resort was America's wealthiest families, the Astors, the Vanderbilts, the Morgans who enjoyed watching major league caliber baseball in a private setting. In early spring Rube left southern Florida with his team to tour the South. Without fanfare Rube Foster debuted his new ball club, which he named the "American Giants," while on this spring training tour in 1911. Foster swung through Florida, Georgia, Arkansas, Texas, Tennessee, Kentucky and Indiana before returning home to Chicago. The American Giants played their first game in Chicago on May 6, 1911, against the Chicago Gunthers, traditionally one of the top teams in the City League, at Gunther Park and won by a 3–2 score.

The American Giants held their home opener at South Side park, the former home of the White Sox (known also as Schorling's Park) on the following Sunday, May 13, 1911. It was a momentous occasion, as the American Giants now had the keys to a major league park. There were locker rooms for home and visiting teams complete with hot showers. There was seating for about 15,000 of the estimated 200,000 potential baseball fans that lived within walking distance. Schorling sunk $10,000 into repairing and renovating the park for the use of the American Giants. Some of the repairs were essential since there had been a fire at the park during the off season. Even though the American Giants rented and did not own the park, as Rube would have preferred, the park would be a key to the success of the American Giants. Under threatening weather 3,000 fans watched the American Giants play the Spaldings (sponsored by Albert Spalding of baseball and sporting goods fame). American Giant pitchers Charles Dougherty and Bill Lindsay allowed only three hits, but lost the inaugural game 5–4, after three errors were made in the field.[4]

The American Giants drew decent crowds, but a few weeks into the season it was apparent that Rube's grandiose vision of a black major league team filling the stands day after day wasn't coming to fruition. In fact Foster's whole deal appeared in danger of going down the Chicago River. Fan excitement generated in the City Leagues just two seasons earlier was fading fast. In 1911, the City League's number one star Jimmie Callahan, player/manager of the Logan Squares and City League organizer, accepted an offer to play for the American League Chicago White Sox. The loss of Callahan was a crushing blow to the City League as both the quantity and quality of play dropped off. Foster never intended to depend on the City League for his livelihood. He was more interested in competition on the national level, however finding worthy opponents and drawing crowds was tougher than anticipated. The American Giants not only felt the pinch from the decline of the City League, but were also squeezed by Frank Leland's Chicago Giants. Foster realized he would face competition from Frank Leland—both on the diamond and in the battle for fans—but was surprised by the ferocity of that competition.

Leland went to his war chest with a vengeance to outbid Foster. Leland's team featured a pitching rotation of "Cyclone" Joe Williams, Walter Ball and "Big" Bill Gatewood. Gatewood, who had first appeared with the Leland Giants back in 1906, would eventually become a steady work horse in black baseball and towards the end of his career coached a young Satchel Paige on the art of pitching. The seasoned veteran Walter Ball defined pitching in early black professional baseball. "Cyclone" Joe had come to Chicago in 1902. Leland's position players weren't shabby either, featuring veterans Harry "Mike" Moore in the outfield and "Home Run" Grant Johnson (whom Leland lured away from Rube) at shortstop.

While Frank Leland had improved on his 1910 team, Foster's team was weaker. John Henry "Pop" Lloyd, who starred for Foster in 1910, followed greener pastures to the New York Lincoln Giants, and was replaced by a youngster from Indianapolis named Fred "Puggy" Hutchinson. Ace pitcher Frank Wickware, Rube's answer to Cyclone Joe Williams, entered into a unique contract arrangement whereby he pitched part-time for both Beauregard Mosely's marginal "Leland Giants" and for the American Giants. While it was better to have Wickware part-time than not at all, this did not fit with the image Rube wanted to project.

As the season got under way Frank Leland's Chicago Giants manhandled the City League teams—claiming a twenty-game winning streak at one point. Frank Leland upstaged Rube by successfully arranging games against the Philadelphia Giants and the Cuban Stars that were played at South Side Park (which was supposed to be exclusively Rube's baseball palace). One of the best games of the season in black Chicago was a pitcher's duel between Leland's "Cyclone" Joe Williams, 26 years old, against 20-year-old Dick "Cannonball" Redding, of the Philadelphia Giants. Redding gave up two runs in the first inning then held the Lelands scoreless the rest of the way, but lost by a 2–0 score.

Rube offered an olive branch to Leland at the beginning of the season, saying he "welcomed the opportunity to play Leland's Chicago Giants at South Side Park." The two kingpins were able to agree on playing each other but agreed on little else, as their feud continued. Foster would accuse Leland of undermining him with "dirty tricks" and expressed fears of an organized conspiracy against his fledgling American Giants. The two teams would meet for a series of games in early July. The showdown, dubbed the "Battle of the Giants," turned out to be the saving grace of the Chicago American Giants' first season.

Local odds-makers put Frank Leland's Chicago Giants at 3–1 favorites, based on their better overall record. Twelve thousand attended the opening game on a hot July day; and the American Giants shut down Leland, winning 8–0. Leland's Chicago Giants returned the favor by shutting out the American Giants 7–0, in the first half of a doubleheader played on July 4th. Foster did his part by putting in a relief appearance, but to no avail. After four games the series was split two games apiece, the fifth game was a see-saw affair that went 12 innings and Rube's American Giants defeated Cyclone Joe Williams by a 7–6 score.[5]

The American Giants won the sixth game of the series by forfeit when the game ended in total chaos after an umpiring controversy. The American Giants were up 4–3 in the eighth inning, there was one out; William Parks had advanced to second for Leland's Chicago Giants, and batter Harry Moore hit a little grounder to pitcher Frank Wickware who tried to catch the lead runner off the bag at second. A run down ensued, the ball appeared to hit the base runner — Parks — as he retreated back to second — then it caromed into the outfield. Parks thought he was safe, although the umpire had not yet ruled, and the ball was still alive in the outfield where Pete Hill picked it up and threw it to first to catch Harry Moore off guard for a would-be third out. While Chicago American Giant first sacker Leroy Grant attempted to tag Harry Moore, Parks dashed for third base and Grant threw to third — even though Parks was assumed out by the previous rundown play. Grant's throw was errant and Parks came into score a would-be tying run.

Both teams protested. Umpire Fitzpatrick was slow to decide then attempted a compromise ruling, but a faction of unruly fans lost patience and threatened violence against the ump. Finally the umpire had to be escorted from the park by police, whereupon the game was forfeited to the American Giants. The series resumed, a few weeks later, after the American Giants made a successful road trip to the East Coast. On July 29, 1911, Foster's team beat Leland 1–0 in a duel between Rube's ever-impressive left hander Charles Dougherty and Walter Ball. The next day Foster sent Frank Wickware to the mound, who won 6–3 against "Big" Bill Gatewood. Foster silenced many of his detractors at that point. Three more games were played and Frank Leland's Chicago Giants actually won two of them, but all told the American Giants won seven games and the Chicago Giants won four and Frank Leland had to pay off a $500 side bet he had made on the games.[6]

While Leland and Foster slugged it out, Beauregard Mosely's so called "Leland Giants" continued to barnstorm the country in a lackluster campaign. Mosely appointed a family member, Burton Mosely, to manage the team. The team was mostly unknowns, save Frank Wickware who pitched a few games for the outfit. Early in the season Mosely's team looked legitimate. They fared well against the West Baden Sprudels (a tough southern Indiana resort team), winning four out of five games in mid–June. Bo' Mosely's team fell apart however and would lose often and by large margins. The season included losses by 22–9 in Louisville, 19–4 in Kansas City, and a 10–0 whipping administered by "Smokey/Cyclone" Joe Williams of the Chicago Giants. William S. Peters' Chicago Union Giants also continued to play against lower tier semi-pro teams around Chicago; rounding out the "Giant" clubs of Chicago.[7]

One highlight of the 1911 season was a benefit game for Provident Hospital, played at the new Comiskey Park, between the American Giants and the Gunthers. Provident Hospital opened in 1891 as a teaching hospital for African American doctors and nurses who were excluded from other medical schools in 1891. While the hospital mostly served the black community, prominent white business people supported it and inter-racial cooperation was a cornerstone of the hospital mission. The Gunthers sent "Bugs" Raymond to the mound. Raymond was a formidable spitballer who had been released from the major league New York Giants. Raymond had natural ability but had one major downfall — his fondness for liquor. He was known to pick up and leave in the middle of a baseball game with a couple of baseballs in his pockets which he promptly exchanged for drinks at a nearby saloon. Raymond pulled the stunt that afternoon against the American Giants, leaving the game halfway through for the barroom. The American Giants came out on top 5–1, and a good bit of money was raised for the hospital. A year later Bugs Raymond died after a drunken brawl at a Chicago ballpark.[8]

The Chicago American Giants' inaugural season may not have lived up to Rube's vision but the team proved viable and able to move forward. Rube Foster came to the forefront as he made his point boldly by declaring independence and raising the flag of the American Giants. Foster had also formulated a model of a black professional baseball league and was just waiting for the opportunity to bring it to life. In the interval between the end of the regular season and the beginning of winter ball, Foster penned another chapter in his ongoing black baseball manifesto that was published in the *Chicago Defender* and other newspapers, a portion of which is excerpted here:

> The downfall of colored baseball in Chicago and throughout the South lies at the feet of Frank C. Leland who is a mere accident in baseball. Trouble began to brew in the organization when he tried to become manager. The men who invested their money in the club thought it advisable to keep me as manager, as I had accomplished in one year what he failed to do in a lifetime. His low dirty undermining tactics against me and his ambition to exterminate me from baseball dug a grave for him in baseball and he is now a detriment to the game....
>
> ... The wild, reckless scramble under the guise of baseball is keeping us down, and we will always be the underdog until we can successfully employ the methods that have brought success to the great powers that be in baseball of present era *organization*.
>
> We have had enough good men associated financially with clubs to insure success, but the same spirit that has existed in Chicago exists there — one man trying to "do" the other. With clubs in St. Louis, Kansas City, Louisville, Indianapolis, Chicago and Detroit operated by businessmen, in an organization, it would be the best thing yet in baseball. There is enough capital in the club owners to put up parks, and let the league own Indianapolis and Louisville. Then we could all reap the benefit. It will pay. We make the same jumps without a league and it is a certainty we could with a league and we would receive better patronage.[9]

1912

During the winter of 1911–1912, some of the American Giants went to Palm Beach and others to Cuba. Rube Foster along with Jimmie Lyons and Leroy Grant played with the baseball club of La Fe, Cuba. Also playing for "Fe" were black baseball stars Cannonball Redding, Spotswood Pole and future major leaguer Adolfo Luque. In Cuba, Foster was cast in the role of a baseball mercenary — an old time hurler with a legendary screwball. Back home he was a high officer better suited to twirling a pencil than a baseball, but he continued to take the mound for years to come. Across the island playing for the Havana Reds were Chicagoans "Cyclone/Smokey" Joe Williams, Preston Hill, Bruce Petway, Grant Johnson along with Jose Acosta — a future Washington Senator. Other Windy City regulars Frank Wickware, Wes Pryor, Jap Payne, and Pete Booker took their spring training in Palm Beach, Florida, representing either the Royal Poinciana or the Breakers hotel. Meanwhile, Frank Leland also took a group of players to Southern California where they joined forces with the African American Occidental of LA to play winter ball.[10]

By the time opening day of the regular 1912 season rolled around the course of infighting between Chicago's black baseball moguls had taken a dramatic change. Frank Leland decided not to field a team in 1912 and instead put his hat in the ring for Cook County commissioner. Despite Rube's successful tenure in Chicago, Frank Leland had always regarded him as an outsider and stayed an arm's length away from him. It is easy to see how Foster would evoke such a response, as he challenged almost everyone he interacted with. His desire to "do it all" — play, manage and own teams — would color Rube's career. Foster was beginning to show the traits of a mad baseball genius. Foster's punishment of Leland's team on the diamond might have been the deciding factor for Leland.

Beauregard Mosely also woke up to reality and wisely left baseball behind. The Chicago City League was virtually extinguished, although there were still several independent semi-pro teams in the Chicago area. This left Rube Foster's American Giants as the premier attraction in Chicagoland black baseball. Foster had been openly critical of the black baseball establishment for years and had anxiously awaited this moment of triumph. Foster was also anxious to test his recent hypothesis that a confederation of Midwestern teams could operate as a league. Rube's opportunity would come in 1912. In a show of unity Frank Leland, Major R.R. Jackson and Beauregard Mosely joined guest of honor Benjamin Davis, the editor of the *Atlanta Independent*— a leading black newspaper of the South — in box seats for the American Giants' opening day on April 21, 1912. The American Giants defeated Rogers Park, a white semi-pro team, in the opener by a 5–1 score with Bill Gatewood on the mound.[11]

With Frank Leland's team out of the picture Foster was able bring pitcher Bill Gatewood and catcher Sam Strothers back to the American Giants. Rube was not able to sign Cyclone Joe Williams, who went to the East Coast to play for the Lincoln Giants of New York. Leland's other starter, Walter Ball, began the 1912 season as an American Giant but moved to the St. Louis Giants. Foster also signed a young pitcher named Louis "Dicta" Johnson (also known as "Spitball" Johnson) who would blossom into a steady performer and a valued arm in the Negro Leagues. Frank "the Ant" Wickware was retained as the ace of the staff, and Rube occasionally pitched himself.

"Candy" Jim Taylor joined the American Giants' infield at third base (replacing Wes Pryor). "Candy Jim" was a legend in the making; he became one of the best third basemen in the history of the Negro Leagues, and later followed his brother C. I. (Charles Ishum) Taylor into the managing ranks. Bill Monroe played second, Fred "Puggy" Hutchinson was the shortstop and Bill Pierce played first. Captain Preston "Pete" Hill played center field, Frank "Pete" Duncan played right, and local legend Charles "Joe" Green, who came over from Leland's defunct team, played left.

The crew played well, and Foster later claimed the team won an unbelievable 112 out of 132 games in 1912. Unfortunately published scores for only about half that many games have been found — making it impossible to document Rube's claim. Rube stepped into his head honcho role with confidence, but others looked on with skepticism, which might explain why the *Chicago Defender* did not fully cover the American Giants. The bread and butter for the American Giants were games against teams like the St. Louis Giants, the Indianapolis ABCs, and the Cuban Stars.

Rube Foster renewed a rivalry with manager C.I. Taylor, whom he had last met in 1909 when the Leland Giants swung through the South. C.I. Taylor had migrated north out of Birmingham, Alabama, to manage the West Baden, Indiana, Sprudels in 1912 (the team was named for a mythical gnome that was said to guard the hot springs at the spa). Rube bested C.I. in 1912, winning all but one of the seven reported contests. The American Giants played against other Indiana teams in 1912, including the French Lick Plutos (another team from the Springs Valley resort spas of southern Indiana), the Abram Giants of Indianapolis and the Indianapolis ABCs.

On July 14, 1912, heavyweight boxing champ Jack Johnson was chosen to throw out the ceremonial first pitch prior to a hotly contested double-header against the visiting St. Louis Giants. Johnson had successfully defended his crown on July 4th against Jim

Flynn in Reno, Nevada. While Johnson was embroiled in legal difficulties, he found popular support in the black metropolis of Chicago. Early that summer Jack Johnson was indicted for "smuggling a diamond bracelet" into the U.S. Also in the summer of 1912 he opened a popular interracial cabaret known as Café de Champion on the South Side. A few weeks later his wife, a white woman named Etta Terry Duryea, committed suicide. It wasn't long after that Johnson was charged with violating the Mann Act, otherwise known as the "White Slave Traffic Act"—supposedly transporting women across state lines for immoral purposes.

Jack Johnson and Rube Foster went way back; they both were large men, born in East Texas, less than a year apart. Jack Johnson actually played professional baseball alongside Rube in Philadelphia when the pugilist saw action at first base with the Philadelphia Giants in 1903–04. Bronzeville gloried in the exploits of Jack Johnson as they gloried in Rube's American Giants. The rivalry with St. Louis drew increased local interest since the St. Louis team included former Chicago area players: Wes Pryor, Walter Ball, Felix Wallace, Jimmie Lyons (who had played in Chicago youth leagues) and the stoic Chappie Johnson who first came to Chicago in 1899 as a member of the Columbia Giants. Extra seats had to be placed on the field to accommodate the overflow crowd. Rube's team won the first contest by an 8–7 tally, but only after overcoming a 4–7 deficit in the bottom of the ninth. The St. Louis team won the second game 5–2, behind the pitching of a young pitcher named William "Dizzy" Dismukes—who was at the beginning of an illustrious career. Dizzy earned his nickname for his tricky submarine delivery.[12]

Some of the one hundred plus victories that Rube claimed in 1912 came against the teams of an upstart renegade white professional baseball league known as the United States League. The USL was formed in 1912 by a Reading, Pennsylvania, coal dealer/politician named William Abbott Witman. The USL attracted a number of marginal major league players. The quality was weak; one of the biggest names was the familiar drinker/spitter Arthur "Bugs" Raymond who was with the Cincinnati franchise. The league got off the ground, but was bankrupt by June and suspended play. Some of the USL teams continued on as independents and played against the American Giants. The American Giants were dominant in the handful of documented games against the "Uncle Sams," defeating the Pittsburgh team 9–1 on June 24th, whipping the Chicago "Greensox" 8–3 on July 20th and 7–0 on August 27th.[13]

The American Giants' biggest test of 1912 was the Cuban Stars. The islanders, behind the pitching of Jose Mendez and Eustaquio Pedroso, took two of three games played against Rube's men over the July 4th weekend. Foster avenged the losses later in the season by sweeping a four game series. There was no "championship" playoff or battle with the top Eastern club. The Lincoln Giants of New York were on par with the American Giants, boasting a lineup that included John "Pop" Lloyd, Spotswood Pole, Ben Taylor (the youngest of the Taylor brothers), Cannonball Redding and Smokey/Cyclone Joe Williams. A showdown between the two teams would have been of great interest, but while Foster had reached a truce with his Chicago brethren there was no peace with the white promoters of the East.[14]

Following the regular season Foster declared the Chicago American Giants "undisputed colored champions of the world" and the team boarded a train to Los Angeles to compete in the California winter baseball league. It was a spectacular trip for the American Giant players, most of whom had only "heard stories" about the western United States.

Upon arrival in L.A. the American Giants were met at the train station by a group of 200 Angelinos. The American Giants' reputation had preceded them and they made a big splash in Southern California. Somewhat surprisingly, and to the delight of Foster, the *Los Angeles Times* newspaper followed the team's every move. The mayor of Los Angeles threw out the first pitch on opening day, November 1. Unfortunately there was also a not so subtle hint of mockery in the praise heaped on Rube and the American Giants. For instance, in an article announcing the season opener, headlined "Winter Ball Starts Today," the *L.A. Times* wrote: "The Winter League will open its season here today … between the American Giants black and the McCormicks white. The Winter League is a varicolored organization three-fourths light and the *residue* dark."

Through the course of the winter season the *L.A. Times* gave credit to the American Giants where it was due, but also reached into a deep bag of racial slurs to punctuate the telling. For instance writer Harry Williams referred to the American Giants as "*brunette babies*" on one occasion, and on another referred to their fans as "*Pickaninnies.*" In telling the story of how pinch hitter James Parks won a game for the American Giants with a 10th inning RBI, Williams led with: "James Edward Parks utility man *imported from the Congo Free State especially for the purpose* broke up yesterdays game … with a red hot single." The writer called Bill Lindsay and Bruce Petway "one of the best batteries ever seen in the sunshine state," and exclaimed "*Wow! How this black boy can pitch….* It was his second victory over the white trash…. His speed was terrific his control almost perfect and his curves calculated to bamboozle the best of them."[15]

The other teams in the California Winter League were the San Diego Bears, the McCormick "Shamrocks" and the Tufts-Lyons team of Pasadena. It was a training/instructional league, but also featured a number of everyday major leaguers including Chief Meyers, Fred Snodgrass, Tillie Shafer and Charley Hall — all Californians — who had weeks earlier wrapped up playing in the World Series with the New York Giants (and the Boston Red Sox, in the case of Charley Hall). The American Giants posted the best record and took the pennant, although they by no means dominated play. Teams were concerned mostly with off-season conditioning, but in one game between San Diego and the American Giants fights broke out and players were ejected — indicating that competition was fierce at times.

Rube was proud of the Giants' performance against the white professionals, as he saw competing against and beating major leaguers as requisite for the success of a professional Negro league. The American Giants were honored in a post-season banquet in Los Angeles given by the "Good Fellows Club," in which the presiding officer proclaimed "the day the American Giants arrived in Los Angeles should be celebrated as, as great a historical event as the landing of Columbus in America." The 1912 season was a success. Rube found a way to generate regional interest in black baseball and picked up games on the fringes of the major leagues. Hopes for a proposed organized national league, dashed in 1911, were rekindled.[16]

Foster wore the hat of owner, manager and player. His prowess as a pitcher was legend, and now his talents as a baseball businessman were blossoming. Foster was a dreamer who set high goals but was careful not to get carried away, and always dealt with the business at hand. The American Giants kept costs down during the regular season by playing mostly home games. Foster eliminated middlemen whenever possible, thereby keeping money in the family of black baseball. Foster employed economy, but also knew when to make an investment. He was a great learner as well as a great teacher and had picked up every trick in the book from friend and foe along the way. The result was that Rube Foster succeeded where others did not. A black baseball league and competition against major leaguers suddenly seemed possible with Foster at the helm.

While his reputation as a shameless self-promoter was well earned, Foster's philosophy went beyond merely winning and personal gain. When it came to organizing black baseball as whole, Foster put the good of the whole first. Thirty-five years later when major league baseball admitted Jackie Robinson it was called baseball's "Great Experiment." Rube Foster began experimenting with integrating baseball much earlier. Foster was relentless in challenging the white baseball establishment (athletically and mentally), all the while deflecting the sticks and stones of racism.

1913

The American Giants' 1912 season continued through the end of the calendar year, what had started as a post-season West Coast trip became an extended mission. The American Giants traded a frigid Chicago winter for a West Coast swing, staying in Southern California until mid–March before heading up the coast towards San Francisco and then to the Pacific Northwest on the North Pacific Railway. They lived up to their bigger than life name and reputation as they dominated teams from San Francisco, Portland, Seattle and Vancouver.[17]

The 1913 team remained mostly intact from the previous year, featuring Bruce Petway behind the plate, Pete Hill in center field, Jess Barbour in right field, Pete Duncan in left, Candy Jim Taylor at third base, Fred "Pug" Hutchinson at short, William Monroe at second, and Bill Pierce at first. The biggest change on the team was the loss of pitcher Frank "the Ant" Wickware who jumped Rube's ball club to star for the Schenectady, New York, Mohawk Giants. It turned out that Wickware was barely missed. Bill Lindsay emerged as the ace, Pat Dougherty was still considered a world class lefty, and a young Louis Dicta "Spitball" Johnson along with veterans "Big" Bill Gatewood and Rube Foster himself rounded out the pitching staff.

While there were great players on the team, there were no prima donnas— except for maybe the manager, who was increasingly referred to as "the Great Rube Foster." Teamwork, coolness and effectiveness became a trademark of the well-oiled American Giant machine that calmly put down opponents. Foster deserved the credit he received for molding the team, but on the diamond there was a core group of players, namely Pete Hill, Bruce Petway and Jess Barbour, who formed the bedrock of the team. This core group quietly went about doing their job year after year and winning games for the American Giants, yet received only scant recognition. The consistent success of the American Giants was built on quiet team players— one of the secrets of Rube's winning formula.

The American Giants returned to Chicago and opened up the regular season against a team from Gary, Indiana, winning 6–4. About two weeks later the American Giants met a team from East Chicago, Indiana, that featured a pitcher who went by the name

"Cy" Young — this was not *the* Cy Young, but probably Charles Young, who later pitched for Buffalo in the Federal League. The American Giants with Bill Lindsay on the mound handed Young and the East Chicago team a 6–1 defeat. The American Giants faced a number of teams from the Hoosier State in 1913. Teams from Indiana's northwest region were a natural match up due to their proximity. The American Giants also battled the Indianapolis ABCs, the French Lick Plutos and the West Baden Sprudels, who represented southern Indiana health resort towns. Foster's longtime rival C.I. Taylor remained in command of the West Baden Sprudels.

When Rube returned to Chicago from the West Coast, he found former standout infielder Dangerfield "Danger" Talbert suffering in poor health and organized a benefit game to assist him. Charles Comiskey and James "Nixie" Callahan of the White Sox both contributed $25 to the fund. Former business manager Beauregard Mosely, who had recently become the first African American to serve on the Electoral College, also made a donation.[18]

It was while touring the West Coast that Rube's friend heavyweight champion Jack Johnson was arrested and jailed in Chicago for violating the Mann Act. It was Judge Kenesaw Mountain Landis who initially refused to grant Johnson bail — citing irregularities with the bail bond. Later Johnson did post bond, and his highly publicized trial would get under way in the spring of 1913. Jack Johnson was found guilty and sentenced to a year in prison and a $1000 fine. However Johnson's attorney convinced the court that Johnson should be allowed to remain free on bail while he appealed the ruling. A week later — while out on bail — Jack Johnson accompanied the American Giants on a road trip — a road trip that happened to include a swing through Canada. Johnson donned an American Giants uniform, blending in with the team, and stepped off the train in Montreal to make his escape. From Canada, Johnson steamed to Paris and resumed his boxing career. At least that is the tale that Jack Johnson told of his flight from injustice. Johnson even elaborated that he had posed as the husky pitcher Bill Gatewood and hired an imposter of like stature to stay at his home so that authorities would not realize he had left. A later investigation by the *Chicago Examiner* newspaper revealed that Johnson had made timely payments (bribes) to federal officials who cooperated in Jack Johnson's road trip as an American Giant.[19]

The American Giants also played against old rivals from the Chicago semi-pro scene who survived in scaled down form: the Chicago Gunthers, the Spaldings, Logan Squares and a new incarnation of Frank Leland's Chicago Giants. Frank Leland swore off the baseball business for the most part, but could not resist taking one last crack at it and put together a semi-pro team for an occasional local contest. For old times' sake the American Giants met Leland's team twice late in the season.

The *Indianapolis Freeman* announced the contests:

> … The Chicago American Giants who have been playing some very fine ball all the season will play at Schorling Park on Sunday. [Sam] Crawford the famous Southpaw twirler will pitch for the Chicago Giants. Frank Leland owner of the team states that he will stake his life on the Chicago Giants and that he has the best team of the two. Seats are now on sale at the box office. Mr. Foster thinks the Chicago boys play good but will not be able to down his men. Both teams have friends and several thousand are expected to attend the game…. [20]

The American Giants took them too lightly and lost both games. Sam Crawford was the winning pitcher on both occasions. In the first meeting the American Giants got eleven hits, but ended up losing 10–3. The American Giants were supposedly fatigued from a long road trip. The rivals met again in September, this time Rube actually took the mound, but he was hammered for six runs in the second inning and the Americans lost by a 9–5 score. Leland proved that Rube could not take his dominance for granted.[21]

Midway through the season, on July 1st, 6,000 fans showed up to see the visiting Sprudels of West Baden, Indiana (population 2,000), take on the Chicago American Giants (population 2,000,000). Before the game both teams took part in a parade. The Giants donned new uniforms, cream color trimmed in blue. The Giants unfurled a banner of bunting with a border of blue with white stars and red lettering that read: "Champions of the California Winter League. Season of 1912–1913. American Giants." Opposing teams saw Rube's bunting as a target and took aim. The West Baden Sprudels won two out of three games from Rube. The Sprudels featured second baseman Elwood "Bingo" DeMoss; they were managed by C. I. Taylor, whose brother Ben Taylor was their first baseman while other brother Candy Jim Taylor played third base for the American Giants.[22]

The American Giants struggled all year long to protect their reputation as "champions." Shortly after C.I. Taylor and the Sprudels left town, the Cuban Stars with Jose Mendez and a young outfielder named Cristobal Torriente took four out of five games from the Giants. Cristobal Torriente, a young hulking slugger, turned a lot of heads and Rube Foster's was one of them. Rube wished he could lure Torriente into the American Giant fold — a wish that he would later fulfill.

The highlight of the season was a "championship" series against the Lincoln Giants of New York. The Lincolns were led by pitchers Cyclone Joe Williams and Dick Cannonball Redding, along with shortstop John Henry Lloyd, and outfielder Spotswood Pole. Foster attempted to sign pitcher Frank Wickware to bolster his staff for the East-West showdown. Wickware had pitched for Rube the previous year, but he had gone over to the Mohawk Giants of Schenectady, New York. The manager of the Lincoln Giants, Eddie McMahon, who also knew of Wickware's talents, approached him to pitch and actually advanced Wickware $100 to pitch for the Lincoln Giants. McMahon was therefore shocked when he arrived at New York's Olympic Field and spotted Wickware suited up in a Chicago American Giants uniform warming up.

McMahon and Foster argued over who had rights to Wickware for an hour before the game was finally called off. A large crowd was justifiably disappointed with the cancellation. The *New York Age* of July 24, 1913, noted:

> Fans inclined to be fair find it difficult to side with Wickware or regard him as a hero. To accept money from one manager and then want to play for another is a piece of reasoning which does not favorably impress those who believe that one should keep his word at all times…. Wickware will do much to injure the progress of baseball among the colored clubs.[23]

McMahon and Foster set their differences aside and the series got under way the next day. Foster's worst fears were realized. The Lincoln Giants with Cyclone Joe Williams on the mound were nearly unbeatable. In the first four games the Lincolns won two games (both with Williams on the mound), one game ended in a tie, and the American Giants took one. The American Giants had battled against Williams before, and the results were familiar. The Lincoln Giants traveled to Chicago as the championship of 1913 continued. Foster tried to counter by bringing Ben Taylor, Steel Arm Taylor and Bingo DeMoss on board. In one game Candy Jim Taylor played third, Ben Taylor played first and Steel Arm

Taylor pitched, but not even the famous Taylor family could bail out the American Giants. Before it was all over, the Lincoln Giants won seven games and the American Giants won five. Joe Williams was the winning pitcher in six of those games.

Fans questioned some of Rube's coaching decisions (he gave Pat Dougherty only one start in the championship), and the wisdom of having taken the team out on the road all year with no time to rest. Rube didn't let the criticism affect him, pointing out to anyone who would listen that he had "acted in the best interests of black baseball."

It was one of the few times in his career that Rube Foster admitted defeat, saying:

"I am one who takes his hat off to the victorious Lincoln Giants. Their great playing and wonderful defense was never surpassed, if equaled, on any diamond."[24]

After the regular season Foster challenged Chicago Cubs manager Johnny Evers to a post-season match. Evers did not dismiss the idea immediately out of hand (many of the Cubs would have liked the extra payday), but Rube was later rebuffed by the Cubbies. Foster still yearned for revenge of the narrow defeat put on his squad by the 1909 Cubs, it was a dream he never let go of.[25]

6

Black Baseball in the Teens (1914–1919)

"Before another baseball season rolls around colored ball players, a score of whom are equal in ability to the brightest stars in the big league teams, will be holding down jobs in organized ball...."
— Rube Foster, May 2, 1914, *Seattle Post-Intelligencer.*

1914

Foster did not spend time crying after suffering defeat at the hands of the Lincoln Giants in the 1913 showdown. Shortly afterward Rube was heard whispering to old friends on the opposing team: "How about heading out West this winter to California, Oregon, Washington and British Columbia in a private train?" Rube's invitation was directed with special attention to Cyclone Joe Williams and John Henry Lloyd, two players who were largely responsible for the superiority of the New York Lincoln Giants. Foster also extended invitations to outfielder Jude Gans, pitcher Lee Wade and third baseman Bill Francis, an old friend from his Philadelphia Giant days. Ah, Rube's power of persuasion proved effective — all of the above accepted. Ben Taylor, who had joined the American Giants as a ringer for the championship series, also accepted Rube's invitation. In mid–March Rube headed out West in a private Pullman coach filled with raw baseball talent, one of the most talented teams Rube would ever manage.[1]

The American Giants opened spring training at Santa Maria, California, against the Portland, Oregon, Beavers on March 21, 1914. The first game ended in a 9–9 tie and the Portland Beavers won the following afternoon by a 5–3 count. Rube had planned to begin the tour in Southern California then work his way up the coast through Northern California and into the Pacific Northwest. The itinerary had to be changed however when Pacific Coast League President Allen Baum voiced objections to prospects of a black team playing against the PCL teams. After Baum's disapproval, games that had been scheduled in San Francisco and Oakland were cancelled. Portland Beavers' manager Walter McCredie disagreed with Baum. A rivalry between the Beavers and American Giants had hatched the previous winter. McCredie appreciated the skills of the American Giants and the large gates they brought in. McCredie spoke out against the color line and extended an invitation to the American Giants to play against the Beavers in Oregon.[2]

The American Giants skirted racial prejudice at the Golden Gate only to again meet up with Jim Crow in Oregon. The American Giants were refused at every hotel in Medford, Oregon, until finally the color line was dropped at a Japanese inn. The American Giants were informed that they would be allowed to sleep at the inn, but would not be allowed to eat there. An argument ensued with the innkeeper who relented and procured cheese and crackers for the American Giants. The *Chicago Defender* ran a banner headline on page one of the April 11, 1914, edition: "Rube Foster's Team Starving In Oregon."[3]

The American Giants continued by rail to Portland and then to Seattle. About 2,500 fans showed up for a Friday game between the American Giants and Seattle. The weekday crowd saw a dandy pitcher's duel; Cyclone Joe Williams struck out 16 Seattle batters and Pete Schneider (who went on to pitch for the next five seasons for the Cincinnati Reds) allowed the American Giants just four hits. The game was all tied at 1–1 going into the ninth frame when Ben Taylor got a hit. Pop Lloyd was the next batter, Seattle catcher Duddy Cadman thought Taylor was set to steal and called for a pitchout. However Lloyd reached his bat across the outside of the plate and slapped the ball down the first base line. Ben Taylor got all the way to third base. Taylor was then able to tag up and score on a fly ball hit by Jesse Barbour and the American Giants held on to win the game 2–1.[4]

The Sunday game was delayed when a throng of fans swamped the ticket booth in disorderly fashion. Not all could fit into Rainier Valley Baseball Park — a group of young fans resorted to physically breaking into the park by prying off a board in the outfield.

Promoters had done a great job publicizing the game, as some Seattle fans thought the American Giants were actual "Giants."[5]

Rube and the American Giants appeased the fans by playing "Shadow Ball" before the game. Pop Lloyd picked up an imaginary baseball, tossed it in the air, and hit it to infielders who fielded the invisible ball and made a play on the baserunner. The punch line came when there was a play at home plate and one of the runners would collide with the catcher (played by veteran Bill Monroe, a real life second basemen), who played the fall guy. The fans were enthralled by the farce although it was one of the few times that the American Giants were reported to have put on a comedy performance.[6]

The visit of the American Giants garnered the attention of the local press. The *Seattle Post Intelligencer* published several feature stories about the visit of the American Giants including an interview with Rube Foster. The headline of the Sunday April 5th *Seattle Post Intelligencer* read: "Will Let Down Bars to Colored Players, says Foster." What followed was an interview Seattle writer Royal Brougham conducted with Rube. Rube stated:

> Before another baseball season rolls around colored ball players … will be holding down jobs in organized baseball…. The Fed's will force it [baseball's integration], in the coming season…. It was last year before the new organization [the Federal League] had cut so much ice in baseball that several big fellows got together and decided to put the league on a basis the same as a big league. The players were to have the same privileges and be governed by the national body. The black teams draw enormous crowds…. But last fall when things slowed up in the new league and it was not thought that anything could be feared from the Feds, the magnates gave up the plan. A few months later, when Gilmour [Fed League founder] and the rest of the live wires began to shout I received a message from one of the

party which mentioned the colored league of last year. He was very anxious to go through with the whole thing. But we had our schedule arranged for this tour, and it was too late. I would not consider the thing. But at that I would not be surprised if the league is organized next year[7] [*Seattle Post Intelligencer*, April 5, 1914].

Rube's remarks grabbed attention, however his proclamation was "wishful thinking." Foster may have been attempting to show leadership by postulating a new state of affairs for colored baseball. Billy Lewis writing for the *Indianapolis Freeman* communicated the sentiments of black baseball's rank and file:

It goes without saying it emphatically that Foster's opinion sounds mighty good to the poor down trodden colored players who have to do so much "tall" figuring in order to make ends meet. But the plain fact of the matter is that Rube has drawn on his imagination for the better part of his opinion. For as much as I hope, and as colored players and people hope, for better days for the colored players there is nothing to warrant what he had to say. Foster is having the time of his life riding about in special cars out west and naturally enough with the distinguished consideration paid him and his bunch of players he feels to give out something worthwhile.

As to the supposed plan for organized ball to put together a league, Billy Lewis conceded that there might have been a grain of truth to Rube's account:

Perhaps Foster was in on the deal and does know what he was talking about. But I confess my ignorance right here I heard of no such scheme. Not at all that it was important that I should have heard of it, but one feels to know about things that are in his line of duty. However it may be that Rube is right. It is hardly reasonable to think that he could [have] born such an elaborate story by himself and still live. Well it was a poor job at any rate true or fiction.[8]

After taking two games from Seattle, the American Giants took a boat across Puget Sound and faced off with the Victoria, B.C., "Bees." They then went on to play Washington State College in Pullman, Washington, and stopped long enough to play at Lewiston, Colorado — as they made their way back to the Windy City to open the regular season on April 26.

Although most of what Rube said to the press in Seattle about the imminent integration of professional baseball was quickly forgotten, there was something to his rendition. Baseball was entering a second genesis in 1914. Babe Ruth joined the Boston Red Sox in 1914 and the curtains began to close on the Dead Ball era. Another event of 1914 was the outbreak of World War I. The war would affect baseball as the U.S. was gradually drawn in and players had to join up. As Rube had alluded to, the competition of the Federal League would force changes in major league baseball. Many top major league players were signed to Federal League teams, creating a second major league. Several Federal League cities built or refurbished ballparks.

Chicago's baseball landscape was forever changed with the addition of Weegham Park at Addison and Clark streets, the home of the Federal League Chicago Whales. After the demise of the Feds, Charles Weegham sold the park to William Wrigley — the rest is history. A Federal League park was also erected in Indianapolis, and even though the Hoosier Feds won the championship in 1914, the team was sold and moved out the following year. Indianapolis Federal League Park then became a choice venue for contests between the Indianapolis ABCs, the American Giants and other top black teams. Foster considered the major league backdrop another step forward in the development of pro-

1914 American Giants. From left to right, front row: George "Chappie" Johnson, Pete Hill, Bill Francis, William Monroe, Horace Jenkins, Bill Lindsay, Jack Watts, James "Pete" Booker, Frank "Pete" Duncan. Back row: Lee Wade, Jess Barbour, Andrew "Rube" Foster, Albert "Hamp" Gillard, John Henry "Pop" Lloyd, and Robert "Jude" Gans. Rube left for the West Coast with a few ringers following the regular season in 1914 (photograph courtesy NoirTech Research, Inc.).

fessional black baseball. Foster's long time rival C.I. Taylor took over as the manager of the Indianapolis ABCs in 1914, forming a very strong black team in the backyard of the American Giants.

The roster of the American Giants was shuffled for the regular 1914 season. Foster found places for the four players he had robbed from the Lincoln Giants at the conclusion of the preceding season. Candy Jim Taylor and Ben Taylor left the fold and were playing for the Indianapolis ABCs. Veteran Bill Francis took over the hot corner from Candy Jim. Jude Gans joined captain Pete Hill and Pete Duncan in the outfield. "Smokey" Joe Williams left the American Giants shortly after they returned from the West Coast, but former Lincoln Giant pitcher Lee Wade was added to the rotation. William Monroe remained at the keystone and Jesse Barbour held down first base. John Henry Lloyd replaced Puggy Hutchinson at shortstop. "Pops" Lloyd had played for Rube Foster previously on the Leland Giants of 1910 — the team Foster called his "best ever." The American Giants again looked poised to dominate black baseball.

The main competition in the 1914 season was against the Cuban Stars and the Indianapolis ABCs. Along with a tough pitching staff featuring Eustaquio Pedroso, Monk Pareda and Jose Junco, the Cuban Stars sported slugger Cristobal Torriente who could single-handedly break a game open. The Indianapolis ABCs of 1914 featured the whole Taylor family: "Candy Jim" Taylor at third, Ben Taylor at first, "Steel Arm" John Taylor on the mound, and C.I. Taylor in the dugout. Both the Cubans and the ABCs held their own with the American Giants. Rube lost his share of games, and while he recognized that competition was good for the business of black baseball — he still hated losing.

The American Giants continued to play against local semi-pros. Frank Leland put together a team — the Chicago Giants — made up mostly of American Giant castoffs who aimed to upset Rube's men. The two teams met in mid–May. Sam Crawford was the starting pitcher for Frank Leland's team. Lee Wade started the "battle of Chicago" for the

American Giants. True to historic form Leland's team kept pace with the American Giants and the score was tied 0–0 through six innings, but the American Giant bats came to life and Rube's team ended up winning 6–0.[9]

Foster, not satisfied with having decimated Nat Strong's Lincoln Giants following the 1913 season, tried a similar trick in 1914 — this time the target was the Mohawk Giants of Schenectady, New York. Midway through the season Rube redefined the meaning of the term "player raid," when he journeyed to Schenectady and convinced the Mohawk Giants to come to Chicago to play against the American Giants. A big crowd came out to see the Mohawk Giants do battle with the American Giants on July 19th, as former American Giant twirler Frank Wickware pitched for the Mohawks in the first of the two-game series.

The American Giants won both games, the real action came *after* the games when Foster arranged to have the Mohawk Giants transplanted to Louisville, Kentucky. Rube's motives aren't entirely clear, but it would appear to be a foray into "farming" players or propping up a franchise in the Midwest in hopes of advancing a league. Before moving the Mohawk Giants to Louisville, Foster saw to it that Frank Wickware was in an American Giant uniform. According to Mohawk Giant historian Frank Keetz, "In Louisville ... they (the Mohawk Giants) had a disastrous experience both on the field and with their paychecks." Moving the Mohawk Giants to Louisville proved to be a disaster. Foster, who often bragged about "never missing a payday," was embarrassed by the episode and swept it under the rug.[10]

There were some surprising developments on the American Giant pitching staff in 1914. Thirty-four-year-old Rube Foster decided to take the mound on a regular basis and was able to hold his own with the kids. Rube relied mostly on a variety of off speed pitches and screwballs but found his groove. Rube shut out the Cuban Stars 1–0, in a one hitter that was spoiled by a Cristobal Torriente double. A few days later Foster shut out the Indianapolis ABCs by a 3–0 count.[11]

Newcomer Lee Wade became the ace on the staff, as Pat Dougherty began to have trouble with his arm. Bill Lindsay, also known as the "Kansas Cyclone," a hard throwing right-hander who had shown great promise the previous season, worked a few games in the first half of the season, but fell ill. Lindsay's illness was serious and tragically he died in Chicago's Provident Hospital on September 8, while the American Giants were in the middle of a big series against the Brooklyn Royal Giants. The series against the Brooklyn Giants was billed in the *Chicago Defender* as the "World Series," but the Brooklyn Giants had no legitimate claim to a championship match. Other than pitcher William "Dizzy" Dismukes, the Brooklyn Giants were a weak team and the American Giants swept them in five straight games.[12]

Following the rout of the Brooklyn Giants the American Giants staged a rematch with Frank Leland's Chicago Giants. The weather was dismal, the crowd was disappointingly small and the American Giants won by a 5–3 score. The personal rivalry between Rube Foster and Frank Leland had started when Rube landed on the shores of Lake Michigan in 1902. While Rube gave the impression of total domination, Frank Leland had gotten the upper hand on a number of occasions and always competed well. The rivalry between the two was drawing to a close. While the American Giants played the Chicago Giants, Frank Leland lay in bed with a serious illness. It turned out it was his deathbed; on November 15, 1914, Frank Leland died.

Frank Leland was one of the most important figures in early black baseball. Leland traced his baseball experience back to the nineteenth century — when baseball had tried to take on a gentleman's air. He mustered the courage and resources to organize a team to compete in the otherwise all-white City League. He forged relationships with the likes of Albert Spalding — one of professional baseball's founding fathers.

While Rube came to be known as the "Father of Black Baseball," Leland was "the grandfather of black baseball in Chicago." In the Chicago black community Leland was not only a baseball man, but also a successful politician and community leader. Every black professional player in Chicago in that era truly owed Leland a debt of gratitude. Leland's funeral service was held at the historic Quinn Chapel, Chicago's oldest black church. The floral bearers were Jude Gans and Mrs. R.R. Jackson — the wife of R.R Jackson, one of Frank Leland's collaborators in baseball and politics. The floral design was a baseball diamond with a link between first base and home plate. The pall bearers were ball players: pitcher Sam Crawford, catcher Pete Booker, pitcher William Gatewood, first baseman Dudley McAdoo, shortstop Guy Jackson and outfielder Joe Green. Joe Green had a special relationship with Frank Leland; he inherited the baseball team and would run the Chicago Giants for many years. It was the second funeral in two months for many in attendance.[13]

Rube made his usual boasts about the superiority of his squad and the growth of black baseball, but black baseball in 1914 fell short of expectations. The American Giants did not face off with St. Louis, which had previously been a big rivalry — the St. Louis organization fell apart. Also missing from the schedule were the Lincoln Giants — due to bad blood created by Rube's raid of the previous season. Rube's pre-season forecast of integration and assimilation of black baseball with the majors proved to be sheer fantasy.

1915

After time off for the holidays the American Giants were back on the rails. This time they opened the 1915 season in March against semi-pro teams in New Orleans before heading to Southern California. Veteran second baseman William Monroe did not make the trip due to illness, and when the American Giants reached Los Angeles they were alerted by telegram that the beloved Bill "Money" Monroe had passed away. Monroe was a veteran and had real presence in the dugout, making jokes and talking it up. He was greatly missed.

The American Giants played a few games in Southern California before heading up the coast to take on the Portland Beavers. Portland manager Walter McCredie appreciated the opportunity to play the American Giants, the rivalry was now in its third year. Earlier in the year McCredie found himself in the midst of a firestorm when he hired Lang Akena, an Oriental/Hawaiian, to play outfield. McCredie bowed to pressure from other Pacific Coast teams who had complained that Akena was "as dark as Jack Johnson" and released Akena. Walt McCredie let Akena go reluctantly and stated: "I don't think the color of the skin ought to be a barrier in baseball.... If I had my say the Afro American would be welcome inside the fold. I would like to have two such ball players as Petway and Lloyd of the Chicago Colored Giants who play out here every spring. I think

Lloyd is another Hans Wagner around shortstop and Petway is one of the greatest catchers in the world."[14]

The games between the Beavers and the American Giants featured a battle between Detroit Tiger 22-game winner Harry Coveleski pitching for Portland and Frank Wickware for Chicago. The games were hotly contested with the Beavers taking four of seven *known* games. Before leaving the Pacific Northwest the American Giants played Victoria, B.C., Tacoma, Seattle and Aberdeen. The American Giants stopped long enough in Omaha, Nebraska, to play a game against a local team before returning to Chicago to open the regular season on April 24th.

The death of William Monroe coming on the heels of the deaths of Bill Lindsay and Frank Leland was emblematic of changes in black baseball; talented young players replaced the old pros and the game evolved. One example of young talent changing the game was the debut in 1915 of teenager Oscar Charleston with the Indianapolis ABCs. From the beginning, Charleston wowed fans with his exceptional strength and quickness. Charleston was later called "among the best players ever" and lifted the ABCs to parity with the American Giants. The American Giants also faced serious competition from the New York Lincoln Giants and the Cuban Stars. The Cubans' answer to Oscar Charleston was Cristobal Torriente and the Lincolns had sluggers Louis "Big" Santop and Spotswood Pole.

The American Giants lost several key players. Pop Lloyd, Jude Gans and Lee Wade, all of whom Foster had pinched from the New York Lincoln Giants, returned to Gotham in 1915 to join the Lincoln *Stars*. (The Lincoln Stars had split off from the Lincoln Giants.) Puggy Hutchinson came back to Chicago to play short, and Rube picked up a young slugger from the ranks of the local black semi-pros—Hurley McNair—who replaced Gans in the outfield. Charles "Pat" Dougherty lost his spot on the team and joined the successor to Leland's Chicago Giants, "Joe Green's" Chicago Giants.

Foster's experiment with farming out the Mohawk Giants to Louisville, Kentucky, failed, but he salvaged the operation by hiring star pitchers Frank Wickware and Dick Whitworth to pitch for the American Giants in 1915. Veteran thrower Bill Gatewood rejoined the team to give additional support and Foster pitched a few games.

After returning from the West Coast, the American Giants found easy pickings among the local semi-pros and took about a dozen straight games. However when the Indianapolis ABCs came to town in June that winning streak ended. The team that Indianapolis manager C.I. Taylor brought to town included, in addition to Oscar Charleston, second baseman Elwood "Bingo" DeMoss, pitcher William "Dizzy" Dismukes, and Ben Taylor at first. On paper the Indianapolis ABCs had the better team, and defeated the American Giants twice in the five game series.

Two weeks later in a series that began on July 4th the Cuban Stars, under the leadership of Augistin Molina, came calling on Chicago's South Side. The Cubans dominated the American Giants—taking six of seven games. "The Giants seemed powerless before the men from the Island," said the *Chicago Defender*. Just like that the American Giants, whose manager often boasted that the team was "the greatest colored team in the country," had a losing record against their peers. The American Giants found themselves in the midst of a classic summertime baseball war when they were awakened by the bitter taste of defeat. It got worse for Rube's men before it got better.[15]

The American Giants took a rare regular season road trip down the line to Indianapolis. On Sunday July 18th the ABCs hosted the American Giants in Federal League Park — the ballpark built for the Hoosier Feds in 1914. The owners of the Federal League Park were more than happy to rent the park out to the ABCs for a major attraction such as the American Giants.

Indianapolis fans black and white crowded the park to see the one and only Rube Foster. The game, which began as a pitcher's duel between Dizzy Dismukes starting for Indianapolis and Frank Wickware for Chicago, ended in a different kind of duel. The American Giants went up 3–2 in the eighth inning on a run produced by a Rube Foster RBI, who inserted himself as pinch hitter for Frank Wickware. Richard Whitworth was brought in to pitch the bottom of the eighth and preserve the Giants' one run lead, but the lanky right hander gave up a hit to George Shively and then walked Bingo DeMoss. Rube threw up his hands and called on old timer "Big" Bill Gatewood to douse the flames. Gatewood faced rookie phenom Oscar Charleston and walked him — loading the bases. With the chips down Gatewood pitched to clean-up hitter Ben Taylor and walked him as well, which scored the tying run. The game was tied at three, the ABCs had bases loaded, no outs in the bottom of the eighth when the nature of the game changed.

A storm was brewing, thunder rumbled in the distance and fine dust blowing around the infield was blinding the players. C.I. Taylor and Rube Foster agreed to have the ground crew sprinkle the infield dirt so that it wouldn't blow around. The ground crew sprinkled the infield between second and third, when the first few raindrops were felt. Umpire Harry Giesel felt that dust blowing around was no longer an issue due to the natural dampness and ordered play recommenced. Rube begged to differ; he felt that the doctoring of the infield had been hasty and uneven and could lend an advantage to the Indianapolis team.

Rube threatened to not bring his players back on the field unless the infield was sprinkled evenly. At that point umpire Giesel declared the game a forfeit to the Indianapolis ABCs. Team captain Pete Hill approached the umpire to restate Rube's case and a melee erupted at Indianapolis's Federal League Park. A sergeant from the Indianapolis Police Department came on the field in an effort to calm things down by restraining Hill. Later, Rube Foster accused that police officer of "hitting Pete Hill on the nose with a gun."

The *Chicago Defender* headlined the story of the forfeited game: "American Giants in Fierce Riot at Hoosier City." The *Defender* distorted one detail of eyewitness accounts in an article titled "Umpire Hits Pete Hill with Gun." The image of an umpire cracking the Chicago American Giant team captain on the head with a gun was an outrage. Readers might have suspected that the *Defender* account was exaggerated; on the other hand fans were struggling to understand how their beloved American Giants could suddenly find themselves on the losing end so often — blaming the ump was a convenient explanation. The *Defender* painted the Indianapolis club as crooked bumpkins who acted without regard to the greater good of black baseball:

> Both teams grabbed bats, the umpire and Pete Hill had an argument and the umpire jerks out a gun and hits "Pete" over the nose. The umpire forfeited the game to the ABCs. Hundreds of people who were betting had scrap. The scene on the diamond was a disgrace. The game was played at the white Federal Park. No more will these teams play at this park. There

was too great a contrast between the gentlemanly playing of the Federal teams and the riot scenes enacted Sunday. Such games mean that baseball in this city will be reduced to low ebb and respectable people will not patronize them. It was a bloody chapter. Another one will kill Afro-American ball playing.[16]

Contrary to the concerns raised by the *Defender*, it would not be the last time Hoosier Federal League Park was utilized by black baseball teams, it was the first of many. (There would be other melees too.) The donnybrook came in the first of a four game series between the Midwestern rivals. The following day an Indianapolis police officer approached Rube Foster during the game and chided him "who started the fight yesterday?" Rube mumbled some words and ignored the cop. Indianapolis's finest responded by uttering profanity, hurling racial epithets and threatening to "blow Rube's brains out." Also during the second game of the series, a usually subdued C.I. Taylor got into a shoving match with American Giant second baseman Harry Bauchman who was sent by Rube to coach third base. Bauchman had decided to straighten out the bag that he found to be crooked. C.I. did not approve of Bauchman's handiwork and first demanded he step back and then physically pushed him back.

The talent laden Indianapolis team took all four games from the American Giants. Rube and the Chicago fans had sour grapes, given the extracurricular activities in Indianapolis and the embarrassing defeats. Rube Foster and C.I. would exchange verbal barbs in the newspapers. Foster called Taylor the "Stool Pigeon of the ABC club." Rube added that Taylor was an "ingrate ... of the lowest kind" who used "low tactics" that "ruined baseball in West Baden." Rube (who had hired C.I.'s brothers for short stints) said "C.I.'s own brothers refused to play for him, because C.I. wouldn't pay them."

C.I. responded to Rube's comments in a letter written to the *Chicago Defender* that was also published in the *Indianapolis Ledger*. Taylor threatened to sue Rube Foster for libel and denied Rube's accusations, but also offered an apology for the events that had taken place in Indianapolis. C.I. Taylor stated that he "only wanted to act as Rube's lieutenant" in the bid to start a Negro baseball league. C.I. attached personal correspondence with Rube over the last year, to demonstrate good will.[17]

Even though there was animosity between Chicago and Indianapolis, in the end the two cities worked closely together to promote black baseball. The *Indianapolis Freeman* newspaper had covered the goings on in black baseball throughout the country, even before the *Defender*. C.I. Taylor would be Rube Foster's righthand man when it came to solidifying the black baseball movement into a league.

On July 24, 1915, Great Lakes passenger steamship called the S.S. *Eastland* docked downtown on the Chicago River and boarded some 2,500 Western Electric employees headed for a company picnic in Michigan City, Indiana. With the full load of passengers the poorly constructed ship listed back and forth then tipped over and dumped passengers into the water — some 800 people died. The *Eastland* disaster was the worst in Chicago history, with more loss of life than the Chicago fire, indeed it was one of the worst disasters in U.S. history. The *Chicago Defender* reported that only three Afro-Americans were on board the ill fated ship, and that they all escaped death.[18]

The American Giants got on track in early August. They battled the Lincoln Stars to a standstill, both teams winning five games in the ten-game series. Some called the series a World Series because of the East vs. West aspect. On August 22nd, the American Giants defeated the Cuban Stars 4–3. It was the first Sunday game they had won in two months; no one could remember a time when Rube had gone two months without winning on Sunday. The two teams met again the following day, Monday, August 23rd. It was a hotly contested game — as the American Giants were hoping to avenge the drubbing they suffered at the hands of the Cubans earlier in the season. In the fourth inning the Cuban center fielder, Cristobal Torriente, was called out trying to steal third and responded by kicking the umpire. Chicago pitcher Sam Crawford intervened and took a swing at the hulking Torriente. The Cubans came streaming out of the dugout and a melee ensued. The police got things under control, remarkably the game resumed and the American Giants ended up winning 3–1. After the game Torriente and Crawford met on the street and a rumble broke out. Bricks, left by workmen who were repairing the streets, were used as missiles by the combatants. Rube Foster finally came on the scene and eventually brokered peace.[19]

At the end of August, Henry "Pop" Lloyd and Jude Gans left the Lincoln Stars after finding out that team owner Jesse McMahon drank their paychecks, and rejoined the American Giants. With Lloyd and Gans on the squad, the scales were tipped in Rube's favor. The American Giants finished out the season in strong fashion, drubbing the Cubans and the St. Louis Stars, although they split two games with local rivals Joe Green's Giants.[20]

Rube dared to proclaim his team champions, but that claim was dubious considering how much the team had struggled. Lucky for Rube, the Lincoln Stars, Cuban Stars and Indianapolis ABCs had simultaneously beat up on each other and it turned out that none of the four teams demonstrated superiority over all three of the others. The season ended in a dead heat between the four powerhouses. This balanced competition was a milestone on the way to league formation. After the regular season, Rube challenged the Federal League pennant winning Chicago Whales led by Joe Tinker (former Cub shortstop immortalized in the "Tinker to Evers to Chance" poem) to a game with the proceeds to go to a local charity. While the Whales did play games against several Chicago semi-pro teams, Tinker ignored Rube's challenge. Rube's hope that the Federal League might be a force in ending the color line in major league baseball was a distant memory.[21]

The American Giants didn't take any time off following the regular season and by mid–October were on their way to the West Coast. The train stopped in Omaha, Nebraska, long enough for the American Giants to split two games from a white professional team made up of Federal Leaguers and minor leaguers. The American Giants continued on to Southern California to play in the California Winter League. While Foster had received a cold shoulder from the head of the Pacific Coast League the previous year, that did not deter him from going back to California and laying down the gauntlet. There was a subtext to the extensive traveling by the American Giants. The travels of the Chicago White Sox, the white major league team also housed on the South Side of Chicago, were widely publicized. Writer Ring Lardner accompanied the Sox to California for a spring training in 1913 and published regular stories in the *Chicago Examiner*. Lardner later used the experiences as the basis for a number of "tongue in cheek" stories in the *Saturday Evening Post*. While the Chicago White Sox captivated white America's notion of a "big-time coast-to-coast travelling ball club," Foster proved the American Giants could do the same. Ring Lardner's tales captured the humorous side of big league baseball, by contrast the stories of the Chicago American Giants' rail journeys were often fraught with the ongoing struggle against hatred and bigotry.

As the train went from Chicago to Indiana, to Kentucky, on to Tennessee, into Georgia and the Deep South, across Texas, through New Orleans, the desert Southwest, into California, north all the way to British Columbia, through the mountains, the Great Plains and back through the prairies to Chicago, the players felt a wide range of emotions. The American Giants were trailblazers; their contribution to the cause of racial equality was unappreciated.

The team that made the journey in 1915–1916 was supplemented with pitchers William "Dizzy" Dismukes of the Indianapolis ABCs, pitcher Andrew "Stringbean" Williams and Jimmy Lyons of the St. Louis Giants. Pop Lloyd and Jude Gans also remained with the club. The added muscle on the mound and depth on the field made the team a formidable opponent on any diamond. Three of the players' wives also made the trip with the team to California: Mrs. Frank Wickware, Mrs. William Dismukes and Mrs. Horace Jenkins. The team also brought along a chef to prepare meals in the private car. The Chicago White Sox had on occasion had some of the players' wives along for the trip, and here again the American Giants demonstrated that the right to roam the country by rail was not reserved for rich white folks.[22]

The American Giants put the finishing touches on the California Winter League championship by beating the "Pantanges" of San Diego on Christmas Day and again on December 26th. The American Giants' journey of 1916 was extensive and they had even announced plans to sail for Hawaii after the California Winter League. The Hawaiian trip fell through however and Rube took the team back east, setting sail for Cuba where they played during the mid-winter. (The American Giants represented the village of San Francisco, Cuba, in the Cuban league).[23]

1916

Instead of taking a month off after the Cuban winter season ended, Rube cast aside any concerns about fatigue and took the team back through Alabama, Mississippi, doubling all the way back to California and up to the Pacific Northwest for another month of spring training. Along the way they met with the Indianapolis ABCs in New Orleans, Oregon Agricultural College in Corvallis, Oregon, and the University of Oregon in Eugene, Oregon. The American Giants mostly rolled over the competition. The journey was one of the longest road trips ever taken by a baseball team. At this point in time Rube Foster did not have a concept of a baseball "season"—baseball was his job and he played it all year long.

The American Giants opened the traditional season in Chicago against the semi-pro West Ends on May 7, 1916, winning 5–2 on their home grounds—which remained South Side Park at 39th and Wentworth (also known as Schorling Field) where the team had played ever since 1910. The American Giants retained the services of Pop Lloyd and Jude Gans for the 1916 season. The pitching staff was deep, with Frank Wickware, Dick Whitworth and Tom Johnson as starters. The American Giants went into the season with a strong veteran team who had been fine tuned by Rube over the winter months. The fervent competition that had arisen in 1915 between the American Giants, the Cuban Stars, the Indianapolis ABCs, and the New York Lincoln Stars continued in 1916. In addition, the St. Louis Giants were more active and engaged the American Giants a number of times, as did the "All-Nations" team of Kansas City, a precursor to the fabled Kansas City Monarchs owned by white businessman J. L. Wilkinson.

About one quarter of the games the American Giants played over the regular season were against the Cuban Stars, who made themselves at home on the American prairie for a summer of baseball. One contest with the Cuban Stars was attended by "Shoeless" Joe Jackson of the Chicago White Sox. "Shoeless Joe," a well known bat aficionado, noticed the bat of Cuban pitcher Jose Junco and bargained to buy it for the exorbitant sum of $6.50. Junco was not known as a particularly great hitter, but perhaps the Cuban stick bore some resemblance to Joe's beloved "Black Betsy"? It was not that uncommon for white major leaguers to take in a game of professional black baseball, and likewise for black players to take in a white major league game. Players and coaches of both races found they could learn something by watching the game played a little bit differently, but Jim Crow had conquered professional baseball. Any hopes of going back to the days when the likes of Bud Fowler, Fleet Walker, George Stovey and others were part of organized baseball with a chance at the big leagues were long lost. It was apparent that *something else* would have to happen if baseball were ever to be integrated.[24]

The cause of black baseball was never far from Rube's thoughts. Even when the American Giants suffered the occasional crushing defeat, Rube took solace in the fact that there was genuine tough competition among his brothers. Rube remained hard at work trying to form a league. The *Indianapolis Freeman* reported that "Rube Foster … represented a wealthy syndicate of Negroes whose object is to buy up Federal League Parks in St. Louis, Pittsburgh and Chicago…." That particular plan did not pan out, but the wheels were turning to create a black baseball league.[25]

The American Giants played virtually all of their games on their home grounds. This was an obvious advantage and it must have tipped a lot of games their way but there was surprisingly little complaining about the cozy arrangement. The American Giants did take long road trips, but for the most part the road trips were taken during the winter and spring training when competition was a bit lighter. The American Giants came out on top in most of these contests and, as had become the pattern, were poised to make their claim as champions of colored baseball. The Indianapolis ABCs would have something to say about the championship of colored baseball in 1916.

In Indianapolis the smoke was slow to clear from last year's season-ending riots—not only the outbreak following the American Giants game, but a separate incident that occurred in a game against local white major and minor leaguers which resulted in the arrests of Oscar Charleston and Bingo DeMoss. Also, in Indianapolis, a rift had developed between white team owner Tom Bowser and manager C.I. Taylor during the off season; the consequence of which was two separate teams calling themselves the Indianapolis ABCs opening the 1916 season.

Taylor's Indianapolis ABCs began the year fractured: rookie phenom Oscar Charleston had been lured away to the New York Lincoln Giants, and Tom Bowser came up with enough cash to sign Bingo DeMoss to the otherwise second-rate Bowser ABC club. Trouble in Indy meant trouble for the greater good of black baseball. Rube Foster was always on guard to defend the reputation of black baseball, so that one day a professional league might be formed. The Indianapolis situation where there were two teams named the "ABCs" gave an unprofessional appearance. The so-called "riots" in Indianapolis the previous season were also the sort of thing that threatened to give black baseball a bad name and would potentially hurt chances for league formation.

Indianapolis, some 200 miles away from Chicago, had become one of the American Giants' main rivals and it was important that it be a healthy rivalry. However, C.I. Taylor and Rube Foster were scarcely on speaking terms. Taylor criticized Rube for patronizing Bowser's ABCs who played a couple of games against the American Giants in June. In mid–July Foster took a trip to Indianapolis in an effort to patch things up. Foster met with C.I. Taylor, Tom Bowser and one of the owners of Indianapolis's Federal League Park. The result of the summit was "useless" in regards to efforts to reunite the two ABC teams—that split remained; but Rube and C.I. did agree to meet in a series of games to be played both in Chicago and in Indianapolis's Federal League Park later in the season.[26]

By the time Taylor's ABCs and the American Giants met it was late August; Bowser's team had closed up shop—allowing Bingo DeMoss to rejoin Taylor's ABCs; and Oscar Charleston left the New York Lincoln Giants to rejoin the ABCs. The Indianapolis team again whole, with Ben Taylor at first, Bingo DeMoss at second, Candy Jim Taylor at third, Oscar Charleston in center and ace pitcher Dizzy Dismukes, was a force to be reckoned with. There was a ground swell of anticipation among fans when the original Indianapolis ABCs of 1916 traveled to Chicago to face Rube's men. The *Chicago Defender* wrote on August 26, 1916:

> One of the most interesting games of the season will be seen Sunday when the American Giants face the Indianapolis ABCs.... The strong Indianapolis team will face one that is equally strong ... Taylor's ABCs have beaten Cuban Stars four out of five, St. Louis Giants three straight, Kokomo with [Geo] Mullin [who had over 200 major league wins] pitching 3 out of 4, the Lincolns of NY four out of five. The question that interests the fans the most is will they beat the American Giants?[27]

While Foster and Taylor had supposedly buried the hatchet, it remained to be seen. The *Chicago Defender* called it "the largest throng that has ever witnessed a ball game on a semi-pro lot." Frank Wickware pitched for the American Giants and Dizzy Dismukes took the mound for the ABCs. The game was a pitchers' duel. Frank Wickware took a 3–0 one-hitter into the ninth inning and the large crowd had thoughts of heading home, when the vaunted Indianapolis ABCs finally showed some life. The ABCs loaded bases after hits from George Shively and Bingo DeMoss, a sacrifice by Candy Jim Taylor, and Ben Taylor was hit by an errant Frank Wickware pitch. The ABCs scored a run after an error from American Giant second baseman Harry Bauchman. The score was then 3–1. Catcher Bruce Petway nearly let a ball get past him, which lured Ben Taylor off of second base—Petway responded by angrily throwing the ball to Pop Lloyd covering second base and caught Taylor napping. Bingo DeMoss who was at third tried to steal home, a rundown ensued; DeMoss came in hard at the plate, which was being covered by first baseman Leroy Grant. Umpire Harry Goeckel waited until the dust cleared to call Bingo— "out!"[28]

Whatever window dressing had been in place to mask the bad blood between C.I. Taylor and Rube Foster was junked. Bingo DeMoss vehemently protested the call, got overexcited and hit the umpire. The American Giant players got in between DeMoss and the umpire and a "riot" was avoided—for the time being. The two teams met again the very next day, and in the second inning Indianapolis manager C.I. Taylor was kicked out of the game for arguing an inconsequential decision by the ump. The American Giants won three of the five games, one game ended in a tie. Part one of Chicago versus Indianapolis 1916 had concluded and the American Giants had handled the ABCs as if they were just another opponent; but the two teams would meet again on Indianapolis's home turf in a fall classic showdown.

The American Giants got a scare when catcher Bruce Petway, who had led the team to victory against Indianapolis, was thought to be badly injured in a game against a semi-pro team from Kenosha, Wisconsin. Petway was replaced by a virtual unknown by the name of Buddy Hayes. Luckily Petway's injury wasn't nearly as bad as originally thought, and the catcher some called the greatest in black baseball was back in action a week later.[29]

Rube Foster became a father again in early October — a daughter named Sarah, after his wife. Family life did not mix that well with the lifestyle of the professional baseball player. The travel schedule and the horseplay that was part of the culture was not conducive to settled home life. Many players remained bachelors or had difficulties with their spousal relationships. In Rube Foster's case it was apparent even to the casual observer that, between the year long baseball schedule and his efforts to organize a league, he would not have a lot of time to spend with his two children. Mrs. Sarah Foster was supportive of Rube's career, and Rube did bring home a bigger paycheck than most of his cohorts; thus Foster managed to be a good father too. Sadly though, Rube's daughter would die at the age of twelve and the tragedy was said to have had a profound effect on Rube's mental health.[30]

It was an eventful autumn, in mid–October the American Giants went on the road and took two out of three games from the All-Nations team in Kansas City. The All-Nations team included Cristobal Torriente, Jose Mendez and pitcher John Donaldson. Then the showdown everyone had been waiting for: the American Giants journeyed to Indianapolis, Indiana, to play the ABCs at the Indianapolis Federal League Park.

The American Giants took game one 5–3. They tried to squeeze in the second game of the double-header, which was started in late afternoon, but it had to be called due to Sunday baseball laws. In game two Dizzy Dismukes pitched for the ABCs and Frank Wickware pitched for the Chicago American Giants. Dizzy held the Giants to only three hits, while the ABCs hit Wickware six times. The only run of the game was scored when the usually infallible Pop Lloyd muffed a grounder and the ABCs won 1–0.

In the third game of the series Rube Foster took his team off the field, due to a dispute with the umpire, thereby forfeiting the game to the ABCs. Controversy reared its ugly head when Indianapolis first baseman Ben Taylor objected to Rube Foster's wearing a baseball mitt while coaching from the first base coaching box. Taylor asked that Rube take the glove off. A debate as to the official rules of baseball on the issue ensued. The next thing that happened was that Rube was tossed out of the game. Rube then removed his team from the game in protest. At the time the score was 1–0 in favor of the ABCs. Dicta Johnson got credit for the victory. Foster had started a pitcher named Rube Tyree whom he had recruited from the All-Nations team when they had played a week earlier.

In game four William "Dizzy" Dismukes allowed seven hits scattered over nine innings, and Oscar Charleston went four for four as the ABCs won by a score of 8–2, putting them ahead in the series 3–1.

After a day off Dizzy Dismukes started for the ABCs in game five. Dizzy got off to a rocky start allowing two runs on three hits in the first inning. Foster sent Rube Tyree out to the mound again, he allowed one run on three hits in the first inning. The American Giants chalked up another run in the second inning to take 3–1 lead, but Dizzy found his rhythm, allowing just one hit between the second and eighth innings. In the third stanza Tyree walked a batter and gave up a single to Jim Taylor, a triple to Oscar Charleston and a single to catcher Russ Powell. The ABCs put three runs on the board to mount a 4–3 advantage. Rube's green recruit Rube Tyree was not panning out and he brought in Frank Wickware for the relief job. The score remained ABCs four and the American Giants three in the bottom of the sixth when the ABCs exploded for seven runs on seven hits and two errors committed by the American Giants. Right fielder James Jefferies hit twice in the inning and Candy Jim Taylor hit a bases loaded triple that made the score 11–3. The ABCs upped the score to 12–3 in the seventh and it looked like the game and series was all but over.

The American Giants did not lie down for the ABCs, and in the eighth inning mounted a comeback. Pete Hill singled; Pop Lloyd walked; Bill Francis, Frank Duncan and Leroy Grant all got hits; and three runs scored. Bruce Petway hit the ball to Jim Taylor who threw Leroy Grant out at second, but Francis was able to score and Petway made it safely to first base. Jude Gans singled and the last batter, pitcher Frank Wickware, also singled. Bases were loaded with one out, and leadoff hitter Jess Barbour was coming up to bat; the score was 12–7.

At that point C.I. walked out to the mound, and motioned for brother Ben to take over pitching duties, and sent Dismukes over to first base. Ben Taylor had rarely pitched, but had thrown with some success when he was younger. Legendary catcher Bruce Petway was taking a sizeable lead off of third as Ben faced batter Jess Barbour, then Powell tore a page out of Petway's book and rifled the ball down to Jim Taylor — picking off Mr. Petway for out number two. Ben Taylor got Barbour out and the scare was over. The Giants scored one more run in the top of ninth, but Ben Taylor came through with the relief effort and the ABCs took the game by a 12–8 score. The ABCs won the post-season series four games to one and therefore claimed the championship. The ghastly head of controversy surfaced again; Rube pointed out that the American Giants had taken four of five games played in Chicago earlier in the season and therefore the ABCs had no legitimate claim to the title. While Rube's argument had some validity, that did not stop the ABCs from celebrating the Western Championship — even if it was only a shared championship. By most accounts the Indianapolis ABCs had the better team. Nineteen sixteen was the high-water mark for the Hoosier franchise; for the American Giants it was one more season marked by average success. Chicago attorney/politician and former City League participant Edward Litzinger made up a *World Champions* pennant, sent it to the team, and congratulated the members of the American Giants with gold pins. Litzinger's gesture was clearly designed to win black votes in the upcoming election and had no basis in fact. Black baseball had evolved considerably, but it remained impossible to decide which team was the best without the benefit of an organized league. The one thing both C.I. Taylor and Rube Foster agreed on was the need to form such a league.[31]

1917

The trauma of World War I was closing in on the U.S. By the time baseball season opened in 1917 the United States had made a formal declaration of war (April 6, 1917). The American Giants were able to get in a productive spring training before the war declaration. For the first time since 1911 Rube did not go to California and instead took spring training in southern Florida at the Royal Poinciana resort at Palm Beach. The American Giants represented the Royal Poinciana resort, whereas the Lincoln Giants represented the Breakers. Indianapolis ABCs Bingo DeMoss and Oscar Charleston joined the American Giants for spring training. Cuban pitcher Juan Luis Padrone, "El Mulo," also joined the American Giant regulars to represent the Poincianas.

The battle between the Palm Beach resort teams was a good one that year. The Breakers featured Spotswood Poles, Louis "Big" Santop, Jimmy Lyons, as well as pitching greats Dick Redding and Smokey Joe Williams. While these were only spring training games, with such a collection of talent, rivalries naturally arose. The two teams played each other fifteen times. The American Giants/ Poincianas won seven games, the Lincoln Giants/Breakers won six games, and two games ended tied.

Rube pulled off a coup by convincing Bingo DeMoss and "Cannonball" Dick Redding to leave their respective camps and join the Chicago American Giants for the 1917 season. The American Giants toured the Deep South, playing in Georgia, Alabama, Mississippi and Louisiana before heading back north. In New Orleans the team was given a tour of the city in automobiles and then entertained with a Creole dinner and a dance.[32]

Meanwhile a committee of legendary black baseball figures from the state of Ohio, including Sol White, Charles Grant, Home Run Grant Johnson and Chappie Johnson, led by Dayton businessman John Potter, announced plans to create a "Negro Baseball League" in January of 1917. Even with the full house of black baseball legends this attempt to create a "Negro League" would fail. There had been attempts to create professional baseball almost every year for the last ten, but those plans always fell through.[33]

The opening day game between the American Giants and a local semi-pro team led by former major league player/manager Jake Stahl was preceded by a parade of marching drum corps and four machine gun trucks. Baseball was married to the flag during World War I — many references to baseball as "America's game," "the National pastime," or the implied synonym of baseball and American patriotism came out of this period. Soon patriotic songs and military parades were common at baseball games.

The Selective Service Act required all men between the ages of 21 and 30 to register for the military draft. The draft was later supplemented to include all men between ages 18 and 45 and one by one almost all of the American Giant players registered at the local draft board — even Rube Foster. The World War would put a slight damper on the game. Rube Foster was determined to go ahead with baseball regardless of the war and Indianapolis manager C.I. Taylor shared Rube's determination. Both skippers scrambled to give their professional baseball teams the look of an "essential industry," and thereby stay in the good graces of Uncle Sam and the general public.

When the war placed the baseball season in jeopardy, traditional rivals Rube Foster and C.I. Taylor called a truce and worked together to ensure that there would be an exciting summer of black baseball. The American Giants played the Indianapolis team frequently during the 1917 season. Working through a promoter, the American Giants met the ABCs in a series of games in major league parks: Cincinnati's Redland Field, Detroit's Navin Field and Pittsburgh's Forbes Field. These were hotly contested games and brought out large crowds of both black and white fans.

The American Giants and ABCs were thrilled to play in the major league parks, but there was clearly an ulterior motive to their invitations into the Roman coliseums—which was to stage patriotic war rallies intended to increase support for the war among black Americans. The American Giants had a role in the wartime propaganda campaign whose message was that "America is worth fighting for since things were getting better for blacks all the time." Of course there were grave questions as to the status of black Americans at the time.

Over the next two years the American Giants would play games to benefit the Red Cross, facilitate patriotic rallies around the flag before games and play against military teams. Not all of the flag waving was coerced (after all the team was called the *American Giants*). Genuine patriotic feelings were stirred when it was friends, family and teammates waving goodbye through the window of a train. The state of Illinois had a black National Guard regiment — the Eighth Regiment, and a white regiment — the Seventh. Both regiments would be called to action. Dave Wyatt described the scene as the Seventh Regiment pulled out of Chicago shortly before the World Series between the Chicago White Sox and New York Giants got under way:

> Who will win [the 1917 World Series] is the slogan nowadays; that is the burning question of the hour. War has been relegated to the background for the time being, not withstanding the fact that the gallant seventh just pulled out bidding us adieu. It was a sorrowful parting; it was a sad, sad heartbreaking scene, especially the sorrow the white boys showed over the uncertain disposition of our colored regiment, the eighth. The colored soldiers marched to the depot with their loyal friends and neighbors. The two have been bosom pals upon each call to arms. They have gone together before and were as loyal as brothers. This time the eighth is left. They are the last out. In which direction they will go is definitely not known. It is possible that both regiments may lose their state identity altogether. This is unfortunate and depressing to the lads as well as thousands of friends and admirers. They had hoped to go together, fight together and die together if it came to that. The youngsters coming out of the same territory were practically reared from boyhood together, now at the most critical stage of their careers, the peculiarities of war preparedness causes a general severing of the friendly ties that bind. It may be for the best interest of our country, but if the two home units the Seventh and Eighth are separated forever, the move no matter what interest at stake is greatly abhorred by thousands.[34]

A by-product of the war was the buildup of manufacturing and increased job opportunities for African Americans in Northern cities. The labor demand set off "the Great Migration," as millions of blacks left the South for Northern cities. Changes occurred on a large scale as blacks and whites interacted on a more frequent basis— some of those interactions were constructive and some destructive. The migration also accounted for more black baseball teams and more black baseball fans in some Northern industrial communities. The Hilldale baseball club of Darby, Pennsylvania (Philadelphia suburb), traces its birth as a professional team to the year 1917. According to baseball historian/author Neil Lanctot, the Hilldale club got on its feet due to the large influx of blacks to the Philadelphia area and also the presence of many major and minor league baseball players who took jobs in the Philadelphia shipyards to fulfill their military obligation.[35]

The American Giants beat their frequent opponent, the Indianapolis ABCs, 15 out of 19 games in 1917. The addition of second baseman Bingo DeMoss and pitcher Cannonball Dick Redding gave the American Giants a decided advantage. John Henry Lloyd remained at shortstop, along with seasoned war-horses Bruce Petway, Pete Hill, Jesse Barbour, Bill Francis, and Jude Gans. Cannonball Redding had good company in the pitching rotation with Dick Whitworth, Tom Johnson and Tom Williams. It was a very strong American Giant team and they crushed the competition in 1917.

Although play was scaled back during the 1917 season (there were only a few games against eastern teams), the American Giants kept busy. In addition to the extended series against Indianapolis, they also faced the Cuban Stars about a dozen times over the season. Other opponents included Joe Greene's Chicago Giants, Chappie Johnson's Dayton Giants, the All-Nations team, a couple of white minor-league aggregations and a team known as the Texas All-Stars. A squad of former major leaguers calling themselves the "Norwoods"—named for the Cincinnati suburb which was their home base—challenged Foster to a game for a side bet, but chickened out after Rube wanted to raise the stakes.[36]

The Cuban Stars came to the United States during the summer and spent much of that time in the Chicago vicinity. Joe Greene, who inherited the Chicago Giants from Frank Leland, remained active on the local semi-pro lots. Teams of minor league and former major league players sometimes offered themselves up as bones to be chewed by the American Giants—there usually would be enough fan interest in the inter-racial games to generate gate receipts. Rube Foster arranged a special "Texas Day" in late July, in which his home state was honored. It was on "Texas Day" that the American Giants battled the Texas All-Stars—who included two notable players in third baseman Henry Blackman and outfielder Floyd "Jelly" Gardner.[37]

Another notable event of the season was a game played for the benefit of Harry "Mike" Moore, the turn of the century star of the Chicago Unions, who was dying of tuberculosis. Teams were drawn from the ranks of the American Giants and the Chicago Giants and the gate turned over to Moore's family. Among the individual donors were Charles Comiskey, Rube Foster and C.I. Taylor; Mike Moore was 42 years old when he succumbed in September of 1917.[38]

While it was largely business as usual for the American Giants, the war forced adjustments and caused uncertainty. It was a new kind of war and no one knew what to expect. There were those who felt that men had no business playing baseball for a living when others were asked to give their life on the battlefield. Among ball players and fans there was a fear that the game might be put on the shelf. The *Chicago Defender* reported on September 8, 1917:

> DRAFT WRECKS RUBE FOSTER'S BASEBALL TEAM. The entire pitching staff of the American Giants, Tom Williams, Dick Redding, Tom Johnson and Dick Whitworth; and catcher George Dixon and first baseman Leroy Grant were ordered to report for the national army.[39]

However the draft did not wreck Rube's team in 1917. Of the five players mentioned by the *Defender* only Tom Johnson was actually taken into the Army; the other four started out the 1918 season on the roster of the American Giants. Johnson was made a lieutenant in the 365th Infantry—probably due to his college education. The opportunity for African Americans to become officers had only recently been won. An early victory for the NAACP was the establishment of the Colored Officers' Training Camp at Fort Dodge in Des Moines, Iowa.

Almost all of the American Giants had registered for the draft — even Rube Foster at the age of 38 registered. It was some time before they were actually called up, Uncle Sam was slow deciding what to do with the black soldiers, but by the summer of 1918 that changed and a number of well known American Giants had joined the armed services.

1918

The American Giants headed for Palm Beach in mid–January to renew their annual tradition of spring training. The American Giants represented the Poinciana resort and the N.Y. Lincoln Giants plus a few ringers represented the Breakers resort. Before the two teams kicked off the Palm Beach resort ball in 1918, a brass band fired up the popular tune of the day "Over There" and everyone hummed along to the catchy refrain "The Yanks are coming, the Yanks are coming...."[40]

John Henry Lloyd did not make the trip with the American Giants, instead over the winter he worked in the army's Quartermaster Depot. Lloyd was replaced by a young recruit from New Orleans University who impressed Rube named Bobby Williams. It was hoped that Pop Lloyd might rejoin the American Giants later in the season but he wound up out East as the captain of the Brooklyn Royal Giants. The Lincoln Giants representing the Breakers resort came into camp with Cyclone Joe Williams, a dandy young infielder from Florida named Dick Lundy, as well as Cuban infielder Pelayo Chacon and Cuban pitcher Juan Luis Padrone. Spring training was tightly contested, with Rube Foster going so far as to get thrown out of one game for arguing with the umps.[41]

After edging out the Breakers, the American Giants took a short tour of the South through Atlanta, Alabama and New Orleans. The American Giants lost pitcher Tom Williams in Montgomery Alabama; he was thrown off the team when Rube Foster saw him boarding the train in an intoxicated stupor. Rube was strict about that sort of thing and said that "college men were the hardest to keep away from the drink." Tom Williams had been recruited from Morris Brown College.[42]

The American Giants caught the Illinois Central train back to Chicago for the regular season in mid–April. The American Giants started out with Bruce Petway and George Dixon behind the plate. (Petway was seeing less action as injuries had taken a toll over the years). Leroy Grant played first, "Bingo" DeMoss was at the keystone, Bobby Williams took over for Pops Lloyd at shortstop, veteran Bill Francis played third; the outfield was made up of Jesse Barbour, Frank Duncan and captain Pete Hill. While Cannonball Dick Redding had pitched for the American Giants during spring training, when the team came north, Redding went east and joined Pops Lloyd with the Brooklyn Royal Giants until his number came up in the draft. Foster relied on Dick Whitworth and Frank Wickware to handle most of the pitching duties. Rube also shored up the staff with two noname pitchers known simply as Keyes and Fields; the first names of both pitchers have eluded even the fine-tooth comb of history.

One of many indications that black baseball would be different in 1918 was the announcement of a baseball game between the 183rd Brigade of Camp Grant, Rockford,

Illinois, and the American Giants slated for late May. The 183rd Brigade advertised a pitching staff of Tom Johnson, Louis "Spitball" Johnson of the Indianapolis ABCs, and Russell Powell, catcher for the ABCs, and it was rumored that "Cannonball" Dick Redding would soon be joining the squad. The Army had requisitioned many of black baseball's top players. However, due to a mix-up, or orders from high command, the announced contest between the American Giants and Camp Grant on May 19th was cancelled. The Camp Grant 183rd team did play the Indianapolis ABCs on May 5th, a contest which the ABCs won handily.[43]

Later in the season a game between a white military team from Camp Grant and the American Giants was arranged. The Camp Grant 86th Division was a collection of major league, minor league and semi-pro players. The American Giants defeated the 86th Division 1–0 behind masterful pitching by Frank Wickware. The *Chicago Defender* reported that Chicago's white newspapers were so embarrassed that Frank Wickware and the American Giants defeated the white 86th that they refused to print the outcome.[44]

The American Giants' roster continued to be chipped away at by the draft as the season progressed. Rube confided to writer Cary B. Lewis of the *Chicago Defender* that he had been hoping to bring in some fresh blood to the team anyway. However, the rebuilding program was at the mercy of the U.S. Army who had first dibs on the pool of players. "Cannonball" Dick Redding was taken in the draft but reported to Camp Upton in Suffolk County, New York, rather than Camp Grant as initially rumored. Bobby Williams, Pop Lloyd's replacement, was himself taken in the draft in late July. Jude Gans and Frank Wickware shipped out a few days later. Foster was able to plug Cuban pitcher/utility man Jose Mendez into shortstop. Foster pulled off another coup when he was also able to sign Cuban slugger Cristobal Torriente as a replacement. Torriente would become something of a fixture in Chicago in the years to follow, although Mendez's career as an American Giant was short lived. Uncle Sam approached Rube Foster about becoming an organizer of baseball among black troops, but Rube turned down the job.[45]

Other wartime measures included surtax on tickets and a prohibition on travel to Cuba—due to the fact that draft registrants had to stay in the country. Government agents checked identification of fans at baseball games in an effort to round up and crack down on men who had not registered for the draft—"slackers," in the parlance of the day.

The previous season's experience prepared the American Giants for coping with the inconveniences of wartime baseball. Through the turmoil the American Giants were able to line up ball games and played an almost normal season. Primary competition was against the Indianapolis ABCs, the Cuban Stars and beefed up Chicago region semi-pro teams. Chappie Johnson's Giants of Columbus, Ohio, and the Dayton Marcos of Dayton, Ohio, also faced the American Giants during the abbreviated season.

Again, the American Giants went on the road with the Indianapolis ABCs and played against each other in major league parks. The tour of big league parks included Forbes Field (Pittsburgh), Griffith Stadium (Washington, D.C.) and Navin Field (Detroit). While on the road the American Giants also faced the Hilldales of Darby (Philadelphia suburb) and the Bacharach Giants of Atlantic City. The Hilldales and the Bacharachs were vanguards in a new generation of East Coast black baseball teams; the Eastern movement would soon challenge Rube's established dominance of black baseball. Both the Hilldales and Bacharachs swept the American Giants on their visits.

According to the national "work or fight" directive, baseball was considered a non-essential industry. Many big league players took jobs in shipyards or related war industries, which allowed them to play baseball on weekends for semi-pro teams. These semi-pro teams would sometimes play against black professional teams, bringing the best ball players of both races together as the color line was crossed.

One of the regional semi-pro teams who faced the American Giants was the Fairbanks-Morse team from Beloit, Wisconsin. Fairbanks-Morse was a train and marine diesel engine builder, the team was nicknamed the "Fairies," and featured Chicago Cub pitcher Zip Zabel as well as Chicago White Sox third baseman Buck Weaver.

The Chicago White Sox won the World Series in 1917. Bronzeville hoped to see the American Giants play against the White Sox. The prescribed racism in major league baseball prevented the two teams, who were literally neighbors, from playing against each other. Following the abbreviated season the American Giants played against some of the White Sox, also ravaged by the draft, including Buck Weaver, Eddie Murphy and Jack Quinn who played with a team in Joliet, Illinois. The American Giants were set to face Hippo Vaughn of the Cubs in late October when the local health department issued orders prohibited large congregations due to the influenza outbreak and the game was cancelled.[46]

The American Giants maintained their winning tradition through the 1918 season, although the U.S. Army's insatiable appetite for pitchers (Tom Johnson, Dick Redding and Frank Wickware were all drafted) proved to be a setback to the team. Rube Foster was lauded as the chief reason the American Giants were able to succeed in the face of unforeseen circumstance. Moreover Rube shepherded the whole cause of black baseball, and came to be known as a leader of his race.

During the last game of the season a boisterous fan relentlessly heckled second baseman Bingo DeMoss. A group of fans had made it their business to ride players on a regular basis. Foster, having been a player himself, was sensitive to the effects of verbal abuse; he was also fearful of what might happen if one of his players responded to the jeers. Foster felt the rowdiness had crossed the line and made a general announcement:

> If I find people who insist on ridiculing my players to the extent of insult, or until it affects their work, this man will have a hard time getting into the park. I do not want his money. I mean to have a team that is out and working all the time and they will not be mollycoddled, but I mean to stand between them and insult.[47]

World War I ended on November 11, 1918, and the American Giants who had served overseas slowly began returning to Chicago. The war presented a deadly threat to the fragile alliance of black baseball teams that later became the Negro Leagues. If the war had continued, full-time black professional baseball teams would have been impossible. Rube Foster cooly dealt with the dire situation as it developed, and against the odds was able to dig in and scratch out a fresh start for the fledgling association of black baseball teams.

1919

For the first time in the history of the team the American Giants did not take spring training. During the off season Rube Foster spent time thinking and planning how to bring back to life plans to create an organized black professional baseball league. Efforts to do so had been going on year after year going back to the turn of the century; Rube was determined to succeed where so many had failed.

There was a lot of ground to make up in this effort. Though the war had ended, a number of players stayed in Europe as part of the occupying force. The Indianapolis ABCs, a chief rival of the American Giants, did not field a team in 1919. Indianapolis manager C.I. Taylor had lost a number of his players to the draft and decided not to open up shop in 1919. The loss of the ABCs was a setback to the organization of black baseball — the games between the American Giants and ABCs had sustained black baseball in 1917 and 1918. Despite the various obstacles Foster forged ahead.

Foster decided to back a new team to be located in Detroit. Wartime labor brought thousands of blacks to Detroit, and Rube figured it was fertile ground to plant another team. Tenny Blount, a light skinned numbers man familiar to Detroit's sportsmen, was installed as the business manager of the team. Pete Hill, who had captained the American Giants since day one, was appointed captain and coach of the newly founded "Detroit Stars." Pete Hill's appointment was a reward for his longtime loyalty to the American Giants and also a gentle way to put the aging center fielder out to pasture.[48]

In late March 1919 there was a jamboree of ball players at Schorling Park on Chicago's South Side. Among the aspirants were players back from a tour of duty in Europe, displaced Indianapolis ABC players now without a team, wide-eyed youngsters from as far away as Texas and seasoned Chicago veterans hoping to extend their careers. Rube Foster and Pete Hill picked the best of the bunch for their respective teams.

Bingo DeMoss replaced Pete Hill as captain of the American Giants and none other than Indianapolis ABC Oscar Charleston was hired to take Hill's spot in center field. Foster also picked up pitcher Lem McDougal, a World War I vet who had previously been with the Indianapolis ABCs. Cristobal Torriente played left field. Leroy Grant, Bobby Williams, Tom Johnson, and Jude Gans were all welcomed back into the fold on returning home from the war. Pitcher Dave Brown and catcher James Brown, both from Texas, impressed Rube enough to make the team. The two had worked together previously in Texas, and were naturally nicknamed the "Brown battery." Dave Brown was rumored to be a fugitive from justice, but he was also a good pitcher, a nice guy; and his checkered past did not stop Rube from signing him. Rube was said to have bonded Dave Brown out of jail on highway robbery charges.[49]

Pete Hill and the Detroit Stars stocked the team with former American Giants: Jose Mendez, Bruce Petway and Frank Wickware. Detroit also came away with second baseman Frank Warfield, a tough player cast off from Indianapolis, and Floyd "Jelly" Gardner who was at the beginning of a long career in black baseball. The Detroit Stars were never referred to as a "farm team," however Rube ultimately held the reins. If for some reason Rube had needed a pitcher he certainly could have brought Frank Wickware from Detroit to Chicago — but that type of circumstance did not present itself.

While Rube's vision of a black baseball league was still off in the distance, 1919 would be an historic year for baseball and an historic year for Chicago. In the majors, Babe Ruth set the single season home run record, with 29 clouts for the Boston Red Sox; the record of 27 had been held since 1884 by Ned Williamson of the Chicago White-Stockings (about half of those over the 180-foot left field fence at Lake Front Park). The game was changing — the "dead ball era" was over. As Rube Foster had predicted, fans were coming back

1919 American Giants. From left to right, (front row) unidentified, Jimmie Lyons, Bill "Lil Corporal" Francis, unidentified, unidentified; (middle row) Dave Malarcher, Bobby Williams, unidentified, John Reese; (back row) Bingo DeMoss, Leroy Grant, Dave Brown, Rube Foster, Oscar Charleston, Dick Whitworth. Rube was able to hoard some talent in 1919, because World War I had caused some teams to cut back (photograph courtesy NoirTech Research, Inc.).

to the ballparks. While the Babe's Red Sox finished near the bottom of the American League, the best team in baseball (though the whole team could muster only 25 homers) was the Chicago White Sox. The White Sox should have waltzed to victory against the Cincinnati Reds, but they lost in a major upset. Later it was revealed that a group of players on the Chicago White Sox conspired to fix the series, in what came to be known as the Black Sox series.

In Northern cities blacks and whites were interacting more frequently at work, at play, in factories, schools, on city streets, restaurants, theaters, athletic fields and everywhere. After thousands of black men had fought for "democracy," it seemed reasonable to expect that blacks might be accepted into American society as equals. If only the American Giants could have faced the Boston Red Sox; Ruth versus Charleston — two of the greatest players of all time. While baseball had helped Americans get through the war, the game missed something — namely competition between its greatest players.

The twentieth century came into full swing: automobiles plied city streets; phonographs, telephones, movies and even airplanes became familiar. *Chicago Defender* sporting editor Cary B. Lewis joked with Rube that perhaps the American Giants could fly to a game in Detroit — a notion which Foster considered as a good publicity measure.[50]

One of the immigrants to Chicago was a Texas woman named Bessie Coleman, who followed her two brothers to Chicago and took up the trade of manicuring. Both of Bessie Coleman's brothers served in France during World War I. When her brothers returned from the war they related to her experiences often related by blacks who fought that war — that in France blacks and women enjoyed more rights than in America. They told her that some French women even flew airplanes and this inspired Bessie Coleman to pursue a career in aviation. The white male flight instructors wouldn't think of teaching a black woman to fly. On the advice of *Chicago Defender* editor Robert Sengstacke Abbott, who told her such opportunities simply weren't available in America, Ms. Coleman saved her money, went to France to study aviation. Eventually Bessie Coleman became the first woman and the first African American to earn the Fédération Aeronautique Internationale pilot's license

The Chicago American Giants did not fly to a game in 1919, and not ever for that matter. The America that black troops returned to was looking backward as much as forward. The Ku Klux Klan reorganized and realized political power. In the neighboring state of Indiana, the governor and the mayor of Indianapolis were found to be on the payroll of the Klan. There was competition between races for jobs, a shortage of affordable housing, and increasingly tension between whites and blacks escalated to violence. So, in the charged atmosphere of post–World War I, any notion of dropping the color line in major league baseball was outside the bounds of reality.

The American Giants of 1919, with Charleston and Torriente batting three and four, was one of the more exciting teams Rube had ever fielded, however the pool of competition had shrunk as other black teams were struggling to get back on their feet following the war. The American Giants did meet traditional Chicago area semi-pro rivals like Joe Green's Chicago Giants, Rogers Park, Gunthers, Fairbanks-Morse, Kenosha (Wisconsin), the Roseland Eclipse and others. The Cuban Stars made their annual pilgrimage to Chicago and played a set of games against the American Giants. On Memorial Day the American Giants had to turn away thousands of fans that couldn't fit into the ballpark for a game against the Cuban Stars. Foster had already started expanding the park, but this incident caused Rube and park owner John Schorling to speed things up.[51]

As the season went on, more players who had been stationed in Europe came back to the states and back to baseball. Dave Malarcher, a Louisianan who had migrated to the Hoosier State and become an excellent utility man for the Indianapolis ABCs, returned home from the war at mid-season clutching a letter from Rube Foster that he had received while stationed in St. Luce, France. Foster got "Gentleman" Dave Malarcher a job with the Detroit Stars. On the East Coast teams like the Hilldale club, the Atlantic City Bacharach Giants and the Brooklyn Royal Giants were thriving. The Dayton Marcos captained by William "Dizzy" Dismukes remained open for business. Black baseball seemed poised for recovery from setbacks incurred during the war.

There was a dramatic turn of events. It was July 27th, 1919; Eugene Williams, a black youth, was swimming near a "white beach" and was attacked by a stone-throwing white male. The youth drowned, and when the police arrived they did not take action against the perpetrator. A riot broke out that would last five days and claim the lives of 23 blacks and 15 whites. The South Side of Chicago became a war zone; children were among the dead, homes were burned, shops looted, there were volleys of gunfire and territorial wars fought over certain neighborhoods. Some of the rioters were white men wearing their army uniforms, and a Chicago commission on race relations pointed a finger at an Irish athletic club, the Ragen Colts, as chief instigators in the rioting. A grand jury charged that the Ragen Colts posed as an athletic club but was really an organization of hoodlums and criminals. The American Giants had met the Ragen Colts' baseball team on the diamond in 1917. At that time the Ragen Colts carried on their roster Ed Corey, a pitcher who later had a cup of coffee with the Chicago White Sox. Another South Side club charged with instigating the riot was the Hamburg Athletic Club, of which a seventeen-year-old future Chicago mayor, Richard Daley, was a prominent member.[52]

The rioting was at the doorstep of the American Giants' ballpark, which would be occupied by National Guard troops. The Atlantic City Bacharach Giants had been scheduled to visit Chicago on August 3rd, the game was cancelled and the American Giants hit the road. Rube's arrangement with Tenny Blount and Pete Hill in Detroit allowed the American Giants to seek refuge in Detroit, Michigan. The American Giants went to Detroit following the riots and played the Detroit Stars in a series of five games—losing four of them.

Foster called a meeting in Indianapolis, where he met with Augustin Molina of the Cuban Stars, Joe Matthews of the Dayton Marcos and Warner Jewell of Indianapolis to discuss the state of black baseball in the face of race riots. It is not known exactly what was discussed—it may have just been a matter of rescheduling games—but Rube clearly didn't see the riots as a threat to his master plan of creating an organized league.[53]

The American Giants then journeyed to the East Coast. In Philadelphia the American Giants split a double-header with the Hilldale Daisies. Tom Williams, who had been booted from the American Giants for drinking the previous year, pitched for the Hilldale club and defeated the American Giants by a 2–0 score allowing only two hits.

The American Giants went on to New York, where they met a team known as Guy Empey's "Treat 'em Roughs" at Dyckman Oval on the north end of Manhattan. Guy Empey was the author of *Over the Top*, a best-selling account of World War I, a screen writer, a well known silent film maker and the father of "famous to-be" pin-up girl Diane Empey Webber. Empey apparently had a generous bank roll, as he signed Pol Perritt, who had won 18 games for the New York Giants a year earlier, and Jeff Tesreau, a New York Giant pitcher with over 100 career wins, plus a number of other big leaguers (some of whom played under assumed names). The American Giants were not intimidated by the big leaguers and defeated the "Treat 'em Roughs" four out of four games. It was said that the movie mogul and World War I vet, despite the unusual team name, was actually a pretty nice guy. Guy Empey was especially "chummy" with those players that had served in the war, his team played against a number of black teams. So even as the American Giants had fled racial violence there was ongoing dialogue with white professional players.

The Hilldale club was scheduled to meet the American Giants in New York City for a series of games but backed out at the last minute. The American Giants stayed at the Allen boarding house at 11 W. 135th Street for a short but welcome vacation in Harlem. Oscar Charleston, who had played for the New York Lincoln Giants in 1916 and was familiar with the city, took advantage of the time off to buy a pair of designer shoes with funds he plied from Rube Foster. It was rumored that a New York promoter tried to convince Rube to move the American Giants to New York on a permanent basis and promised to build him a $100,000 stadium — Foster wasn't interested. [54]

The American Giants left after a week in New York and headed back to Chicago on the Pennsylvania Railroad. A big homecoming was planned for the American Giants who were scheduled to meet the Cuban Stars for a series of games over the Labor Day weekend. Fans who held tickets for the game that had been postponed due to the riot were allowed to exchange their tickets for the gala welcome. There wasn't an empty seat in the house as fans came out in droves to welcome home the American Giants. Park owner John Schorling was relieved to have the team back home as he had gone a month without the gate receipts.

A makeshift Indianapolis ABC team came to Chicago for a game in September and gave the American Giants a scare before ABC pitcher Hurland Ragland balked in the game winning run in the thirteenth inning. The Dayton Marcos with Dizzy Dismukes on the hill also visited Chicago in September. The American Giants beat the Marcos with Andrew "Stringbean" Williams pitching. "Stringbean" Williams had started the season with the Marcos, but Rube hired him away before the team went on the road trip following the riot. Earlier in the season Stringbean Williams had pitched for the Dayton Marcos in a win over the American Giants. Rube Foster's relationships with the struggling team in Dayton and grassroots supporters in Indianapolis went beyond moral support or advice; Foster was almost certainly providing some form of financial support to the struggling teams.

The American Giants went back out on the road to St. Louis, Kansas City and Birmingham, Alabama, before returning to Chicago for a finale against the Cuban Stars in October. By the end of the season things had gotten pretty much back to normal for the American Giants. The riot hardly fazed Rube, who in the days immediately following remained busy laying the groundwork for an organized league. Foster had taken several key steps in 1919 toward forming a Negro baseball league. By investing in Detroit, supporting Dayton and Indianapolis, holding meetings, then taking a late season road trip to St. Louis and Kansas City, Rube Foster had assured that a black baseball league, at least in a modest form, would soon be feasible.

7

These Were the Negro Leagues (1920–1924)

Chicago, Chicago, that toddlin' town…
On State Street, that great street, I just want to say
They do things they don't do on Broadway…
More colored people up in State Street you can see,
Than you'll see in Louisiana or Tennessee;
Chicago, the town that Billy Sunday could not shut down….
— Songwriter Fred Fisher

1920

Chicago Defender Sports Editor Cary B. Lewis wrote in October 1919: "There is every indication that next season baseball fans of America will have a circuit of western clubs…. The circuit will be owned and controlled by Race men. It has been seen now that baseball is a financial proposition among our people and men of money in every town are willing to back such a proposition." Lewis predicted there would be teams in Chicago, Detroit, Indianapolis, Cleveland, Dayton, and Kansas City, and the Cuban Stars would be a traveling team. Cary Lewis had gotten the scoop straight from his old friend Rube Foster. Foster was fervently working behind the scenes drawing up blueprints for a Negro baseball league.[1]

Foster had reached certain "foregone conclusions" as to what steps must be taken in order for a Negro baseball league to stand a chance of viability. Rube was keenly aware that he held the keys to a black baseball league; he had a sense of history and knew his place. An effective but sarcastic diplomat, Rube shared his feelings in a treatise titled *"Pitfalls of Baseball"* that was serialized in the pages of the *Chicago Defender* during the hot-stove league of 1919–20 for public consumption.

"Pitfalls of Baseball" rambled on for six weeks. It was dry, with lapses in grammar and laced with mean-spirited criticism. Foster criticized almost all of the owners, players and black baseball impresarios of the day. Rube stated: "Baseball as it exists at present among our owners is a disgrace to the name of good honest sportsmanship…. I have seen every ball club for the past fifteen years wrecked by different owners." He proceeded to name owners going all the way back to 1902 (including Walter Schlicter, Nat Strong, C.I. Taylor, John Connors and others)—pointing out how over ambition and wishful thinking brought down a great number of black teams: the Cuban Giants, the Philadelphia Giants, the Lincoln Giants, the Indianapolis ABCs and others.

Foster stated the obvious when he pointed out that the practice of players jumping from team to team posed a danger to organized black baseball. Rube reminded that both players and owners shared responsibility. Players reneged on commitments, certain owners had gotten "greedy" in the zealous attempt to lure players away from their contracts. Rube lamented the lack of cooperation between the East Coast baseball teams and the Western teams—another roadblock to creating a league. He laid out in detail the economic challenges facing black baseball, from the cost of ballparks, the day to day operations and the need for fiscal responsibility. Foster reasoned that since "colored" managers, owners and fans could not raise enough money to fund stadiums, "whites" would have to partially bankroll black baseball, and unfortunately "wealthy whites" would stand to profit from colored baseball.

The last installment of Rube's serial coincided with the announcement of a meeting of black baseball owners and organizers to be held in Kansas City, Missouri, in February of 1920. The agenda was to organize a Negro baseball league. Some of those in attendance included C.I. Taylor of Indianapolis, Tenny Blount of Detroit, Joe Green of the Chicago Giants, Lorenzo Cobb of St. Louis, and J. L. Wilkinson, the white owner of the K.C. Monarchs. Representatives of the Dayton Marcos and the Cuban Stars were also present. Sportswriters from the major black newspapers—Dave Wyatt of the *Indianapolis Freeman*, Charles Marshall of the *Indianapolis Ledger* and Cary B. Lewis of the *Chicago Defender*—joined the organizing committee. The writers were charged with documenting and publicizing the proceedings. Elisha Scott, a black attorney from Topeka, provided legal counsel (Elisha Scott was the head of the "Scott, Scott, Scott and Jackson" law firm who later filed the landmark *Brown vs. Board of Education* case).[2]

W. A. Kelly of Washington, D.C., was apparently the only interested party from the East Coast to make a showing. Rube's original plan for the league had teams from the East Coast playing in one division and Western teams playing in another division, with division winners meeting in a World Series. Nat Strong of New York was the kingpin of East Coast black baseball and without Strong's cooperation there was no way that an East Coast circuit would be formed. Nat Strong was notoriously self interested and usually at odds with Rube Foster, so no one held their breath at the prospects of his joining the effort to create a black baseball league. Nat Strong did however send a letter to the delegation stating he "was ready to do anything to promote the best interests of baseball all over the country." Strong's words were appreciated, but taken with a grain of salt—as financial commitments and concessions were the order of the day. The gulf between Strong and other managers would not be bridged so easily. The idea of an East Coast division of the Negro National League was put on the back burner.

Foster shocked the assembly by producing a dossier, previously kept secret, which contained a corporate charter and articles of incorporation for a National Negro Baseball League that had already been filed in Illinois, Michigan, Ohio, Pennsylvania, New York and Maryland. There was still much work to be done; the sportswriters and Elisha Scott stayed up all night drafting the constitution of the Negro National League. Finally an agreement was reached and representatives from the participating teams signed the document and anted up the agreed upon $500 bond. Provisions of the league constitution prohibited players from jumping teams, disallowed the practice of "borrowing" players, allowed owners to make trades and sanctioned fines against violators.

Initially it was announced that the league would not commence until a full year later, in 1921, in order that each team would have enough time to either buy or lease a suitable ballpark. (Rube held out hope that black baseball teams could get away from being dependent on white ballpark owners.) However the newly appointed Negro National League owners decided to go ahead and make arrangements to play in rented ballparks in 1920 as they normally would have, so league play commenced a year ahead of schedule.

It was suggested that the teams in the NNL be equalized by distributing some of the star players throughout the league. Rube had been able to corner the market on ball players in 1919 because many black baseball teams closed up shop during the war. At the Kansas City convention it was proposed that a collection of black sportswriters would select the players for the teams based on "relative strength" and arbitrate contract disputes. The sportswriters went so far as to publish their proposed equalized team rosters. However in the end team owners were not prepared to sacrifice governance over their respective teams.[3]

There were some minor adjustments to team rosters prior to the start of league play. The *Chicago Defender* of March 20, 1920, declared: *"The wisest move made by Foster was in distributing the stars to various clubs, equalizing the playing strength and each series will be better attended."* In reality the roster changes were minor and the distribution of players had more to do with the re-launching of black baseball following the World War than it did with equalizing the teams.

John Donaldson and Jose Mendez went from Detroit to Kansas City. Both players had long been associated with the All-Nations team of Kansas City and had landed in Detroit only due to the fact that the 1919 K.C. team disbanded early because of World War I. Oscar Charleston naturally went from the American Giants back to Indianapolis where he was born and had played most of his career. Likewise Charleston had joined the American Giants in 1919 only because C.I. Taylor mothballed the Indianapolis ABCs during the war.

There were some other changes to the American Giants' roster prior to the 1920 season. Pitcher Dick Whitworth was said to have been "assigned to Detroit" as a part of equalization measures (there was even a sendoff for "Whit" according to the *Chicago Defender*), but on the way to Detroit "Whit" detoured to Philadelphia and signed with the Hilldale club. This chagrined Foster as he viewed it as one more example of the type of "contract jumping" that hurt organized black baseball. Veteran third baseman Bill Francis (who had played ball with Rube in Philadelphia back in 1904) also jumped to the Hilldale club prior to the 1920 season.[4]

Rube quickly patched the holes in the roster. Pitcher Tom Williams, who had been booted from the team two years earlier for drinking, convinced Rube he was sober enough for the starting rotation. The other starters were lefty Dave Brown, who came into his own as the ace of the staff in 1920, and World War I vet Lieutenant Tom Johnson.

"Gentleman" Dave Malarcher, who Foster had farmed out to the Detroit Stars the

1920 American Giants. From left to right, (front row) Jim Brown, Otis Starks, George Dixon, Dave Malarcher, Dave Brown, unidentified, John Reese, unidentified; (back row) Cristobal Torriente, Tom Johnson, unidentified, unidentified, Rube Foster, Bingo DeMoss, Leroy Grant, Tom Williams, Jack Marshall. The American Giants finished on top of the NNL in 1920, the inaugural year of the circuit founded by Rube Foster (photograph courtesy NoirTech Research, Inc.).

previous season after recruiting him from the battlefields of France, became the everyday third baseman for the American Giants. Malarcher was a disciple of Rube Foster's baseball science. Malarcher was also a switch hitter who could play any position (including catcher and pitcher). Joining Malarcher in the infield were: Bingo DeMoss at second base, Leroy Grant at first, and Bobby Williams at shortstop; George "Tubby" Dixon shared catching duties with Jim Brown.

The 1920 American Giant outfield was led by power hitting center fielder Cristobal Torriente who joined the American Giants after winning the batting title in Cuba during the winter season. Torriente hit around .400 for the Almendares Blues and had faced a number of white major league pitchers who spent the winter in Cuba as part of an "All-American" team. Cuban fans were so delighted when Torriente smacked a towering three-run homer off Philadelphia Athletic pitcher Bob Geary to win a game that they showered the field with money.[5]

Joining Torriente in the outfield was veteran Jude Gans in left. A loquacious young hustler known as Floyd "Jelly" Gardner became the starting right fielder in late July replacing John Reese, a Morris College grad, who had jumped from Hilldale at the start of the season. Before league play got under way Rube traveled East, stopping in Philadelphia and New York to make one more attempt to convince the East Coast baseball magnates to join the Negro National League. Even if the Eastern teams could not be persuaded to join, Rube figured he would at least promote the league and possibly schedule a few games.[6]

The response of the Eastern owners to Rube's overtures was less than enthusiastic. Nat Strong backed out of his initial pledge of support for the league. Ed Bolden, owner of the Hilldale club, who had an ongoing disagreement with Foster over the contractual rights to certain players, was suspicious of Rube and wanted nothing to do with the league. Only the Atlantic City Bacharach Giants were interested in cooperating with the NNL and were accepted as "associate members." There would be no "east and west conferences" in the NNL in 1920, though later in the season the Bacharachs would travel west to face several of the league teams.[7]

Since Rube was busy working out the details of the Negro National League, the Chicago American Giants did not hold their usual winter/spring training in 1920. Instead the American Giants held open tryouts in March and worked out with Joe Greene's Chicago Giants. The preparations were completed and the Negro National League opened for business. The first ever NNL game was held on May 2, 1920, in Indianapolis, between the ABCs and Joe Green's Chicago Giants. The American Giants played their first NNL game on May 9, 1920, against Joe Green's Chicago Giants. Black baseball had long suffered with a lack of organization, so the inauguration of the NNL was a giant step. For opening day in St. Louis a large parade paced by marching jazz bands had fans perched on housetops and hillsides watching. The stands were packed and fans were ushered onto the grass where they completely surrounded the field — 2,000 fans had to be turned away. Similar scenes were repeated on opening day in Indianapolis, Detroit and Kansas City. Just one year after the Chicago race riots had left black baseball in total disarray the Negro National League had unmistakably come to life.[8]

The banner of the Negro National League had great psychological and symbolic importance, however many of the same problems that affected black baseball before the creation of the league remained. A conscientious effort was made in the inaugural year to be patient and not to expect too much, too fast from the fledgling league. Most of the NNL teams had played against each other for years; it wasn't as if they were starting from scratch. The lax structure permitted the league to focus on playing baseball and assured that black baseball would continue regardless of obstacles. Team owners were forced by the league to work together for the good of the whole. The schedule was unbalanced; the teams did not play each other an equal number of times, nor did they play the same number of "league" games. There were issues with availability of ballparks. Weaker teams had trouble scheduling games against the powerhouses since crowds were smaller and less interested when weaker teams played. The teams were free to play outside of the league so long as they didn't do business with teams that had violated league contracts. With the commencement of "league play," schedules and standings determined by winning percentage were published in black newspapers (occasionally in white papers) which invited the public to follow teams more closely. Large crowds turned out for the best match ups. Under the auspices of the Negro National League black baseball was on the road to becoming an American institution.

The league was new, but the players, managers and teams were familiar. Also familiar to the black baseball combatants was the dominance of the American Giants who—as usual—were the team to beat. Both Kansas City and Indianapolis did their best to collect talent equal to the American Giants. Kansas City Monarch owner J. L. Wilkinson culled the Monarchs together from the best black players from the All-Nations team, which he had previously managed, and recruited players from the black 25th Infantry army team. The Monarchs of 1920 included Jose Mendez, John Donaldson, Dobie Moore and Hall of Fame pitcher Wilbur "Bullet" Rogan. The recruits from the 25th Infantry team were heartily endorsed by Kansas City native Casey Stengel, who had barnstormed against the team and was impressed. C.I. Taylor supplemented his already strong Indianapolis ABC team, which included his brother Ben Taylor and Oscar Charleston, by leveraging a buyout of a San Antonio team which brought Henry Blackman and Raleigh "Biz" Mackey to the ABCs—two more black baseball greats.

The talent of the Monarchs and the ABCs would not be enough to overcome the well-oiled American Giants machine. When the percentages were tallied toward the end of the season the Chicago American Giants had a commanding .777 winning percentage, well ahead of Detroit, Indianapolis and Kansas City, who were hovering over the .500 mark. St. Louis and the Cuban Stars (who played in Cincinnati) were just below .500. The Dayton Marcos and Joe Greene's Chicago Giants, the have-nots of the NNL, were the cellar dwellers—lacking a strong fan base and depth on the field.

There had been a changing of the guard on the American Giants with long time captain Pete Hill and Bruce Petway out of the picture. Leroy Grant, Jude Gans, Bobby Williams and Frank Wickware carried the torch. A hallmark of the American Giants was that they were not dependent on a star player to carry the team. After players like Smokey Joe Williams, John Henry Lloyd, Ben Taylor or Oscar Charleston left the American Giants, the team continued to win. While the American Giants came out on top, they did not rout the competition. Partial records show that the American Giants just barely edged KC in head to head games, and beat Indianapolis five times, lost three times and two games finished tied due to darkness. Even the lowly Dayton Marcos managed a stunning upset over the American Giants early in the season.

The Bacharach Giants, featuring pitcher Dick "Cannonball" Redding, shortstop Dick Lundy, third baseman Oliver Marcelle and right fielder Jesse Barbour, grabbed a westbound train in August 1920 to do battle with a number of NNL teams. Redding and Barbour both previously played for the American Giants. The participation of the Bacharach Giants as associate members of the league showed that Rube could get along amicably with the East Coast teams and that the Negro National League was truly "national," stretching from New Jersey to Missouri. Cannonball Redding was still one of the best pitchers in baseball, even after serving in the military for most of the previous season. Redding's presence helped make the Bacharachs one of the best teams in black baseball and a threat to the American Giants' supremacy.

There were differences between the baseball cultures of the Eastern and Midwestern states. One reason that owners Nat Strong and Ed Bolden did not jump at joining the NNL was because they did not need the support of the league to be profitable — the urban scenes of New York and Philadelphia provided ample opportunities. In the fall of 1920 Ed Bolden's Hilldale club actually squared off several times against a barnstorming major league team that featured Babe Ruth — proof that Bolden's organizing skill rivaled Foster. The East-West rivalry had grown over the years going back to1904 when Rube Foster left Philadelphia.

When the Bacharachs visited Chicago in August an incident occurred that caused the *Chicago Defender* to declare that the "ill mannerisms of the Bacharachs must be stopped immediately." Bacharach player Oliver Marcelle tried to charge the mound when he was nearly struck by a wild pitch delivered by Tom Williams. When Marcelle came back to the plate two innings later, according to the *Defender*: "with his back toward the boxes on the left side of the grandstand he proceeded to make immoral movements with part of his body that would resemble a hoochy-coochy dancer. Fans might stand for this sort of treatment in the East, but not here...."[9]

In October the American Giants went East to meet the Atlantic City Bacharach Giants for a series of games played in Philadelphia's Shibe Park and Brooklyn's Ebbetts Field. The exhibition series was a dress rehearsal for what Rube envisioned as the black World Series. The Bacharachs gave the American Giants a run for the money; published accounts of the exhibitions, though incomplete, state that both teams won three of six games. The first season of the Negro National League was a success, insofar as a full season was played, there was good competition between the teams and the rules of the league were respected. The NNL did not disintegrate into bickering and broken promises—Rube Foster was largely to credit.[10]

Earlier in his career Foster had earned a reputation as the bully from Chicago who raked in the dough as the king of black baseball. While that reputation stuck, Foster changed his business tactics in response to challenges created by World War I and the subsequent race riots. Foster realized the value of promoting and supporting black baseball outside of Chicago. The American Giants played more road games. Rube gave direct support to franchises in Detroit and Dayton, Ohio. He crisscrossed the country meeting with friend and foe in a tireless effort to make the league a reality.

While Rube Foster had achieved fame for his feats as a pitcher, and defined greatness as a manager, it was the creation of the Negro National League that was his crowning achievement. It was during this period that Foster earned his reputation as the "Father of Black Baseball." Rube became the great shepherd of the black baseball teams, guiding the flock to a greener pasture. The good shepherd was also as tough as a Texas sheriff and knew how to lay down the law. Rube Foster's leadership abilities helped him win over detractors and succeed where others had failed.

Foster wore the hats of NNL president, team owner and team manager. Not only did Rube have "multiple irons in the fire," he also faced conflicts of interest. Foster had to render judgment when there were disagreements between different members of the league—even when that disagreement involved the American Giants. If there was a dispute regarding umpiring, complaints about scheduling, questions on enforcement of contractual obligations or any interpretation of NNL rules—it was Rube Foster who set policy. Foster also administered the treasury of the Negro National League—10 percent of all gate receipts were earmarked for the league operating fund. Even when there was no conflict of interest there was always the appearance of a conflict. The Negro National League was no democracy. Rube Foster was in charge.

The Negro National League was just one of several major developments in the national game of 1920. In the white major leagues George Herman "Babe" Ruth was sold by the Boston Red Sox to the New York Yankees and set an unbelievable record with 54 home runs in one season. Chicago found itself at the center of the baseball universe. In September of 1920 a Cook County grand jury was called to investigate allegations that the Chicago White Sox had fixed the 1919 World Series. By the end of October indictments had been handed down on eight Chicago White Sox players, the infamous "Eight Men Out"—also known as "the Black Sox." The Black Sox scandal eventually led to the appointment of federal judge Kenesaw Mountain Landis of Chicago as commissioner of baseball. (Landis later enforced dictums that major league players could not compete against professional black baseball teams.)

The post-war boom and fruits of the industrial revolution ushered in the "Age of Jazz." Chicago was in the crosshairs of change and events of the 1920's would permanently shape the city. The city bustled with cars and trains. Marketplaces and entertainment venues were frenetic as the post-war boom put more money into people's pockets. Yet while the Roaring Twenties were marked by excess, the decade was greeted with the enforcement of Prohibition. One of the leading proponents of Prohibition was Billy Sunday, a former outfielder for the Chicago White Stockings turned evangelist.

While Prohibition was the law, local law enforcement was known to turn many a blind eye to the activity on Chicago's South Side. Cops freely accepted bribes and law enforcement was often done only for show. South State Street was a long carnival of stores, restaurants, cafes, cabarets, concert halls, underground drinking, gambling and prostitution establishments ablaze with the lights of store fronts making it bright enough to see—even though there were no street lights.

Al Capone arrived in Chicago in 1920. Political corruption, prostitution, gambling and hard drinking were woven into the fabric of Chicago. Prohibition only seemed to make Chicago thirstier. As one verse of the famous song "Chicago: that toddlin' town" goes, Chicago was "the town that Billy Sunday could not shut down ... after all, it was Capone's town!" Famed jazz pianist Earl Hines recalled raids on the Sunset Club where he performed:

> A lot of money passed under the table, but the police would raid the Sunset and we would all have to get into the patrol wagon and go down to the police station every night. All we did is sign and go back to finish the rest of the night. I stood up in the wagon so often on those trips, I finally decided to run and get a seat when the police came.[11]

The "Great Migration" continued; the lure of job opportunities and the bright lights of State Street drew Southern blacks. The Illinois Central train brought blacks from the Deep South to Chicago on a daily basis. Joe "King" Oliver, fabled cornet player and progenitor of New Orleans "jazz," moved to Chicago in 1919 and joined "The Original Creole Orchestra." A couple of years later, King Oliver invited Louis Armstrong to join his band. As Chicago's black population swelled, whites and blacks interacted more frequently, though the city remained segregated. Through jazz many white Chicagoans developed an appreciation of black culture as they ventured into the cabarets and "black and tans" of the South Side. Even as the industrial North received masses of black immigrants from the South and some cross-cultural mixing was taking place, the social and economic gains achieved by blacks were met with resentment by some whites. In the 1920s the Ku Klux Klan reorganized and were especially active in the Midwestern states like Indiana and Illinois. A chill hung in the air of race relations as the Klan threatened, and sometimes engaged in, general violence against blacks.

Chicago was awash in the twentieth century. A great many changes had taken place since the city rebuilt following the Great Fire. There was ungodly turmoil along the way, but turmoil was the norm in Chicago. The transition to a modern industrial city was a natural course. Things like gangsters, gambling, jazz, pedestrians crushed under street-cars, clashes between conservative Midwestern culture and brutal urban culture marked "Chicago." In July of 1920 pugilist Jack Johnson, who had fled the country disguised as a member of the American Giants baseball team, surrendered to U.S. authorities and was sent to prison in Leavenworth — where he waited anxiously to return to Chicago. The Negro National League did not capture the general public's attention in the same way as Babe Ruth, the Black Sox, Jack Johnson, Louis Armstrong, Al Capone, Billy Sunday, cars, phonographs and movies. Nonetheless the league became a fixture in the black urban community in the nineteen twenties; another accouterment of the Jazz Age.

A meeting of the Negro National League was held in Indianapolis the first week of December 1920. It was announced that teams represented at the meeting had drawn a combined total of over a million fans in 1920. Hilldale owner Ed Bolden, who had only a few months earlier accused Rube Foster of "a belligerent attitude," and "attempting to boycott the Hilldale club," put aside his reservations and joined the Negro National League as an "associate member." Bolden was joined at the meeting by representatives from the Atlantic City Bacharach Giants, Pittsburgh and Cleveland as well as the NNL core members — a positive sign of the league's vitality.

Pittsburgh and Cleveland were not granted league membership, however they were offered general protection under the umbrella of the "League Constitution." It was declared "the Constitution of National Association of Colored Professional Baseball Clubs is effective and will be the executive body from which the Western Circuit and all other Circuits affiliating will be governed." The master plan called for Pittsburgh and Cleveland to procure home ballparks before joining the league. The Dayton Marcos were moved to Columbus, Ohio, and Joe Greene's Chicago Giants were allowed to remain in the league although they would basically play all of their games on the road. Rube remained the "strongman" of the league, as he was re-elected league president — the responsibilities of secretary and treasurer went along with the executive office. Overall the cooperation displayed at the year-end league meeting was encouraging and all signs pointed to Rube Foster's vindication as the true leader of organized black baseball.[12]

1921

Following the year-end meetings Rube retreated to Hot Springs, Arkansas, for much needed recuperation after working three jobs during the 1920 season — owner, manager and league president. Pitcher Tom Williams, who had done the lion's share of the pitching in the 1920 campaign, also "took the water cure" in Hot Springs. Center fielder Cristobal Torriente went back to Cuba for winter ball. John McGraw, manager of the New York Giants, brought a group of major league ball players that included Babe Ruth down to Cuba that winter; the "Babe" was a legend in Cuba as well. He was reportedly paid $2,000 a game and ticket prices had to be increased to foot his bill. On November 4, 1920, Torriente and the Alemendares team defeated McGraw's crew and the Sultan of Swat by an 11–4 score. The game was longed talked about on the island (similar to Petway's pegging out of Ty Cobb), because Torriente blasted three home runs while the Bambino went hitless. Torriente hit the home runs off of George "Highpockets" Kelly, a Hall of Fame first baseman but not a regular pitcher; in addition Torriente hit a double off of Babe.

(Alemendares pitcher Isidor Fabre deserves the credit for holding Ruth hitless.) Torriente was one of the greatest power hitters in black baseball history — in elite company with the likes of Oscar Charleston and Josh Gibson, and was nicknamed by some "the Black Babe Ruth."[13]

In late January, following the retreat to the Hot Springs spas, Rube gathered up most of the American Giants and headed to Palm Beach, Florida, to renew the tradition of taking spring training while playing for the entertainment of the wealthy guests of the Palm Beach Royal Poinciana and Breakers resorts. Frank Warfield, normally a second baseman and who had played with the Detroit Stars in 1920, joined the American Giants for the trip and filled in for Torriente who remained in Cuba. The American Giants represented the Royal Poinciana resort. Players from the Hilldale club such as Phil Cockerel, Louis Santop, Bill Francis along with John Henry "Pops" Lloyd represented the Breakers. The American Giants finished up in Palm Beach in mid–March, then swung through the South playing games in Georgia, Tennessee, Alabama and Arkansas, following the well-worn path taken in previous years. Before leaving the state of Florida first baseman Leroy Grant was married in Jacksonville; some of his teammates were attendants in the ceremony.[14]

Prior to the season a white baseball promoter named Andy Lawson of Boston proposed a new "Continental League" in which states rather than cities would have franchises. Lawson was interested in forming an association with Rube Foster and other black baseball teams. He went so far as to announce that he would "place a Colored team [in Chicago]." Lawson was working under the irrational assumption that Foster would be interested in joining. While Lawson was taken seriously by some (interest in owning franchises was shown in a number of states — Pennsylvania (Pittsburgh), Michigan (Detroit), Indiana (Indianapolis), and Maryland (Baltimore), to name a few), he was ridiculed by the major league baseball establishment. Andy Lawson went on record in the *New York Times* stating that there were many black ball players equal to or better than the average major leaguer. The proposed league was dubbed the "Black and Tan League" by the black press. Lawson had a minor association with the Federal League in 1914 and had favored integrating that league, as did Rube Foster. Foster welcomed any attention paid to professional black baseball. No agreement between the Continental League and the Negro National League was made, due in large part to the fact that the Continental League of 1921 never got off the ground. Foster continued to hope that there would be some movement in major league baseball towards racial integration; in the mean time all energy and resources were put into the fledgling Negro National League.[15]

Plans laid out for the 1921 NNL season were more ambitious than the inaugural season, although the familiar challenges facing black baseball and requisite allowances meant that league operations were at times disorganized. An interesting season took shape as quality baseball was played throughout the league and several teams had a shot at the pennant. Oscar Charleston, probably the single best player in the league, was lured away from his hometown Indianapolis ABCs to the St. Louis Giants. Charleston almost single handedly put the St. Louis team into contention for the NNL crown. Another legend, John Henry "Pop" Lloyd, took up the reins as manager of the new team in the league: the Columbus Buckeyes, who took the place of the Dayton Marcos. The Eastern associate members, the Atlantic City Bacharachs and the Hilldale club, played more games against the regular NNL teams which added to the league's vitality.

There was only one major change in the American Giants' roster for 1921: Jude Gans returned to New York, where he began his career, to become manager of the Lincoln Giants. Gans was replaced by Jimmy Lyons, who had played in Chicago as a youth, but most recently was with the Detroit Stars after returning from European wartime service in 1919. The American Giants opened the second NNL season with a three-game series against the Kansas City Monarchs at Schorling Field beginning on May 7th. Rube's men would have taken all three games had it not been for three fielding errors, which ruined a one-hitter tossed by Tom Johnson.[16]

The American Giants struggled on the road in 1921. St. Louis took six out of eight games played on their home field. The American Giants traveled to Cincinnati in late July where they played the Cuban Stars at Redland Field — the only active major league park on the circuit. (John Beckwith of Joe Green's Chicago Giants was credited with being the first player to put a ball over the left field wall of Redland Field — a feat accomplished May 21, 1921.) The American Giants were shown up by the Cubans in Cincy, losing back to back games, then faced an additional loss when outfielder Jimmy Lyons somehow fell 25 feet down an open elevator shaft at the hotel the team was staying at in Cincy, sustaining serious injuries.[17]

Despite setbacks on the road the American Giants were able to dominate teams in the Windy City. The standings remained close all season long, but in the end the Chicago American Giants claimed the NNL championship, though it was by a very slim margin (just .005) over the St. Louis Giants. Given the closeness of the race it might have been reasonable to have a playoff. Even after the establishment of the NNL the "championship" was awarded on a subjective basis, since schedules remained unbalanced. There was no vocal protest against the American Giants' claim to the 1921 NNL pennant, although there was some grumbling. The general public overlooked the fact that Rube Foster, president of the NNL, awarded the championship to Rube Foster, manager/owner of the Chicago American Giants, two years in a row.

Under the regimen of an organized league, the American Giants had planned to scale back the number of games played against Chicago area white semi-pro teams. However in July, Rube met with heads of Chicago area semi-pro leagues who were anxious to resume the tradition of play in the so-called "City League." The way was cleared so that the American Giants and other NNL teams could play against Chicago semi-pro teams when scheduling allowed. Among the local white teams the American Giants played in 1921 were the Chicago Magnets, the Progressives — representing Commonwealth Edison, Briscoe Motor Company, the Logan Squares, the Pyotts (formerly known as the Gunthers) and the Singer Sewing Machine Company. Following the time-honored tradition the semi-pro teams usually featured one or two former major leaguers as their calling card.

The American Giants met the Singer Sewing Machine team of South Bend, Indiana, on July 24, 1921, at Schorling Park — on "Eighth Regiment Day," in honor of local black troops who had served in World War I. The pitcher for Singer was Walter Halas, brother of "Papa Bear" Halas of Chicago Bears pro football fame. Halas had been a star in baseball, basketball and football at the University of Illinois and was the coach of the Notre Dame baseball team in 1921. Halas lasted just three innings against the American Giants who sent him to the showers up 5–0, and eventually won by an 8–0 score.[18]

In October the American Giants went east to play against the Hilldale club and the

Bacharach Giants, a dry run for the planned future "East-West World Series." On this trip east the American Giants were in for a rude awakening. They lost two of three games against Hilldale and split eight games with the Bacharach Giants. Rube said he regarded the post-season games against the East Coast teams as mere exhibition matches; he reminded everyone that the American Giants had won the NNL pennant. The American Giants played with their regular season roster, with the addition of pitcher Elvis Holland who Rube picked up from Detroit for the tour.

In all the years Foster had managed the American Giants, beginning in 1907, only once (in 1913, when defeated by the Lincoln Giants in post-season series) did he concede "*the championship*." In 1916, when the Indianapolis ABCs won more games from the American Giants in post-season series, Rube refused to acknowledge them. Though Foster had an interest in seeing that the Negro National League he founded was run fairly and that there was some parity between the teams in the league, he continued to take "*winning the championship*" very seriously. Rube's penchant was sometimes carried to an extreme and he was seen by some as obnoxious.

On the whole the NNL was an overwhelming success in 1921. The league was competitive, fans followed the teams throughout the country and some of Rube's nay-sayers were ready to eat their hats. It looked like Rube Foster had found the path to baseball's Promised Land. Most importantly the NNL was no longer just an idea or a sketch on a pad; the NNL had a life of its own, with characters, drama and sustainability.

Rube Foster, the American Giants and the NNL were sailing along just fine, but choppy waters lay ahead. Following the autumn journey to the East Coast, in which the American Giants fell to the Hilldale club, Rube took the team down to New Orleans for yet another extension of the 1921 season — the so called "Championship of the South" — and from there the team planned to catch a boat to Havana. As the trip to New Orleans was a bit more low-key, Rube arranged for his wife and daughter (both named Sarah) to catch a train and join him for short vacation.

Rube and the American Giants headed south down the Eastern seaboard through Atlanta. Rube, who had traveled hundreds of thousands of miles by rail, was in for a big surprise when he reached Atlanta. When the American Giants' special train (which consisted of a locomotive, baggage, diner, and three Pullmans) pulled into the station on the afternoon of November 3rd, officers of the Atlanta police department boarded the train and arrested Rube Foster, charging him with fraud. The charges were based on the claim of Ben Harris, a player with whom Rube had brief contact the previous year. Harris claimed that Rube had recruited a number of players from Atlanta, promised them $125 a month plus a share of gate receipts. Harris had gone so far as to hire a white attorney, Roy Drennan, to pursue claims against Foster.

Within hours Foster was bailed out by his well connected friend R. J. Davis, the editor of the black newspaper the *Atlanta Independent* (which was the organ of the Odd Fellows society). Rube said that the charges were "totally unfounded." In all likelihood there was a germ of truth to Ben Harris's claim — it was Foster's style to talk things up. After posting bond Rube and the American Giants loaded back onto their special train and pulled out of the station — just as President Warren Harding pulled into the station on *his* special. [19]

Rube went on to New Orleans, his wife and daughter met him there as planned. The American Giants called off the trip to Cuba. Political turmoil and a crash in the sugar market dimmed prospects for Cuban baseball in 1921. Instead, Rube, his family and the American Giants headed back to Chicago. Rube's five-year-old daughter Sarah said good-night to all the players before going to bed in the sleeper car. When the sun came up in the morning Rube's normally gregarious daughter had trouble waking up. Mrs. Foster was worried and tried to apply first aid. When they reached Chicago, little Sarah was rushed home and a doctor was called. The physician informed Mr. and Mrs. Foster that their young daughter had a leakage in her heart apparently caused by a toxic substance. A few hours later Rube's five-year-old daughter died.

Rube grieved deeply for his daughter, but within days was back to the business of running the Negro National League. Foster wrote a series of four articles for the *Chicago Defender* outlining his view of the current state of affairs in black baseball. [20]

The articles were in the same vein as his previous essays, which had been published off and on in the *Defender* since 1910. While the success of the NNL was undeniable, Foster guarded against overconfidence and addressed upcoming challenges. Each of the four essays tackled a separate topic: "What Baseball Needs to Succeed"; "Why Colored Baseball Owners and Managers Have Been a Failure"; "Colored Baseball Players as I Know Them"; and "Colored Umpires."

Foster's tone was pessimistic as he played devil's advocate. He repeated many of his long held views that managers and players were too self centered and too greedy. He stated that many of the managers were "failures," while relating the story of one unnamed team that wrote bad checks to players. Rube revealed that "some of our leading baseball clubs of the country [are] managed by men who cannot either read or write." According to Foster, only he himself and Indianapolis manager C.I. Taylor possessed the necessary business and baseball skills required to succeed.

Rube singled out ballplayers who had come from college, stating: "they have proven to be the greatest whisky drinkers," and often were ignorant of the rules of the game. Rube also suggested that players consider a "readjustment in ... salary," due to the "industrial depression that has hit the entire country" (referring to the decline in manufacturing jobs at the end of World War I).

While criticizing others, Foster still managed to put feathers in his own cap. He reminded readers, "the American Giants would be an even greater financial success without the league," but that as a 'duty to the race' he reduced the American Giants' cut of the gate on the road to promote the league. Foster couldn't understand how the other managers floundered, since in his 16-year managing career he had "yet to find a player that is hard to manage" and "not had one to disobey any instruction given him."

Most surprising to some, Foster stated his case against hiring black umpires:

> To be official umpire the first great step for the umpire is to study the disposition and temperament of the players with whom he comes in contact; to be a good judge of' human nature, to know the baseball rules their interpretation and to be HONEST and SQUARE. These qualifications are sadly missing in the umpires that I have seen perform. We need umpires of the Race very badly and can use them to great advantage.... They don't know all the technicalities of baseball rules to make efficient umpires, yet the more they umpire the better they will be. There must be a beginning. It would, however, be unfair to give them positions unless we were in position to give them the protection they will need in doing their work. [21]

The issue of hiring more black umpires would be revisited in years to come.

1922

Not everyone appreciated Rube's candor, but the articles made a good jumping off point for discussions at the league meeting. After meeting in Kansas City and Indianapolis in previous years, the 1922 NNL meeting was held in Chicago at the Appomattox Club in late January. Since Chicago was headquarters for black baseball, a fair amount of pomp was put on for the meeting. Alderman Major Robert R. Jackson, who had managed the Chicago Unions in 1889 and was one of those who had sparred with Rube when he had declared independence from Frank Leland in1907, was the "toastmaster" for the meeting. Members of the black press such as writer Dave Wyatt of the *Chicago Whip*, Robert Abbot, publisher of the *Chicago Defender*, Q. J. Gilmore of the *St. Louis Argus* and Ira Lewis of the *Pittsburgh Courier* (to name a few) addressed the assembly. C.I. Taylor was among the managers who spoke before the assembly in a speech titled "Perpetuating the Game." Rube spelled out the issues facing the league, similar to the articles he recently had published in the *Defender*, in his speech titled "Around the Circuit." Foster underscored the need for "business sense," given the uncertain economic situation.[22]

When the talk ended, the NNL had made a few changes. The Pittsburgh Keystones and Cleveland Tate Stars were granted league membership. The Columbus Buckeyes and Chicago Giants were dropped; both teams had struggled and threatened to drag down the league. The Cuban Stars' agreement to use Cincinnati's Redland Field was not renewed, so the Cuban Stars would play all of their games on the road. As of the late January meeting Ed Bolden, manager of the Hilldale club, was undecided as to whether or not he would remain in an association with the league; but by the beginning of the season had rejoined. Despite the bleak picture Rube Foster had painted of the state of affairs, the league forged ahead for another season. In Chicago, Detroit, Indianapolis and Kansas City the league was healthy. The fact that the league had a life of its own, able to withstand various challenges, was noteworthy.[23]

The league meeting adjourned; the managers went back to their respective towns to regroup for the upcoming season. Shortly after returning to Indianapolis, owner/manager C. I. Taylor, the vice-president of the NNL, fell ill. It was a bitterly cold winter and there had been a flu epidemic. C.I. Taylor's illness turned out to be serious. Just three weeks after the league meeting the NNL brass was reunited for the somber occasion of C.I. Taylor's funeral. Rube Foster, still shell-shocked by the November death of his own daughter, gave a eulogy for C.I. Taylor at the Bethel A.M.E. church in Indianapolis on February 27, 1922. C.I. Taylor died at age 47. He was out of the "old school," a hardworking baseball man, a true believer in the Negro National League and had played a vital role as the league vice-president. The death of C. I. Taylor, one of the few people Foster had faith in, was another challenge for the league to overcome.

C.I. Taylor's wife Olivia Taylor took over the ownership of the ABCs, his brother Ben Taylor took over the field management. "Candy Jim" Taylor, also a brother of C.I., was manager of the Cleveland Tate Stars— newly inducted into the NNL.[24]

There were some minor changes to the roster of the American Giants for 1922. Utility player Dave Malarcher was ordered by his doctor to sit out due to a torn ligament near his heart. Rube hired another top utility man, John Beckwith, to take Malarcher's spot. Beckwith had been with Joe Green's Chicago Giants since 1916. He was a husky player who swung a thirty-six-inch bat like it was a toothpick—he went down in history as the first player ever to hit a ball over the left field wall of Cincinnati's Redland Field. Like Malarcher, Beckwith could play any position on the field. Unlike Malarcher, who was one of the most polite and well spoken players in the history of the Negro Leagues, Beckwith was known for violent outbursts, drunkenness and a general lack of clubhouse chemistry. (On one occasion Beckwith badly beat an umpire and had to flee prosecution from police.) Rube gave Harry Jefferies, who also had played with Joe Green's Chicago Giants in 1921, a tryout at first base, but once the regular season got going Leroy Grant took the job back.[25]

Rube also reworked the pitching rotation. The American Giants acquired "Huck" Rile, a strong young pitcher also adept as a hitter, from the disbanded Columbus Buckeye team and had high expectations for him. Also joining the team was veteran Cuban pitcher Juan Luis Padrone, "El Mulo." Padrone picked up the nickname "Mulo" for his slow-moving change-up pitch, and was considered one of the truly great Cuban pitchers. Padrone was also an impressive outfielder and hitter in his prime. Rube signed back Dick Whitworth who had jumped to Hilldale in 1920. The signing of Whitworth served notice to Ed Bolden, owner of the Hilldale team, that he had better conform to the governance of the NNL organization or face losing his top players. (Before the season started Bolden capitulated, but Whitworth stayed with the American Giants.)[26]

Dave Brown was the only starter that remained in the rotation from the previous season. Jack Marshall, who had pitched fairly well for the American Giants in 1921, was dealt to the Detroit Stars. Tom Johnson was not able to play due to health problems and Tom Williams went to the Lincoln Giants of New York. In addition to Huck Rile, Juan Luis Padrone, Dick Whitworth and Dave Brown, Rube signed a young pitcher named Aubrey Owens, who was also a dental student at Meharry Medical College of Nashville, Tennessee.

The difficult 1921 season came to an end, and the American Giants headed to New Orleans for spring training. Before going into camp Foster was called upon to settle a disagreement between the St. Louis Stars and the Indianapolis ABCs, regarding the contractual rights to sign Oscar Charleston. Rube ruled in favor of Indianapolis and Oscar went back to his hometown team. St. Louis signed a hometown player of their own that year—James "Cool Papa" Bell.

The American Giants had a productive spring training sparring against the local New Orleans Crescents and the Cuban Stars who steamed over via Key West, Florida. The American Giants dropped their May 6th NNL opener to the Kansas City Monarchs by a 5–1 score. Newcomer Ed "Huck" Rile gave up two doubles to Hurley McNair, a triple to Jose Mendez and a home run to Walter "Dobie" Moore. K.C. pitcher Rube Currie allowed only two hits and notched the win.

The second game of the season, on May 7, 1922, had a bizarre outcome. A large crowd came out for the Sunday game; when one of the ticket gates was closed some fans began stepping over a barrier into the higher price boxed seats, then more fans began to follow suit. The game got under way but fans kept pushing forward, some of them actually on the field. In those days it was not that unusual for a small number of fans to be allowed to stand on the field out of the way in foul territory. The crowd was so large and out of hand that several times during the game fans actually encroached into fair territory. At one point the fans interfered with a ball hit into right field and the umpire awarded K.C. hitter Jose Mendez a double. The crowd protested the umpire's decision and remained unruly as the game continued. In the top of the eighth inning the Monarchs went up by one run. But in bottom of the eighth the hometown American Giants battled back to tie the game and the excitement was too much for the overwrought fans. It was just the bottom of the eighth, the game was merely tied, but fans began running on the field yelling and throwing hats in the air, women screaming. When the ninth inning started efforts were made to keep the fans off of the field, but when one group of fans was moved back, another moved back on to the playing surface. Finally both managers agreed the game had to be called.

The decision to call the game was greeted by further outbursts from the unruly, drunken fans that were throwing seat cushions and pop bottles. The episode fit the storyline of South Side Chicago in the 1920's. According to the *Chicago Defender*, "[P]atrons of the park have not only brought whisky there, but have sold it in the rest room. The actions of the women in the ladies' restroom Sunday, according to reputable witnesses, is not fit to put into print." John Schorling, owner of the park, went to authorities to increase security for future games. Measures were to include more police officers, confiscation of "hip liquor," and plain clothes officers who would infiltrate the gambling rings known to conduct business at the park.[27]

The American Giants finished out the series against the Monarchs with two one-run victories. Dick Whitworth notched a 2–1 win over Monarch Clifford Bell. Cristobal Torriente (normally the center fielder) pitched nine innings of a ten inning thriller in which he helped his cause with a ninth-inning three-run homer to tie the game at four apiece — then reliever Huck Rile put the American Giants ahead 5–4 with his game winning RBI in the tenth. In the same game Dave Malarcher, who had recently been under doctor's orders not to play, was badly spiked by KC shortstop Dobie Moore while attempting to steal second and had to be carried off the field directly to Provident Hospital. Malarcher's injury landed John Beckwith back into the American Giants' starting lineup.

The battle for the NNL flag was again hotly contested. Indianapolis started league play with an 11–1 record and it looked like the American Giants might be taken off the throne. Indy sported high profile talents like Oscar Charleston, Biz Mackey, Ben Taylor, Dizzy Dismukes and Henry Blackman. The ABCs had trouble keeping up the blistering pace. In early June, C.I. Taylor's widow Olivia Taylor made the trip to Chicago with the team she owned so that she might discuss league business with Rube. She sat in a box seat with Mrs. Foster, only to see the ABCs drop both games of the two game series against the American Giants.[28]

The American Giants struggled against Kansas City all season. On a road trip to Kansas City, on June 18th, the American Giants were shellacked 19–5, which was their worst ever defeat. Future Hall of Famer Wilbur "Bullet" Rogan delivered the lacing but the American Giants sealed their own fate by committing seven errors.

By July it was a four-way race between Indianapolis, Chicago, Detroit and Kansas City. The American Giants took four straight games from Indianapolis in mid–July (extending their record against Indy to 6–0) and snuck into first place. The pennant race was far from over though, and it appeared there would be a "fair fight" for the championship with a strong possibility that the American Giants might finally have to cede the throne.[29]

The American Giants passed up the customary trip to the East Coast, but the Atlantic City Bacharach Giants and Hilldale both paid visits to Chicago. A bit of history was made on August 16, 1922, when the American Giants were involved in one of the longest games ever in Negro League history. The Bacharachs, featuring John Henry "Pop" Lloyd and Dick "Cannonball" Redding, met the American Giants in the rubber game of a five-game series. Harold Treadwell was the starter for the Bacharachs and Huck Rile started the game for the American Giants. The game was scoreless through four innings; in the fifth Rube pulled Huck Rile and brought in Dave Brown. The game remained scoreless through nine innings. In the ninth, John Beckwith left the game after being spiked and was replaced by Dave Malarcher who had been on the shelf most of the season with injuries. The teams went back and forth, inning after inning, late into the afternoon, neither team able to score — although both had opportunities. The score remained tied at nil through nineteen innings. In the bottom of the twentieth inning Cristobal Torriente walked, was advanced on the sacrifice of Bobby Williams and then brought home on a hit by Dave Malarcher. Amazingly Bacharach pitcher Harold Treadwell went the distance.

Three days after the historic tug-of-war against the Bacharachs, the Hilldale club came to town. Another piece of history was made as Hilldale pitcher Phil Cockrell tossed a 5–0 no-hitter against Rube's men. Cockrell's performance gave Hilldale owner Ed Bolden a measure of satisfaction, in a season that otherwise fell short of his expectations. The Hilldales won just three of nine games on their western road trip and Bolden was disgruntled with the high cost of traveling to Chicago, when compared to the easy money to be had in the Philadelphia metro area.

The 1922 Negro League pennant race remained crowded for the balance of the season. Indianapolis, Detroit and Kansas City all ended up winning more league games than the American Giants; however, when the number of games won was divided by the number played — the American Giants had the higher winning percentage. Negro National League President and Secretary Rube Foster did the long division, certified the numbers and for the third time in the three years, awarded his team the championship title.

Even as the Negro National League matured into a full fledged professional league, all the teams continued to play occasional non-league games. Barnstorming continued to be the lifeblood for all of black baseball. During the 1922 season American Giant non-league opponents included stalwart Chicago semi-pro teams Rogers Park, Logan Squares and the Pyotts; House of David (Benton Harbor, Michigan, religious sect noted for their long hair and beards); and other semi-pro teams — who usually sported a former major league pitcher. (The American Giants beat former White Sox pitchers Dickie Kerr and John "Lefty" Sullivan, and former Cubs pitcher "Long" Tom Hughes.)

Rube announced with some excitement that the American Giants would play two games against the American League Detroit Tigers. Unfortunately the game against the Detroit Tigers did not come off— owing to bad weather and logistics which prevented rescheduling. While the American Giants' game versus the Tigers was nixed, several other NNL teams did face major league competition following the 1922 season. The Indianapolis ABCs faced the AAA Indianapolis Indians, the Cleveland Tate Stars played two games against the Cleveland Indians, St. Louis Stars played against the Detroit Tigers, and the Kansas City Monarchs faced a barnstorming crew that included Babe Ruth. Putting a chink in the color line was always a high priority for Rube Foster.

Season-ending league meetings were held again at Chicago's Appomattox Club. The meeting started off civilly on December 7, with a prayer in memory of C. I. Taylor, but then came the fireworks in a busy three-day session. The Pittsburgh Keystones, who were bankrupt and did not send a delegate to the meeting, were dropped from the league. The Cleveland Tate Stars could not come up with their dues and were voted out of the league. The N.J. Bacharach Giants did not bother to send a delegate, which brought an end to their three-year association with the NNL.

Ed Bolden attended the meeting but only for the purpose of submitting the resignation of the Hilldale club from the NNL. Bolden was fed up with the terms of his "*association*" with the NNL and was hatching plans to start a separate league in the East. Bolden also requested the return of his $1000 bond, but that request was denied. Foster stated that the "bond would only be returned if Bolden's proposed Eastern League would sign an agreement to respect the rights and contracts of the NNL."

The subject of general discipline among the players was addressed; Rube suggested that teams implement strict rules for "bed times" and "prompt reporting to the ballpark." Rube also took the opportunity to lecture those in attendance on the importance of professional business practice and accurate bookkeeping. Before the meeting was closed Rube was re-elected league president and treasurer (though he had made some noises at last year's meeting about not wanting the presidency), Detroit owner Tenny Blount was named vice-president, and Kansas City owner J. L. Wilkinson was made secretary. Olivia Taylor (C.I.'s widow) attended the meetings and was offered the job of vice-president, which she declined; she did however accept appointment to the board of directors. Some minor trades were approved and the board voted to erect a memorial to C. I. Taylor.[30]

1923

There were a lot of loose ends to be worked out prior to the season. Would Rube and the league be content with a Negro National League that did not extend to the East Coast? Would there be an effort to replace the teams and associated teams that had left league? *Chicago Defender* sportswriter Frank A. Young had mounted an aggressive campaign for the league to hire black umpires. Eroding economic conditions in the black community brought on by the decrease in postwar employment was another ongoing concern for black baseball.

Two weeks after the Negro National League meeting in Chicago, Ed Bolden held a meeting in Philadelphia on December 16, 1922. Bolden called together the principals of Eastern clubs—the Original Bacharach Giants, Baltimore Black Sox, Brooklyn Royal Giants and New York Lincoln Giants—and announced the formation of the "Eastern Colored League." Soon after the formation of the ECL, the hot-stove league sizzled with rumors that a large number of NNL players would be jumping East.[31]

A group of players went to Cuba to play in the winter league including Oscar Charleston, Dave Brown, Oliver Marcelle and John Henry Lloyd. When the players returned from Cuba it was rumored they would all be jumping to the Eastern circuit. Huck Rile was named by the *Chicago Defender* as an "agent for the Eastern Association." Another rumor had it that Indianapolis owner Olivia Taylor had "traded Oscar Charleston to Rube Foster, but that Charleston would jump east anyway." A bizarre rumor circulated through Chicago on March 5, 1923, that Rube Foster had "dropped dead at 35th and State Street"; phone calls jammed the *Chicago Defender* office attempting to get more information, and telegrams of sympathy were sent — the report was a hoax. While the rumors of Rube's demise were greatly exaggerated, there was a vein of truth in most of the other hot-stove chatter.[32]

One of the first defections from the NNL was Ben Taylor, field manager of the ABCs. Ben Taylor had a disagreement with in-law Olivia Taylor stemming from an incident in which Ben took it upon himself to organize a post-season game without informing Olivia or the league. Rube Foster was put in the awkward position of referee of the family feud and handed down a $200 fine on Ben Taylor. Ben Taylor had other differences with Olivia as well, and decided to break away from the ABCs. He tried to organize a NNL team in Cincinnati, but was unsuccessful and instead worked out a deal in Washington, D.C. Ben founded the Washington Potomacs, and leased Griffith Stadium — home of the American League Washington Senators. The Washington Potomacs were independent and not members of the ECL in 1923, nonetheless Taylor threatened to take with him some of the top players in the NNL whom he had long standing relationships with, including Oscar Charleston, Biz Mackey, Henry Blackman and others.[33]

Several more top NNL players would leave for the Eastern Colored League. Frank Warfield went from Detroit to Hilldale, Biz Mackey went from Indianapolis to Hilldale, Dave Brown thumbed his nose at the American Giants and went to the New York Lincoln Giants and was joined by Rube's number two pitcher Ed "Huck" Rile. The departure of Dave Brown, who had become the pitching ace for the storied American Giant franchise, understandably drew Rube's ire. Foster responded by letting the general public in on his disloyal twirler's little secret — that when he had hired Dave Brown back in 1919 he had posted a $20,000 bond to get him out of a Texas slammer where he was held for robbery.[34]

Foster termed the conflict with Ed Bolden and the Eastern Colored League a "baseball war." Not since the Federal League had raided Major League baseball in 1913 had a similar battle raged between competing baseball leagues. Foster and Bolden duked it out in the pages of black newspapers throughout the country. Foster blasted Bolden for doing business with Nat Strong, who Foster said "has taken 10 per cent from the gross earnings of colored ball clubs for over twenty years, has never built a fence for them to use and never will." Foster also recalled for his black audience that "Nat Strong [and] ... the whites took the players and paid them such small salaries as two fifteen cent meals a day."[35]

The fight between Foster and Bolden went no-holds-barred. Bolden responded indignantly: "Why does he (Foster) not publish the fact that Schorling Park and the American Giants are property of John Schorling, for whom the park is named and Foster is but a chattel of his white boss? Why does he not publish the fact that the secretaryship of the Western Association is held by Mr. Wilkinson, who is one of the opposite race?" Bolden resurrected all of the criticism that had been heaped on Rube Foster over the years.

Disgruntled players and managers came out of the woodwork to get in their two cents. The thrust of the character assassination was that Foster was a strong-arm dictator who ran the NNL as his personal fiefdom. Even Foster's friends sometimes referred to him as "the baseball czar." W. S. Ferance, a secretary for the St. Louis Stars who was privy to the league's business meetings, published a supposed exposé of Rube's ruthless ways. Ferance claimed that the league itself was "nothing more than a booking agency for the benefit of one man." Recalling the league's organization meetings, Ferrance stated: "The late C.I. Taylor and Charles Mills were the only two men that had nerve enough to fight the one man booking agency. Taylor and Mills were ... bitter against giving any one man five percent of all games played by the eight clubs. Mr. Rube Foster ... received $11,200 for his work the 1920 season and the league nothing ... not one penny." Commenting on the record-keeping of the NNL, Ferrance wrote: "The batting and fielding averages of clubs and players and the standings in the pennant race, if there is one, is what every fan would like to know and read. We all remember in St. Louis concerning the averages mailed out from 'League Headquarters' a real joke."[36]

Foster did not respond to the criticisms point by point, he did however challenge Ed Bolden to a public debate. Bolden accepted the challenge and suggested Rube "take the Hilldale's $1000 security deposit, rent the Academy of Music in Philadelphia, charge admission and give the proceeds to disabled ball players." However the spectacle of a formal debate never took place. Foster tried to rise above the fray by taking a paternalistic approach. He reminded the public of his long record of success as a player and manager. Rube readily admitted that he had profited from his hard work in baseball and stated: "I will not try to stop a raid on our players," but added "at the proper time will drive a blow that will not be easy to get rid of. I do not fear Nat Strong or any man in the baseball business."[37]

While the battle against the upstart Eastern Colored League was being fought, the responsibilities of shoring up the failing NNL franchises and preparing the American Giants for the season ahead also fell on Rube. Before the season got under way new franchises were established in Milwaukee and Toledo. Instead of the traditional journey south for winter/spring training, Rube called open try outs in Chicago. Forty-three players, including the returning veterans, went into camp at Schorling Field, which was opened to the public. Among the aspiring players Rube found two young arms, Alabaman George Harney and Kentuckian Lewis Wolfolk, who would both put in mound work for the American Giants; most of the other aspirants went home. Also in camp were three black umpire candidates, as Rube lent conditional support to the campaign for black umpires headed by Frank Young of the *Chicago Defender*. Among the candidates for the ump job was Tom Johnson who had trouble returning to playing form after the war.[38]

The American Giants' outfield remained steady with Cristobal Torriente in center, Jimmy Lyons in left and Jelly Gardner in right. The infield was equally impressive; a healthy "Gentleman" Dave Malarcher held down third base, Bobby Williams was at short, Bingo DeMoss was at the keystone and John Beckwith earned the starting job at first displacing Leroy Grant — who rode the bench for most of the season.

By contrast the pitching staff was weak. For years Foster had relied on a patchwork of aging journeymen pitchers (some of whom struggled with drinking problems) and young "flash in the pan" throwers. The strategy was good enough for three consecutive championships, but in 1923 the American Giants' pitching struggled. The team lacked an ace; Tom Williams was brought back for another stint but was well past his prime.

At the eleventh hour Foster issued a bulletin from the league offices: "All baseball players who signed to play the 1923 season with clubs of the Western Circuit of the NNL and who jumped their contracts and went East to play, will be barred from baseball in the NNL forever, unless they return or apply for reinstatement on or before the 28th day of April 1923." Rube's ultimatum and amnesty may have swayed Huck Rile to return to Chicago after jumping to New York with Dave Brown at the outset of the season. When the maligned Ed "Huck" Rile rejoined the team he assumed the role of the team's top starting pitcher.

Other pitchers on the staff going into the 1923 season included Aubrey Owens (the dental student who had shown promise in 1922), Jack Marshall (who started a number of games for Rube in 1921), Luther Farrell and Harry Kenyon (both acquired from Indianapolis). Rookies Lewis Wolfolk and George Harney were also put into the starting role. Rube had especially high hopes for Wolfolk, who was given a lot of work early in the season. Late in the season Rube hired Louis "Dicta" Johnson and Fulton Strong who were absorbed from the failed Milwaukee Bears franchise. This pitching committee would show a few sparkles, but lacked the kind of overpowering strength of a Pat Dougherty, Tom Johnson, "Cannonball" Dick Redding, Dick Whitworth, Frank Wickware or Rube Foster himself in their prime.

Rube did take a swipe at bringing a top pitching talent aboard for 1923. He wrote a personal letter to Ed Bolden's star Phil Cockerell — who had thrown two no-hitters for the Hilldales the previous season. Stealing Cockerell from Bolden might have also been Rube's attempt at "a mighty blow against the East," as he had earlier promised. Cockerell remained loyal to Hilldale and turned the letter over to Ed Bolden — Rube's mighty blow had not been struck.[39]

Pitching had been a concern for the American Giants since the onset of World War I. For the most part Rube was resolute in not getting in a bidding war for top pitchers — this had been his philosophy even before the rise of the Eastern Colored League. He preferred to scout unknown, under-appreciated talent and drive a bargain. Late in the 1923 season Foster landed a great pitcher from out of nowhere that took even him by surprise — his half-brother Willie Foster.

When the hot stove finally cooled and the season was set to begin, an assessment of damage caused by the baseball war wasn't as bad as originally feared. The top player in the NNL, Oscar Charleston, did not jump to the East, and reports that Charleston had been traded to the American Giants proved baseless. The Negro National League did lose some star power, but the league stayed intact. Chicago, Detroit, Indianapolis, Kansas City and St. Louis remained strong core teams of near major league caliber. In the bigger picture there were some positive signs for the growing enterprise of professional black baseball. The creation of the Eastern Colored League was an expansion of organized black baseball and a vindication of Rube Foster's long held view that organization was practical. At that point in time, however, it was impossible for the Western and Eastern circuits to see beyond their differences.

Competition was again close in the fourth season of the Negro National League. Indianapolis, who lost Biz Mackey and Ben Taylor to the Eastern Colored League in the carnage of the East-West baseball war, had enough power left to jump into first place early in the season. The pennant race bunched up as Chicago, Kansas City and Detroit challenged Indianapolis for the top spot. By late June the American Giants worked their way back to their familiar perch at the top of the standings. Their stay at the top was short lived though as the Kansas City Monarchs eclipsed them in the standings a few days later. By late August, the American Giants dropped to third place (behind Kansas City and Detroit) and it became apparent they would not win the pennant.

The Toledo and Milwaukee franchises were going broke; both would fold before season end. Signs of weakness were also seen in Indianapolis. When the fourth-place ABCs visited the American Giants for a two game series, they did not have a player available to play first base for the second game of the series. Rube bailed out the ABCs by dealing veteran American Giant first sacker Leroy Grant to Indianapolis after the Saturday game. Grant played against the American Giants in an ABC uniform on Sunday afternoon. Although Grant had spent most of the 1923 season on the bench, seeing him in a different uniform shocked some observers.

Foster was questioned by the press about the Giants' lackluster season and the sale of Leroy Grant. Foster took the bait and stated he was "beginning to wreck the once great machine that represented the American Giants." The comment might have betrayed Foster's underlying wishes, but he was not in a position to rebuild the team at that time. The "deal" to send Leroy Grant to Indianapolis was a loan, not a sale, as he was back with the American Giants within the month.[40]

The practice of "loaning" players had gone on occasionally in the days before league play, usually to bolster a team in the post-season for contests against white major leaguers. Loaning players during the regular season was considered bush league and this was not the image that Rube wanted the league to project. Rube made the exception given that the ABCs were being run by a widow and Leroy Grant's services were not really needed by the American Giants.

While the league lost the Milwaukee Bears and Toledo Tigers, the Birmingham Black Barons and the Memphis Red Sox were brought under the umbrella of the NNL as associate members late in the season. On the way back from a rare August trip into the Deep South to play the Birmingham Black Barons, the American Giants went by way of Memphis where they stopped to look over a flashy pitcher with the Memphis Red Sox named Willie Foster. Willie Foster was Rube's half-brother. Rube was able to use his leverage as league president to rustle him out of Memphis for a tryout in Chicago. Willie Foster had actually tried years earlier to convince Rube to give him a tryout, but Rube had rejected him.[41]

Willie's first appearance as an American Giant was against the league leading Kansas City Monarchs and Wilbur "Bullet" Rogan. Willie gave up two runs in the first inning, he walked a batter and made an error. Brother Rube had Willie yanked in the second inning and lectured him on the art and craft of pitching. Willie Foster saw limited action for the American Giants for the remainder of the season. While Willie Foster did not produce any great results (and could not possibly bring the American Giants back into the pennant race), observers noted that Willie Foster was a promising talent with a great future ahead of him.

The Kansas City Monarchs, with the strong pitching of Wilbur "Bullet" Rogan, Bill Drake and Rube Currie, were able to hold on and take the pennant from the American Giants. Rube's feelings were hurt when he found out that some of the American Giants' players held a secret meeting after the season in which they drafted an anonymous letter stating that "players did not try to win the pennant" because Rube did not pay them fairly. The anonymous letter was mailed to the local black newspapers. While taken off guard by the accusation, Rube responded calmly, explaining how players were compensated (generous by his accounting) and pointing out that "lax playing ... if true ... did not cause the Giants to lose the pennant." Rube displayed good sportsmanship in conceding that the Kansas City Monarchs deserved the pennant, although he commented that they had "fattened up their winning percentage by playing more games against Milwaukee and Toledo."[42]

The American Giants again played a slate of games outside of the Negro National League. Rube entered into an agreement to play a series of games against three Chicago white semi-pro teams, the Pyotts, Logan Squares and Normals. The semi-pro teams were quite happy to play games against the American Giants because a lot more fans attended the games. Rube apparently took the city championship seriously, as he made a deal to bring Oscar Charleston to the team for the post-season. The outfield then consisted of Oscar Charleston, Cristobal Torriente and Jelly Gardner: one of the hardest-hitting black outfields of that era. The "City Series," as it was called, boiled down to a climax between the Pyotts and the American Giants in October. The Pyotts, with former Washington Senator pitcher Dolly Gray on the mound, beat the American Giants and claimed the city championship, although the American Giants charged "crooked umpiring."

The season finale for the American Giants was a three game series against the American League Detroit Tigers. The American Giants hadn't played head to head against a major league team since they met the Cubs for a three game series back in 1909. A lot had changed in those fourteen years; the Chicago American Giants had established themselves as the greatest black baseball team of all time, the Negro National League had been formed, the game itself was played differently, but one thing had not changed — the color line in major league baseball.

Rube had added Oscar Charleston to his post-season roster and also tried to get Kansas City pitcher Wilbur "Bullet" Rogan on board to bolster the team against the Tigers. Rogan declined the offer, probably because the Monarchs scheduled a post-season showdown themselves against a barnstorming crew led by Casey Stengel. The Detroit Tigers had finished second to the Yankees in the AL pennant race. Ty Cobb did not make the trip, but the rest of the regular team played, including twenty-one-game winner George "Hooks" Dauss and Hall of Fame outfielders Harry Heilmann and Heinie Manush.[43]

In the first game of the series, played on October 20, 1923, the American Giants and Dicta Johnson had a 2–0 shutout going through four innings. An error by American Giant catcher Jim Brown in the fifth inning allowed the Tigers to tie the game, but the American Giants put two more runs on the board in the bottom of the fifth and regained the lead. In the sixth inning Jim Brown made another error, which led to Detroit scoring three runs and taking a 5–4 lead. Oscar Charleston scored a tying run in the eighth inning; the game remained tied though nine innings then was called for darkness. In the second game the American Giants battled the Tigers for eight innings. The ninth inning started with the Tigers winning 3–1, but Detroit put four insurance runs on the scoreboard in the top of the ninth and took the game 7–1.

Rube got some bad news prior to the start of game three; Oscar Charleston and Cristobal Torriente had left to play in Cuba, and would not be available for the final game. George Harney, the young pitcher Rube had fielded in pre-season tryouts, would face twenty-one-game winner George "Hooks" Dauss of the Detroit Tigers. Harry Kenyon and Jimmy Lyons filled in for Torriente and Charleston. This unlikely bunch defeated the Detroit Tigers 8–6, reaffirming for the Chicago American Giants' faithful that their team could defeat a major league team and bringing a somewhat disappointing season to a cheerful close. The American Giants' triumph came on a Monday afternoon, and since the players had all agreed to play for a share of the gate, Harney's cut was set at a mere $5.00. Rube reached into his pocket and gave George Harney $20 as a bonus— such were the economics of black baseball, and Rube's attention to the bottom line.[44]

1924

League meetings were held in two sessions, one in Chicago in December and another in St. Louis in February. Rube was again elected president of the league. Black umpires were given a vote of confidence to continue in1924, despite some controversial episodes and complaints late in the 1923 season. The Birmingham Black Barons, who had been taken in as "associate members" of the NNL during the 1923 season, were granted full membership status. The Kansas City Monarchs were officially proclaimed the 1923 pennant winners.

One subject of discussion at league meetings was "what to do about the Eastern Colored League?" The ECL did not collapse as Rube had predicted, rather it was thriving and expanding. The Washington Potomacs and the Harrisburg Giants joined the ECL, and the easterners resumed their raids on the NNL. The Indianapolis ABCs were most vulnerable to the overtures from the East. Oscar Charleston accepted an offer to become player/manager for the Harrisburg Giants. Other Indianapolis ABC starters Crush Holloway, Connie Day and Henry Blackman joined the Washington Potomacs. Indianapolis had been an anchor for the NNL; the decimation of the franchise and the loss of Oscar Charleston were major blows to the league. (Oscar had last played in the post-season with the American Giants— so there was some question as to whether he jumped from the ABCs or the American Giants.) Despite the bad experience with Indianapolis, it was decided that the best reaction was no reaction. Foster refused to get into an escalating salary war with the East, knowing that, left unchecked, a salary war could lead to the demise of the league. Foster saw the practice of raiding players as an admitted failure in scouting and development. Foster told his players that if they were fool enough to believe the promises of the Eastern teams they could go, "but don't expect to come back."

Following the meetings Rube left for Hot Springs, Arkansas, to "boil out." It was common knowledge that Rube Foster was an overzealous worker; the recuperation was sorely needed. The American Giants players took the Illinois Central south two weeks later, meeting Rube in Benton, Arkansas. According to the *Chicago Defender,* when the team arrived in Benton "the whole town, white and colored, turned out to welcome the American Giants…. The folks shook hands with the big fellow and Mrs. Foster and wished them good luck on their journey. Baskets of hot biscuits and fried chicken and old fashioned southern cornbread were given to the players."

The team loaded up the train and headed for Houston. Rube was well known in many parts of Texas and spring training was a homecoming. In his mid-forties, subtle changes in Rube's outlook were evident. The success of the Negro National League was a fact, as was that of the legendary American Giants. The fact that Rube was able to graciously concede the pennant to Kansas City in 1923 had a calming effect. Rube could relax, puff on his meerschaum pipe, rub his belly and revel in success. The American Giants hadn't spent the spring in Texas since 1909 — the trip gave Foster some perspective.

Over the next month they worked their way through Texas, playing amateur and college teams in Waco, Calvert, Waxahachie, Marshall and Dallas, though some of the games had to be cancelled due to rainy and unseasonably chilly weather. In Rube's hometown of Calvert, businesses closed up early when the American Giants came to town so that everyone could attend the game.[45]

The American Giants did not have any problems defeating the local teams in Texas; meantime Rube tinkered with the lineup in preparation for the regular season. Even before spring training, Rube made a minor effort to trim dead wood from the team. He sold John Beckwith's contract to the Homestead Grays. Beckwith's antics had raised the ire of the black umpiring crews, and his play was inconsistent. Jimmy Lyons, the World War I vet beloved by the Chicago faithful, had not been the same since he fell down an elevator shaft in Cincinnati and he too was not invited to spring training. Rube tried to weed out the pitchers he had used the previous season: Dicta Johnson, Harry Kenyon, Jack Marshall and Fulton Strong were left behind.

Rube did have high hopes for two new faces in camp, pitcher Harold Treadwell and catcher Bobby Roth. Treadwell had made his mark as a pitcher for the Atlantic City Bacharach Giants, and left an indelible impression on Foster when he pitched 20 straight innings against the American Giants in 1921, only to lose by a 1–0 score. Bobby Roth, a young catcher originally from New Orleans, had been picked up from the failed Milwaukee Bears. The American Giants were in need of help behind the plate, since John Beckwith, who had backed up Jim Brown the previous season, had been let go. Rube even held out hope that Roth might have the ability to take the starting job. Foster had not forgotten Brown's miscues that had cost a game against the Detroit Tigers. Treadwell and Roth saw a lot of action in spring training so that Rube could look them over.

Overall, roster changes were minor. While Rube had talked about "rebuilding," when the chips were down he put stock in experience and the American Giants remained a veteran squad. Bingo DeMoss, Bobby Williams, Dave Malarcher, Cristobal Torriente, Jim Brown and Leroy Grant were all back. Cristobal Torriente steamed over from Cuba following the winter season in late March and joined the American Giants in Waco. Torriente arrived with a long face as his steamer trunk had been broken into on the trip from Havana and some of his golden baseball mementos were stolen. Of the position players, Floyd "Jelly" Gardner was the new kid on the block, having joined the team in 1920.[46]

The question mark hanging over the season (again) was pitching; but, being a fabled pitcher himself, Rube Foster was confident that by hook or crook he could put together a competitive pitching staff. Juan Luis "El Mulo" Padrone was back with the American Giants after a year hiatus. Ed "Huck" Rile kept his place in the rotation. Veteran Tom Williams was given another chance after a so-so year in 1923. George Harney, the young Alabaman who had defeated the Detroit Tigers, signed a contract extension. Foster spotted a young pitcher in Texas named Ed "Buck" Miller and invited him to join the team in Chicago. Dick Whitworth, who had suffered in a hospital the last year and had a serious drinking problem, was given the opportunity to pitch in a few games. Willie Foster and Aubrey Owens missed spring training and the first month of the season, but joined the team before the summer months to fortify the staff. Even though Rube had put emphasis on pruning and cultivating his pitchers, for the most part it was the same pitching staff the American Giants had employed in the previous two seasons. Waiting to do battle in the NNL were the Kansas City Monarchs, armed with pitchers Wilbur "Bullet" Rogan and Bill Drake. The 1924 pennant race promised to be interesting.

The American Giants left Texas and headed north, stopping in Memphis to play a play a series before returning to Chicago. The American Giants home opener was against a local white semi-pro team, which had become tradition; this time it was a team made up of some of the better

The one and only Rube Foster, clutching a pipe and a magazine, reclines for just a moment in his office (photograph courtesy NoirTech Research, Inc.).

local amateur players called the Chicago Blues. The American Giants put a 13–2 thumping on the Blues on a chilly Easter Sunday. The Kansas City Monarchs were the first NNL team to visit the South Side in 1924 and they whipped Rube's men in four straight games. K.C. went on to win six more games in a row from NNL foes, giving them a commanding lead. The American Giants got off to a slow start and a month into the season found themselves in fifth place behind Detroit, Birmingham and St. Louis.[47]

The face of the black baseball was changing. The addition of Birmingham increased the travel requirements. A meager team from Cleveland with the backing of the stoic Sol White, who called themselves the "Cleveland Browns" anted up and joined the NNL. The situation with Indianapolis worsened when many of the players who had threatened to jump made good on those threats and team owner Olivia Taylor went into debt with Rube Foster. Midway through the season the once proud Indianapolis ABC team was forced to close up shop, and was replaced by the Memphis Red Sox.[48]

The league was spread a bit thin, but previous fears that the whole league might collapse were vanquished. The NNL was entering its fifth season. Contrary to Rube Foster's and *Chicago Defender* sportswriter Frank Young's predictions that the generous salaries of the upstart Eastern Colored League would cause the league to fold, Ed Bolden's ECL was expanding. Organized black baseball was a permanent installation. With the issue of survival dealt with, baseball fans turned their attention to hopes for a showdown between Eastern and Western teams on the diamond.

The ECL clearly had won a couple of rounds off of the diamond, by decimating the Indianapolis team, by proving resilient to financial pressures and by not suffering with the defection of top players. Even as the center of black baseball attention drifted slightly eastward, there were new stars shining in the NNL. The Detroit Stars had power hitter Turkey Stearnes, the St. Louis Stars had base stealer Cool Papa Bell and rookie shortstop Willie Wells—all of whom ended up in the Hall of Fame. The Kansas City Monarchs were the class of the NNL. They were led by Hall of Fame pitcher Bullet Rogan and bolstered by strong field play from the likes of Dobie Moore and Newt Allen. The Monarchs had strong community support and were somewhat protected from the raids of the ECL by distance.

The American Giants had some stars too like Torriente, DeMoss and Malarcher. In true American Giant blue-collar fashion the team worked their way out of the deep hole they had found themselves in early in the season. Willie Foster and Aubrey Owens joined the team in May, adding backbone to the pitching rotation. Veteran Juan Padrone would throw three complete game shutouts over the season and it looked like the pitching might cut the mustard. The American Giants got back into the race, mostly at the expense of weaker teams. By July 4th the American Giants were in second place a few games behind the Kansas City Monarchs. As predicted the pennant race came down to a duel between Chicago and Kansas City.

Rube's crew had their chances to overcome the Monarchs when they played them head to head, but were not able to get over the hump. Kansas City stayed stingy and led the league from wire to wire. An unexpected announcement came as the season drew to a close. Rube Foster and Ed Bolden opened a line of communication. Both men realized that the greater success of black baseball depended on cooperative agreement between the Eastern and Western circuits. The pair were spurred on by J. L. Wilkinson, owner of the Kansas City Monarchs, and Quincy Gilmore of the *Kansas City Call* black newspaper—who hoped to cash in on K.C.'s success as the NNL champs by playing the winner of the ECL.

Given the feuding of the last two years and the long-standing tensions, it was remarkable how much progress was made, and how quickly, once the two sides negotiated. Foster went so far as to recruit Major League Baseball Commissioner Judge Kenesaw Mountain Landis to arbitrate between the two factions. (That Landis's participation could have been construed as major league baseball's sanctioning of black baseball was apparently of no concern.) Rube traveled to New York to meet with the Eastern heads in September. In the end Landis was not involved in direct negotiations. More surprises were forthcoming as the spirit of equanimity prevailed and both sides signed an historic agreement. The terms allowed players to remain with their current team, cash value of any legitimate contract that had been "jumped" was to be paid to the wronged team, and members of both leagues agreed to honor the contracts of the other league going forward in perpetuity. With those issues dealt with, the way was cleared for a World Series between the two leagues.

With a few quick strokes of the pen one of Rube Foster's ambitions neared realization. In the process of reaching the agreement Rube proved that he was capable of putting the good of the league ahead of his own self interest. Rube left Chicago while his team was still playing to attend the meeting. The American Giants would not compete in the World Series, so earlier charges that Rube acted only to promote his own team also proved groundless. The first World Series between the NNL and ECL was played by the Kansas City Monarchs and Hilldale. The series opened up on October 3, 1924, in Philadelphia. An ambitious best of nine game series was planned with some of the games to be played on neutral fields in Baltimore and Chicago. It was decided that the black umpiring crews who had presided during the regular season would not be used, due to perceived bias.

Prior to the beginning of game three in Baltimore, Rube Foster shook hands with Ed Bolden to publicly signal the truce. After playing three games in Kansas City, the series moved to Chicago for a dramatic conclusion knotted at three games apiece. It took ten games (one of the games ended in a tie) and went down to the last inning with the Kansas City Monarchs winning the crown. It was an exciting championship series though attendance fell short of expectations and players were disappointed with the payout.[49]

8

The End of One Empire, the Beginning of Another (1925–1930)

> The ax fell and heavy upon the heads of several players of the American Giants this week. Heroes of many a battle will be surprised when they find the "chief" as Rube is often called has sent them the "not wanted" note.
> —*Chicago Defender*, March 7, 1925.

> The American Giants are World Champions…. Fans leaped over the box seats and rushed on the diamond to pick Jelly Gardner and Sandy Thompson up and carry them off the field on their shoulders. Frank Young,
> —*Chicago Defender*, October 16, 1926.

1925

The character of the American Giants had changed in the preceding two seasons. Performance was down as they played second fiddle to the Kansas City Monarchs. Rube was not able to swing any blockbuster deals. His quiet settlement with Ed Bolden and the ECL was a bit out of character. While the American Giants were given a lavish welcome when they held spring training in Texas in 1924 and had even considered making Texas their permanent spring training locale, Rube elected to forgo spring training altogether in 1925.

One underlying reason for the changes was the prevailing economic conditions in the black community. As an experienced team owner and the NNL commissioner, Rube Foster was keenly aware of the bottom line. Foster had talked about economic depression as early as 1921, as black Americans were affected by a decline from the wartime build up and jobs lost to returning white troops. Player salaries and travel expenses rose at the same time many fans were hurting in the pocketbook. Rube stuck to the straight and narrow of fiscal responsibility — which meant some compromises.

The stabilization and expansion of organized black baseball into cities like Harrisburg, Birmingham and Memphis was ambitious considering the economic conditions. The lofty goal of integration with major league baseball remained. Even against a backdrop of financial uncertainty organized black baseball forged ahead. The Negro National league laid ambitious plans at the annual league meetings held in St. Louis prior to the 1925 season.

Indianapolis rejoined the league under new ownership, there was also new owner-ship in Detroit, while Memphis scrambled to come up with the funds to pay their annual dues. The Birmingham Black Barons stayed in the league, proving that it was possible for a city from the Deep South to support a big time black baseball team. Chicago, Kansas City, St. Louis and the Cuban Stars were all back for 1925. It was decided that the sched-ule would be divided into two 50 game halves, with the winner of each half facing off in a playoff to determine which team would represent the NNL in the World Series.[1]

Rube Foster prepared to trim the roster. In keeping with the spirit of cooperation with the Eastern Colored League, members of the Negro National League agreed to a nar-rower interpretation of the reserve clause. Beginning in 1925, it was agreed that no player could be kept on a team's reserve list unless he was paid a salary. This meant that Rube had to release a large number of players— some of whom had been associated with the American Giants for many years. To some extent the releases were a mere formality, how-ever, as most of the affected players would not have played anyway.

The most notable transaction was sending Ed "Huck" Rile to Indianapolis. Rile had pitched respectably for the American Giants in 1924. To balance competition in the league, as Rube had occasionally done in the past, Rile was moved to Indianapolis. The question was "could Rube afford to let Rile go?" Harold Treadwell, who had been something of a disappointment the previous season, was also shipped to Indianapolis.

Pitcher Lewis Wolfolk, Rube's find of two years earlier (who saw almost no action in 1924), was handed walking papers. Leroy Grant, a fixture at first base for Chicago since 1917, was unconditionally released. Venerated American Giants veterans George "Tubby" Dixon, Jack Marshall, Tom Williams, and Dick Whitworth, whose better days were well behind them, were all put out to pasture.[2]

The long list of players released gave the impression that Rube had cleaned house, but in fact the product put on the field was similar to the previous year. Bingo DeMoss remained at second, Bobby Williams at short, Dave Malarcher at third, Jim Brown behind the plate, Floyd Jelly Gardner and Cristobal Torriente in the outfield. The core pitching staff was familiar, with Willie Foster, George Harney, Aubrey Owens and Juan Luis Padrone. (Rube again had to wait until Willie Foster and Aubrey Owens finished up the spring semester at their respective colleges before they joined the squad).

There were a few new faces at the start of the season. John Hines, who Rube recruited out of Wiley College in 1924, became the back-up catcher and saw some utility work. Foster tried George McCallister (acquired from the Birmingham Black Barons) at first base to start the season, but still early in the season McCallister was sent to Indianapo-lis. Rube gave young second baseman Will Owens a try at second base, but he was not able to oust the legendary Bingo DeMoss and he wound up back in his hometown of Indianapolis with the ABCs.

Among the aspiring pitchers Rube tried out were James Gurley (acquired from Mem-phis), William McCall (cast off from Kansas City), Eddie "Buck" Miller (recruited from Rube's home town of Calvert, Texas) and Frank Stevens (who had last pitched with the Toledo Tigers in 1923). Foster remained hopeful he might come across a diamond in the rough. There had been a weak spot in the outfield, going back to 1921 when Jimmy Lyons fell down an elevator shaft in Cincinnati. For a fleeting moment in 1923 Chicago had flirted with the notion of hiring Oscar Charleston to tend the gardens along with Cristobal Torriente and Jelly Gardner. That was not to be, as Oscar went eastward. For part of the 1925 season Rube experimented with Torriente at first base — leaving an even bigger hole in the outfield. The holes in the outfield were often filled by one of the pitchers — this was common practice in the Negro Leagues. Many of the pitchers hit respectably in those days. For example Juan Padrone was known as a slugger in Cuba, and twice led the Cuban League in batting average. Kansas City's Bullet Rogan — the top pitcher in the NNL at that time — often batted in the cleanup position.

Rube hired Louis Dicta Johnson (aka Spitball Johnson), who had formerly pitched for the American Giants and the Indianapolis ABCs, as pitching coach. There was no indication that the hiring of "Spitball" Johnson was for a workshop on his trademark pitch, although George Harney also became well known for his spitter. Foster hoped the right mix of youth, experience, and coaching would get the American Giants past the Kansas City Monarchs.

The American Giants ceremoniously kicked off the 1925 season against the white semi-pro Chicago Blues. The Blues sported two pitchers who had cups of coffee in the majors — Dave Black (Bosox) and Spencer Heath (Chisox). Newcomer Frank Stevens started the game for the American Giants and won 5–3.

The American Giants opened the NNL season on the road in Alabama at Rickwood Field against the Birmingham Black Barons. Rube's men swept the Black Barons four games straight, before heading north to Memphis. After splitting a series with Memphis, the American Giants held their NNL home opener against the Kansas City Monarchs. Juan Luis "El Mulo" Padrone picked up where he left off the previous season, pitching a 1–0 shutout against the Kansas City Monarchs to kick off the home stand. Padrone, a member of the Cuban Baseball Hall of Fame (along with teammate Cristobal Torriente), was one of the greatest pitchers of the era. His pitching career started in 1900, he was a contemporary of boss Rube Foster, yet he was still able to fool batters with his change up.

The second home game of the season, held on Sunday May 10, brought out one of the largest crowds ever for an American Giants game. Some 18,000 fans showed up, management ordered the ticket window closed early, and the overflow crowd spilled out around the playing field. Ace pitcher Bullet Rogan started for the Monarchs; the American Giants started youngster Eddie "Buck" Miller. If Foster was going to challenge the Monarchs he had to get some production out of his young players — so the game shaped up to be a good early test.

Kansas City got on the board first, scoring one run in the second inning on a Hurley McNair hit and stolen base, then an error by shortstop Bobby Williams. The American Giants came back in the fourth and scored two runs on back to back doubles from Bingo DeMoss and James Gurley. Gurley's two bagger scored DeMoss, he was then advanced by a Torriente sacrifice and brought home on a Dave Malarcher single.

In the sixth inning fisticuffs broke out when Frank Duncan took out catcher John Hines on a play at the plate. Duncan was out by a goodly margin on a nice throw from center by Torriente, but when the dust settled Hines's trousers were ripped three inches above the knee by Duncan's spikes. The benches cleared, pandemonium erupted, but Chicago's finest were able to get things under control. Duncan took seven stitches to the face.

In the seventh KC first baseman Lem Hawkins singled off of Buck Miller and Rube sent George Harney in for relief, but Hawkins scored on an Oscar "Heavy" Johnson single to tie the game at two runs apiece and the game went into extra innings. The home team finally wrapped things up in the twelfth, when Torriente tripled to center, and was brought home on a sac fly off of Dave Malarcher's bat.

The fans got their money's worth, although the fight that broke out in the sixth inning marred the game. Outbreaks of violence in the ballpark often occurred when there were large crowds on hand, and it was the sort of thing that threatened to give black baseball a bad name. The incident prompted *Defender* sportswriter Frank Young to declare: "We are appealing to the president of the league and the directors to set their foot down hard on any unnecessary rough play…. We are sure that a fine or suspension or both will whip the unruly ones into place."[3]

The American Giants upended the defending champions three out of five games and were off to a good start for the season. The Detroit Stars, skippered by legendary former American Giant backstop Bruce Petway, were also off to a good start and surprised the Fosterites—taking three straight when they came calling on the South Side.

After the drubbing by Detroit, the American Giants skirted down the line to face the reconstituted Indianapolis ABCs. The ABCs of 1925 were a far cry from the teams of old, talent-wise; but the rivalry lived on and the ABCs were fired up for the contest. Indianapolis shocked Chi-town by winning two of three games. Both losses came courtesy of Harold Treadwell, one of the pitchers Rube had sent to Indianapolis prior to the start of the season.

On the morning of the last of the three-game series in Indianapolis, when the American Giants awoke at the boarding house of Frieda Eubanks on the near west side of Indianapolis, Rube Foster did not get up with the rest of the team. Normally Rube was one of the first ones to greet the dawn, and as the morning wore on the players became concerned at the absence of their fearless leader and began to search the house. Finally Bingo DeMoss aided by some of the other players broke down the bathroom door, where they found Rube Foster passed out, lying against the gas heater, his arm badly burned, the odor of natural gas heavy in the air.

Rube was rushed to the hospital. Bingo DeMoss placed a long distance call to Sarah Foster and urged her to "come at once if you want to see Rube alive." Mrs. Foster caught a train to Indianapolis. Rumors spread that Rube had died, but he was resuscitated. With their skipper unconscious and possibly dying the American Giants suffered an embarrassing 10–4 loss at the hands of the ABCs. When he came to, he could not remember what had happened. The remainder of the team left Indianapolis on a train to Kansas City for a five game series. Rube brushed off the near death experience and returned to Chicago with Mrs. Foster the next day. Against doctor's orders Rube insisted on catching a train to Kansas City to join his club.[4]

The American Giants had fallen to fifth place in the seven-team NNL race and desperately needed some wins against first-place Kansas City to pick up ground. The trip to Kansas City turned out to be disastrous, however, as the American Giants lost all five games. The American Giants fell to sixth place and fans began to ask, "what's the problem?" Rube had become a more gracious loser over the last two seasons. He had also quietly answered critics by settling with Bolden, by playing more games on the road, and by not leveraging his position as league president to enrich the American Giants. The change in Rube's disposition was refreshing; however, with the team struggling, the hometown fans were a bit uncomfortable with the new order.

The great chief's wisdom was drawn into question. Rube's biographers agree that his near asphyxiation had a profound negative effect on his overall health. Some also think that his judgment was impaired immediately following the incident, and that the impairment affected how he managed the team. Rube's management style and dugout calls over the last three years had warranted some legitimate scrutiny: Did Rube properly develop his young prospects? Had Rube been fair to his half-brother Willie? Had he exercised good judgment in moving players out of Chicago? Had he been too cheap? Had he kept up with the game? Rube remained passionate about bunting even as the home run was becoming a mainstay of the game.

Studying the grand master at work evoked time honored baseball discourse, but critiques of Rube's judgment at this juncture were not on the merits of a complex strategy. A different and bizarre picture came to light. According to one account, Rube occasionally lapsed into a stupor where he would deliver signals to his players openly — without trying to disguise them — allowing the opponent to see what was coming. The brief loss of oxygen to the brain (if that is what happened) was yet another straw on the camel's back; the signs of fatigue had been there for years.[5]

The fact that the team stumbled out of the gate couldn't all be laid at Rube's feet; the veteran players had to shoulder their share of the blame. As it turned out the team would mount a comeback. Despite the disappointment of losing five straight in Kansas City, flirting with last place, and the unpredictable health of Rube, they went back to Chicago and took three out of four games from the Memphis Red Sox to lift themselves above Indianapolis in the standings. When the Birmingham Black Barons came North the following week the American Giants took them three out of four times. The Cuban Stars were next on the menu, again the American Giants beat them three out of four. With the strong showing in June, the American Giants finished the first half of the season in third place behind St. Louis and Kansas City.

Under the rules adopted in 1925 they still had a chance to win the second half of the season and go to the NNL championship series. Rube tinkered with the lineup midseason. William Ware, another of Rube's recruits from Texas, was given the starting job at first base; this would allow Torriente to concentrate full time in the outfield. Bill Francis — a contemporary of Rube Foster — came out of retirement and played third base. Dave Malarcher moved over to second while team captain Bingo DeMoss was out of the lineup for most of July and August, for an unknown reason. Although the team had brought in some fresh young players, most of the roster changes were out of necessity and netted no noticeable improvement.

While the team held their own during the second half of the 1925 season they were not in championship form. As the American Giants lagged behind St. Louis and Kansas City in the standings Rube tried more and more combinations of new players and lineups. A parade of aspiring young talents came through the South Side. Leroy Stratton, acquired from the Birmingham Black Barons, spent time at third base. A young rookie named Leroy Taylor was brought on to play outfield. Submarine pitcher Webster McDonald came over from the failed Washington Potomacs franchise and became a mainstay in the pitching rotation. "Big" George Mitchell and "Wee" Willie Powell also made brief appearances on the mound for the American Giants. Both Mitchell and Powell would eventually go on to prolific careers in black baseball, however their work for Rube in 1925 was very limited and could be characterized as a "try-out." George Dixon, who had been waived in the spring, was brought back to catch a few games. James Gurley and Frank Stevens (who had pitched and played outfield during the first half of the season) were both sent to the struggling Indianapolis franchise.

The position players were moved around as if on a merry-go-round. John Hines might appear at first base, in the outfield or behind the plate. Starting catcher Jim Brown was also called on to fill in at outfield or first base. When Bingo DeMoss came back in late August, the career second baseman spent some time playing in the outfield, and pitchers continued to help out in the outfield as well. Some of the moving around of players was done to relieve older fatigued players, or simply to get a good look at a young player, and some of the shuffling could be chalked up to nervous management.

The second half of the NNL season ended with the St. Louis Stars taking first place honors. "Candy" Jim Taylor was at the helm of St. Louis, who sported two show stoppers with "Cool Papa" Bell and Willie Wells. Kansas City defeated St. Louis in a playoff series to see who would represent the NNL in the World Series. The Monarchs had inherited the throne left vacant by the American Giants as they went on to play in their third consecutive Negro League World Series. A freak accident kept Monarch ace Bullet Rogan out of the 1925 World Series against Ed Bolden's Hilldale Daisies and the ECL wrested the championship of black baseball away from the NNL.

Rube's men held off the Detroit Stars to lay sole claim to third place, which, under the league rules, entitled them to a fractional share of the World Series purse. The World Series purse however was a pittance as the increase in the cost of rail travel/meals depleted the overall proceeds.

1926

In January of 1926, for the first time ever, there was a joint meeting of the NNL and ECL, which was held in Philadelphia. Each league met in separate sessions first and then came together for a joint session. In the joint session teams from both leagues were able to iron out differences. Ed Bolden was elected chairman of the joint conference, replacing Rube — although Rube remained president of the NNL. Preliminary reserve lists for teams in both leagues were drawn up. There was one early trade announced. Rube Currie, who had pitched the previous season with the Hilldale club, was released back to J. L. Wilkinson and the Kansas City Monarchs, from where he originated; Wilkinson turned around and dealt Currie to the American Giants.

Over the next few weeks it was revealed that Rube was doing some horse-trading. He had considered for several years that the window was closing on the careers of his veteran players. Foster had chipped away at the aging staff, but was loath to part with marquee players. However, during the hot-stove league of 1925, Foster traded away Cristobal Torriente, Bingo DeMoss and Bobby Williams. These were the "Giants" of the American Giants. Cristobal Torriente, among the greatest sluggers in the history of black baseball, was traded to Kansas City. In exchange Rube received from Kansas City George

Sweatt, a talented all-around athlete, he had earlier received a proven arm in Rube Currie.[6]

Bingo DeMoss had captained the team since 1919 and was one of the greatest second basemen in the history of the Negro Leagues. Bingo was a great bunter and base-thief and a phenomenal fielder, however he was a step slower in his late thirties. Rube sent Bingo to Indianapolis where he would become a successful player-manager. Bobby Williams had had to fill the rather large shoes of Hall of Fame shortstop John Henry Lloyd since 1918. While Bobby Williams never lived up to Rube's hope that he had found the next "Pop" Lloyd, he had been a consistent performer and was a fan favorite. Bobby Williams was also sent down to Indianapolis by Rube, but Bobby ended up jumping his contract and going to the independent Homestead Grays.[7]

There would be more player movement before the 1926 season got under way. Rube sent veteran Juan Luis "El Mulo" Padrone to Indianapolis. The departure of Torriente, DeMoss and Williams was earthshaking. Both Torriente and DeMoss were legends, who some baseball historians would have enshrined in Cooperstown. While rebuilding the team was an unavoidable fact of life, these veterans still had productive years ahead of them. There were those who credited Rube with creating parity in the league by beefing up the Indianapolis team. On the flipside, the exchange of older players for younger players was seen as a shrewd, even underhanded, move on Rube's part. On a few previous occasions Foster stated that he had moved players to different teams in order to achieve parity in the league — this stood in direct opposition to his duty as manager of the American Giants to field the best team possible. It stood to reason that any sweeping adjustments to achieve parity should have been overseen by a neutral third party, but league president Rube Foster never instituted such a system.

There was a realignment of the Negro National League prior to the season, when a renegade Negro Southern League was formed — Birmingham and Memphis joined the NSL. Other teams in the Negro Southern League included New Orleans, Nashville, Atlanta, Montgomery, Albany (Georgia) and Chattanooga (the Chattanooga Black Lookouts hired a lanky young pitcher that year by the name of Leroy "Satchel" Paige). The NSL did not have an agreement with the NNL or the ECL. The Southern League was deemed an "outlaw" league and open season was declared on the players from the South. Rube took advantage and grabbed a few players from Birmingham and Memphis.

When the dealing was said and done the American Giants sported a much different look. Several players were called on to fill utility roles on the new-look Giants. William Ware held on to his spot at first base, Dave Malarcher — promoted to team captain — played at both second and third base. Newcomer Charles Williams (acquired from Memphis) took Bobby Williams's place at shortstop. Stanford Jackson (also acquired from Memphis) played at third and outfield. John Shackelford (another of Rube's recruits from East Texas's Wiley College) would join the club at third base after he completed the spring semester. George Sweatt alternated between the outfield and second base. James Thompson, acquired from Birmingham, was given an opportunity to play outfield. Veteran Floyd "Jelly" Gardner anchored the outfield. Catchers Jim Brown and John Hines were often called on to fill in at first base or the outfield, when not behind the plate.

The position players of the new-look American Giants were young, malleable, and a far cry from the legendary American Giants of yore. While the position players were a question mark, the pitching staff was in good shape and the American Giants could count on quality starts from Rube Currie, Willie Foster, Webster McDonald, Willie Powell and George Harney. Robert Poindexter (acquired from Birmingham) and Roy Tyler were given a chance to show their stuff on the hill early in the season. Tyler came to the American Giants directly from Leavenworth Prison. Rube Foster signed parole papers as "First Friend." Tyler had excelled as one of the best players on the Leavenworth Prison black baseball team called the "Booker T's" and had become a personal friend of Jack Johnson. Jack Johnson probably recommended Tyler to Rube. Tyler also played in the outfield, but did not stick.[8]

"Gentleman" Dave Malarcher piloted the American Giants to back-to-back Negro League World Series wins in 1926–27. Malarcher's specialty as a player was third base, but he could play any position on the field, including pitcher and catcher. Malarcher was immune to many of the foibles that befell his comrades. He was happily married, well read, enjoyed clean living and was successful in business after baseball (photograph courtesy NoirTech Research, Inc.).

Winter baseball and a spring training mission down South were again impractical for the American Giants in 1926. A few players went independently to sunnier climes to play baseball but the American Giants did not travel as a team. Workouts were to be held at Schorling Park as soon as the Chicago weather allowed. Old Man Winter was particularly slow in getting out of Chicago in 1926 and baseball practice was repeatedly delayed into mid-spring. Just a few years earlier it had been routine for the American Giants to journey to the Pacific Northwest, California, Palm Beach, Florida, or Cuba. Not taking the excursion removed an element of the excitement of being an American Giant, it was also a reminder of the disparity between the white major leagues and the Negro leagues.

The American Giants held their own in the first half of the season. They won series against Detroit and St. Louis; then swept both the Cleveland Elites and Dayton Marcos—lesser teams who had rejoined the league.

The roster moves seemed to be working as they were nipping at the heels of the first place Kansas City Monarchs. The American Giants' bid for a pennant hit a snag when they went head-to-head against Kansas City. In back to back five-game series with the Monarchs in June, the American Giants lost nine games. The American Giants muddled their way through the rest of June and finished the first half of the season disappointingly off the pace in fourth place.[9]

Rube maintained an outward appearance of confidence and gave the impression that he had recovered from the gas-induced stupor of a year earlier. Rube even pulled off a high powered meeting with American League president Ban Johnson and New York Giants manager John McGraw regarding his proposal that major-league teams play against the American Giants when they were in Chicago on an off-day. Rube was rebuffed by the big leagues; Commissioner Kenesaw Mountain Landis had let his feelings on the subject be known on several occasions in the past.[10]

While Rube had been able to maintain a collected outward appearance, beneath the surface, trouble was brewing. Rube's grueling schedule was legend; everyone marveled, "how did he do it?" His close friends and family knew that the stress and strain was taking a toll on Rube — this became apparent as Rube began to demonstrate bizarre behavior. In one instance Willie Powell said he saw Rube chasing imaginary fly balls outside his apartment. Also during the summer of 1926 Foster backed up his roadster (an Apperson Jackrabbit) and ran over a female pedestrian. Those close to Rube pleaded with him to take a long rest.

At first Rube resisted the idea of a vacation in the middle of baseball season but finally relented. The American Giants began the second half of the season without Rube Foster, who retreated to the hinterlands of Michigan for a prescribed vacation. Dave Malarcher took over field management of the team, and in the first series of the second half of the season, the American Giants took five straight games from the Dayton Marcos including a no-hitter thrown by Rube Currie.

The *Chicago Defender* began to refer to the American Giants as "Rube's Orphans" — an allusion to the Chicago White Stockings, who following the loss of their leader Cap Anson were known as the "Orphans." Dave Malarcher proved to be an able skipper as the American Giants racked up wins in Rube's absence.

Foster returned from Michigan two weeks later. There was no pressing league or team business at the time, but Rube insisted "baseball needs me more now than ever before." Sadly Rube's two-week vacation did not have the desired effect, as his erratic behavior continued. In August of 1926 Rube had a severe episode in which he destroyed furniture in the family apartment. Upstairs neighbor outfielder George Sweatt overheard Mrs. Foster pleading with Rube to stop. Sweatt ran downstairs to assist Mrs. Foster, who had to call the police to subdue Rube. Rube reportedly wielded an ice pick and threatened a friend; he was subsequently arrested and confined to a mental health facility for observation. After eight days of observation Foster was declared mentally irresponsible and committed to the state hospital in Kankakee, Illinois. The event sent shock waves through the world of black baseball.[11]

While Rube was being subdued the American Giants were in Kansas City with an opportunity to claim sole possession of first place in the battle for the second half of the season playoff spot. Willie Foster, who had become the ace of the rotation under the

Malarcher regime, pitched the American Giants to a 14–1 victory to open the series. George Harney dueled Bullet Rogan to a 1–0 shutout victory in game two of the series. The American Giants took three of five games in Kansas City to move into first place and had finally taken a series from Kansas City after a long drought.

Negro League owners gathered in Chicago to decide how to handle Rube Foster's departure. Quincy Gilmore, a business manager for the Kansas City Monarchs, weaseled his way into the meeting and made a pitch to become the head of the league. Gilmore proposed that the Negro National League members should heavily promote themselves through the white press to increase interest and attendance — as he had some success in getting the *Kansas City Star* to cover the Monarchs. Some were afraid that the loss of Foster would set Negro League baseball back fifteen years. The fear was prompted precisely because of "Johnny come lately" characters like Gilmore. The *Chicago Defender* immediately wrote an editorial pointing out Gilmore's naïveté, noting he wasn't even a member of the executive board. The *Defender* also gently reminded readers that it was the black press that was the lifeblood of black baseball. Gilmore's bid was voted down and Dr. George B. Keyes, a co-owner of the St. Louis Stars and the league vice-president, took over Rube's duties. The league directors also passed a motion to go ahead with the league schedule, playoffs if necessary and the World Series against the ECL.[12]

The American Giants had to fight for their lives to stay atop the standings and qualify for a playoff with Kansas City. A victory by the St. Louis Stars over Kansas City in the last game of the season allowed the American Giants to claim first place and forced a playoff. The playoff was a best-of-nine format and the first four games were played in Kansas City. Before the playoff got started the American Giants lost catcher Pythias Russ, who had to get back to school in Texas. The Kansas City Monarchs also lost a player, second baseman Grady Orange, who went South to teach school. That a ballplayer would forego the chance to play in the Negro League World Series for school is not surprising considering the paltry sum paid out to players in the previous World Series.

The American Giants lost the first three games of the series and it appeared their fate was to be sealed by the heavily favored Monarchs. Rube Currie twirled in game four and helped his own cause by doubling in two runs in the eighth as the Giants eked out a 4–3 win. The remaining games were to be played in Chicago. Bullet Rogan started game five on Saturday September 25th for the Monarchs and chalked up an easy 11–5 win, giving the Monarchs a 4–1 advantage in the series. The Chicago faithful figured the season was over, but the American Giants fought back. Rube Curry threw a 2–0, two-hit shutout on Sunday. Monday's contest was rained out, but on Tuesday George Harney came out with a 4–3 win, although he needed two runs in the bottom of the ninth to pull it out. The Monarchs still needed only one win to go to their third straight World Series. The series was to be decided Wednesday September 29th — the teams agreed to play a double-header if necessary.

Bullet Rogan started game eight for the Monarchs and Willie Foster took the mound for the American Giants. The two Hall of Fame pitchers battled for eight innings without allowing a run. Finally in the bottom of the ninth Stanford Jackson crossed the plate to win the game for the American Giants and even up the series. Dave Malarcher took a poll among his players as to who should pitch the second half of the twin bill and they all voted for Rube's brother. Bullet Rogan, who was a tough competitor, wanted to settle the score — so he too pitched both ends of the double-header. Due to approaching darkness it was agreed by both teams that the ninth and final game would go only five innings. The American Giants exploded for three runs in the first inning, then two in the second, as Willie Foster held the Monarchs scoreless. There was no more scoring the rest of the way, and the American Giants defeated the Monarchs 5–0 in an amazing playoff comeback. Years later, on a survey received from the Baseball Hall of Fame in Cooperstown, Willie Foster counted the back-to-back wins over Kansas City as his greatest achievement in professional baseball.[13]

Immediately following the game the American Giants left on the Pennsylvania Railroad to Atlantic City for the Negro League World Series. On October 1st, after a lengthy opening ceremony that included former Atlantic City Mayor Harry Bacharach, his brother Ike Bacharach and other politicos, the World Series between the Atlantic City Bacharachs and the American Giants got under way. Rube Currie started the game for the American Giants and Arthur "Rats" Henderson started for the Bacharachs. The American Giants took a 3–2 lead into the seventh inning, when Bacharach Luther Farrell hit a ball well over the right field fence to tie the game — it would have been the go-ahead run had player-coach Dick Lundy not been thrown out stealing earlier in the inning. Darkness was falling quickly, and the umps wanted to call the game after eight innings with the score tied, but Atlantic City insisted on one more inning. Neither team was able to score in the ninth and the first game of the World Series ended in an unsatisfying tie game. *Chicago Defender* sportswriter

Willie Foster, the half-brother of Rube Foster, was one of the greatest left-handers in Negro League history. He tried to join Rube's American Giants as a young teenager, but was rebuffed. A few years later however he became the star pitcher for the American Giants. After baseball, Willie worked for many years at Alcorn State College as a coach and athletic director. Willie Foster was elected to the National Baseball Hall of Fame in Cooperstown on March 5, 1996 (photograph courtesy NoirTech Research, Inc.).

Frank Young placed the blame on the ECL officials, who "started the games too late and delayed them even further with the opening ceremony."[14]

Frank Young followed the American Giants eastward and sent play by play reports via wire to the *Chicago Defender*, which posted the dispatches in a plate glass window at its offices at 3435 Indiana Avenue. The *Defender* published a photo of a mob blocking traffic as they clamored to see the scores, and reported that thousands more called the *Defender* office to get the scores over the phone. The crowd on Indiana Avenue was excited to see Young's report on the second game. In game two the American Giants sent Bacharach lefty Claude "Red" Grier to the showers in the second inning after scoring seven runs. The Giants had to hold on to win the first decision of the series by a 7–6 score — George Harney started the game, Webster MacDonald came on to save it.[15]

Game three was played in Baltimore on an unseasonably warm day. After being shelled a day earlier Red Grier started the game for the Bacharachs. The pressure was on Grier to redeem himself and he exceeded all expectations when he threw a no-hitter — although he did walk five batters. Webster MacDonald started for Chicago and took a pounding, giving up ten runs before being pulled in the eighth. Dave Malarcher finally threw in the towel and brought in Sam Crawford to mop up. Crawford had helped coach the team a bit in the springtime under Rube Foster, but had not actually pitched for the American Giants for many years. The game ended with the score 10–0 in favor of the "Bees." Malarcher was criticized for not having given the ball to Willie Foster to start that game.

With the series knotted at one game apiece, Willie Foster got the start in the next game, which was held in Philadelphia's Baker Bowl. "Rats" Henderson started for the Bacharachs. Chicago shortstop Stanford Jackson made a throwing error in the fifth inning that ended up costing four runs and spoiled the 3–0 shutout Willie Foster had going. Stanford Jackson scored a tying run in the eighth inning on a passed ball charged to Atlantic City catcher William "Fox" Jones. The game was called for darkness with the score tied at four apiece.

Game five was again held at Baker Bowl. Rube Currie started for the American Giants and Alonzo "Hooks" Mitchell started for the Bacharachs. Rube Currie was going along fine with a 3–0 lead in the fifth inning, when the Bacharachs exploded with seven hits and notched six runs. Currie was pulled, but the damage was done and the American Giants lost by a final score of 7–5. Chicago fans felt that Malarcher should have relieved Currie sooner. "Wee" Willie Powell, who had come to the American Giants by way of the Windy City sandlots, had a dream come true as he was named the starting pitcher in the sixth game — but he was knocked around by Atlantic City. "Red" Grier, starting for the third time in the series, notched seven strikeouts and got the win by a 6–4 tally.

The Atlantic City Bacharachs had a 3–1 lead in the best-of-nine series, however the series seemed much closer as two games had ended in stalemates. The two teams took the Pennsylvania Railroad to Chicago's South Side where the fall classic resumed.

Willie Foster started the first game back in Chicago and Hubert Lockhart started for the Bacharachs. Foster got his first World Series win, after being involved in two deadlocks, albeit on a bottom of the ninth run scored by Dave Malarcher who was singled in by cleanup hitter John Hines — the final score 5–4.

The following day Rats Henderson took the mound for the Bacharachs and delivered a three-hit 3–0 shutout; George Harney was the losing pitcher. The series then stood 4–2 in favor of Atlantic City—they needed only one more win to claim the championship. Rube Currie started the ninth game of the series for the American Giants and Red Grier started for the Bacharachs—it was the fourth game Grier had been called on to start. Dave Malarcher had been careful to rest his pitchers. Fatigue became an issue, as did the cold damp Chicago autumn weather. The ninth game of the series was won by Rube Currie, who held the Bacharachs scoreless for seven innings—the final score was 6–3.

The next day's scheduled game was rained out, giving both teams an extra day of rest. When play resumed on October 13th, Dave Malarcher sent Willie "Pigmeat" Powell to the mound, who had seven days' rest. Bacharach player-coach Dick Lundy started Arthur "Rats" Henderson, it was his fourth start and fifth appearance of the series. The American Giants chalked up seven runs in the fourth inning—sending Henderson to the showers. Meanwhile Willie "Pigmeat" Powell held the Bacharachs scoreless through nine innings to tie the series at four games apiece.

The rubber game of the series went as scripted: Hubert Lockhart took the mound for the Bees while Rube's brother Willie Foster was entrusted with the ball for the Giants. It was a suspense thriller, as Willie Foster allowed the Bacharachs to load the bases in the first inning but pitched out of the jam. In the third and fourth innings the Bacharachs had runners in scoring positions, but Foster with the aid of his gutsy fielders kept the Bacharachs scoreless. In the eighth inning the Bacharachs again loaded the bases, but could not put a runner across the plate. Meanwhile Hubert Lockhart was even more effective against the American Giants, allowing only two hits in the first eight innings. The bottom of the ninth commenced with the score 0–0. The storybook ending came on a Jelly Gardner single, followed by a Dave Malarcher sacrifice bunt. The American Giants celebrated their first official Negro League World Series championship when Sandy Thompson, after fouling off four pitches and taking a couple of balls, lined one into center field to bring in Jelly Gardner. Chicago fans rushed on to the field to carry off their heroes and there was a bit of celebrating on State Street.

Willie Foster, in the words of *Defender* writer Frank Young, was "destined to fill the shoes of his brother Rube as a great pitcher." Dave Malarcher had recaptured the American Giants' "magic" and proven himself a capable field manager. The retooling of the team roster (and to some extent the whole league's rosters) by Rube Foster seemed brilliant in hindsight.[16]

However the loss of Rube Foster made the championship bittersweet. The American Giants were proud to bring the championship home to Chicago, although many who attended the games in Chicago did not root for the home team, according to writer Frank Young. The financial reward for winning the World Series of Black Baseball was again meager. Frank Young of the *Defender* estimated the winners' share of the purse at $10.55 per ball game and flatly stated "The World Series of 1926 was a joke." Frank Young continued, "No club will want to win the pennant in the National League next year to waste two good weeks in the fall. That is if there is any National League in 1927. You heard me— I said IF there is any...."[17]

There were many obstacles on the road ahead: increased expenses, decreased attendance and the fact that major league baseball had shut the door on any hope for integration. Rube Foster had worked almost single-handedly behind the scenes to address these types of issues. With Rube Foster gone from the scene, many feared that organized Negro League baseball would disintegrate. Chicago American Giant fans were curious as to who would be running the local team in Rube's absence. By default, ballpark owner John Schorling held the purse strings of the American Giants, while Dave Malarcher would remain field manager. The thought of a white owner didn't sit well with those who pointed to the American Giants as the pride of black Chicago. No one seemed to know whether it was possible that Rube might recover, come back and pilot the team or the league. Many questions remained unanswered.

1927

John Schorling and Rube Foster's wife Sarah Foster represented the American Giants at a three-day joint meeting of the NNL and ECL held in Detroit on January 11–13. Mrs. Foster stated that "Rube is improving and I expect him to be active in league affairs next season." Sarah Foster's report on Rube was roundly welcomed, but it was apparent that black baseball was moving right ahead without Foster. Many of the owners were all too eager to swoop in on what had been Rube's territory.

It came out later that during the meeting John Roesink (white owner of Detroit's Mack Park) held a dinner for white owners only which included George Rossiter and Charles Spedden of Baltimore, James Keenan of the Lincoln Giants, Nat Strong of the Brooklyn Royal Giants, J. L. Wilkinson of Kansas City and John Schorling of the American Giants. Roesink, like Schorling, had hoped to expand his role as landlord to include team ownership and this was a subject at the whites-only banquet. Although Roesink failed in his bid to take ownership of the Detroit Stars, just the thought of black baseball being infiltrated by whites, and Eastern whites at that, sent a chill through the hearts of the Chicago American Giants' faithful. While Rube Foster had done business with white businessmen for years, his imposing presence left no doubt who was in charge — things were different now.

Two weeks after the Detroit meeting, the NNL met separately in St. Louis and elected black Judge William Hueston of Gary, Indiana, to the post of league president replacing Foster. The election of Hueston was the result of a consensus that someone outside of baseball head the league — similar to the role played by Kenesaw Landis in major league baseball. The fact that the league president was an African American from the Chicago area reduced fears the league would be taken over by outside interests.

In other business, the Indianapolis ABCs were forced to drop out of the NNL, but Birmingham and Memphis were allowed back in the league after a year's absence. It was also agreed that players who had been property of Memphis and Birmingham prior to 1926 would revert to their respective former teams. There would be a game of musical chairs before the season began to get players back to their proper teams. The NNL and the American Giants then set about attempting business as usual without Rube Foster — something that had never happened before. The team did not take spring training as a team, although Willie Foster and George Harney went to Los Angeles to pitch in the winter league for the Philadelphia Royal Giants. An odd thing happened in L.A. when, following the winter season, several Negro League players went on a barnstorming tour of

Hawaii and Japan. Originally it was rumored that Foster and Harney would head to the South Pacific. Foster and Harney opted not to get on the boat; but Frank Duncan of Kansas City, Andy Cooper of Detroit, Biz Mackey of Hilldale and Rap Dixon of Harrisburg did make journey. The players were not treated as Negro League ambassadors by the league; on the contrary it was considered a serious contract violation. The rules of the league stated that any player who jumped contract would be banned for five years. New commissioner William Hueston was faced with a decision as to whether or not to enforce the ban against the globe-trotting players—that decision would be delayed until the players returned in mid-season.[18]

Before the start of the season Rube's widow Sarah Foster was backed into a corner by John Schorling as she tried to assert that Rube was the team owner and her own rights as Rube's guardian. Schorling dismissed and ignored Mrs. Foster, which left a bad taste in the mouths of the Fosters' friends. Rube, who was meticulous with most of his correspondence, did not have an enforceable written agreement with Schorling. Rube Foster was essentially robbed of his interest in the team, although the business was probably profitable only in his hands. Black newspapers reported matter-of-factly, "Doctors at the hospital for the insane in Illinois say that 'Rube' is incurable, which means he will never return to the diamond."[19]

Schorling made good on his pledge to keep the team mostly intact. Field manager Dave Malarcher went about assembling the roster for the orphaned American Giants. William Ware, who had been at first base much of the previous season, was unconditionally released. Outfielder James Thompson, who had seen limited action the previous season, went back to Birmingham. Kansas City offered to send Cristobal Torriente back to Chicago for George Sweatt and another player (which would have been a reversal of last year's exchange), but Schorling vetoed the deal.[20]

By far the biggest change to the American Giants' roster was the loss of Floyd "Jelly" Gardner, who held out for a higher salary then jumped to the Homestead Grays. Malarcher scrounged to fill the outfield positions. Wesley Hicks, recruited from the local semi-pro Gilkerson Giants—jokingly dubbed "the new Babe Ruth" by the *Chicago Defender*—was given a tryout in the outfield. Oland "Lou" Dials came back to Chicago from California with Willie Foster and George Harney following the winter baseball season and was also given an audition. Dials had played briefly under Foster two years earlier, but left to pursue higher education. Malarcher finally decided on former pitcher Walter "Steel Arm" Davis to replace Gardner. The third outfield position was held by John Hines, with the assistance of a committee of utility players.

John Shackleford rejoined the team at shortstop, Charles Williams played second, Jim Brown, long-time catcher for the American Giants and the player with the most seniority of any on the team, was penciled in as the starting first baseman. Catcher Pythias Russ rejoined the American Giants after completing the spring semester at Sam Houston College. James Bray, a recruit from the cross-town Joe Green's Chicago Giants who Rube had looked at few years earlier, was activated as a back-up catcher. Dave Malarcher held down the hot corner along with his coaching duties. The team was a work in progress, roster changes were made throughout the season and most of the players were called on to play a utility role as needed when injuries occurred. While the position players were a rag-tag bunch, the pitching rotation was kept intact from the championship season.

1927 Chicago American Giants. From left to right, captain/manager Dave Malarcher, Stanford Jackson, Ernest Powell, Larry Brown, John Hines, Eddie Miller, James Bray, Nat Rogers, Charles Williams, Earl Gurley, James Brown, Webster McDonald, George Harney, Willie Foster, Walter "Steel Arm" Davis, Rube Currie, Sam Crawford, George Sweatt. Under the capable leadership of Dave Malarcher the American Giants won back-to-back world championships in 1926–27 (photograph courtesy NoirTech Research, Inc.).

Willie Foster was in the prime of his career after big wins in the 1926 playoffs and World Series. Backing Willie Foster were George Harney, Rube Currie, Willie Powell and Webster MacDonald. Calvert, Texas, product Eddie "Buck" Miller returned to the American Giants after spending a season with the Indianapolis ABCs.

The American Giants had what it took to set the pace in the Negro National League in the first half of the season, although they lacked style in getting the job done. After the American Giants struggled at home in a series against the Kansas City Monarchs the *Chicago Defender* wrote:

> The American Giants won the championship of the first half of the National race, but they had no easy time in so doing.... Chicago is not the team Kansas City is. There is not the smooth working combination at 39th Street Park. No one seems to know what to do and it takes three or four men to decide whatever strategy is to be used. Rube Foster could have won all the games the Giants have lost. But Rube isn't on the bench and the Chicago team isn't putting into use what he taught them.[21]

Despite sloppy field play the American Giants had enough pitching and hitting to edge out Kansas City and cop top honors in the first half of the season. Shortly after the second half of the season began John Schorling quietly conveyed ownership of the team to William Trimble, a white racetrack owner and florist from Princeton, Illinois. Trimble was not the type that American Giant fans had hoped to see succeed Andrew "Rube" Foster. The loss of Foster continued to reverberate throughout black baseball, still the American Giants and the Negro National League went about business as usual. Commissioner Hueston was called on to make some executive decisions with the credibility of the league hanging in the balance. The players who journeyed to Japan and Hawaii returned to the United States in July. While official league rules called for a five-year suspension (a rule aimed at ending contract jumping) the commissioner lightened up and called for a thirty-day suspension and $200 fine. However it was reported that three of the four (Biz Mackey, Rap Dixon and Andy Cooper) totally disregarded the sanctions and went right back to playing. Only Frank Duncan of the Kansas City Monarchs respected the rule of law. While Hueston was disrespected in this instance he enforced punitive actions in a number of other cases. Hueston enforced fines on players of $5 for delaying the game and $25 for being ejected. Hueston tossed out the results of a crucial 12-inning game between Chicago and the Detroit Stars that had apparently been won by the American Giants because a player who had been pinch-hit for returned to the field to play. Hueston received high marks from the usually critical *Chicago Defender* sportswriter Frank Young for maintaining discipline and speeding up play.[22]

Competition in the NNL remained tight between Chicago, Kansas City, St. Louis, Detroit and Birmingham. Top talent was distributed throughout the country. Detroit had Turkey Stearnes and Cristobal Torriente and was managed by Bingo DeMoss. St. Louis had "Cool Papa" Bell, Willie Wells and "Dizzy" Dismukes and was managed by "Candy" Jim Taylor. Bullet Rogan anchored the Kansas City Monarchs. Oscar Charleston was out East with the Harrisburg Giants. Frank Warfield, Phil Cockerell and Biz Mackey were among those with Hilldale. With the outstanding talent in St. Louis and Detroit it was surprising that in the second half of the season the chief competition came from the Birmingham Black Barons. The Black Barons had acquired a young pitcher from the Chattanooga Black Lookouts named Leroy Paige, nicknamed "Satchel." Paige's mentor in Birmingham was former Chicago Leland and American Giant pitcher "Big" Bill Gatewood.

In late July utility player John Hines was lost with a broken arm, which sent Dave Malarcher scrambling to find a replacement. Malarcher worked a sketchy deal to get catcher Larry Brown and outfielder Nat Rogers from the Memphis Red Sox. Brown and Rogers were two of the best players on the struggling Memphis team; the additions bolstered the American Giants in their run up to the post-season.[23]

The Birmingham Black Barons edged out the American Giants for honors in the second half of the season, which set up a playoff to see which team would go to the World Series. The Black Barons had something of a home-field advantage in the series. The first three games of the series were held in Birmingham. When the series resumed in Chicago many of the fans were pulling for the Birmingham club — due to the fact that there was a large number of recent immigrants from the Deep South. Despite the popular sentiment the American Giants won the playoff handily, taking four out of five games. Satchel Paige started game two for the Black Barons, but was not a factor as the American Giants drove him from the mound in the third inning and won the game 10–5.[24]

The American Giants opened the 1927 World Series in Chicago on October 1st. Prior to the first game there was a motorcade from the *Chicago Defender* office through the South

Side to the ballpark. City Alderman Louis B. Anderson, the black political power broker backing Mayor William H. Thompson, threw out the ceremonial first pitch. The American Giants took the first four games of the series. The Bacharachs were without their ace Arthur "Rats" Henderson, who injured his arm late in the season. Willie Foster led the way winning game one, Willie Powell took game two, George Harney took game three and Webster MacDonald won game four. All four pitchers pitched complete games.

The best-of-nine series went to Atlantic City for completion. Due to the fact that most of the Bacharach fans were workers in the Atlantic City hospitality industry, the weekday games weren't played until three o'clock — the earliest folks could get off of work to attend. The late starting time irritated the Chicagoans because it increased the likelihood that games would be called for darkness. The American Giants hoped to wrap things up quickly then get back home to make some money playing the local white semi-pros. The Bacharachs did not give up easily and took three straight on their home field — another game ended in a tie. The American Giants finally put the Bacharachs away in the ninth game of the series. The head umpire for the 1927 Negro League World Series was Sherwood "Sherry" Magee — a former major league outfielder. The American Giants thought that Magee was a lousy umpire and felt they would have wrapped the series up quickly were it not for his "bad calls."

In the first full year without Rube Foster the American Giants had faced down the best teams in black baseball. They had won their second World Series in a row and taken back the mantle of the glory years under Rube Foster. Considering the challenges the team had overcome, the accomplishment was impressive. Unfortunately the claim to black baseball's world championship by winning the "World Series" rang hollow. The Negro League World Series itself rang hollow. The fall classic again was a financial disappointment even though commissioners William Hueston and Isaac Nutter of the ECL took the basic step of eliminating the third and fourth place teams' share of the skinny World Series purse. The integrity of the play itself was drawn into question. The *Defender* noted that "players have refused to keep in shape, some would be seen on the streets in the early hours of morning, with a hard game to be played later in the day." The Eastern league would be troubled by major financial problems and dissension — just as Rube Foster had once predicted. In a strange twist, Edward Bolden, the founder of the ECL and former league president, suffered a nervous breakdown in September of 1927. Bolden's breakdown, coming a year after Rube Foster's, served as evidence that the work involved in running the league was overwhelming.[25]

1928

The general decline in quality of Negro League baseball operations not withstanding, the American Giants had distilled a very fine team in 1927. Pound for pound the team was not equal to the great teams led by Rube Foster, but the attack from the mound by Foster, Harney, MacDonald and Powell was noteworthy.

It was during the Jim Crow era that black baseball let go of the slim hopes that major league baseball might integrate and instead tried to be a "separate but equal" league. The reality was that the Negro leagues were "separate and *unequal.*" While wealthy white Americans bought new cars and feathered their nests with the latest electrical appliances, black Americans struggled to put food on the table. Organized black baseball would have to adapt to the deteriorating economic conditions. In league meetings, Commissioner Hueston announced that all teams must reduce rosters to 14 men — a measure taken to reduce the cost of rail travel. Meanwhile, after the league meetings, William Hueston stated "the league was in better financial circumstances than ever before." This was a lame attempt by Hueston to sweep problems under the rug.[26]

Signs were everywhere that the Negro National League and the American Giants were on the brink of disaster. Star player George Sweatt conditioned during the winter months in Chicago by playing basketball, but when the season rolled around he decided to work at the post office because of the low pay offered by owner William Trimble. Trimble was too busy with non-baseball business to attend league meetings. Trimble had mentioned paying for the team to train in Shreveport, Louisiana, but backed out. The American Giants looked extremely uncomfortable in a team photograph of the "World Champion American Giants," seated as a team with white team owner William Trimble sitting in front and center where Rube Foster would have been.[27]

Pitcher Rube Currie, whom Chicago had claimed rights to, refused to sign a contract. Currie eventually signed with the Detroit Stars, but the American Giants did not receive compensation. Webster MacDonald initially refused to sign a contract because he wanted to play in Philadelphia, where he lived off-season. Mac finally did sign with the American Giants team, but within in a few weeks jumped to an independent mixed race team in Little Falls, Minnesota. Meanwhile the Hilldale club, who had anchored the Eastern Colored League, broke their ties with organized black baseball in hopes of making more money playing locally and barnstorming. The very existence of the Eastern circuit was then placed in jeopardy. Surprisingly Trimble was able to sign Jelly Gardner, who had spent the previous season with the New York Lincoln Giants, but in August Gardner jumped the team for Cumberland Posey's Homestead Grays.[28]

If financial problems, mismanagement and disloyalty weren't enough, once the season was under way the American Giants were stung by injuries. In mid–May player/manager Dave Malarcher broke a bone in his shoulder putting a tag on a runner at third base. The injury also prevented Malarcher from managing the team for a few weeks and the reins were turned over to pitcher George Harney. In June the other seasoned veteran on the squad, Jim Brown, underwent surgery and was out for several weeks. Outfielder/first baseman Walter "Steel Arm" Davis, a recent addition to the American Giants who had played a big role in the pennant drive of 1927, went down with a serious ankle injury in early June. Second baseman Charles Williams broke his sternum after colliding with teammate outfielder Reuben Jones and had to sit out for two weeks.[29]

Despite the radical changes the American Giants managed to stay competitive; after all, Rube Foster had fielded the core of the team. Willie Foster, Willie Powell and George Harney remained with the team and provided ample firepower on the mound. It was left up to Dave Malarcher to patch the holes and retool. When Malarcher was not available to play third base, Stanford Jackson filled the position. Pythias Russ anchored the infield at the shortstop position. Bobby Williams, who had been let go by Rube two years earlier, returned to play a limited back up role at short and third base. Early in the season Malarcher tried Red Haley (who may have been a relative of *Roots* author Alex Haley) at second base. Although Red Haley played well Charlie Williams won the job at second base. Later in the season Haley was traded to Birmingham. John Hines took over catching duties as Larry Brown was back with Memphis. Jim Brown was the first baseman, but also helped out behind the plate. Several other catchers were brought in: Tommy "Dixie" Dukes played on his summer break from college, shortstop Pythias Russ filled in when needed, a catcher named Hancock caught one game, James Bray rejoined the team to catch in two or three games, and Mitch Murray (acquired from St. Louis) became the regular catcher towards the end of the season.[30]

Malarcher bolstered the team with the acquisitions of first baseman Lem Hawkins from Kansas City, outfielder Reuben Jones and left fielder James "Sandy" Thompson from Birmingham. Outfielders Nat Rogers and Oland "Lou" Dials also saw action during the season. Several other players were with the American Giants for local exhibition games, in what was often a confusing lineup. In the pitching department Harold Treadwell came out of retirement to rejoin the team, Eddie "Buck" Miller was a regular in the starting rotation, and Owen "Buzz" Smaulding was picked up from K.C. and made a couple of quality starts for the American Giants.

Black baseball reverted to the wild trading and contract jumping of the days before league organization. On one occasion when the Birmingham team visited Chicago, the manager of the Black Barons,' Charles Wesley, sent Satchel Paige and Robert Poindexter back home on a train for violating team rules and for suspicion of trying to join the Chicago team. In the space of the one year Rube had been out of the game some of his "irrational fears" had been realized: namely, control of the team had been wrested away from African Americans and the league was in danger of folding. The Eastern Colored League did collapse in late June, but the Negro National League trudged along. League President William Hueston did his best to appear impartial administering league by-laws even when it was unpopular in Chicago. He ruled that Larry Brown and Nat Rogers, acquired by the American Giants in 1927, were actually property of Memphis. He also overruled the American Giants' claim to Rube Currie and allowed him to sign with Detroit.[31]

The St. Louis Stars, with "Cool Papa" Bell, Willie Wells, George "Mule" Suttles and "Candy Jim" Taylor as player/manager, set the pace in the NNL during the first half of the season. The American Giants, backed by their quality pitching staff, managed to scratch out a first place finish in the second half of the season.

Due to the fact that the ECL had disbanded there was no World Series in 1928. Instead St. Louis and Chicago played a best of nine championship series. The American Giants won the first two games of the series but St. Louis bit back and took the series that went down to a deciding ninth game. The American Giants relied a bit too heavily on Willie Foster, who pitched in five of the nine games. The offensive attack of the St. Louis team was too much — even for Willie Foster.

Malarcher and some of the Chicago faithful insisted that the short left field in St. Louis is what allowed the Stars to win the series. "Candy Jim" Taylor scoffed at Malarcher's assertion and agreed to meet the American Giants in a rematch to prove the point. Both teams apparently had every intention of playing the rematch, but arrangements fell through at the last minute. Instead the American Giants closed out the season with a series of games against local semi-pros. They took two games from a team known as the Duffy Florals, who were led on the diamond by Buck Weaver, the third baseman on the infamous 1919 Chicago Black Sox. Willie Foster matched up against Jim "Hippo" Vaughn in one of the games. Vaughn had led the Cubs to the 1918 World Series with 22 wins, but had retired from baseball in 1921. The American Giants also took two games from a team known as Jimmy Hutton's All-Stars, who were a collection of aspiring white minor league players.[32]

1929

In early 1929 the remnants of the Eastern Colored League and the Homestead Grays regrouped into what was called the Negro American League. Quincy Gilmore, who had been the secretary of the NNL, announced that he was leaving the NNL to form the "Texas, Oklahoma and Louisiana League." Jelly Gardner went to California to play winter ball, teaming up with Bullet Rogan, Chet Brewer, Turkey Stearnes, Biz Mackey, Newt Allen and other well known Negro stars to win the California Winter League championship. Willie Foster returned to school during the off season. Some of the other American Giant players— Jim Brown, Johnny Hines, Buck Miller and Sandy Thompson — experimented with indoor baseball played at the Eighth Regiment Armory in Chicago in January. Owner William Trimble let it be known that he was more concerned with vacationing in Florida, horse racing and the outcome of a certain boxing match than he was with the operation of the American Giants.[33]

Dave Malarcher was patently offended by Trimble's style of management and began making plans to leave baseball to concentrate full time on his insurance and real estate business. Trimble had never officially made Malarcher the manager of the team, nor compensated him additionally for those duties. Malarcher, with Bobby Williams at his side, presented his concerns and gave an ultimatum to Trimble in a special meeting. The meeting was unproductive and Malarcher made good on his threat to leave the team. Catcher and first baseman Jim Brown was appointed the "captain," and took up the field management duties.[34]

The reorganization of the Eastern League as the Negro American League and the creation of the Texas, Oklahoma and Louisiana League were not done in concert with the Negro National League. This meant that the problem of players jumping from one league to another potentially threatened organized black baseball once again. (Some of the players on Negro American League reserve lists were also claimed by western teams.) However due to the diminished financial resources for owners on both sides of the Alleghenies there was no price war for baseball talent.[35]

Money was the overriding concern for players and management. Word came that American Giants Pythias Russ, George Harney, John Hines and Rube Currie had all passed the Civil Service exam and would follow George Sweatt to work full-time in the Postal Service. Trimble acted as if he couldn't care less if the players quit and announced himself that he figured the players "would play with the Quincy Street Station team." Trimble was quick to point out that Willie Foster had returned a signed contract; as if that was all he needed to win.[36]

The rumored defections were not a bluff. An independent team called simply the "All-Stars" with George Sweatt, Rube Currie, George Harney and James Bray played local semi-pro ball in 1929. Dave Malarcher also had a semi-pro team he called the "American Eagles." With highly regarded players dumping the American Giants in favor of sand-lot ball, it seemed the Negro National League had seen the end of its glory days under Rube Foster.[37]

Trimble's American Giants moved forward even with the wind in their face. Trimble got Jelly Gardner to re-sign, and he joined Jim Brown and Willie Foster as core veterans on the team. At the last minute Pythias Russ and Buck Miller had a change of heart and opted to play for the American Giants. Several players who had been brought in to patch things up midway through the previous season, including Lem Hawkins, Reuben Jones, Buzz Smaulding and Harold Treadwell, did not return in 1929. Aspiring youngsters and second tier veterans were brought in to fill in holes. Among the new faces were pitchers Harold "Yellow Horse" Morris, Robert "Frog" Hosley and Herbert Gay, all of whom were part of the regular pitching rotation. Herbert Gay's brother, known only as W. Gay, also saw limited action on the mound. Jack Marshall, in his third stint as an American Giant, was a regular on the mound. Local favorite Willie Powell was shot and seriously wounded in a hunting accident at the hands of his father-in-law in the fall of 1928. Powell hoped to make a comeback and pitched in a few games for the American Giants. Robert Poindexter came back to the American Giants for a stint late in the season. He was released from the Memphis club after shooting teammate James McHaskell in a St. Louis boarding house. McHaskell's baseball career ended when he had to have his legs amputated, Robert Poindexter claimed the shooting was accidental and avoided criminal prosecution.[38]

Journeyman Harold "Harry" Jefferies was brought on from the disbanded Cleveland Tigers to take Malarcher's spot at the hot corner. Charlie Williams played short, Saul Davis was at second, captain Jim Brown played first, Pythias Russ was behind the plate; Sandy Thompson and "Steel Arm" Walter Davis joined Jelly Gardner in the outfield. Following the precedent established after Rube broke up his team of legends in 1926, most of the players also played a utility role.

Despite the problems facing the NNL, Commissioner William Hueston stayed positive and remained resolute in his efforts to run business as usual. Hueston declared "the league schedule would be followed to the letter." Fines and disciplinary action were promised against players/teams violating league rules. Hueston had hired an independent unnamed baseball expert to grade the quality of league play. The expert reported that the quality of play was "Class A," that "the league has some of the greatest natural talent yet seen," and that "three teams were one or two players away from major league quality."[39]

The product put on the field in 1929 was, as Hueston's office stated, "a few notches below major league caliber" and playing schedules were followed closely. A typical five game series consisted of a Saturday afternoon game, a double-header after church on Sunday, then games on Monday and Tuesday. Considering the problems that beset black baseball, particularly the Chicago American Giants who anchored the Negro Leagues for many years, the degree of organization was impressive. For once the league lived up to its billing.

The American Giants played second and third fiddle most of the season to Kansas City and St. Louis, but remained competitive. Many Chicago fans were taken aback by all the changes since Rube's departure, and crowds were thinner. *Defender* writer Frank Young noted that on occasion he saw more black fans filing through the turnstiles at

Comiskey to see the White Sox in action than were in attendance for the American Giants.[40]

To the relief of most everyone there was no World Series again in 1929. Kansas City won both halves of the NNL season to take the crown uncontested. Instead the American Giants hosted a series of barnstorming games. The players preferred the barnstorming games because, unlike the World Series, they could make a little money. Some of the barnstorming games of 1929 were especially captivating, involving the top players in black baseball and some noted major leaguers. The sterling magic of black baseball came back to life in October 1929, just as American financial markets were set to plunge and white America joined black America in economic depression.

The formerly unwelcome independent Homestead Grays made their first trip ever to Chicago in October of 1929. When the Grays arrived, the American Giants were waiting with a virtual NNL All-Star team. Ringers included "Cool Papa" Bell, Willie Wells, Mule Suttles of Detroit and Theodore Radcliffe of Detroit. The Grays sported legend Oscar Charleston as well as pitcher Smokey Joe Williams. But the Grays were unprepared for the onslaught of the westerners who took six straight games, five of them shutouts.[41]

The same team of NNL All-Stars faced off with a crew of major leaguers culled mostly from the ranks of the Cleveland Indians and Detroit Tigers. The major leaguers, whose roster included Hall of Famers Charlie Gehringer and Harry Heilmann, fared only slightly better than the Grays and were defeated in four out of six contests by the Chicago American Giants enriched with the NNL all-star players.[42]

The defeat of the major leaguers certainly would have warmed Rube Foster's heart, if he had been informed. Nothing was heard from Rube in baseball circles. There was an effort to petition the governor of Illinois for Rube's release, but Sarah Foster felt strongly that he should remain hospitalized. Some of the players occasionally visited Foster in Kankakee. Rube would be given a pass off the grounds for a day. On at least one occasion the players drove Rube's old sports car down from Chicago so that Rube could have the pleasure of tooling around.[43]

It was not surprising that a team made up of the very best players in black baseball could defeat a white major league team. Barnstorming black baseball teams had defeated big league teams for as long as anyone could remember, yet thus far those displays of superiority had not brought the major leagues any closer to opening the door. The close of the twenties was a critical time for black baseball. The master plan laid out by Rube Foster lay in shambles. Some of the brightest stars had simply picked up and left the American Giants. Unsavory white businessmen had infiltrated the ranks of Negro League organizers. The Negro League World Series was abandoned under financial strain. Yet the last ten years of organized black baseball had been a step forward, and the Negro National League — though diminished — continued.

1930

The "good old days" of black baseball were of little concern to the up-and-coming young players. Veteran players and managers who depended on the Negro Leagues for their livelihood had no other options. League President William Hueston didn't flinch when he predicted the 1930 season would be "the best year in the history of the league both financially and in the quality of play." Hueston was a jurist but not a baseball man.[44]

Newly installed Memphis Red Sox manager Candy Jim Taylor, who began his professional baseball career at the turn of the century, offered a differing view of the state of black baseball. Sounding "Fosteresque," in a published statement Candy Jim stated "players don't care enough for the game to stay in condition. The most they care for is the 1st and the 15th when pay day rolls around." Taylor was critical of Hueston's cost-cutting decree that teams be allowed to carry only 14 men, observing that "when a player was hurt he had to continue to play. A pitcher with a sore arm could not rest." Candy Jim also came down hard on the practice of hiring hometown umpires and the trend of business people, like W. E. Trimble, usurping the management duties from qualified baseball men like Dave Malarcher, Dizzy Dismukes, Bruce Petway and others.[45]

Though most observers agreed with Candy Jim Taylor, the tenth season of the NNL got under way with no changes to the governing rules established under Judge William Hueston. Some of the NNL teams held spring training sessions: Detroit went to Nashville, Memphis and Kansas City trained in Texas. The Chicago American Giants fielded a mediocre team in 1930. Veterans Jim Brown, Willie Foster and Jelly Gardner returned — the team lacked any notable young players. Crowds were thin and getting thinner, not only in Chicago but throughout the country. As economic conditions worsened fewer could afford to attend games. With less money coming in from ticket sales year after year, the league faced a downward spiral. Kansas City Monarchs owner J.L. Wilkinson experimented with a way of improving attendance — night baseball.

Wilkinson purchased a portable lighting system that consisted of telescoping light poles, held down by cables and powered by a generator on board a bus. The light poles were strapped on to trucks and went with the Monarchs as they traveled by caravan from town to town. Typically crowds for Saturday and Sunday games were respectable, but weekday attendance was weak. The ability to play games at night allowed workers to attend after work. The initial novelty of night baseball was popular with fans, and to keep the fans coming Wilkinson dramatically lowered ticket prices from the normal 60 cents to 25 cents. The strategy worked and attendance at ball games increased for the first time in years.

The first night game in Chicago was held on June 21, 1930, when the Kansas City Monarchs came calling with their 135-kilowatt lighting system. The first night game was delayed 40 minutes due to a blown fuse and the next night's game was a 12-inning affair peppered with whining that lasted until 1 A.M. the following morning. Despite the irregularities the Chicago fans loved night baseball — which would only seem natural considering Chicagoans' well known propensity for night life. Shortly after the conclusion of the night games against Kansas City, owner William Trimble announced that he would install lights at the American Giants' home field. Trimble, normally a cheapskate, made haste and the lights were put up in the park within six weeks. The American Giants also followed the example led by Kansas City and lowered ticket prices.[46]

Night baseball invigorated the American Giants, but it was not enough to cure the ills that continued to mount. The American Giants found themselves in the cellar of the NNL, and even at lower ticket prices fans lost interest. The *Defender* stated that dropping off of attendance was "due to the [poor] play of some of these men, who have practically no following, except for their immediate families, and the rowdyism on the part of some players who should be in the prize ring instead of on the ball field."

In one incident, the visiting Birmingham Black Barons protested when an umpire at first called Chicago base runner Rap Dixon out, but reversed the call when he saw that the catcher Bill Perkins had dropped the ball. The Black Barons insisted that the original call was correct and threatened to leave the field unless the reversal was reversed. The arguing went on for over ten minutes, before the American Giants ownership pressured the field manager (at that time Willie Foster) to let the Black Barons have their way and resume the game. Later that evening, Satchel Paige came inside with three pitches aimed squarely at Eddie "Buck" Miller's head; on the third pitch, Miller charged out to the mound with a baseball bat. Paige ran, while Miller chased him with his bat. Fan support had declined to the point where most of the fans in attendance were white. Those few fans in attendance showed their disgust by leaving. According to the *Defender,* most of the fans asked said "they would not come back."[47]

A semi-pro team who called themselves simply the "Colored All-Stars" with former American Giants Dave Malarcher, George Sweatt, George Harney, Rube Currie and James Bray occasionally made the rounds on the local lots. This semi-pro team was a reminder to the American Giant players that those experienced veterans did not consider the current version of the team worth their time.

The problems in Chicago were as bad or worse in other Negro League cities. Birmingham and Memphis, despite having competitive teams, did not draw fans after the heat of July arrived. The *Defender* pointed out that the league really could not afford to pay the salary of President William Hueston, as none of the teams were operating in the black. The paper declared: "The league is like a drowning man — someone must save it."[48]

With the American Giants in second-to-last place at the halfway point in the season, owner Trimble dismissed Jim Brown as manager and handed the reins to Willie Foster. Willie Foster fared only slightly better than Jim Brown and managed to finish the second half of the season in third place. Ownership and management of the team and ballpark was sold to two new investors — the new owner was Charles Bidwell and the new park manager known as Kelly. Bidwell had apparently shared an interest in horse/dog racing with William Trimble. Trimble had put the team on the block for $26,000 — the hard assets consisted of a lease on the ballpark and uniforms. While Trimble had offered to negotiate a payment arrangement, no member of the black community was interested. Although lights had been added to the ballpark it was still the same physical park that the Giants had played in since 1910. After Schorling sold the team, the park formerly known as South Side Park and Schorling Field was usually referred to as the "Giants Park." The new investors offered to lend some financial support to Willie Foster so that he could rebuild the team. At the end of the season Foster did some housecleaning by letting go of Buck Miller, Robert Hosley, George Mitchell and Charles Williams.[49]

Foster then began recruiting ringers for the barnstorming season. Barnstorming had been the staple of black baseball before the organization of the Negro National League. When hard times fell on black baseball, barnstorming again became the centerpiece of black baseball. The Homestead Grays returned to Chicago in 1930, this time sporting a roster that included Oscar Charleston, Josh Gibson, Judy Johnson and 53-year-old Smokey Joe Williams—who occasionally pitched a game for the Grays. All of the above were eventually inducted into the Baseball Hall of Fame. As might be expected the Grays had no problem defeating the American Giants, taking four of five games. Willie Foster managed to win the one eleven-inning game from the Grays. Smokey Joe Williams struck out ten batters, the American Giants committed two errors and went down to the elder moundsman by a 3–1 count in another contest.

Prior to the season finale against major league barnstorming teams, the American Giants recruited Satchel Paige, Oscar Charleston, Judy Johnson and George Scales to bolster the team. For the second year in a row Earl Mack, son of legend Connie Mack, brought a team of major leaguers that included Charles Gehringer (Detroit Tigers), Harry Heilmann (Cincinnati Reds), Lefty O'Doul (Philadelphia Phillies), Art Shires (Washington Senators) and others for a series of games.[50]

The Negro Leaguers won three out of four games. According to the *Defender,* Art Shires of the Senators and "Steel Arm" Davis of the American Giants "kept the stands in an uproar by their clowning." Comedy, like barnstorming, was another stand-by for black baseball that was employed during hard times. With white and black players joining in providing comic relief, fans and players could take a break from the recent economic news and temporarily bridge the racial divide. While the team played in American Giant uniforms and called themselves the American Giants, the post-season barnstorming team was a de facto All-Star team. The concept of an "all-star" team proved popular in Chicago, and later on in the 1930's the annual Negro League All-Star game would become the premier attraction for fans. Conquering a barnstorming major league team was another feather in the cap for black baseball, but the tenth season of the Negro National League looked like it could be the last. Chicago was the home of black baseball and the steady decline of the American Giants' franchise was a sign of trouble ahead.[51]

The American Giants saw two recent players taken by death in 1930. Utility player Pythias Russ, an all-around athlete who ran track and played basketball and football at Sam Houston College in Texas, died after a long bout with tuberculosis in his home town of Cynthiana, Kentucky. Robert Poindexter, who had shot a teammate a year earlier, was himself the victim of a fatal stabbing. His killer explained that he fought off Poindexter who was swinging a milk bottle at him in a street fight.[52]

In December of 1930 the American Giants and the Negro National League were dealt a potential deathblow. Rube Foster died on December 9, 1930. Exactly what had become of Rube while he was locked behind the gates of the Kankakee asylum is unknown. It was said that he experienced delusions that he would somehow be involved in the major league World Series. The Illinois Eastern Hospital for the Insane was known for its "Cottage Plan," in which patients were housed in groups of about 30 per cottage; the cottages were laid out around a central building like a small village. Most of the patients performed some kind of work at the institution. Rube probably received "hydro-therapy" which was widely used in Illinois at the time. The Illinois mental health system had a policy of "no physical restraints" at the time. Recreational therapy was also encouraged, and it is possible that Rube even had a chance to play ball on the grounds of the asylum. The cause of death was listed as "General Paralysis of the Insane." According to medical literature, General Paralysis of the Insane, also known as paresis, is a manifestation of untreated syphilis that can occur 15–20 years after the original infection. Records show that close to 30 percent of all patients admitted to mental hospitals at that time were diagnosed with paresis. In fact the Illinois State Hospital was so overwhelmed with General Paralysis of the Insane (GPI) cases at one point that they routinely sent out form letters stating:

> Indications are that _____ is suffering from paresis, a disease called softening of the brain. This is a condition for which there is no cure and for which there is but one ending, namely death.... We are, indeed, sorry to have to offer you this rather gloomy outlook. We feel, however, that under the circumstances nothing else would be justifiable, as it is only fair that you should in a measure, realize the hopelessness of the situation.[53]

Although it might seem to fit the life style of a rambling baseball man, there is nothing in the official record indicating Rube had syphilis. A nurse making the rounds discovered him dead at 9:00 P.M. the evening of December 9th; two hours earlier he had bathed and gone to sleep. Further details of Rube's death at the age of 50 are unknown. Foster had suffered with respiratory problems throughout his life, he had been affected by near asphyxiation in 1925, and he was somewhat overweight — it is not known if these other health issues played a factor in his death.[54]

Rube's body lay in state for two days at Washington Undertaking Parlor and thousands paid respect. The funeral was held at St. Mark's African Methodist Episcopal church at 50th and Wabash, and burial was at Lincoln Cemetery. It was a wintry Chicago day, the church overflowed with mourners, there were huge floral offerings including a "huge baseball made of small white chrysanthemums with roses making up the seams weighing over 200 lbs." The funeral service was held at three o'clock Sunday, December 14, the same hour at which baseball games had traditionally started at the ballpark. Rube was eulogized by Pastor John Redmond, who had known Rube for years. A solo by Mrs. Mabel Malarcher and a benediction closed the church services. At the graveside Rube's family, former players and close friends stood ankle deep in snow as Rube was lowered into the grave.[55]

Rube left the world like a king.

9

Life After Rube (1931–1939)

"Rube Foster was a great man, a truly outstanding athlete … to leave this man out of the Hall of Fame would be a big joke."
— Normal "Tweed" Webb, quoted in the
Congressional Record, July 9, 1975.[1]

1931

Even though Rube Foster had not been involved in baseball the last two years of his life, his death was a psychological blow to black baseball, especially in Chicago. Black baseball would never be the same. Negro League baseball survived as an institution, but it was much different from the model laid out by Rube Foster. In the 1930's team buses replaced train travel. The fragile agreements and contracts that disallowed players jumping from team to team cracked under the pressure of tough economic conditions. Increasingly ownership was made up of hustlers, numbers men and speculators. The Annual East-West All-Star game, founded in 1933, replaced the Negro League World Series as the premier event of the season. Rube Foster probably rolled in his grave at the style adopted by the Negro Leagues in the 1930's.

A new crop of stars had come on the scene, names like Satchel Paige, Josh Gibson, Buck Leonard and Martin Dihigo. The call for integration of the major leagues came loud and often. African American athletes like Joe Louis and Jesse Owens captured the hearts of sports fans in the thirties and black baseball wanted nothing less.

The African American baseball movement witnessed the death of its patriarch Rube Foster and resolved that his extraordinary efforts would not go in vain. Rube's funeral was held in December 1930, by the time New Year rolled around the "would be" baseball moguls had already backed away from the role of being Rube's successor. Charles Bidwell, who had taken over ownership from William Trimble halfway through the previous season, treated the American Giants like a pot he lucked upon in a poker game and was at a loss about what to do next.

Many of Rube's hand picked disciples had abandoned the American Giants well before his death, and threatened to overshadow the American Giants with impromptu semi-pro teams called the "All-Stars" or the "Independents." The one major exception had been Rube's half-brother Willie Foster, who had been favored by the team's owner-

129

ship. Willie had served as both the pitching coach and the manager of the American Giants to finish out the 1930 season. Willie Foster had always marched to the beat of his own drummer and had no qualms about going against the grain of cohorts like Dave Malarcher, George Sweatt, Rube Currie and George Harney who had left the team with disdain. (The Hall of Fame pitcher also never felt awkward missing spring training in favor of attending classes.)

In the numbness following Rube's death, Willie Foster set the tone by announcing his resignation as manager in January of 1931. Stating "I can not pitch baseball and manage a team as it should be managed," Willie Foster packed his bags and left the Windy City for Cum Posey's Homestead Grays. The American Giants had typically opened the season on Easter Sunday, but for the first time since 1910 the American Giants did not come out to the ballpark to greet the spring — as if mourning the passing of Rube Foster.[2]

Pennants remained at half-staff for just a few weeks, before a team known as the "Chicago Independents" composed of former American Giants was formed. The Independents included players like Dave Malarcher, Stanford Jackson, Hallie Harding, Nat Rogers, George Harney and Luther McDonald among others. The "Independents" could not acquire a lease on the ballpark and were forced to play exclusively on the road. Finally Dave Malarcher assumed the leadership role and remade the team as the "Columbia American Giants" (a name borrowed from the early history of black baseball.) Malarcher had the connections to secure a lease on the familiar South Side ballpark and so Chicago would be home to American Giant baseball in 1931 after all. The Columbia American Giants held their home opening on Memorial Day (known as Decoration Day at that time) against the Nashville Elite Giants. Malarcher shared his high hopes of "restoring the team" to its former luster and "doing away with unsportsmanlike conduct." Malarcher's plans were moderated by the reality of the Great Depression. The elaborate plans for a Negro League envisioned by Rube Foster were placed on the back burner as the first priority was just keeping a team on the field. The Negro National League of 1931 held a shortened, disorganized season, without a regular schedule or playoffs. The Columbia American Giants squared off against traditional rivals from Detroit, Indianapolis and St. Louis during the month of June. After a July 4th series with the Cincinnati Tigers — not even two months into the American Giants' season — Dave Malarcher decided to drop out of the Negro National League. Malarcher's Columbia American Giants continued to play a limited schedule as an independent semi-pro team. It was a mediocre season by American Giant standards, but the tradition had survived the downturn.

In October of 1931, the "Old Roman" Charles Comiskey died. The *Chicago Defender* noted his passing: "Comiskey employed over 50 Africans — more than any other major league team. That no Race players wore the colors of the White Sox was hardly the fault of Comiskey...." Also in October of 1931 Al Capone was convicted of tax evasion and sentenced to 11 years in prison. In April of 1931 author Richard Wright, whose literary masterpiece *Native Son* tells the story of a black Chicago youth consumed by the injustice of a segregated society, published his first short story, titled "Superstition," in *Abbott's Monthly Magazine* (named for *Defender* publisher/editor Robert Sengstacke Abbott).[3]

In November of 1931, a rumor surfaced that J. L. Wilkinson, owner of the Kansas City Monarchs, was working on a deal to move the Monarchs to Chicago, and that Quincy Gilmore, the ambitious K.C. business manager, was waiting in the wings to take over the

Negro National League commissionership when Judge William Hueston resigned. Worries and rumors swirled during the hot-stove league as the prospects for Negro League baseball in Chicago in 1932 looked doubtful.[4]

1932

Hueston resigned as head of the Negro National League that had essentially collapsed anyway. Pittsburgh Crawfords owner Gus Greenlee led efforts to create a new Negro League called the East-West League — which was to consist of an eastern conference and western conference. Teams in the eastern conference included the Pittsburgh Crawfords, Homestead Grays, Hilldale, Baltimore Black Sox, and Newark Browns. It was hoped that Chicago could be induced to join the league, so that a western conference would be practical, however there were no interested organizers in Chicago.

Kansas City owner J.L. Wilkinson gave serious consideration to moving the Monarchs to Chicago (a shock to the Kansas City faithful), but decided that the terms of the lease offered at South Side park were unacceptable. The park owners were trying to sell the park, and offered only a two-year lease — too short a horizon for Wilkie. In addition to Wilkinson, two other financiers showed interest in the Chicago black baseball market — Abe Saperstein and Robert Cole.[5]

Abe Saperstein was the London-born promoter of a Chicago black basketball team called the Savoy Big Five, which became the Harlem Globetrotters. Saperstein was unable to secure a lease at the park, but proposed taking the American Giants on the road as a traveling attraction. Saperstein hired veteran Jim Brown to manage the team, which he called "the Rube Foster Memorial Giants." Saperstein hoped to hire Satchel Paige and Willie Foster as an unstoppable pitching combination to take the country by storm. The Foster Memorial Giants traveled South for a spring road trip, but soon fell apart, although they were reorganized briefly as Jim Brown's "Cleveland Cubs." (Jim Brown was the former catcher and manager of the American Giants.) While Saperstein's ambitious plans fell through, he later achieved unparalleled success in the arena of sports promotion with the Harlem Globetrotters. Saperstein stayed interested in promoting black baseball teams too and was a booking agent for several teams. At one point Saperstein was part-owner of the Cincinnati-Indianapolis Clowns — a team that eventually did take the country by storm. Years later Ted "Double Duty" Radcliffe called Saperstein "the best friend I ever had," and related stories of a number of personal favors Saperstein had granted — including paying for the funeral of a teammate.[6]

Saperstein might have been heir apparent to Rube Foster's American Giants, had it not been for a hard working enterprising black undertaker named Robert A. Cole. Robert Cole worked his way up from a Pullman porter to become the head of the Metropolitan Funeral Home Association. The Funeral Home Association sold insurance policies which guaranteed burial, and later became a full-fledged insurance company called the Metropolitan Assurance Company. It was a tough sell during the Great Depression, but hard work and a large clientele on Chicago's South Side allowed the company to succeed. Whereas most saw investing hard earned money into professional black baseball as foolhardy, Cole saw a hidden opportunity in baseball.

Robert Cole put up the money to secure a lease on the ballpark and hired Dave

Malarcher to manage the team. Additionally Cole refurbished the stands and the press box and added a loudspeaker system to the ballpark, which won the praise of many. Robert Cole's interest in the American Giants was roundly welcomed. Cole brought with him a trusted assistant named Horace G. Hall. Hall was a good business manager and supposedly had some baseball experience, though he was not known to have played in the Negro Leagues. The *Defender* sponsored a contest to rename the team, but settled on "Cole's American Giants." The team was commonly called the Chicago American Giants, technically under Rube Foster the team was officially known as the "American Giants."[7]

Robert Cole put up enough money so that both Willie Foster and Turkey Stearnes could be brought back into the fold. The American Giants leaned heavily on Willie Foster, but the pitching staff also included right handers Melvin "Putt" Powell and Willie Powell (not related) who turned in consistently good work. Willie Powell, remarkably, had fully recovered from a shotgun blast to the face in 1928. The American Giants also signed pitcher/utility man Joe Lillard. Lillard's regular job was as a star running back for the National Football League Chicago Cardinals. There was no strict color line in effect in professional football at that time. Another new face on the American Giants was third baseman Alec Radcliffe. Alec, the younger brother of Ted "Double Duty" Radcliffe, had a steady glove and was a good hitter. E. C. "Pop" Turner, who had played one game for the American Giants back in 1930, became the regular shortstop. "Boise" Jack Marshall (not to be confused with the 1920's era pitcher named Jack Marshall), a veteran of local semi-pro teams, was brought on to cover second base. Familiar American Giant veterans filled out the squad: Walter "Steel Arm" Davis played first base, Sandy Thompson and Nat Rogers helped out Turkey Stearnes in the outfield. The American Giants tried out one catcher after another during the season, including Ameal Brooks, Robert "Buddy" Campbell, Andrew Drake, Walter Harper, veteran John Hines and Clarence "Spoony" Palm.

Robert Cole had worked a minor miracle in putting the American Giant team back together, thus joining the ranks of the many unsung heroes of Negro League baseball.

Cole's American Giants were able to win the pennant for first place in the first half of the season — playing for the first time in the Negro Southern League. The venerable Negro National League had gone belly-up.

The Nashville Elite Giants won the second half of the season and met the American Giants in a season ending playoff. The *Chicago Defender* announced that the series would be broadcast play by play by the National and Columbia broadcasting systems, however there was no follow up story on the broadcast and it is not known if it actually took place. Cole's American Giants struggled to win the Negro Southern League series against Nashville four games to three.[8]

1933

Franklin Roosevelt got the nod in the Democratic National Convention held in Chicago in 1932 and went on to win the presidency. When Roosevelt took office in 1933, millions were unemployed, wandering the countryside looking for odd jobs. That Negro League baseball even survived the Great Depression was no small feat. Robert Cole's first year as owner had been successful. It turned out that two players from that '32 team — Turkey Stearnes and Willie Foster — would later be inducted into the Hall of Fame. Even more impressive was Gus Greenlee's Pittsburgh Crawfords, whose 1932 roster included, among others, "Cool Papa" Bell, Oscar Charleston, Josh Gibson, Judy Johnson and Satchel Paige — all Hall of Fame inductees.

Chicago had a preview of the New Deal when the World's Fair returned to Chicago in 1933. The World's Fair of 1933 was known as "The Century of Progress" to commemorate the incorporation of Chicago in 1833. With sponsorship from wealthy Chicagoans and large corporations like Chrysler, Ford, General Motors and Time Magazine, a bold "city of the future" was created on Lake Michigan immediately south of the downtown area, from 12th Street to 39th Street — just blocks from Bronzeville. The buildings featured modern architecture that would become a common theme during the intensive public works of the New Deal. Similar to the Columbian Exposition of 1893, African Americans were not fully represented at the fair. An independent African and American Exhibit was installed at the National Pythian Temple at Thirty-seventh and State streets— away from the main World's Fair village. A separate "Negro Day" was held August 12, 1933, which might have been well intentioned, but stirred up bad feelings and was poorly attended.

The sports editor for the *Chicago Tribune*, Arch Ward, proposed that major league baseball hold an "all-star" game in connection with the World's Fair. Using his influence the idea was approved and the first ever Major League All-Star game was held at Comiskey Park on July 6, 1933. Robert Cole had rescued the American Giants the previous season by renewing the lease on the ballpark, but while Chicago was in the world spotlight, the American Giants suffered a major setback. A group of Chicago promoters pooled money together to lease Schorling Field, for purposes of converting the park into a dog racing track. The change was sudden and unexpected. The team was kicked out and work began to turn the venerated American Giants' ballpark — also known as South Side Park, home since the White Sox moved out in 1910 — into a dog track.

The American Giants played a couple of games at "Mills Stadium" on the west side, but the result was a financial failure. Robert Cole might have had other options, such as finding another ballpark or playing exclusively on the road, but oddly enough elected to move the team to Indianapolis, Indiana. The Indianapolis ABCs (owned and managed by Candy Jim Taylor), began the 1933 season with an agreement to play in Perry Stadium, the two-year-old home of the AAA Indianapolis Indians. After only 1,100 fans turned out for opening day, Candy Jim announced that he was fed up with the lack of support and moved the team to Detroit — which created the vacancy for the American Giants. Although Cole's American Giants arguably had drawing cards that the ABCs lacked, they also faced the prospect of smaller crowds in Indianapolis.[9]

Robert Cole's willingness to make a go of it in Indianapolis, Indiana, when he was shut out of Chicago was a testament to his strong will and determination. Although Cole's American Giants' uniforms still read "Chicago," they set up shop in Indianapolis. The American Giants joined a newly formed Negro National League, which was actually the former East-West League headed by Gus Greenlee and had no kinship to the league founded by Rube Foster. Organizationally Negro League baseball was in disarray, with a number of teams either folding or going it alone as barnstorming outfits. The lack of struc-

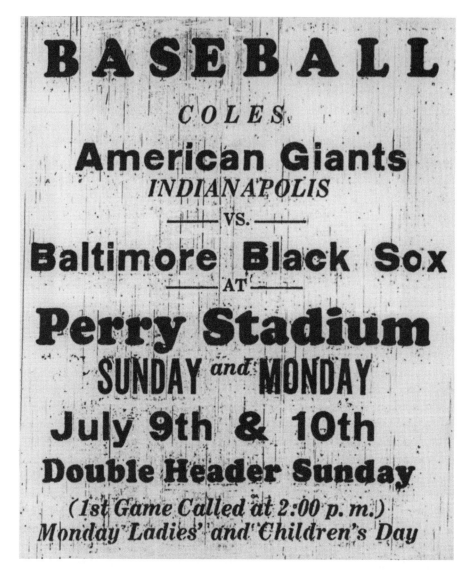

BASEBALL
COLES
American Giants
INDIANAPOLIS
VS.
Baltimore Black Sox
AT
Perry Stadium
SUNDAY and MONDAY
July 9th & 10th
Double Header Sunday
(1st Game Called at 2:00 p. m.)
Monday Ladies' and Children's Day

Advertisement from the *Indianapolis Recorder*, July 1, 1933. The American Giants' ballpark was bought out by gamblers who wanted to turn it into a dog racing facility. Owner Robert Cole decided to play home games in Indianapolis in 1933. The dog racing scheme went bust and the American Giants returned to their home field the following year (photograph *Indianapolis Recorder*).

ture allowed players to jump teams and allowed owners to hoard talent. Gus Greenlee managed to keep "Cool Papa" Bell, Oscar Charleston, Josh Gibson and Satchel Paige in his stables—which can only be described as an unfair advantage.

While Robert Cole was unable to find a ballpark in all of Chicago, he had no problem finding supplementary talent for the team roster. Notably, Willie Wells, Mule Suttles and Quincy Trouppe all joined Cole's American Giants while the team was based in Indianapolis. The trio had played for the pennant winning St. Louis Stars in 1931 and then the short lived Detroit Wolves in 1932 — both teams were victims of the economic downturn. Rube's disciple "Gentleman Dave" Malarcher remained at the helm, along with Turkey Stearnes and Willie Foster, giving the team their greatest assemblage of talent since the early twenties.

Willie "the Devil" Wells was the top shortstop in black baseball in that era. A native of Austin, Texas, he had been taken under the wing of fellow Texan Rube Foster when he came up North. The pair got together to discuss the fine points of the game — even though Wells never played for the American Giants during Rube's tenure. George "Mule" Suttles was one of the greatest power hitters in Negro League history. He swung a 50-ounce bat and was known for his tape-measure homers in parks all over the country.

Quincy Trouppe was just beginning his legendary career when he came on board with Cole's American Giants and was not even the first-string catcher; but some 19 years later Trouppe joined the major league Cleveland Indians. Trouppe's stint with the American Giants was cut short when, following a game against the Columbus Blue Birds, a sly member of the opposing team by the name of Double Duty Radcliffe collared Quincy and let him know about an opportunity to play with an integrated barnstorming team in Bismarck, North Dakota. Trouppe went to Dave Malarcher to ask for his release; Malarcher called Chicago to check with business manager Horace Hall, who okayed the deal, although the American Giants retained "league rights" to Quincy Trouppe. Duty chuckled when he heard Quincy "asked permission to jump" — as he played with five different teams in 1933.[10]

The American Giants were able to collect these players because there weren't as many places for players to go to. There weren't many teams to play against either. Not surprisingly the pennant race boiled down to a battle between the Pittsburgh Crawfords and Cole's American Giants. By the American Giants' tally they felt they should have been awarded the pennant for the first half of the season, but "not so," said league commissioner Gus Greenlee — who also happened to be the owner of the Pittsburgh Crawfords. The tables had been turned on the American Giants, who for many years had benefited from having manager Rube Foster at the head of the Negro National League.

At a mid-season Negro National League meeting called by Gus Greenlee the idea of an East-West All-Star game was floated among club owners. The idea had been mentioned before, but the success of the first ever Major League All-Star game in conjunction with the Century of Progress World's Fair gave added incentive for a Negro League All-Star tilt. Robert Cole was appointed the go-between to the Comiskey Park owners. While the American Giants played home games out of Indianapolis in 1933, interest in black baseball ran high in Chicago and it was decided the All-Star game would be a hit. Fans chose the players by sending in ballots published in the *Chicago Defender* and *Pittsburgh Courier*. It came as no surprise that the East squad was dominated by the Pittsburgh Crawfords and the West squad dominated by Cole's American Giants.

On September 10, 1933, some 20,000 fans braved an early afternoon thunderstorm and came out to Comiskey Park to see the first annual Negro League All-Star game. Willie Foster pitched an 11–7 complete game victory for the Western team. The East was without their ace Satchel Paige, who snubbed the event, and East manager Pop Lloyd was forced to name veteran Sam Streeter the starter. The game lived up to billing as a star studded affair, with notables "Cool Papa" Bell, Oscar Charleston, Josh Gibson, Judy Johnson, Dick Lundy, Biz Mackey, Turkey Stearnes and Willie Wells all playing. Willie Foster hit legend Oscar Charleston two times with inside pitches — indicating that the game was hotly contested. Mule Suttles hit a game tying home run in the fourth, and tied the game up again in the sixth with an RBI double, before the West squad took control of the game.

On the whole the game was a great success—only slightly tarnished by the absence of Satchel Paige and the gloomy weather. What started off as an exhibition game to spur baseball excitement during the Great Depression eventually grew to become an annual tradition and a premier event in black sport. Excitement generated by the Negro League All-Star game overshadowed the pennant race almost immediately. A new and different day was dawning for Negro League baseball—called by some the "Modern Era of Negro League baseball." In the Modern Era emphasis shifted away from teams to individual star players—some of whom would eventually land major league contracts.[11]

1934

The scheme to run dog races in the American Giants' ballpark failed. Illinois governor Henry Horner went along with dog racing, but was dead set against betting on the dogs. True, Chicago went wild with the end of Prohibition in 1933 but gambling remained illegal. In order for the American Giants to reclaim the ballpark they first had to reconvert the facility back to a ballpark from a dog track. Owner Robert Cole put up the necessary funds to fix the park and retain the best players. The pitching staff included Willie Foster, Willie "Sug" Cornelius and Ted Trent. Among the position players: Turkey Stearnes, Willie Wells, Mule Suttles along with Alec Radcliffe. Utility player Joe Lillard was able to concentrate a bit more on baseball, as the National Football League, which had been partially integrated, decided that blacks could no longer play in the league. Dave Malarcher remained skipper.[12]

Prevailing economic conditions remained grim and black baseball struggled in most cities, but the American Giants' return to Chicago was a positive sign. Teams in the Negro National League included the Philadelphia Stars, Newark Dodgers, Nashville Elite Giants and Cleveland Red Sox. Missing from the league mix were teams from Kansas City, St. Louis, Indianapolis and Detroit. The face of Negro League baseball was much different than it had been in the days of Rube Foster's Negro National League. Gus Greenlee's Pittsburgh Crawfords maintained a virtual all-star team with players like Satchel Paige, Josh Gibson, "Cool Papa" Bell, Oscar Charleston and Judy Johnson. Exhibition/barnstorming games again became staples in the Negro Leagues.

Among the exhibitions during the 1934 season was a post-season barnstorming trip by Dizzy Dean's All-Stars against various Negro League teams. The American Giants fell to Dean's All-Stars by a 13–3 score in a mid–October game. The independent Kansas City Monarchs, with the addition of American Giants Willie Foster and Turkey Stearnes, played in the *Denver Post* tournament against the "House of David" team who had recruited Satchel Paige as their ace. House of David and Paige came out on top in that tournament. The House of David team, with Hall of Famer Grover Cleveland Alexander as pitcher, played an exhibition game earlier in the year in Chicago, which featured a game of "donkey" baseball. While there was little if any redeeming value to "donkey baseball," the widespread interest in black baseball pointed to an underlying healthiness in the business of black baseball.[13]

The most important exhibition of the year was again the Negro League All-star game, held at Chicago's Comiskey Park. The Western team was composed mostly of Chicago American Giants players and the Eastern team was composed mostly of Pittsburgh Crawfords players. A crowd of 30,000 filled the park and saw the Eastern squad led by Satchel Paige defeat the West led by Willie Foster by a 1–0 score. Actually neither Paige nor Foster started the game. Slim Jones of the Philadelphia Stars started for the East and Ted Trent of the American Giants started for the West but the two Hall of Famers did come on to pitch the last three innings.

There was a playoff for the championship of the league between the Chicago American Giants, who finished in first place for the first half of the season, and the Philadelphia Stars, who finished in first place in the second half of the season. The Pittsburgh Crawfords, even with their stacked deck of talent, did not make the playoffs, probably because ace Satchel Paige was more concerned with barnstorming engagements. In those days Leroy could single handedly fill a stadium. Satch shut out the American Giants three different times in 1934. The absence of Paige and the Crawfords was evidence that playoffs did not represent the best of black baseball. Another indication that the championship series was of diminished importance was the fact that the playoffs were actually interrupted for the purpose of playing exhibition games.

Shortly before the playoffs, Negro National League head Gus Greenlee called Chicago Giant owner Robert Cole to a special meeting in New York. Cole hopped a plane to meet with Greenlee, who laid out his plan to have the American Giants, Pittsburgh Crawfords, Philadelphia Stars and New York Black Yankees meet in a four team double-header at Yankee Stadium. Greenlee predicted a crowd of over 30,000 for the big event. The game in Yankee Stadium came off as planned and was a great success. Ted Trent went the distance for the American Giants in the first game, beating the Black Yankees 4–3. The event at Yankee Stadium was so popular that another four team double-header was scheduled three weeks later in the midst of the playoff championship. The supposed World Series between the Chicago American Giants and Philadelphia Stars would not generate anything near that amount of fan interest, so it made sense from a business standpoint to schedule the games in Yankee Stadium.[14]

The American Giants had a three games to one lead in the championship series against the Philly Stars, but Philly clawed back to tie the series after back to back wins in Philadelphia. As it happened the intermission in the championship series to play the four game series at Yankee Stadium came with the series tied at three games apiece. The deciding game of the series went to the Philadelphia Stars who won on a 2–0 shutout by Slim Jones. Dave Malarcher disputed the outcome and filed two separate protests with the league. Malarcher based one protest on an obscure league rule, which stated that a championship game should not be played at night. The other protest was in regards to umpires who did not eject Jud Wilson after he threw a roundhouse punch at umpire Bert Gohlson. The reason Gohlson gave for not ejecting Wilson was that he "didn't see who did it." The commissioner agreed with Malarcher that the umpire's action, or lack thereof, was "unjustifiable" but did not feel it should change the outcome. Both protests were thrown out and the Philly Stars were awarded the championship. The incident caused Dave Malarcher, who had long been disillusioned with the administration of the Negro National League, to mull retirement.[15]

1935

Following the 1934 season it was announced that Cole's American Giants had traded away Joe Lillard and outfielder Nat Rogers to Abe Manley's Brooklyn Eagles. When Joe Lillard, the two-sports professional athlete who made a major contribution to the American Giants in 1934, got word that he had been traded to Brooklyn he stated flatly "I'll quit baseball for good unless I am returned to the Chicago American Giants." Lillard's stand-down of management had become commonplace in 1930's era black professional ball.[16]

As part of hot-stove league jockeying, Robert Cole offered a contract to catcher Quincy Trouppe, who was touring with a basketball team during the off-season. Trouppe reportedly wired that he would sign with the American Giants for the 1935 season. However Trouppe was a no show in the spring and instead stuck with the independent Bismarck, North Dakota, Cubs. Trouppe had made a name for himself with Neil Churchill's integrated barnstorming outfit and even took credit for bringing Satchel Paige to the Bismarck Cubs. Paige was credited with winning 134 of 150 games he started for the Bismarck team. Satch used the association with Neil Churchill to leverage the bidding for his talent; his rambling around during the mid-thirties became the stuff of folklore.[17]

There were many who had begrudged Rube's strong-arm tactics but in hindsight the Negro National League of the twenties looked like clockwork compared to the freewheeling of the thirties. A lack of discipline from league executives on down to team owners, managers and players led to many odd situations where a player would be traded from one team to another, but simply decide not to go to the new team. Even with the new footloose style of the 1930's, Negro League baseball remained serious business. Owners made investments in their clubs even as the economy struggled. The names had changed, owners like Gus Greenlee, Cum Posey, Robert Cole, Abe Saperstein, Abe Manley, had taken the place of Rube Foster, C.I. Taylor, Ed Bolden, and J. L. Wilkinson as the movers and shakers in black baseball.

As expected, Dave Malarcher stepped aside as manager of the American Giants prior to the season. An educated church going man with high standards of professionalism, Malarcher decided that he had seen enough of the shaky deals endemic in black baseball. His experience working closely with Rube Foster and C.I. Taylor made him an irreplaceable figure and he would be sorely missed.[18]

Despite Malarcher's departure, Robert Cole remained committed to the success of the American Giants. Cole put more money toward fixing up the American Giants' turn of the century ballpark which was in constant need of repair. Cole tapped catcher Larry Brown, whose professional experience dated to 1919, to manage the team. He also hired Wilson "Frog" Redus, a hard-hitting outfielder who made his mark with the St. Louis Stars during the heyday of the NNL. Redus followed in the footsteps of Willie Wells, Mule Suttles and Quincy Trouppe, who had all been with the St. Louis club back in 1931. Catcher Jim Brown, whom Rube Foster had brought to Chicago in 1918 and Abe Saperstein had hired to pilot the short lived "Rube Foster Memorial Giants," was lured back to Chicago where he served as assistant manager to Larry Brown. In addition to managing the team, both Larry Brown and Jim Brown actually put on the catching gear and got behind the plate. Jim Brown also played at first base just as he had in the twenties under

Rube Foster. Catching duties were also handled by Richard "Subby" Byas, a local product new to the American Giants in 1935 who looked young enough to pass as a bat boy.[19]

The raw talent on Cole's American Giants compared to the talent on some of Rube's best teams. Outfielder Turkey Stearnes, shortstop Willie Wells and pitcher Willie Foster all were eventually enshrined in Cooperstown. The supporting cast wasn't bad either. Outfielder George "Mule" Suttles was compared with Josh Gibson because of his ability to hit the long ball. Hard-hitting third baseman Alex Radcliffe was a perennial All-Star who would set the career record for most Negro League All-Star game at-bats. At that time right-handers Ted Trent and Willie "Sug" Cornelius had mound repertoires superior to that of Willie Foster, who suffered with nagging arm soreness and was nearing the end of his career. The right side of the infield was a bit weaker, with the aging Walter "Steel Arm" Davis sharing duties at first base, and William "Jack" Marshall at second. Things had changed since Rube's departure, but the team still bore the maker's mark. Most of the players had served, at least for a short spell, under Rube a decade earlier.

Cole's American Giants took spring training in Texas then opened up the season at home against the New York Cubans who were managed by Martin Dihigo. The opening game was held at an alternative field because workmen had not completed the work at the American Giants' park. In addition to managing the team Dihigo struck out eleven batters and scored two runs for the Cubans. Sug Cornelius held the Cubans to only five hits and the American Giants won by a 4–3 score.

The American Giants' first big test of the season was a four game series against the Pittsburgh Crawfords. The lineups sounded like a "who was who" in black baseball. Batting leadoff for the Crawfords was Cool Papa Bell, Dan Bankhead batted second, followed by Oscar Charleston, Josh Gibson batting cleanup and Judy Johnson batting fifth. The heart of the American Giants' batting order was similarly strong with Willie Wells, Turkey Stearnes and Mule Suttles. The American Giants split the four game series with the Crawfords on the strength of the pitching of Sug Cornelius, who won the first and last games of the series.

During the 1930's era of black baseball the lineups of heavyweight teams were usually star-studded. The aura of black baseball shifted from that of a ball club representing a city to the cult of the glamorous twentieth century star athlete. The consolidated league was entertaining and competition was good. Professional black baseball had built on a generation of its own stars. There were the wise old owls of black baseball holding up the fort. For example, Ben Taylor managed the Brooklyn Eagles, "Candy Jim" Taylor managed the Columbus Elite Giants, Dick Lundy managed the Newark Dodgers and Sam Crawford managed the independent Kansas City Monarchs. There were players nearing the end of their career: Oscar Charleston, Biz Mackey, Phil Cockerell and Willie Foster to name a few. There were the players in their prime like Satchel Paige, Josh Gibson, Cool Papa Bell, Leroy Matlock , Double Duty Radcliffe, Willie Cornelius, Ted Trent and others. Then there were new kids on the block like Homestead Gray first-sacker Buck Leonard, Brooklyn Eagle pitcher Leon Day and Newark Dodger Ray Dandridge (all of whom eventually found their way to Cooperstown).

The annual All-Star game was made more interesting when the Pittsburgh Crawfords were put into the West along with Chicago American Giants, yielding a heavy hitting team for the West. Although the league was now based on the East Coast, with teams in Pittsburgh, Philly, New York, Brooklyn, and New Jersey—along with Columbus and Chicago—the big All-Star game remained firmly planted in Chicago's South Side at Comiskey Park. Twenty-seven thousand fans packed Comiskey for the third annual classic. The fans got their money's worth, as after nine innings the All-Star Game was knotted at 8–8 and remained knotted until the eleventh inning. With two outs in the bottom of the eleven, Eastern manager Webster McDonald elected to intentionally walk cleanup batter Josh Gibson to face Mule Suttles. Mule made him pay with a dramatic 3-run walk-off homer to the delight of the local fans. American Giant ace Willie "Sug" Cornelius was credited with the win although he pitched only one inning.

The Negro National League at that time consisted of only one division, did not have a balanced schedule and was a league in name only. The American Giants were the only team in the Negro National League at that time from the old circuit, although they also played games against independent teams in Kansas City, Detroit and Cincinnati. The American Giants played .500 ball through most of the season, which was respectable considering the frequent encounters with the likes of the Pittsburgh Crawfords.

The American Giants under Rube Foster had been built on a careful system of scouting and mentoring. Robert Cole's strategy for building the team consisted mainly of opening his pocket book. The two men were different in most respects, but both were good businessmen. Bob Cole, unlike Rube, was not dependent on the success of Negro League baseball for a paycheck and considered his involvement more of a speculative venture. Cole's primary occupation was running the Metropolitan Funeral Home Association as a successful company. The day to day demands of running the American Giants eventually became disruptive to Cole's primary business interests and half-way through the 1935 season Cole decided to turn operations over to assistant Horace Hall.

Cole relied on Dave Malarcher's guidance to run the team when he took over in 1932 but had gradually shifted more responsibilities to Horace Hall. Cole kept his post as treasurer of the Negro National League, but sold his interest in the team to Hall. By the August All-Star break, Horace Hall was officially deemed the owner of the American Giants. One of Horace Hall's first acts was to announce that the American Giants did not intend to participate in the Negro National League the following season.[20]

The Chicago American Giants did not vie for the championship of the Negro League, but instead took on the Kansas City Monarchs in a series of games to close out the season. The Monarchs, who were playing independently of the Negro National League, pulled off a coup by signing Satchel Paige. The Monarchs used Satchel to pitch a few innings in every game in order to draw fans to the park. A nice crowd turned out at Comiskey Park on a chilly Sunday afternoon, September 22, 1935, to see Willie Foster pitch against Satchel Paige. Paige pitched well through five innings, struck out eight batters, allowed one hit and no runs—but after manager Sam Crawford rested Satch, the Giants piled on seven runs. Willie Foster pitched a complete game and allowed only one run in the 7–1 victory. The American Giants then went out on the road to play a series of games against the Monarchs in Omaha and in Kansas City. Star players Willie Wells, Mule Suttles and Turkey Stearnes also did some barnstorming later in the fall and played in the California winter league.

The American Giants, and other baseball teams, found themselves pushed off the front of black sports pages by the "Brown Bomber" Joe Louis and the "Buckeye Bullet"

Jesse Owens. Joe Louis became a hero when he knocked out former heavyweight champion Primo Carnera on June 25, 1935, and took the crown outright by defeating Max Baer on September 24, 1935. Ohio State track and field star Jesse Owens made headlines when he shattered world records for the 100 yard dash, broad jump and 220 yard dash at a Big Ten track meet on May 25, 1935.

The emergence of Joe Louis and Jesse Owens as black Americans on the international stage prompted more calls for integration of baseball. *Chicago Defender* sportswriters Al Monroe and Dan Burley peppered their columns with calls to end the "color line." The *Defender* cornered Chicago Cub president Phil Wrigley and Chicago White Sox vice-president Harry Grabiner on the subject of integration and the possibility of their respective teams playing against the American Giants. Wrigley, who became owner of the Cubs in 1934, sidestepped the question, deferring to Commissioner Kenesaw Mountain Landis. Harry Grabiner avoided the *Defender*, which had sought to confirm a statement attributed to him that "the White Sox play only white teams."[21]

1936

Horace Hall began his first full year as the owner of the American Giants in 1936. Hall announced ahead of time that he did not intend to compete in the Negro National League due to the high expenses of traveling to the East Coast. During the hot-stove league rumors swirled as to the future of the American Giants. One report stated that boxer Joe Louis, who had recently seen a good payday after knocking out heavyweight champ Max Baer, would be rebuilding the Detroit Stars and raiding the American Giants' roster. Louis reportedly received a large volume of mail from aspiring players when the rumor broke. Joe Louis would sponsor a Detroit softball team, but had no ambitions to raid the American Giants.[22]

The American Giants were raided nonetheless. Willie Wells and Mule Suttles were picked up by Abe Manley's Newark Eagles. Turkey Stearnes wound up with the Philadelphia Stars. Willie Foster, in the twilight of his career, joined the Pittsburgh Crawfords. Third baseman Alec Radcliffe, a mainstay on the American Giants since 1932, left the American Giants for the Cuban Stars, but after some wrangling came back into the fold in July. It was no surprise that the American Giants lost these star players, as Horace Hall stated he was looking to do things on the cheap.

Hall prematurely announced his confidence that Satchel Paige was close to signing with the American Giants. However Satchel wanted nothing to do with Hall's American Giants and by-passed the Windy City on his way from the Kansas City Monarchs back to Greenlee's Pittsburgh Crawfords. Hall may have entertained illusions, or delusions, of dealing to build a team around Satchel Paige, but in the end took a more modest approach.[23]

Veteran Bingo DeMoss, who had been out of baseball for a number of years, replaced Larry Brown as skipper. Horace Hall worked the grapevine to establish rapport with a number of the American Giant old timers. Dizzy Dismukes and Jim Brown assisted Bingo DeMoss with managing duties, while Jimmy Lyons was retained as a front office advisor. DeMoss took the team down to New Orleans for spring training and held tryouts for the numerous vacancies on the team. The American Giants did hang on to pitchers Ted Trent and Willie Cornelius who anchored the team. Wilson Redus remained in the outfield, otherwise the American Giants was mostly a crew of fresh faces. Management introduced a crew of literal "no-name" players to the Bronzeville faithful. A photograph of the new infield was published in the *Chicago Defender* on May 16, 1936: McCall at first, Lebeaux at second, James at shortstop and Prince at third — no first names were given.[24]

The drop off in the level of talent from 1935 to 1936 was steep indeed. Chicago went from being great team loaded with Hall of Fame talent to a regional act. The American Giants announced they were playing in the newly formed Southern Baseball Association — this loose association was not truly a league. The 1936 American Giants ended up playing an abbreviated season against the likes of the Claybrook (Arkansas) Tigers, the Kansas City Monarchs, Cincinnati Tigers, St. Louis Stars and a number of regional semi-pro teams. The American Giants even stooped to playing against the State Prison team in Joliet, Illinois, at least that was what the team called itself — there is some question as to whether the team was actually from a prison.[25]

Horace Hall's fire sale was initially unpopular, but the frugal approach was also a breath of fresh air in an era when deep pockets had become the primary force in running a baseball team. After all, one of Rube's axioms was that competition should be balanced. Chicago baseball fans were sophisticated enough to appreciate the beauty of the game and looked down their noses at the greedy ways of Gus Greenlee. The American Giants and other Midwestern teams were able to use the hiatus from playing against the Eastern teams to regroup the old alliances.

One of the highlights of the season was a "Rube Foster Memorial Day." The benefit featured a game between a team of old-time American Giants like Walter Ball, Jim Brown, Bingo DeMoss, Jelly Gardner, George Harney, Jimmy Lyons, Dave Malarcher, Bruce Petway and an old-timer white team led by former White Sox/Logan Squares manager Jimmy Callahan. Included on the white team was 70-year-old Fred "Crazy" Schmidt, whose best days were pitching with the Baltimore Orioles back in 1893.[26]

Despite the fact that the American Giants were not part of Gus Greenlee's Negro National League, the fourth annual Negro League All-Star game was held in Chicago. The Western team was made up entirely of American Giant and Kansas City Monarch players. Some of the American Giants on the All-Star team made the team with less than stellar credentials. For example, catcher Subby Byas and outfielder Herman Dunlap played regularly for the American Giants, but were not regarded as star players. The Eastern squad, with Satchel Paige and the gang from Pittsburgh (Josh Gibson, Cool Papa Bell, Judy Johnson, Jimmy Crutchfield, Sam Bankhead, Leroy Matlock), won the game by a 10–2 score. A crowd of thirty thousand packed Comiskey for the All-Star game, which continued to be the centerpiece of black baseball.

Exhibition was front and center but the whole season was not a carnival. The American Giants faced some worthy competition among their regional opponents. The Kansas City Monarchs had a young standout named Willard Brown, who eventually played briefly with the Major League St. Louis Browns, along with a stable of wily veterans like Bullet Rogan, Newt Allen and Andy Cooper. The Cincinnati Tigers had a number of young talented players including Porter Moss, Howard Easterling, Rainey Bibbs and Olan "Jelly" Taylor. The abilities of Cincinnati's young players far exceeded those of the no-name youngsters of the American Giants.

Black baseball was pushed down the sports pages to make room for Jesse Owens' four gold medals in the Berlin Olympics. Jesse Owens' success made it clear that blacks must inevitably join the major leagues. More and more baseball scribes, both black and white, were hitting home with convincing arguments as to why the color line should fall in major league baseball. The *Defender* reprinted a column by *New York Daily News* writer Jimmy Powers in which he called for integration of baseball. The *Defender* also reprinted an article by Ted Benson of the Socialist *Sunday Worker* paper in which he exposed the "emperor's new clothes"—specifically the drawers of National League president Ford Frick. Frick stated, "I do not recall one instance where baseball had allowed either race, creed or color to enter in the question of the selection of its players."[27]

During the hot-stove league representatives of clubs from Chicago, Kansas City, Cincinnati, Memphis, St. Louis, Birmingham, Indianapolis and Detroit met at the centrally located crossroads of Indianapolis to discuss the formation of a new western alliance. Horace Hall was the chairman of the conference; icon J.L. Wilkerson represented Kansas City, Dick Kent and G. B. Key represented St. Louis, Dr. John B. Martin and his brothers Dr. B. B. Martin and W. S. Martin came up from Memphis. Promoter Abe Saperstein, *Defender* sports editor Al Monroe and alderman Major R.R. Jackson also descended from the Windy City to participate. Major Jackson, a Spanish-American War veteran, was the elder statesman—his involvement with Chicago black baseball dated all the way back to the 1889 Chicago Unions. The result of the gathering was the formation of the Negro American League. Major Jackson was appointed league commissioner. Not since the historic 1920 conference in Kansas City to form the Negro National League had such a well-organized meeting of the western black baseball minds occurred. Horace Hall, as chairman of the organizing committee, showed that he was no fly-by-night operator. Hall also announced in December that he had signed Candy Jim Taylor to manage the American Giants for the upcoming Negro American League campaign.[28]

1937

If there was one manager in black baseball that could single handedly make a difference in the fortune of a team it was Candy Jim Taylor. Taylor retooled the American Giants. The no-name infield was gone, replaced by slightly more memorable first baseman Zack Clayton and shortstop Timothy Bond. Jack Marshall was convinced to return to the fold after spending the 1936 season with the Philly Stars and Alex Radcliffe held down third. Willie Cornelius and Ted Trent were the one-two punch on the mound. Willie Foster returned to Bronzeville to pitch in a handful of games for the locals. Fan hopes of bringing Mule Suttles and Turkey Stearnes back into the fold were dashed, however Stearnes did appear in a few games for the American Giants after the struggling Detroit Stars franchise closed up shop.

The Negro American League had shortcomings—which were to be expected in the first year of operation. In the Eastern circuit, still known as the Negro National League, many of the top players including Satchel Paige, Josh Gibson, Cool Papa Bell, Sam Bankhead, Leroy Matlock, Luis Tiant, Chet Brewer and others were lured to the Dominican Republic to play for dictator Rafael Trujillo's team. Trujillo used the national treasury to offer the players huge payments that they could not refuse. The annual All-Star game at Comiskey was devoid of the major stars who had left the country, slightly tarnishing the classic. On June 22, 1937, at Comiskey, heavyweight fighter Joe Louis defeated James "Bubba" Braddock to take the world championship. Joe Louis's defeat of a white champion fueled more discussion and expectations for an end to the color line in major league baseball. Despite shortcomings, black baseball enjoyed a major renaissance in 1937. With teams stretched from Kansas City to New York and from Birmingham to Chicago, Negro League baseball blanketed the country. Fans and organizers even waxed nostalgic for the return of the Negro League World Series. The worst effects of the Great Depression appeared to be receding and a new era of black baseball was dawning. Negro League baseball in this new era was "fatter" than it had been during the height of the Rube Foster era.

Horace Hall's renewed investment paid some dividends as the Chicago American Giants went to the top of the Negro American League standings. Larger crowds returned to the park, putting wind back into the sails of organized black baseball. The NAL pennant race was competitive as Cincinnati, Chicago, Kansas City and Memphis all fielded respectable teams. The NAL season was divided into halves. The American Giants finished the first half of the season in a dead heat with the KC Monarchs, and just barely finished on top in the second half of the season. It wasn't until after the second half of the season that a determination was made on how to settle the tie for the first half of the season. After a back and forth discussion with league commissioner Major R.R. Jackson, it was decided that the American Giants would meet the Kansas City Monarchs in a seven-game series to settle the issue.[29]

The playoff was to be staged in Chicago, Kansas City and on neutral fields in Dayton, Indianapolis and Milwaukee. Willie "Sug" Cornelius started game one of the series, held at Duck Park in Dayton, Ohio, and gave up four runs in the first inning. "Sug" held the Monarchs scoreless the rest of the way and the American Giants ended up with a 5–4 win. The second game turned out to be a classic in the annals of Negro League baseball, as the two teams battled 17 innings, on a cold September evening in Chicago. Veteran manager-pitcher Andy Cooper went the distance for the Monarchs. Willie Foster pitched seven innings before he sustained an injury when he was hit in the chest by a ball off the bat of Bullet Rogan, and Willie Cornelius finished the game for the American Giants. In the bottom of the seventeenth, a fan grabbed a ball from Kansas City right fielder Willard Brown, and Willie Cornelius tried to dash home from third base to score the winning run. The umpire noticed the interference, however, and the game was called a tie as an eerie wintry scene descended on the park. The series was subsequently shortened to five games from seven, and Kansas City took three games straight to lay claim to the first-half pennant.

By the time the playoff was completed it was decided that there was no need for a second playoff to decide the overall champion of the NAL. Instead it was decided that the Monarchs and American Giants would put together a team made up of the best players from both teams to face the best players from a combined team of Homestead Grays and Newark Eagles from the NNL in a nine game series. The odd match was dominated by the Eastern team who took seven of the nine games. The so-called "World Series" was not widely followed by fans or the press. Frank Young, writing for the *Defender*, stated "I cannot see where it can be called a World Series." Young pointed out that the World

Series in the days of Rube Foster was based on competition and organization, but that this was merely an "intersectional or inter-league series" drummed up by four club owners. Young did note that Eastern baseball at that time was indeed a step ahead of the West.[30]

1938

The excitement created by the launch of the Negro American League and the rejuvenation of organized play among the teams of the Midwest was measured. Soon after the NAL opened for business fans remembered the shortcomings of the previous Negro National League. Along with rhetorical complaints about the lack of organization, sneaky back office deals and poor officiating, fans were questioning the very nature of a separate Negro League. The Negro Leagues had their roots in the previous century and were a concession to the forces of segregation in the Northern states. The commissioner of the Negro American League, Major R.R. Jackson, had managed the Chicago Unions way back in 1889 — the question had to be asked "had anything really changed in all those years?" Baseball was, after all, only a game. Questions of moral conscience were immediate and several events in 1938 cast light on the complexity of Negro League baseball.

Time magazine's "Man of the Year" in 1938 was Adolf Hitler. Boxer Joe Louis defeated German heavyweight Max Schmeling on June 22, 1938, before 70,000 fans in Yankee Stadium and was heralded a hero by both black and white Americans. On July 30, 1938, New York Yankee outfielder Alvin "Jake" Powell was interviewed on Chicago's WGN radio station prior to a Yankees vs. White Sox game. When asked in the interview about what he did in the off season, Powell remarked that he "kept in shape cracking niggers over the head as a police officer in Dayton, Ohio." The *Chicago Tribune*, owner of the station, was deluged with complaints from black Chicagoans. Baseball commissioner Kenesaw Mountain Landis suspended Jake Powell for ten days for his conduct. When Powell returned to play in Washington, D.C.'s, Griffith Stadium, he was pelted with pop bottles by angry fans.

The outcry against Jake Powell and the rallying behind Joe Louis was evidence of a subtle shift in racial attitudes. By 1938 seating at most major league stadiums was integrated. It was "hip" among some Chicago blacks to check out the White Sox. *Chicago Defender* writer Frank Young expressed his personal displeasure at the large number of blacks who were supporting the Chisox and not supporting the American Giants, complaining:

> Baseball games are not being supported by our group. The depression may have had something to do with it. The recession may have something to do with it now. Neither the depression or the recession has anything to do with the young Negro who prefers to spend his money to see two all-white teams play in the major league which draws the color line…. The Negro club owners are paying out more than the individual ball player is drawing through the turnstiles.[31]

The chorus of newspaper writers white and black calling for the integration of baseball continued to swell. The only way for Negro League baseball to succeed was to bring about the end of its own existence, by succeeding to integrate the major leagues. It is hard to think of another major American institution with a similar mission. The owners ponied up the cash to fund a league that they hoped eventually would be eliminated.

Players and coaches pursued their careers in a league that they would just as soon see fold up. Of course Negro League baseball had always been in this predicament, but by the late 1930's there was a nexus of the old school and a more progressive new school of thought. It was against this backdrop that the Chicago American Giants went to work in 1938.

The team went down to Florida and toured the South for spring training. Candy Jim played the role of a seasoned baseball skipper and talked about scouting fresh players, making trades and winning a pennant. Willie Cornelius and Ted Trent anchored the pitching staff. Willie Foster was not signed and went to play for a white semi-pro team in Elgin, Illinois. Turkey Stearnes started out as the center fielder for the club, but Candy Jim decided Turkey was not in his best form and released him mid-season. A few years earlier Candy Jim had cut a young prospect named Josh Gibson, who he said "would never make a catcher." In the cases of Turkey Stearnes and Willie Foster in 1938, Candy Jim's judgment seemed to be correct as both men retired shortly thereafter, though fans were disappointed to see them go. Alec Radcliffe remained at third base, Richard "Subby" Byas backstopped and played first, Wilson "Frog" Redus roamed left field, and Herman Dunlop was back in right field.

"Candy" brought in some new faces. Outfielder Billy Simms was acquired from Kansas City and took Turkey Stearnes's spot in center field. Junius "Rainey" Bibbs was brought in from the Cincinnati Tigers to cover second base. A fresh recruit from New Orleans named William "Billy" Horne was the starting shortstop when the season began but was replaced by Ormand Sampson who was lured from the Atlanta Black Crackers.

As the season progressed more changes were made. Candy could not settle on a permanent backstop. Subby Byas had trouble making the throw to second, was converted to a first baseman and replaced by Paul Hardy. When Hardy ran into problems behind the plate, shortstop/utility man Ormand Sampson replaced him. Halfway through the season Sampson was set to go back to the Atlanta Black Crackers but jumped to the Mexican League. Candy then traded second baseman Rainey Bibbs to Kansas City for legend Frank Duncan, who had put in a complete career as the regular catcher for the Monarchs. (Duncan should not be confused with the player by the same name who played for the American Giants in the 1910's.) Second stringers like first baseman Ed "Pep" Young and outfielder Robert Smith were also used behind the plate. Luther Gilyard, who had come to the American Giants the previous year, started about half the games at first base. The pitching staff was supplemented with Tommy Johnson of Clayton, Missouri, Jess Houston of Cincinnati, and a rookie right hander named Percy Forest.

The American Giants pulled off a ho-hum season. Highlights included an exhibition trip with the Kansas City Monarchs through Manitoba, Canada, and an exhibition against the Monarchs in Milwaukee's minor-league park. The American Giants also dropped two exhibitions against the Palmer House Indians (representing the famous Palmer House Hotel of Chicago). The Palmer House team was made up mostly of former American Giants. Like the American Giant teams of recent years, the 1938 team relied heavily on the throwing of "Sug" Cornelius and Ted Trent.

In the spring of 1938, the greatest power hitter to play for Rube Foster's American Giants, Cristobal Torriente, died of tuberculosis, penniless, living in New York City. His body was returned to his native Cuba for interment. The annual East-West Negro League

All-Star game was again held at Comiskey. The starter for the West was Willie Cornelius, who was joined by teammates Alec Radcliffe and Frank Duncan. The Western team won on the strength of Memphis Red Sox's Ted "Double Duty" Radcliffe's relief effort by a 5–4 score in front of 30,000 fans, although some of the top players in the East were forced to sit out by their team owners who feared injury.

1939

The American Giants again bussed down to Florida for spring training in 1939. Most of the core veterans returned: Alec Radcliffe kept his spot on the hot corner, "Frog" Redus roamed left field, "Sug" Cornelius was the ace on the staff and Ted Trent also returned. Most of the regulars from the previous season were also back, including second baseman Billy Horne, shortstop Joe Sparks, utility man Richard "Subby" Byas, first baseman Edward "Pep" Young and outfielder Herman Dunlop. Candy Jim finally found a back-

East-West All-Star game 1939: 40,000 turned out on August 6, 1939, to see one of the closer All-Star games. The West won 4–2 on an eighth inning two-run homer hit by Dan Wilson of the St. Louis Stars. Some well-known stars that played included Josh Gibson, Willie Wells, Buck Leonard, Leon Day, Mule Suttles, Hilton Smith and "Double Duty" Radcliffe. Players (save Satchel Paige) did not get a windfall from the All-Star game, although owners and organizers did (photograph courtesy NoirTech Research, Inc.).

stop that he could put faith in when he landed Lloyd "Pepper" Basset. Basset had been with the Pittsburgh Crawfords in 1938, where he had filled the shoes of Josh Gibson. The Crawfords folded due in part to players like Gibson, Paige and Bell jumping to Latin American teams. While Bassett gave stability to the lineup, early in the season Candy Jim tried out new players like an alchemist searching for a secret formula. There were a number of fresh recruits, including outfielders Ernest Smith of Rochelle, Louisiana, Charles Robinson of Atlanta, and Jack Miles, as well as pitchers Pierre Rogers and John Ford Smith. Other new players included infielders Lester Lockett from Birmingham, Howard Easterling from the Cincinnati Tigers and Red Hale from Detroit. Randolph "Lefty" "Bob" Bowe, from Burkesville, Kentucky, who had seen limited action with the Monarchs in 1938, became a regular in the American Giant pitching rotation.[32]

Why did Candy Jim put so much effort into molding a team? What did they play for? The money was insignificant. Competition for the pennant or even victory in post-season playoff carried only bragging rights. The players were celebrated in their communities, although many blacks had adopted the white major league teams of their cities, and even this small measure of celebrity was dimming. Some players hoped they might actually one day play in the major leagues, and a few actually would (Monte Irvin of the 1939 Newark Eagles and Roy Campanella of the Baltimore Elites for example). Baseball has long been imbued with poetic mystery and here again the magic of the diamond had cast its spell on black baseball. Candy Jim, the players and team owners, like gears in a clock, did what came natural — they played baseball even when it didn't make sense.

In their long efforts to "make things work," Negro League baseball owners had stumbled upon the means for survival. The method involved juggling bills, leases, and contracts and cashing in big at the annual All-Star game. The Great Depression was coming to an end, and as Americans went back to work they had a little more pocket change to spend on leisure. The economics of professional baseball at all levels has always been shrouded in mystery, as book cooking and number fudging are traditional back office staples. According to the books, team owners weren't making money, but they were almost breaking even. There were always just enough resources to keep Negro League baseball in business and it seemed that things could continue in this fashion indefinitely.

For the all the dugout jockeying Candy Jim had only a .500 record to show for it. Alec Radcliffe, Pepper Bassett and Billy Horne were all named to the All-Star team, but the American Giants lacked a big magnetic star player. While the American Giants had the foundation of their storied past and could count on at least *some* support from the black metropolis, the team had again fallen into mediocrity. Negro League team owners tried to coax an extra golden egg from the goose who layed the golden egg of the All-Star game, by holding an additional East-West game in Yankee Stadium. The West won the All-Star game at Comiskey and the East won the game at Yankee Stadium. The fact that the All-Star games were held in major league parks of the nation's largest cities was a highly visible sign of change.

For all the faults with Negro League baseball, some of which made up the basis for crude stereotypes, there was no denying that black baseball was an important social force with a vital mission. Racial justice issues came to the forefront of American society in 1939. African American opera singer Marian Anderson had planned to give a concert at Constitution Hall in Washington, D.C. The Daughters of the American Revolution, who owned Constitution Hall, would not allow blacks to perform. With the aid of Eleanor Roosevelt, Marian Anderson performed in front of 75,000 people at the Lincoln Memorial on Easter Sunday. The National Baseball Hall of Fame in Cooperstown threw open its doors in June of 1939. It goes without saying that the Hall of Fame did not recognize the great black players in the game. Writers continued to press the case for integration of baseball. The pivotal episode of the twentieth century began with the outbreak of World War II in 1939. In November of 1939, the *Defender* published a picture of UCLA halfback Jackie Robinson, captioned "the most dangerous halfback on the Pacific Coast."[33]

10

Democracy Invades Baseball (1940–1946)

"Organized baseball's unwritten but effective practice of exclusion, against some players because of their color helps to spread the "master race" theory among Americans on a mass basis."

— John Sengstacke, general manager,
Chicago Defender (1943).

"Democracy has finally invaded baseball."

— Frank A. Young, after learning of
Jackie Robinson's signing.
Chicago Defender, November 3, 1945.

1940

The founder, publisher and editor of the *Chicago Defender*, Robert Sengstacke Abbott, died on February 29, 1940. Abbott had been one of the most influential members of Chicago's black community. He was born on the Georgia Sea Islands in 1870, the son of former slaves; he studied at Claflin College in South Carolina and the Hampton Institute and received a law degree from Chicago's Kent College. Robert S. Abbott abandoned his law practice and founded the *Chicago Defender* newspaper in 1905. The *Defender* eventually grew to be the nation's greatest black newspaper. The *Defender* was the primary means by which the masses were able to follow the American Giants and black baseball. The reins of the *Defender* passed to his nephew John H. Sengstacke. Among the famous literary voices that wrote at one time or another for the *Defender* were Ida B. Wells, Richard Wright and Langston Hughes. Richard Wright's masterpiece *Native Son* was published in 1940. The main character in *Native Son* was Bigger Thomas, a black youth from Chicago's South Side, who murders a rich white girl from Chicago's well-to-do North Side. The book was a best seller and American readers came to identify with the struggle of the real life Bigger Thomases against a prejudiced society.

Organized Negro League baseball entered the third decade of existence facing many of the same challenges that existed in 1920. Issues such as preventing players from jumping contracts, securing ballparks and the general struggle to maintain financial solvency persisted. Some of the very same cast of characters who played key roles in the fledgling days of the Negro National League and Eastern Colored League were still at it. Among the hard core were J.L. Wilkinson, owner of the KC Monarchs, Ed Bolden, owner of the Hilldale club and Philadelphia Stars, skipper Candy Jim Taylor and others. For a select few Negro League baseball had provided steady employment and a full career.

There were some new faces on the scene too — such as white promoters Ed Gottlieb and Abe Saperstein who used their connections to profit from an increase in black baseball's popularity in the 1940's. Even though the Negro League All-Star game held annually in Chicago was the centerpiece of black baseball, the movers and shakers in black baseball were based on the East Coast. Among the high profile impresarios were Effa Manley (Newark Eagles), Cum Posey (Homestead Grays) and Tom Wilson (Baltimore Elite Giants). The new crop of moguls was bent on extracting a profit from black baseball and an uptick in the economy put this pie-in-the-sky almost within reach. By contrast Chicago American Giants' owner and Negro American League officer Horace Hall maintained a low profile and had even begun to scale back his investment in the American Giants.

For most of the twenty years of the Negro Leagues, professional baseball was no closer to being integrated than it had been at the turn of the century. The death of Rube Foster and the onset of the Great Depression were further setbacks to the cause, but hope sprung eternal in the Negro Leagues. By 1940 the call for integration of the major leagues was loud and steady. Public opinion against fascism in Europe created sympathy for the plight of African Americans. Increases in black populations in Northern cities and an improving economy gave hope that the color line might yet fall.

Candy Jim Taylor left his post as manager of the American Giants for the Birmingham Black Barons — Candy had started his professional baseball career way back in 1904 with the Birmingham Giants. Candy Jim had provided some stability over the last three years but his won-loss record was only average by Chicago American Giant standards. He had relied on a small core group of veterans and was not able to develop any brand new star players. Owner Horace Hall named veteran outfielder Wilson Redus player/manager to start the 1940 season.

Wilson Redus took the American Giants into spring training in Arkansas. By the time Redus returned to the South Side three of his best players — Willie Cornelius, Pepper Bassett and Alec Radcliffe — had left the team. Cornelius and Bassett had jumped to the Mexican League; Radcliffe was playing with the local semi-pro Palmer House Stars. Palmer House sported nearly a full roster of former Chicago American Giants including Frank Duncan, Norm Cross, Kermit Dial and Subby Byas. Unfortunately for manager Wilson Redus there was one negative development after another for the American Giants in 1940. It was probably the weakest American Giant team to date. The whole of Negro League baseball had weakened as most of the top players had jumped to the Mexican League. The Western Circuit of the Negro American League consisted of the Chicago American Giants, Kansas City Monarchs, Birmingham Black Barons, Memphis Red Sox, St. Louis–New Orleans Stars, Cleveland Bears and Toledo-Indianapolis Crawfords (the dying embers of Gus Greenlee's Pittsburgh Crawfords.) Other than Satchel Paige, the best player in the Negro American League was pitcher Hilton Smith of the Kansas City Monarchs — who could have played in Mexico but chose not to. Rookie Clifford "Connie"

Johnson was a rising star with the Toledo-Indianapolis Crawfords — he eventually made it to the major leagues as a pitcher for the Chicago White Sox and Baltimore Orioles. Otherwise the talent level in the Negro American League had decreased even further in 1940.

Satchel Paige upstaged the Negro League organization by arriving by plane from Mexico City to start off the season barnstorming with his Satchel Paige All-Stars. Meanwhile Effa Manley of the Newark Eagles still wanted to enforce a contractual claim to Paige dating back to 1938 when Gus Greenlee, disgusted with Satchel's jump to the Dominican Republic, sold her the contract. The front office chumps were placed in a quandary. Satchel refused to play for Manley, but it would clearly be unprofitable to ban Paige altogether because of his drawing power. In the end Satchel was granted status as "property of the Negro American League" though he continued to play for the barnstorming "Satchel Paige All-Stars," a team owned by KC Monarch owner J. L. Wilkinson. Paige had about "pitched his arm off" in Latin America — working almost every day. The normally confident Satchel even worried himself that he had lost his stuff but he miraculously regained his strength. Satchel Paige became an American celebrity in the 1940's. Articles were written about him in national magazines like *Time*, *Life* and the *Saturday Evening Post*. Leroy was a special case; while the rank and file Negro League players (who stayed in the United States) labored in cramped buses, Leroy might catch a plane or drive his Cadillac. Paige could single handedly change the fortunes of a club owner by packing the house.

In 1940 a barnstorming team known as the "Ethiopian Clowns" arrived on the scene to do battle with the Negro League teams. The Clowns had connections with booking agents Abe Saperstein and Syd Pollock and were able to arrange bookings, raid teams and even impress a critical audience with their playing ability on the field. While the name "Ethiopian Clowns" and the comedy routines were offensive to some, American Giants' owner Horace Hall and other owners thought that business concerns outweighed cultural sensitivities. Games against the Clowns became a staple. The Clowns swept the American Giants in a two-game series held in June.

Among catchers the American Giants hired to replace Pepper Bassett were Rossie Dawson, Ernest Smith, Harry Else, Johnny Dawson, and Ulysses Brown. Randolph "Lefty" Bowe was promoted to the ace of the staff, Tommy Johnson and Willie Hudson (picked up from Cincinnati) rounded out the rotation. Manager Wilson Redus was joined in the outfield by two newcomers, Henry Merchant and Donald Reeves. Henry "Speed" Merchant was a rookie, he later went on to star for the Indianapolis Clowns where he was a teammate of Hank Aaron among others. Donald Reeves was dubbed the "Home Run King" by the local press and according to one account hit 50 home runs over the course of the season.[1]

At one point in the season the Chicago American Giant players threatened to go on strike. The labor dispute came about when first baseman Ed "Pep" Young and Donald Reeves asked business manager Dave Malarcher for an advance on their pay. Malarcher thought their request unreasonable and decided the two players needed to be let go. At the time team owner Horace Hall was in New York for a joint meeting of the Negro American League and Negro National League. Malarcher called a meeting of the players at the park for an announcement. Malarcher also invited two police officers to the meeting —

apparently because he anticipated some trouble. Donald Reeves did not attend the meeting although Pep Young was present. Malarcher stated that he could not "get along in a business way" with Ed Young. Over the protests of manager Wilson Redus, Malarcher went on to announce that Reeves and Young would be paid in full but let go from the team. The players united around Reeves and Young and went on strike, at least until Horace Hall returned two days later. When Horace Hall returned he sided with the players, both Reeves and Young were reinstated. Dave Malarcher had overstepped his authority, he was handling some business for the team, but did not have the authority to hire and fire players. Even if Hall had wanted to stand behind Malarcher's action he would have had a difficult time replacing the two players. Later in the year however reserve outfielder Billy Simms asked for an advance of his paycheck to cover living expenses, and was let go.[2]

The weekend before the annual All-Star game the American Giants faced off in a double-header against the Toledo Crawfords in a benefit for the NAACP. Heavyweight champ Joe Louis threw out the first pitch, Jesse Owens gave an exhibition between the two games. Oscar Charleston was the skipper of the Toledo Crawfords and Ohioan Jesse Owens was the business manager. The American Giants also made a donation from the gate directly to former players Ted Trent and Herman Dunlap who had fallen on tough times and illness. Ace pitcher Randolph "Lefty" Bowe was not particularly moved by the American Giants' generosity. Bowe picked up and left for the Ethiopian Clowns who were set to play in the annual *Denver Post* semi-pro tournament.

Despite clubhouse turmoil and player raids from Mexico, the American Giants managed to play .500 ball. The All-Star game was held at Comiskey August 18 in front of a nice crowd of 25,000 who braved bad weather. American Giants Donald Reeves and short-stop Leroy Morney were named to the Western All-Star team. The West went down to an embarrassing 11–0 defeat. A nervous Leroy Morney made four errors, which helped the East to their biggest win ever. Buck Leonard was 3 for 4 for the East, who also saw most of their traditional stars taken south of the border.

Satchel Paige was ruled ineligible to play the game because he didn't actually play in the Negro American or Negro National leagues. The fact that Paige did not play was a blow in favor of the historically weak ownership hegemony. True, the general public would have clamored for Satchel, but players had become more emboldened in their flouting of league rules and here the league had shown some backbone. At the time there was a backlash against Satch who had become a darling of the patronizing white press. Frank Young reminded readers that "the game itself is bigger than Paige," and wrote that making an exception "would not only set a bad precedent but it would kill both leagues."[3]

When Satchel Paige did visit Chicago in September for an exhibition game, the venue was the American Giants' regular home field South Side Park, not Comiskey. The American Giants had already returned 6,000 grandstand seats they had been renting, forcing thousands to view the game from awkward positions perched on cardboard boxes. After a Labor Day series with the Memphis Red Sox, management rushed from the park after paying the visiting team in a desperate attempt to put the money toward an unsatisfied tax bill. The American Giants had been collecting federal taxes on tickets, but not remitting the proceeds to the U.S. Treasury.[4]

The setbacks mounted for the American Giants. The 1940 American Giants under

Frog Redus never stood a chance against the Kansas City Monarchs in the NAL pennant race, but no one was closely keeping track. Normal strictures of organized league play, such as schedules, standings, statistics had slipped by the wayside amid distractions. Chicago fans did not strenuously object when the Ethiopian Clowns or a hotel semi-pro team knocked off their American Giants. Fans loved to attend the All-Star game and were not particularly concerned that the great players were from Kansas City or the East Coast and not Chicago. American Giant fans came out to be entertained, to pass time or for cultural immersion — the outcome of the games was less important. A similar phenomenon occurred with Chicago's other professional baseball teams, the White Sox and the Cubs.

On Christmas Eve, December 24, 1940, vandals set fire to South Side Park, which was already in a dilapidated state. South Side Park had been the home of the American Giants since 1910. It was known as a pitcher's park due to the far-fetched outfield fences. The world champion 1906 Chicago White Sox, who played in the park, were known as the "hitless wonders" — they hit only three home runs all year in the park. It was the park where Rube and Willie Foster earned Hall of Fame credentials. It was an historic landmark in the history of Negro League baseball. Yet, no one shed tears when South Side burned, as there was universal agreement that the old wooden ballpark had outlived its usefulness. The destruction of the ballpark in 1940 was emblematic of what seemed also to be the destruction of the American Giant team.[5]

1941

There was a joint meeting of the Negro National League and the Negro American League at Chicago's Hotel Grand at 412 E. 47th Street in February. Three items dominated league business: the status of players who had jumped to Mexico, Satchel Paige, and the Ethiopian Clowns; there was no consideration given to staging a World Series between the two leagues. After heated debate it was agreed that players who had jumped to Mexico and wanted to return would be granted amnesty if they paid a $100 fine and returned before May 1. It was also agreed that Satchel Paige would be eligible for the All-Star game, although Effa Manley protested as she steadfastly maintained Paige had violated his contract and league rules. A motion was passed that all teams in the associated Negro Leagues would be banned from playing the Ethiopian Clowns team. The Ethiopian Clowns had advertised themselves as "Colored World Champions," a claim not backed by either league. Owner Syd Pollock and the Clowns were also accused of violating league contracts by raiding signed players. The name and the antics of the team remained a sore spot with most of the owners who considered it an insult.[6]

Among those not amused by the Clowns was Negro American League president Dr. J. B. Martin. Doc Martin was a pharmacist/entrepreneur from Memphis. He had operated a drugstore and a funeral home and dealt real estate in Memphis's black community. Doc J.B. Martin, joined by brothers Dr. B. B. Martin and Dr. William Martin, approached baseball as another business proposition. The Memphis Red Sox were notoriously cheap when it came to paying players, however the team was one of the more stable franchises in black baseball during the Great Depression era. In 1940, the influential Dr. J.B. Martin ran afoul of the Memphis mayor/strongman "Boss" Ed Crump. After facing repeated harassment from Memphis city hall, J.B. Martin picked up and moved to Chicago in 1941. Relying on shrewd business skills, Doc Martin would prosper in Chicago. In years to come he would create a business empire that eventually came to include a firm hold on Chicago's black baseball enterprise.

The Windy City remained black baseball's capital city, home to the sacred cash cow of the annual All-Star game, home to the Negro American League president and the so-called "commissioner" of black baseball. The commissioner of black baseball was a community elder, former alderman Major R. R. Jackson, whose involvement in Chicago black baseball went all the way back to the Chicago Unions of 1889. Major Jackson was an "unpaid volunteer" who offered to arbitrate differences between the NNL and NAL; however the eastern based Negro National League never recognized him. Paradoxically, the hometown team of black baseball's mecca did not have the most basic necessity — a playing field. The American Giants had been through this before in 1933 when their ballpark was turned into a dog track.

Majority owner Horace Hall was nonchalant about the lack of a ballpark. The commissioner and NAL president were similarly unconcerned. There were sketchy plans to rebuild the park, but no urgency. Frank Young of the *Defender* was enraged and wrote: "we have a ballpark which wouldn't be a credit to the Negroes of Chittlin Switch, Mississippi." One group of investors got together to rebuild the park but were scared off when they found out that the American Giants still owed $2,800 in back taxes on tickets. Another proposal was made to build a park from the ground up, if NNL president J.B. Martin would guarantee the authorization of a brand new franchise in Chicago— Martin refused. The American Giant brain-trust came up with a solution, which was simply to rent Comiskey Park for a few engagements and otherwise send the team out on the road.[7]

The return of key personnel made the American Giants a respectable baseball team once again. "Candy" Jim Taylor was brought back to manage the team in 1941. Willie Cornelius and Pepper Bassett came back from Mexico, which instantly restored the team's credibility. The American Giants welcomed back third baseman Alec Radcliffe from the Palmer House team and also obtained pitcher Ted Alexander, formerly of the Palmer House team. Jimmy Crutchfield, a one-time fixture with the Pittsburgh Crawfords, took last year's player/manager Wilson Redus's spot in the outfield. The American Giants also signed a kid from Memphis named Art Pennington to play outfield who turned out to be a real find. Other new faces included pitchers Charles "Lefty" Shields and Gentry Jessup, who would become regular starters for the American Giants in the years to come. The American Giants were vastly improved in 1941 from 1940, although they still had a long way to go to compete with their chief rival the Kansas City Monarchs. Candy Jim took the team down to Florida to get into shape for the season — whatever it might bring.

The American Giants met the Monarchs for the home opener at Comiskey on May 18, 1941. Singer/actress Ethel Waters threw out the first pitch and sang before the game. Satchel Paige pitched a complete game for the Monarchs, winning by a 3–1 score over Willie Cornelius. Renting Comiskey was more expensive and that cost was passed on in the way of higher ticket prices, which created the risk that fewer fans would attend. Game promoters tried to lure fans in by adding an attraction or reason to attend the game. The American Giants would play only four home dates in 1941. Ethel Waters was featured for

1941 Chicago American Giants. From left to right, (front row) Oscar Boone, John Lyles, Curtis Henderson, Candy Jim Taylor, Jimmie Crutchfield, Bill Horne, and Sug Cornelius; (back row) Willie Ferrell, Henry "Speed" Merchant, Don Reeves, Willie Hudson, unidentified, Lloyd "Pepper" Bassett, Alvin Gipson, Art Pennington and Ted Alexander (photograph courtesy NoirTech Research, Inc.).

the chilly opener, a week later the double-header against St. Louis was called "Rube Foster day." A double-header with Memphis in June was supposedly a benefit for the "Big Brother Club of Chicago." The season-ending home game on August 31 versus the KC Monarchs and Satchel Paige was a benefit for the Provident Hospital. The crowds for these games were smaller than hoped and it wasn't at all clear to what extent the charities actually benefited. Frank Young commented that "[O]n what was billed as 'Rube Foster day' folk who came out would have stayed home if they knew that all Mrs. Sarah Foster, widow of the Rube Foster who built Negro baseball, received was a bouquet of flowers."[8]

An overflow crowd of some 51,000 did attend the East-West All-Star game at Comiskey. For the first time since 1936 Satchel Paige showed up at the August Classic — a two inning relief appearance for the West. The Eastern squad included Roy Campanella, Monte Irvin and Buck Leonard. Four American Giants were included on the Western squad: Jimmy Crutchfield, Pepper Basset, Billy Horne and Willie Hudson. The East won the game by an 8–3 score.

The American Giants played a number of games on neutral fields. They played the New York Black Yankees at Indianapolis, the St. Louis Stars at Cincinnati's Crosley Field, the Jacksonville Red Caps in Terre Haute, Indiana. They also met archrival Kansas City in Terre Haute, Canton, Huntington, West Virginia, and in Detroit. The game against Kansas City held at Detroit's Briggs Stadium, in which Satchel Paige pitched KC to an

11–4 win, brought out 39,500 fans, one of the largest crowds ever to see a Negro League game in the Motor City.

The 1941 season was a great success when compared to the failures of the 1940 season. Improving economic conditions and the presence of Satchel Paige were factors in bringing out large crowds to NAL games at major league parks in Chicago, Detroit and Cincinnati. There was quite a contrast between games where a major league facility was packed to the brim and the typical Sunday crowds of the rickety old wooden ballparks.

This taste of success fueled the American Giants' aspirations to achieve a big league atmosphere. Outspoken writers calling for integration of major league baseball like Lester Rodney of the *Daily Worker*, Wendell Smith of the *Pittsburgh Courier*, Jimmy Powers of the *New York Daily News*, Shirley Povich of the *Washington Post* and Sam Lacy of the Baltimore *Afro-American*, among others, were determined to see changes come about.

The American Giants lost two notable former players in 1941. Legendary catcher Bruce Petway passed away July 4, 1941. Walter "Steel Arm" Davis, a dependable hitter for the American Giants from 1924 to 1935, was shot to death in an altercation at a tavern on Chicago's South State Street on November 30, 1941.

The U.S. began to make preparations for the possibility of being drawn into war,

East-West All-Star game 1941: 50,485 turned out to see Satchel Paige pitch. Satch pitched only a couple of innings and his Western squad went down to an 8–3 loss. There is no question that Chicago was the most important city in black baseball, especially so after the establishment of the annual East-West All-Star game in 1933. The classic was played from 1933 to 1960 (photograph courtesy NoirTech Research, Inc.).

and the military draft was instituted. A build up in defense-related industries was under way and the issue of discrimination against black workers came to the forefront. Pioneering black labor leader Asa Philip Randolph (founder of the Brotherhood of Sleeping Car Porters—who had successfully negotiated a contract with the Pullman Company in 1937) threatened to organize a massive strike and march on Washington if the federal government did not act to end discrimination in the defense industry. President Franklin Roosevelt responded by issuing Executive Order #8802 on June 25, 1941, which prohibited discrimination in the defense industry. The time was ripe for change — and the biggest of them came about on December 7, 1941, when the U.S. was drawn in to World War II.

1942

World War II changed everything. The country went back to work during World War II, building ships, aircraft, armored vehicles and weapons. Chicago was a natural center for the wartime boom. Workers were needed in factories, soldiers were recruited, trained and shipped out. African Americans made up part of this work force, although they had to fight bigotry just to get thankless jobs in service to the country. An important part of the top secret Manhattan Project was undertaken in Chicago, when Italian physicist Enrico Fermi successfully created the first controlled nuclear reaction at a secret lab under the bleachers at Stagg Field at the University of Chicago on December 2, 1942.

When the war escalated there was some question whether or not professional baseball at any level would be played. The Office of Defense Transportation (ODT) asked teams to reduce travel. Rationing of gas and rubber, which was necessary for the team buses, went into effect. The lights were dimmed in stadiums to guard against the possibility of enemy pilots bombing American cities. However, Franklin Roosevelt himself came out in favor of keeping baseball going in a letter he wrote to Commissioner Kenesaw Mountain Landis. In what was dubbed the "Green Light Letter" Roosevelt wrote:

> I honestly feel that it would be best for the country to keep baseball going. There will be fewer people unemployed and everybody will work longer hours and harder than ever before. And that means that they ought to have a chance for recreation and for taking their minds off their work even more than before. Baseball provides a recreation which does not last over two hours or two hours and a half, and which can be got for very little cost.[9]

Roosevelt was speaking primarily of the recreational value of major league baseball, but he had earlier affirmed by executive order the rights of blacks to work in the defense industry — the right to recreate was assumed. The Negro Leagues were also granted grace and allowed to continue. Black baseball sported a higher profile in the forties. National magazines glamorized Satchel Paige and he became the first black baseball player whose name became a household word. Fans came out to the ballpark for entertainment in great numbers during the forties, just as Roosevelt had suggested. The changed economic environment was a by-product of the global war, which gave Negro League baseball a much-needed shot in the arm. Those activists pushing for integration in the major leagues latched on like bulldogs to a prowler. Their steadfast determination embodied the American Spirit, a manifest destiny of full integration. The already convincing arguments laid out against baseball's color line were framed against the background of a war against racism in which Americans of all ethnic backgrounds were killed.

In March of 1942 Kansas City Monarchs Jackie Robinson and Nate Moreland, accompanied by a writer from the *Pittsburgh Courier*, asked Jimmie Dykes, the manager of the Chicago White Sox, for a tryout at the White Sox training camp in Pasadena. Dykes agreed to let them work out and he had some complimentary things to say about Jackie and Nate, but in the end rebuffed the pair. Dykes stated, "The matter is out of the hands of us managers…. We are powerless to act … it is strictly up to the club owners and Judge Landis." This episode proved, as the *Pittsburgh Courier* had theorized, that the color line existed even though it might not have been written into the by-laws of major league baseball. History might have been different if Jimmy Dykes and the White Sox organization had gotten behind an effort to sign Jackie Robinson. History might also have been different if Cap Anson had not protested against George Stovey in 1887, if Charles Comiskey had not protested the signing of Charles Grant in 1902, or if Kenesaw Mountain Landis had negotiated with Rube Foster.

The American Giants started off the 1942 season on a positive note when Candy Jim Taylor was successful in signing 39-year-old Cool Papa Bell. Cool had played in the Mexican League since 1938, where he was one of the top players in the league. He had been one of the top players in the United States prior to going to Mexico. Cool Papa Bell was the first big name player to play for with the American Giants since the days of Turkey Stearnes and Willie Foster.[10]

The improved American Giants went south for spring training, as was the normal routine, although some major league teams stayed closer to home for spring workouts due to wartime restrictions. Talk of building a new ballpark, which had been rumored a year earlier, ceased. The American Giants were resigned to renting Comiskey for a few dates during the year and otherwise playing on the road.

The American Giants had an okay team in 1942; in addition to Cool Papa Bell, Alec Radcliffe rejoined the team and pitcher Leroy Sutton added some depth in the rotation. The American Giants were no match for the Kansas City Monarchs who had a devastating pitching staff that included Satchel Paige, Hilton Smith and Clifford "Connie" Johnson. The Monarchs also had soft-spoken steady hitting first baseman John "Buck" O'Neil providing on-field leadership. Many years later, in 1962, Buck O'Neil came to the Windy City as coach for the Chicago Cubs; he was the first black coach in the majors. The Monarchs ran roughshod over the rest of the NAL field and swept the Homestead Grays in the so-called Negro League World Series.

The functional integrity of the Negro Leagues remained in decline, despite the fact that the owners and league officials stayed busy. Fines were imposed on players who had jumped to Mexico. League teams were prohibited from playing the Ethiopian Clowns, whose antics were judged detrimental to Negro League baseball. Rulings came down from high on a regular basis. The Negro Leagues worked with the Office of Defense Transportation to keep the turnstiles open, proving they had legitimacy in the eyes of the federal government. In 1942, for the first time since 1927, there was a Negro League World Series between the eastern and western leagues, though the pennant race leading to the series was virtually non-existent. Organized black baseball, led by Tom Wilson, president of the Negro National League, and Doc J. B. Martin, president of the Negro American League, had some successes in 1942; yet the most basic functions of any athletic league, such as schedules, standings and statistics, went neglected.

The regular season games became mere interludes to the big exhibition games. On May 10, 1942, the Chicago American Giants opened up their home season with a double-header against the Kansas City Monarchs at Comiskey Park. World heavyweight champion Joe Louis's wife Marva Louis threw out the first pitch, Bill Bojangles Robinson demonstrated his ability to run backwards around the base paths, and Dave Malarcher's wife Mable Malarcher sang the National Anthem. A nice crowd braved the chilly weather to see Hilton Smith and Satchel Paige take the two games from the home crowd. This glitzy big-tent style with added attractions had begun to displace the old style tug-of-wars played in dusty parks as the image of Negro League baseball.

Whenever well known white major league players were thrown into the mix the crowds were even larger. A crowd of 30,000 turned out on May 24, 1942, when Satchel Paige and the Kansas City Monarchs visited the friendly confines of Wrigley Field to face off against Dizzy Dean and his former major league All-Stars. Bob Feller was among those big leaguers that were announced, but at the last minute Feller was required by the U.S. Navy and missed the game. Wrigley Field on Chicago's North Side had previously been off-limits to Negro League teams. The change in policy, brokered by promoter Abe Saperstein, was a sign that the color line was weakening.

A local activist group calling themselves the Citizen Committee for Negroes in the Big Leagues targeted Chicagoans Philip Wrigley and Kenesaw Mountain Landis. The bi-racial committee included Catholic Bishop Bernard Sheil and longtime *Defender* sportswriter Frank Young, as well as local judges and politicians. Put on the spot, the "chewing gum king" went so far as to predict "Negroes will be in the big leagues — and soon. That is a certainty."

After being petitioned and addressed loudly in the press by Lester Rodney of the *New York Daily Worker*, Commissioner Landis directly addressed baseball's race issue, stating: "There is no rule against major league clubs hiring Negro baseball players ... Negroes are not barred from organized baseball by the commission and have never been since the 21 years I have served."

Landis's words rang empty but events of 1942 signaled a change in major league baseball's attitude. The Pittsburgh Pirates and Cleveland Indians said that they would arrange for tryouts of black players, although they later reneged on the commitment. Increasingly, average white Americans became aware of the injustice of baseball's color line and cared enough to give at least lip service to the cause of ending it.[11]

1943

During World War II attendance increased and owners saw the unfamiliar sight of black ink on the bottom line. Efforts to bring down the color line in 1942 did not yield immediate results but prospects of an integrated major league entered the realm of possibility — even probability. Black baseball was in uncharted waters. Negro American League president and American Giants' part owner Doc J.B. Martin worried well in advance what would happen to the business side of Negro League baseball if the color line should fall. Ironically the Negro League owners had an interest in maintaining the status quo. Big league owners also profited from the increased interest in the Negro Leagues because they rented out major league parks.

It was surprising that black baseball prospered, as it looked as if the war might shut down the league altogether. The ODT issued a new order banning the use of private buses for the transportation of baseball teams in order to conserve gas and rubber supplies. Doc Martin flew to Washington, D.C., to meet with Joseph Eastman, director of the ODT, to plead for an exception to the order for Negro League baseball. Homestead Grays owner Cum Posey and Washington Senators owner Clark Griffith, who had arranged the meeting with Eastman, joined Martin. The teams of the East had less at stake than the NAL, because the teams were grouped closer together with ready access to railways. Martin returned from the meetings confident that the ODT would grant an exception, however a few weeks later Martin received a telegram from Eastman stating:[12]

> After full consideration of your request of special consideration of *general order ODT 10-A.* Regret to advise special busses cannot be made available for transportation of baseball teams during coming season. Urge your cooperation in utilization of existing transportation services to make possible continuous operation of league.... Joseph Eastman.[13]

The Negro American League decided to go ahead with baseball with the idea that the schedule would be consolidated and that trains and commercial bus lines would be utilized if necessary. The owners met at Chicago's Hotel Grand to draw up the schedule. The Negro American League of 1943 included clubs from Kansas City, New Orleans, Birmingham, Memphis, Cleveland, and Chicago, and for the first time the Ethiopian Clowns (known as the Cincinnati Clowns) were granted official status as a NAL member. As a precondition to joining the league the Clowns agreed to drop the painted faces and minstrel acts, however after a short time the Clowns defied the league and went back to using a comedy routine during league games. Travel by train would be very expensive, travel by bus—especially in the South—was impractical. Doc Martin was joined by other owners, particularly the ownership of the far flung Kansas City Monarchs, in lobbying the ODT for relief from travel restrictions. Kansas City marshaled different resources including a large petition drive and the help of Senator Harry S. Truman to pressure government. Eastman and the ODT initially refused to budge but midway through the season did offer relief. The ODT formally acknowledged that the NAL faced difficulties using public transportation in the South when granting an exception for the NAL to use buses for travel of 2,000 miles per month. Among the arguments that had weight with the ODT was the economical recreational value of baseball referred to by Franklin Roosevelt in his letter to major league baseball.[14]

The mere acknowledgement by the U.S. government of the cultural value of Negro League baseball was a landmark. Negro League baseball would gain even more status from the U.S. government when, on July 17, 1943, the Army dedicated a new baseball field at Fort Huachuca in honor of Rube Foster. Rube's widow Sarah Foster was present along with Brigadier General Benjamin O. Davis for the dedication of Rube Foster Memorial Field. Fort Huachuca was the traditional base of the Buffalo Soldiers and was the home of the 93rd Infantry—the first black division activated in World War II. More than 15,000 fans packed into the stadium to watch the Fort Huachuca Service Command team play the 92nd Division team. It was a simple gesture, but a pleasing one to the legions who remembered Rube.[15]

A number of Negro League players were sent off to fight in World War II, most notably for the American Giants was All-Star outfielder Jimmy Crutchfield. Candy Jim Taylor

Ted "Double Duty" Radcliffe: born July 7, 1902 — died August 11, 2005. "Candy Jim" Taylor: born February 1, 1884 — died April 3, 1948. Double Duty was one of the most interesting characters to come out of the Negro Leagues. He generously shared his Negro League experiences with several generations of fans. Candy Jim's career stretched almost the whole breadth of segregated baseball — much of it with Chicago. The young woman's identity is unknown (photograph courtesy NoirTech Research, Inc.).

did not return to manage the American Giants in 1943; instead he ended up as manager of the Homestead Grays. Cool Papa Bell also ended up with the Homestead Grays, the result of a trade in which the American Giants received Lloyd Davenport from the Cincinnati Buckeyes and Ted Radcliffe from the Memphis Red Sox. Bell was supposed to join the Red Sox but jumped to the Grays. The Homestead Grays of 1943 had a dominating lineup including, along with Cool Papa Bell, Josh Gibson, Buck Leonard, Sam Bankhead, Jud Wilson, Roy Partlow and Ray Brown.

"Double Duty" Radcliffe was named player/manager of the American Giants, but he had his work cut out for him. Jimmy Crutchfield and Cool Papa Bell had been the two best players on the team. Outfielders Lloyd "Ducky" Davenport and Art "Superman" Pennington took over as the top offensive assets on the team. The third outfielder was John Bissant who had been with the team off and on for a couple of years but was now in a starting role. In the pitching department the American Giants were still forced to rely heavily on the aging Sug Cornelius who had carried the franchise through most of the previous decade. Gentry Jessup was the ace on the staff; Leroy Sutton and Charlie "Lefty" Shields rounded out the rotation. (Shields had tried to jump to the Homestead Grays but was ordered back to the American Giants by league officials.) Ralph Wyatt was the regular shortstop. The keystone position was a revolving door handled by Bill Charter, Henry Smith and Herbert Buster. Ed " Pep" Young — one of the more tenured American Giants — played first base. Double Duty's brother Alec Radcliffe anchored the infield at third base and Duty himself was the primary catcher during the 1943 season.

The American Giants' season was highlighted by a victory over the Great Lakes Naval Station team and a night game played at Comiskey Park. The Great Lakes Naval Training Station Blue Jackets were managed by Hall of Fame catcher Mickey Cochrane; Johnny Mize — also a Hall of Famer — played first base along with a number of quality major league players. Gentry Jessup pitched for the American Giants and took the Blue Jackets by surprise, winning 7–3 as the American Giants amassed 19 hits against the major league pitching. About 10,000 fans attended the game held north of Chicago, only a small contingent among them American Giant backers. On the evening of September 2, 1943, the American Giants suffered a 2–0 loss against the Memphis Red Sox under the lights at Comiskey Park. It was the first time the American Giants had played a night game at Comiskey.[16]

The team was respectable but still no match for the dominating Kansas City Monarchs or the Homestead Grays. The Monarchs of 1943 were sidetracked by both the transportation situation and the loss of several top players to the armed forces, but still shut out the American Giants back-to-back when the teams met for a two game series. The American Giants finished the season below the .500 mark and were challenged by all the teams in the NAL. In the abbreviated war-time season the American Giants managed to qualify for a five game playoff against the Birmingham Black Barons to see which team would represent the NAL in a post-season match against the NNL champion Homestead Grays, but lost two games to three. The rules for the championship series were altered to allow American Giants Double Duty Radcliffe and Gentry Jessup to play for the Birmingham Black Barons while shortstop Ralph Wyatt was loaned to the Homestead Grays in an attempt to make things look equal. Candy Jim and the Grays, behind the hitting of Josh Gibson, won the series four games to three.

The far-reaching effects of the war framed the summer of 1943. The saying "Double V," victory at home and abroad, was the call to action for black America. Fairness in employment and housing were two of the major issues at home. On June 23, 1943, a race riot broke out in Detroit in which 34 people were killed. The riot was the result of crowding, housing discrimination and unfair labor practices inflicted on the thousands of blacks who had immigrated to Detroit during the wartime buildup. The American Giants played a double-header against the Memphis Reds for the benefit of the NAACP at Comiskey Park on September 5. During the 1940's the NAACP saw enormous growth in its membership. The association cooperated with the Congress of Industrial Organizations (CIO) in an effort to win jobs for black Americans. The NAACP also lobbied Eleanor Roosevelt and Franklin Roosevelt to integrate the armed forces.

Black baseball served its purpose as an escape from the trying conditions on the home front in black America. Some 51,700 fans showed up for the Negro League All-Star game held August 1 at Comiskey. Satchel Paige led the West to a 2–1 victory; Double

Duty Radcliffe, Alec Radcliffe and Lloyd "Ducky" Davenport represented the American Giants on the Western squad. On July 18th a four team double-header was played at Wrigley, billed as "Satchel Paige Day," before about 25,000 fans. Satchel pitched for the Memphis Red Sox in an exhibition game against the New York Cubans. Satchel was loaned to Memphis for the game, which put some money into the coffers of the struggling franchise. Doc J.B. Martin's brothers W. S. Martin and B. B. Martin owned the Memphis team — the game did not count in the official standings and no ethical questions were raised. Then again on August 14 a four team double-header was played at Wrigley Field. The first game featured Satchel Paige and the K.C. Monarchs against the Cleveland Buckeyes and hard-hitting Sam Jethroe. The second game was a contest between the Memphis Red Sox and the Birmingham Black Barons.[17]

Standing-room-only crowds notwithstanding, baseball was a mere pass-time; the battle for civil rights for African Americans was front and center. Among the gestures toward the Negro League establishment during the 1943 season were acknowledgment from the ODT, the dedication of Rube Foster Field at Ft. Huachuca, a night game held at Comiskey and a series of Negro League games held at Wrigley. However there was no follow-up to the specific matter of the proposed tryouts for Negro League players that were supposed to have taken place the previous season. To the growing coalition of activist sports writers like Lester Rodney, Wendell Smith, Frank A. Young, Ira Lewis, Sam Lacy, Rollo Wilson, Dan Burley, Chester Franklin and others, the slight from major league baseball in regards to the tryouts was disturbing. The goal was to have the doors to major league baseball open soon, and to that end it was important to know whether the friendly gestures toward the Negro Leagues were sincere or patronizing.

The activist coalition did have a breakthrough however when a delegation was seated for the annual meeting of organized baseball. John Sengstake, general manager of the *Chicago Defender*, Judge Kenesaw Mountain Landis, Paul Robeson, and several leading black sportswriters were among those who attended. This was more than a gesture, it was a meeting that specifically addressed the color line in baseball. Landis went on record in regard to the color line, stating:

> I do reiterate what I said in June 1942, that there is not now, nor has there ever been any baseball rule — written or unwritten — prohibiting the use of Negroes in organized baseball. This is the first time such a question has been brought into the open and I don't know what might come of it. I do know that the step is a healthy one and should clear the air for all concerned.

The usually reserved John Sengstake did not mince words in his presentation to the gathering:

> Organized baseball's unwritten but effective practice of exclusion, against some players because of their color helps to spread the "master race" theory among Americans on a mass basis. If the principles, which our committee will present, are accepted by your great body of distinguished and respected Americans, America will be moving toward a larger strength for our great nation. One of our basic strengths, I believe, is in the readiness of Americans to meet squarely their obligations and to unite. Unity is the demand of the hour. It is our belief that no organization, truly representative of the American philosophy of fair play, can justify any bars, either psychological or real, which are predicated upon color, race, creed or national origin.[18]

The meeting gave a platform for many of the age-old arguments against the color line which had long been ignored by major league baseball. The subject of what would happen to the Negro Leagues in the event of integration was also broached. However there was no finding or end result to the meeting, much less a commitment to integrate the major leagues. In Chicago the local Committee for the Integration of Negroes in White Major League Baseball met with Cubs owner Philip Wrigley for the second year in a row. Wrigley, employer of a large number of blacks in his chewing gum factories, stated that the Chicago Cubs "would scout Negro ball players this coming season to watch the play in the Negro Leagues in order to get first hand information." Wrigley also admitted that he personally thought it was inevitable that major league baseball would integrate, but qualified that, saying "I don't think the time is ripe now. The middle of the war isn't the spot to make such a departure from custom."[19]

1944

By 1944 Doc J.B. Martin's takeover of the American Giants and the NAL apparatus in Chicago was complete. When he first arrived in Chicago in 1941, in addition to being the president of the NAL, he was referred to as a part-owner of the American Giants. In 1943 he held the title of secretary-treasurer of the Chicago American Giants; by 1944 he was both president and owner of the American Giants as well as NAL president. Martin, like Horace Hall and Rube Foster before him, had consolidated power as both owner and head of the league. Unlike Rube Foster, Doc Martin did not play baseball and he clearly put his business interests first. Also unlike Rube Foster, Doc Martin was never accused of using his position to unfairly benefit the American Giants. The reason those accusations were never leveled was because the team's performance on his watch was so lackluster suspicion was never warranted. The tycoon's relationship with the team personnel was sometimes cold and distant. The players responded in kind and were not particularly thrilled to play for the American Giants. Those who challenged his authority met with a swift axe. There were occasional locker room jokes and barbs pointed at those who played for the rich doctor.

Doc Martin was a hard boss to work for, but he was also the man who rescued the American Giants from possible demise. The team had struggled mightily during the 1930's following Rube's death. After South Side Park burned, there was no telling what might have become of the American Giants without Martin's injection of cash. Martin was never very well liked—certainly never lionized like Rube Foster, but there was a tacit understanding that Martin was the right man to head the American Giants.

Doctor J.B. Martin's administration by iron fist set the tone for the remaining existence of the American Giants franchise. Shortly before the 1944 season, negotiations between Doc Martin and manager Ted "Double Duty" Radcliffe broke off. Double Duty headed for Birmingham and the American Giants received pitcher Gready McKinnis from the Black Barons in the deal. Ted's brother Alec expressed interest in managing the team; he was the elder statesman on the team and felt that he should be the heir apparent for the managership. When Alec Radcliffe, who had signed as a third baseman, was not offered the position he responded by leaving the team. Mound veteran Willie "Sug" Cornelius was offered the job, but he reported to the U.S. Army during the off-season. Finally, just before the season was to begin, the crafty sage Bingo DeMoss was signed to manage the American Giants. DeMoss's tenure didn't last long in this go-round as American Giant skipper; by mid–June he was dismissed at the behest of business manager R. S. Simmons. DeMoss was replaced by the latest American Giant hotshot, Lloyd "Ducky" Davenport.[20]

Jimmie Crutchfield concluded his service with the army and rejoined the American Giants in the outfield. Pitching was handled by Gentry Jessup, Leroy Sutton and Gready McKinnis. Gentry Jessup emerged as the marquee pitcher for the American Giants of the 1940's, following in the long lineage of heavy duty American Giant hurlers of previous decades that included Sug Cornelius, Willie Foster, George Harney, Frank Wickware and Rube Foster.

Ducky Davenport, Gready McKinnis and Gentry Jessup were named to the Western squad for the All-Star game. Gentry Jessup wound up being the winning pitcher in the 7–4 win over the East. The 1944 All-Star game was in danger of being cancelled when the Eastern squad threatened to strike unless their pay was increased. Satchel Paige demanded that he be paid more than the other players, or else he would not play. The game organizers relented and increased the players' pay, but Satch was not appeased and did not play.

Shortly after the All-Star game Ducky Davenport, along with Art Pennington and Gready McKinnis, decided to accept advance money from Gus Greenlee to play on his reconstituted Pittsburgh Crawfords. Once he caught wind of the contract violation and disloyalty, J.B. Martin dealt Davenport to Cleveland, then suspended Pennington and McKinnis. Outfielder John Bissant was named player/manager. The team went through four managers in less than a year, a sign of just how shaky the team had become.[21]

The news that Cubs owner Philip Wrigley planned to actively scout the Negro Leagues during the 1944 season created some anticipation. There was a bit of skepticism as to whether or not Wrigley would follow through, and it seemed unlikely that the color line would fall on the North Side of Chicago before it did on the South Side. Wrigley didn't have to go far to see the best talent in the Negro Leagues—for the third year in a row Satchel Paige and the Monarchs played at Wrigley Field. The best players in Negro League baseball were showcased and scouted at Wrigley, but the Cubs were in no hurry to hire an eligible black candidate.

The Cubs went to the World Series in 1945 for the first time since 1908, but lost to the Detroit Tigers after being up two games to one with four games to play at Wrigley. That series was later remembered for the "Curse of the Billy Goat." The supposed curse came about when longtime Cubs fan William Sianis brought his pet billy goat to the World Series game, was kicked out, and stated "Cubs not going to win anymore." As it turned out the Cubs did not get back to the World Series in the twentieth century. The color line would not drop at Addison and Clark until 1953 when Ernie Banks and Gene Baker joined the Cubbies.

Fans began to suspect that Negro League owners shared an interest in keeping baseball racially divided. Major league baseball not only did not grant tryouts to black players, as promised in 1942, they actually poured salt into the wounds of bigotry by hiring under-qualified players to shore up teams during the war. The Cincinnati Reds, for instance, hired 15-year-old pitcher Joe Nuxhall. Meanwhile the likes of Satchel Paige, Hilton Smith and Don Newcombe could have been tapped from the Negro Leagues. The American Giants saw a number of wartime players too. Herbert Barnhill, catcher, Kendal Felder, infielder, and Willie "Brooks" Wells Jr., shortstop/outfielder, were among the new players to spend some time with the American Giants in 1944.

On November 25, 1944, after a long illness, MLB commissioner Judge Kenesaw Mountain Landis died of a heart attack. Landis was widely lauded as the man who saved major league baseball following the 1919 Black Sox scandal. For the 24 years of his tenure as commissioner he dodged the question of the color line in baseball. Ironically his *New York Times* obituary headlined that he "Freed Slave Athletes," a reference to his rulings which limited the practice of keeping qualified major league players in a team's farm system. In the black community Landis was better known for preventing major league teams from playing barnstorming games against Negro League teams.[22]

There was a bit of irony in the fact that co-existing within the Chicago community there was the bulwark of Negro League baseball as well as the heavy handed major league commissioner often working against each other. In 1942, Landis had made a somewhat disingenuous statement that "there was no color line in baseball." A year previous to his death he met with the Negro Newspaper Publishers Association to discuss the proposition for the first time. Some of Landis's critics laid the color-line issue at his feet and hoped that after his passing progress might be made.

1945

Major league baseball's foot dragging had gone on for two years after the Pittsburgh Pirates and Cleveland Indians had promised to arrange tryouts of qualified black players. Public statements from the likes of Kenesaw Landis, Philip Wrigley, and Clark Griffith as well as acknowledgement from the executive branch of the U.S. government had teased advocates of integrated baseball with a few crumbs of hope. When the rites of spring came in 1945 the sense of anticipation was double — not only was there baseball, but there was also some measurable progress in putting down Jim Crow. The fight against racism at home and abroad produced results. The New York State legislature passed the Ives-Quinn act, which specifically prohibited employers from refusing employment because of race, creed, color or national origin. The passage of the law was aimed primarily at the defense industry, but was pounced on by activists as a way of forcing MLB owners to open their training camps.

On April 6, 1945, Dave "Showboat" Thomas of the New York Cubans and Terris McDuffie of the Newark Eagles showed up unannounced for tryouts at the Brooklyn Dodger training camp in Bear Mountain, New York. The two players were accompanied by activist sportswriters Joe Bostic of Harlem's *Peoples Voice* and Nat Low of the *New York Daily Worker*, both considered Communist newspapers—who were sure to get a story one way or another. Unbeknownst to Bostic and Low, Branch Rickey actually was scouting black players at the time. Rickey was taken aback by what he saw as an ambush, but in the end he allowed the two players to work out. "Showboat" Thomas and "Elmer the Great" McDuffie suited up in Dodger uniforms and worked out under the watchful eyes of Branch Rickey and Leo Durocher. Thomas and McDuffie were older veteran players, perhaps capable of playing at the major league level, but were not seriously considered for the Dodgers.[23]

A few days later, on April 16, Jackie Robinson (KC Monarch shortstop), Sam Jethroe (Cleveland Buckeye outfielder) and Marvin Williams (Philadelphia Star second baseman) were to work out at Boston's Fenway Park. This wasn't so much a tryout as it was an exhibition. The tryout was delayed by a couple of days due to the death of President Franklin Roosevelt on April 12. The Red Sox had no intention of hiring a black player, but agreed to stage the "tryout" as the key bargaining chip in gaining the approval of a Boston city councilman to play baseball on Sundays. The Red Sox, long cursed for allowing Babe Ruth to slip through their hands, passed on Jackie Robinson and ended up being the very last major league team to integrate, in 1959, when infielder "Pumpsie" Green was brought up.

On April 24, 1945, Kentucky senator Albert "Happy" Chandler was elected to replace Kenesaw Landis as the commissioner of major league baseball. Chandler told the *Chicago Defender*, "I don't believe in barring Negroes from baseball, just because they are Negroes. I believe all players should be given a chance to prove their prowess and be given tryouts for the big leagues."[24]

On April 30 Nazi dictator Adolf Hitler committed suicide, signaling the German surrender, which came on May 8. On the same day as Germany's surrender the *New York Times* ran a story about the formation of the United States Negro Baseball League. The press conference announcing the league was given at Brooklyn Dodger president Branch Rickey's office. Apparently insensitive to the half-century struggle of Negro League baseball, Rickey used the press conference as an opportunity to take a cheap shot at established Negro Leagues. Rickey bashed the NAL/NNL as a "disorganized operation without by-laws, schedules and written contracts." While Branch Rickey claimed he had nothing to do with the USL other than as the operator of Ebbets Field, he was secretly working behind the scenes on a plan to procure the best black players for the Brooklyn Dodgers.[25]

The USL was nothing new, it was the brainchild of Gus Greenlee who had been hankering to get back into baseball after the collapse of his powerful Pittsburgh Crawfords back in 1938. The league consisted of six marginal franchises: the Pittsburgh Crawfords, Detroit Motor City Giants, Philadelphia/Hilldale Daisies, St. Louis Stars, Atlanta Black Crackers and Chicago Brown Bombers. The Hilldale-Philadelphia team, which was moved to Brooklyn, was coached by legend Oscar Charleston and one-time American Giant pitcher Webster MacDonald. Bingo DeMoss was the coach of the Chicago Brown Bombers. The commissioner of the league was John Shackleford, formerly a third baseman for the American Giants back in 1926, who gone on to practice law in Cleveland. The teams of the USL were routinely described as "semi-pros" by the black press.

The criticisms Rickey leveled at the established Negro Leagues were all true and well known, but even casual observers were aware of the new league's shortcomings. Problems with scheduling, statistics, contracts did not go away. Even as the writing on the wall began to read that integration was coming and that Negro League owners had best get their house in order — very little changed. In fact in some instances things had gotten worse. Players tried to jump from team to team, Satchel Paige refused to pitch in the All-Star game, Josh Gibson was suspended, and worse yet there was a series of violent outbreaks at ballparks in 1945. On June 17, in a game at Wrigley Field between the Memphis Red Sox and Indianapolis Clowns, a near riot broke out after Memphis' third baseman, upset at being called out, struck an umpire. The management decided to raise the rental fee at the friendly confines to a not so friendly $5,000, which effectively priced Negro League teams out. The incident at Wrigley was one in a string of many, in fact on the very same day several American Giant players charged an umpire who got confused and called a force out at home safe. A month later, on July 17, Birmingham infielder Piper Davis was suspended, fined and banished from the All-Star game after he attacked an umpire in Cleveland after a close call.[26]

The added pressure of major league baseball breathing down the necks of Negro League ball clubs did not seem to help matters. Negro League team owners from both the NAL and NNL thought the time might be right to appoint a truly neutral commissioner. The officials got together in Chicago on June 12 to vote on two different candidates. William Hueston from Gary, Indiana, former president of the old NNL who had succeeded Foster in 1927 had the support of many of the Eastern based NNL teams. The other candidate was Frank Church, a wealthy politician and old friend of Doc Martin's from Memphis. The owners could not come to a consensus and lost valuable time in the effort to prepare for the possibility of integration.[27]

While the spring of 1945 marked historic progress, at the outset of the season there were still questions as to whether or not the ODT would allow teams to travel by bus, and whether or not Uncle Sam would allow men to play baseball rather than fight. The ODT relented and professional baseball was allowed — with certain restrictions. Major league baseball was forced to cancel their annual All-Star game and travel was limited, forcing teams to take spring training close to home. Negro League teams were limited to 2,000 miles of bus travel through Southern states per month.

In 1945 Candy Jim Taylor was back as manager for the third time. He had managed the team from 1941 to 1942 and also from 1937 to 1939. Candy was credited with winning two Negro League championships back to back in 1943 and 1944 while he was the skipper of the Homestead Grays. Although the 61-year-old did have some health problems there was no question that he was a capable manager. The team was a mixture of legitimate major league caliber players, a few grizzled veterans, wartime replacements and true prospects. Pitchers Gentry Jessup and Gready McKinnis led the way for the American Giants in 1945. Art "Superman" Pennington batted in the cleanup position and provided the excitement on the offense. Teenager Clyde McNeal from San Antonio, Texas, spent some time at shortstop — he proved to be more than just a replacement player, years later he joined the Brooklyn Dodger minor league system. Jesse Douglass was at second base, he too later played minor league ball. San Diegan Walter McCoy, fresh out of the army, became a workhorse for the American Giants on the mound and also eventually played minor league ball.

The American Giants held their own in the Negro American League, which consisted of teams in Chicago, Birmingham, Cleveland, Cincinnati/Indianapolis, Memphis and Kansas City. They did not show the flash of champions and were frequent victims of the Cleveland Buckeyes. The Buckeyes, owned by Erie, Pennsylvania, hotelier Ernest Wright, featured hard-hitting outfielder Sam Jethroe and catcher/manager Quincy Trouppe along with former American Giants Archie Ware and Ducky Davenport. Talentwise the American Giants were not that far behind the Buckeyes, but were not able to do the necessary things to give them a run for the money. It was another ho-hum season.

By the mid–1940's the Chicago American Giants baseball team had stopped being competitive from season to season — "just another team" in the words of Frank Young. The local black press complained that management would not put a "first rate club" on the field despite the large patronage at Comiskey Park. Baseball has always been a game textured as much by the endurance of losing as well as the glory of winning. Perhaps the American Giants were affected by their surroundings in the black metropolis. There were more distractions in Chicago than in places like Memphis and Birmingham. Whether it was cabarets, card games, women, theaters, museums or other diversions, whatever the reason, something kept the American Giants back from reaching their old form. The American Giants became lovable losers—haunted by the ghost of Rube Foster.

The American Giants did not have gang-busting stars like Satchel Paige, Jackie Robinson, Monte Irvin, Sam Jethroe or Roy Campanella, though years later a number of the American Giants were signed by major league organizations to play on farm teams—an indication that maybe the talent was better than thought by the peanut gallery.[28]

On Sunday July 29 the annual East West All-Star game was held at Comiskey Park. Pitcher Gentry Jessup was the only American Giant to play in the classic, the shortstop for the West was Jackie Robinson. A few days later, on August 6, an atomic bomb was dropped on Hiroshima, Japan, presaging the end of World War II. On August 24 the Kansas City Monarchs came to Chicago for a double-header. In attendance at the game was Clyde Sukeforth, scouting on behalf of Branch Rickey and the Brooklyn Dodgers—although Rickey told Sukeforth the scouting was for the Brooklyn Brown Dodgers. Rickey requested Sukeforth to report back on Jackie Robinson and inquire about setting up a possible meeting, but Jackie had recently hurt his shoulder and was out of the lineup for the Chicago game. Though Sukeforth was not able see Jackie play that afternoon, he used the opportunity to pass the message that Branch Rickey was interested in meeting him. Since Jackie would have to sit out a few games anyway, Rickey seized on the opportunity and a few days later Jackie Robinson had his historic meeting with Branch Rickey in New York. After Jackie Robinson signed with the Montreal Royals on October 23, 1945, *Chicago Defender* writer Frank Young declared: "Democracy has finally invaded baseball."[29]

Branch Rickey had not negotiated with the owners of the KC Monarchs for the rights to Jackie Robinson, much less paid them. Shortly after agreeing to terms with Jackie Robinson, Branch Rickey rustled pitcher John Wright (who technically wasn't under contract) from the Homestead Grays. Then Rickey had the audacity to snatch catcher Roy Campanella and Donald Newcombe from the Newark Eagles following the 1945 season — claiming they were not under contract for 1946. Now the alarm was rampant that major league baseball would run roughshod over Negro League contracts. As president of the Negro American League, Dr. J.B. Martin became the point man in a crisis that could determine whether or not black baseball would survive. The gravity of the situation meant that his other duties as owner of the American Giants took a back seat.

1946

Doc Martin, along with NNL president Tom Wilson, met with major league baseball commissioner Happy Chandler and NL president Ford Frick at MLB headquarters in Cincinnati's Carew Tower in January of 1946 to discuss ways that the Negro American League could bring their structure in line with major league baseball. Martin returned from the meeting with blank contracts for all team owners worded identically to the major league contracts in hopes that the major league clubs would respect their contracts. Doc Martin actively petitioned executives in major league baseball in an effort to ensure that the Negro Leagues would receive fair treatment. Martin received some support from Clark Griffith and Larry MacPhail, who had a vested interest in maintaining the status quo, and were against seeing Rickey getting a leg up. These efforts didn't hurt matters, but by no means was the crux of the issue addressed. Going forward the relationship with MLB would be a constant battle. When pitcher Roy Partlow was signed by the Dodgers in mid-season the Philadelphia Stars received a $1,000 payment — raising hopes that maybe Negro League baseball might find a way to profit from the integration of the major leagues after all.[30]

While Jackie Robinson and pitcher John Wright worked out with the Montreal Royals and Brooklyn Dodgers in Daytona Beach, the American Giants took a bus to Jackson, Mississippi, for spring training. Candy Jim Taylor was back as manager. Before spring training ended, three key American Giant players — pitcher Gready McKinnis, outfielder Art "Superman" Pennington and infielder Jesse Douglass — turned in their uniforms and hopped a boat for Mexico from New Orleans. In a common modus operandi, agents from the Mexican baseball league secretly approached key players with promises of money. At the time the Mexican millionaire Pasquel brothers were in the midst of a campaign to lure both Negro League and major league players south of the border. Doc Martin immediately announced that the players would be subject to a five-year suspension from Negro League baseball, as was the league rule at the time. Threats from the Mexican leagues, in tandem with the watchful eyes of the major leagues, made Martin's job all the tougher.[31]

Candy Jim shuffled the lineup to deal with the loss. Ed "Pep" Young, a player of average abilities who had been with the American Giants from 1936 to 1942, was back as the cleanup hitter and starting first baseman. Clyde Nelson became the regular third baseman and was one of the top hitters in the Negro American League, which earned him a trip to the All-Star game. Ralph Wyatt, who had been a bright spot on the American Giants during the forties, began the season as the starting shortstop. Wyatt was among those recruited by agents from the Mexican baseball league, but he remained loyal to the American Giants. Wyatt was criticized by the *Chicago Defender* for not running out a ground ball, which resulted in a double play in a situation where the Giants might have been able to score, costing a game to the Birmingham Black Barons. A month later Wyatt refused to accompany the team on a road trip and was subsequently sold to the Cleveland Buckeyes. Clyde McNeal, who had come to the American Giants as a 17-year-old in 1945, took over the shortstop position and showed great promise. Gentry Jessup and Walter McCoy were the top two pitchers on the club and Jessup was a selection for the NAL All-Star team. Jessup turned in an exceptional performance on May 12, 1946, when he pitched all twenty innings of a 3–3 tie game against the Indianapolis Clowns at Comiskey Park. Jessup did not walk a single batter and struck out a mere 13; Ed "Peanuts" Davis pitching for the Clowns also went the distance. There was speculation that Gentry Jessup might be considered for a major league tryout.[32]

There was also a host of young and inexperienced players with the American Giants in 1946. Among the lesser known: William Charter and Sam Seagraves (both catchers); Harold Millon (aka Mello), Wilbur "Dolly" King and Bernell Longest (infielders); Clarence Locke, Grover Hunt, and Herman Howard — who all helped out with pitching duties.

The American Giants regularly faced tough competition in the Negro American League against the likes of Dan Bankhead of the Memphis Red Sox; Sam Jethroe of the

Cleveland Buckeyes; Willard Brown, Connie Johnson, and Hank Thompson of the KC Monarchs— who all eventually played in the big leagues. As fate would have it, every team in the Negro American League of 1946 would have at least one player who eventually went on to play in the major leagues— except for the American Giants. The American Giants were not as good as the other teams in the league and finished the season at the bottom.

While the American Giants flailed in 1946, Jackie Robinson had taken the stage in organized baseball with a remarkable aura of success. Jackie Robinson made his minor league debut in Jersey City, N.J., on April 18 and went four for five with a homer and scored four runs, leading Montreal to a 14–1 victory over the Jersey City Giants. Robinson and the Montreal Royals drew large crowds when they played on the East Coast, but did not compete directly with teams of the Midwestern Negro American League for fans.

By the end of the 1946 season five former Negro League players were in the Dodger organization: Don Newcombe, Roy Campanella, Roy Partlow, John Wright and Jackie Robinson. Something had changed in baseball. Given the long track record of false hope, disappointments and injustice that had come to define the Negro Leagues, no one pronounced the end of segregated baseball. There was a wait and see attitude. Would the Dodgers promote Jackie Robinson? How would Negro League baseball "fit in" to the new order if the major leagues did in fact integrate? Only time would tell.

11

The Collapse of a Dynasty
(1947–1953)

Jackie Robinson was the magnet, which drew 46,752 paid admissions to Wrigley Field Sunday, May 18th. Wrigley had the largest attendance since it abolished field crowds in 1936. The fans were packed in. Twenty thousand were turned away.
> —*Chicago Defender*, May 24, 1947.

Negro baseball is on the ropes facing a knockout blow unless Negro fans will rally to its support and save it for next year.
> —Luix Virgil Overbea, *Chicago Defender*,
> September 9, 1950.

1947

Homestead Grays catcher Josh Gibson suffered a stroke and died at the age of 35 on January 20, 1947. Gibson was one of the most admired and feared hitters in the history of baseball. Gibson personified the Negro Leagues, and his death —coming shortly before the integration of major league baseball — was like the strike of a kettledrum as the orchestra built to a crescendo. As expected, Branch Rickey called Jackie Robinson up from the Montreal Royals to the Brooklyn Dodgers in the spring of 1947. The piercing of the color line in major league baseball was the next percussion.

Roy Campanella, Don Newcombe, Roy Partlow and John Wright had all joined Jackie Robinson in the Dodger organization in 1946. It was clear that time was marching past Negro League baseball. There was a period of time when Negro League owners, managers and players weren't at all sure what the future might hold, so they tried for a while to go on as if nothing had happened.

Candy Jim Taylor set about in 1947 making trades, scouting players, sending out contracts; filling out the American Giants' roster in fine tradition. On a visit to Uniontown, Kentucky, Candy Jim signed a 220 lb., 6 foot 2 inch pitcher named Earl Bumpus who had been with the Black Barons and also inked George Harris, a catcher who had been with the Pittsburgh Crawfords. Candy also tried to woo hard-hitting Lucius Easter but was unsuccessful.[1]

Candy Jim traded steady hitting third baseman Clyde Nelson to the Cleveland Buck-eyes for the slightly more experienced outfielder Buddy Armour. Armour would represent the American Giants in the 1947 All-Star game. Veteran Alex Radcliffe was given a chance to earn a spot at third base, but was replaced by a younger player named Jacob Robinson. Another trade involved sending outfielder Walter Thomas to the Birmingham Black Barons, for first baseman Lyman Bostock. Bostock had been an All-Star for the Black Barons in 1941, but spent the next four years with the U.S. Army. Bostock returned to form and was a bright spot for the American Giants in 1947. Lyman Bostock's son Lyman Bostock Jr. went on to become a major league player in 1975 and was one of baseball's first highly paid "free agents." Sadly, Lyman Bostock Jr., who was with the California Angels, was killed by a deranged gunman while driving to visit his uncle in Gary, Indiana, after a game against the White Sox at Comiskey Park on September 23, 1978. Candy Jim also tried out Thomas Turner at first base, on the recommendation of pitcher Walter McCoy, who had served with Turner in World War II. Thomas Turner played behind Lyman Bostock and his playing time was limited. Many years later, in the 1990's and into the twenty-first century, Tommy Turner toured the Midwest educating groups from baseball historians to school children with first hand accounts of life in the Negro Leagues. Tommy's buddy Walter McCoy was a starting pitcher for the American Giants in 1947, along with Gentry Jessup, Earl Bumpus, Leonard Johnson and Clarence Locke.

According to Frank Young, McCoy had led the NAL in strikeouts in 1946 with 108 K's (eight more than second place Connie Johnson), he also led in categories for most hits allowed, most walks and most batters faced. Walter McCoy, who is from San Diego, is said to still enjoy playing baseball at age 83 in the year 2005. Another San Diegan, John Ritchey, was the regular catcher for the American Giants in 1947. Other American Giant players in 1947 included pitchers Riley Stewart and Harry Rhodes and infielders Burnell Longest, Jesse Warren, and Clyde McNeal.[2]

The American Giants went to work in the Negro American League against the likes of the K.C. Monarchs, Indianapolis Clowns, Birmingham Black Barons, Memphis Red Sox and Cleveland Buckeyes. The NAL had trimmed a lot of fat, and the American Giants faced tough competition in each and every game. For the American Giants to win they needed to get good pitching and a bit of luck. The results were predictable as the American Giants finished with a losing record at the bottom of the league standings. Among their losses was a 7–2 loss to the Harlem Globetrotter baseball team in an exhibition game and a forfeit to the Indianapolis Clowns due to the team bus's breaking down on the road. Earlier in the season the Memphis Red Sox narrowly avoided sacrificing two league games when their bus broke down in Cincinnati. However, Red Sox owner Dr. B. B. Martin chartered a plane to fly the team from Cincy to Memphis in time for the double-header. Doc B. B. Martin was a little freer with the money than was his brother J.B., who seemed to pride himself on thriftiness.[3]

For haggard veterans like Candy Jim Taylor, 1947 was another bump in the very bumpy road of Negro League baseball. It was a bit tougher for the fans and the media to look at Negro League baseball with the same enthusiasm as in years gone by. The love of the Negro Leagues remained, but the outcomes of games and the league standings were unimportant. By 1947, the *Defender* rarely printed a complete American Giants box score. By contrast, the *Defender* and other black newspapers regularly printed capsules of Jackie

Robinson's batting average and fans followed his exploits daily. While fans might not have been enthralled with the Negro Leagues circa 1947, major league scouts knew that the league was still rife with talent and regularly attended games.

When the Brooklyn Dodgers visited the Cubs on May 18, 1947, it was the largest single-game paid attendance in Wrigley Field history (46,572); some 20,000 fans were turned away. Black folk who had never ventured north of the Chicago River flooded the North Side in hope of witnessing history. There were concerns well in advance of the game that the Bronzeville crowd might turn out in big numbers and be unruly. Frank Young wrote:

> Jackie Robinson will be in Chicago Sunday and Monday May 18 and 19. There shouldn't be the necessity of devoting this column to unwarranted actions of Negro baseball fans as a whole, yet we cannot avoid warning our fans that they are MORE on trial than is Robinson who has and will continue to acquit himself well.... Negro fans who go to Wrigley Field might as well understand now, once and for all times, that the management there will not tolerate whisky drinking, profane language and boisterous conduct from anybody.... Don't tell us that all our fans are Sunday school members and behave like Emily Post would have. Tain't so— not a "jug full." One Sunday in Cincinnati's Crosley Field the police hauled a man and woman out of the stands. They had a market basket with whiskey and gin and paper cups.... And on April 27th at Comiskey Park after the game a grandma was found helpless in the grandstand. She was full of her hootch and had been smoking reefers. The Negro fans can do more to get Jackie Robinson out of the major leagues than all the disgruntled players alive.[4]

Fortunately Frank Young's concerns turned out to be unfounded as the overflow crowd was well behaved.

Larry Doby made his major league debut at Comiskey Park on July 5, 1947, as a pinch hitter with the Cleveland Indians. Chicagoan Bill Veeck was responsible for hiring Doby, and manager Lou Boudreau (who was also from the Chicago area) congenially welcomed Larry Doby to the Indians as they posed for pictures at Comiskey. Flashbulbs were popping. Over 50,000 fans and a bevy of major league scouts were on hand for the 1947 All-Star game held on July 27 at Comiskey. Among the future major leaguers who played were Monte Irvin, Minnie Minoso, Sam Jethroe, Quincy Trouppe and Dan Bankhead. American Giants Gentry Jessup and Buddy Armour played for the West— rumor had it that the White Sox considered signing Jessup, but nothing came of it.[5]

By mid–July 1947, Robinson and Doby were joined in the majors by K.C. Monarchs Hank Thompson and Willard Brown who signed with the St. Louis Browns. Late in the season Memphis Red Sox pitcher Dan Bankhead joined the Brooklyn Dodgers—who incidentally made it to the World Series.

Jackie Robinson was not the first black player in the big leagues (that honor belongs to either William White of the Providence Grays or Fleet Walker of the Toledo Blue Stockings). By most accounts Robinson was not the most talented candidate from Negro League baseball, either. It turned out, however, that Jackie was the best person to lead the way to the integration of major league baseball. The Baseball Writers Association named Jackie Robinson the "Rookie of the Year" in 1947; he was presented the award at the Regal Theatre in Chicago on November 12, 1947. Nineteen forty-seven was the first year of the award, which was originally known as the J. Louis Comiskey award—in 1987 the award was renamed the Jackie Robinson award.

The wall had tumbled down, but black Chicago was on the outside looking in at Brooklyn, Cleveland and St. Louis. Chicago was the key locale in the story of the integration of baseball, yet neither the White Sox nor Cubs had a black player on their roster. Following the 1947 season, Chicago American Giant catcher John Ritchey, who ended up leading the NAL in batting with a .378 average, attended an open tryout for the Cubs at Wrigley. The Cubs liked what they saw and asked him to report for minor league assignment. The *Defender* speculated that Ritchey would likely be assigned to the "Class A" Iowa team as he had two years' experience in the Negro American League. It isn't clear whether Ritchey had in fact been offered a contract by the Cubs, or what terms were offered. Ritchey ended up signing a minor league contract on his own with his hometown San Diego Padres of the Pacific Coast League. The Padres were not obligated to buy out his contract from the American Giants, but as a goodwill measure wrote a substantial check to Doc Martin.[6]

The lifetime followers of the American Giants would have to wait to see one of their own in the big leagues. All the while there were suspicions that owner Doc Martin might be opposed to integration. Fans who could recall the epic battles between Jimmy Callahan's Logan Squares and Rube Foster's American Giants could not understand why the Sox or Cubs would not jump at the chance to bolster their roster and attendance with one of the proven star players of the Negro Leagues. The atmosphere in the Negro

Doc Martin on the tarmac getting set to hop a plane. Doc Martin was head of the Negro American League when integration occurred and thus was thrust into an important role as negotiator for African American professional baseball players (photograph courtesy NoirTech Research, Inc.).

Leagues in 1947 was markedly changed. The fan base had deteriorated, the major leagues threatened to raid rosters, as did the Mexican Leagues, even the traditionally loyal black press patronized black baseball as if it were a few cards short of a full deck. Despite the set-backs, the Negro Leagues remained a "professional" baseball organization. Doc Martin pointed out that players in the Negro Leagues were paid more than players in the minor leagues. Negro League team owners began to deal directly with major league teams. The selling of players to major league organizations soon became a cottage industry for Negro League owners, and was the biggest new source of cash since night baseball.[7]

Candy Jim Taylor had seen nothing like 1947 in his 46 years of service to the game. To see youngsters like Jackie Robinson and Larry Doby play in the big leagues was special for him. Candy could trace his connection to Chicago baseball back to 1910, when Frank Leland hired him as a ringer for his Chicago Giants. Nineteen forty-seven would be Candy's last season, he missed several weeks due to illness and had to attend to his sister who died in Cleveland that summer. While Taylor was out, veteran outfielder John Bissant took over as interim manager. Candy had won championships as the manager of the St. Louis Stars and the Homestead Grays, but lightning never did strike for him in Chicago. He was never given the talent to work with in Chicago, as owner Dr. J.B. Martin made a business decision not to compete on salary with the Mexican Leagues or the aggressive Negro League owners.

1948

Candy Jim was not asked back as manager following the 1947 season; the 63-year-old skipper had decided he would take a job as the manager of the Baltimore Elite Giants — a job previously held by his brother Ben. Candy never joined the Elite Giants, he had been sick off and on the last few years and died at Chicago's People's Hospital, April 3, 1948. Candy Jim, one of the grand-daddies of black baseball, left quietly. Even at his funeral not a condolence was read or one word spoken as coming from any of the 12 clubs in organized Negro baseball. He was buried in an unmarked grave in Chicago's Burr Oak Cemetery. In the year 2004 a group of baseball historians working with the cemetery staff had a headstone placed on James "Candy" Taylor's grave, along with those of several other players interred at Burr Oak.[8]

Quincy Trouppe was acquired from the Cleveland Buckeyes to be the player/manager. Trouppe had played with the American Giants briefly in 1933 — in the intervening time he had become one of the more seasoned members of the black baseball fraternity. In addition to catching Satchel Paige with Neil Churchill's Bismarck Cubs, he also played with Kansas City, the Indianapolis ABCs, and the Cleveland Buckeyes, but notably he had become a star in Latin American baseball. According to legend, Mexican millionaire Jorge Pasquel arranged to have 80,000 Mexican workers loaned to the U.S. for the war effort, in exchange Pasquel asked that Quincy Trouppe and pitcher Theolic Smith be allowed to play ball for his team in Mexico. Quincy Trouppe brought with him four recruits from Puerto Rico when he came to the American Giants: outfielder/catcher Bienvenido Rodriguez, outfielder Alfonso Gerard and pitchers Rafaelito Ortiz and Roberto Vargas. During spring training Trouppe also persuaded James Pendleton, a young shortstop from

Asheville, North Carolina, to join the American Giants. Eventually Trouppe, Vargas and Pendleton would all see action in the major leagues.[9]

It was also during spring training 1947 in Birmingham, Alabama, that Quincy Trouppe was tipped off about a young kid named Willie Mays. Trouppe offered Mays a tryout, but Willie informed him he was too young to sign a contract and had to check with his father first. To which Trouppe said, "have your father get in touch with me in Chicago, and we'll send you the expense money to come on up and join us." On his arrival in Chicago, Trouppe had a letter waiting for him from Mays. Trouppe pitched to Doc Martin his idea of advancing $300 to Willie Mays to come to Chicago for a tryout, but Martin vetoed the plan.[10]

Even with Quincy Trouppe at the helm the American Giants could only tread water in the Negro American League. Robert Vargas and Rafaelito Ortiz bolstered the pitching staff, which had become overly dependent on the aging arm of Gentry Jessup. Pitchers Riley Stewart, Harry Rhodes and Earl Bumpus stayed with the club, but Walter McCoy was conspicuously absent. McCoy continued his career in the Pacific Coast League and in Mexico. Lyman Bostock left the American Giants, his spot at first was filled by John Williams who quit his job as a cop with the Hot Springs, Arkansas, force to join the team. Clyde McNeal, in his fourth year in the American Giants' infield, manned second base for the American Giants. Marlin Carter, who had been a standout for the Memphis Red Sox at third, was lured to the American Giants. Newcomer James Pendleton proved to be something special at shortstop and Quincy Trouppe himself was one of the best in the game. The outfield lacked any big sluggers, something that had been missing for several years; Sam Hill, John "Mule" Miles, John Bissant, Bienvenido Rodriguez and Alfonso Gerard played the outfield.

Quincy Trouppe energized the American Giants, but any excitement created by the new look was overshadowed by the attention garnered by blacks in the big leagues. The *Defender* led the chorus directed at the owners of the Cubs and White Sox, especially the White Sox who had a unique relationship with the American Giants. In an article titled "White Sox Needs Negro Player like Larry Doby," *Defender* writer William Warren pointed out:

> The Negro White Sox fans are becoming concerned. They are between two thoughts, i.e. is the Comiskey group downright prejudiced, or are they determined not to spend any money for ball players white or black? The White Sox management, ought to have been the first in line as far as the Fair Employment Practices Law is concerned.[11]

The annual Negro League All-Star game was usually the biggest draw of the year at Comiskey. Even an American Giant Sunday double-header during this era of mediocrity sometimes turned out a larger crowd than an average Sox game. One school of thought was that the White Sox should just go ahead and hire one of the established stars in the Negro Leagues— someone like Quincy Trouppe, "Cool Papa" Bell or Satchel Paige. The other school of thought advanced was that care should be taken to scout and develop a young player. The White Sox were indecisive and did neither. Meanwhile the Cleveland Indians did what black Chicagoans had called for — they went ahead and signed the 42-year-old Satchel Paige. When the Cleveland Indians came to town on August 13, 1948, Satchel Paige was named the starting pitcher for the Tribe. A crowd of 51,013 turned out, which was the largest crowd ever for a night game at Comiskey, and 15–20,000 fans were turned away. Satchel pitched a complete game shutout and allowed only five hits. Larry Doby salted the game away for Satch and the Indians with a triple, a single, two steals and two runs scored. Many of the 51,000 were cheering for the Indians. Words were unnecessary, what happened that night in Chicago was triumphant. The Cleveland Indians went on to win the American League pennant and the World Series; the White Sox finished in last place.[12]

The American Giants put together a hastily planned thirty-sixth anniversary celebration at Comiskey in late July. Preacher and civil rights leader Reverend Archibald Carey was to throw out the first pitch for the big anniversary game—only he was a no-show. Master of ceremonies and American Giant general manager Roscoe Simmons called Rube's widow Sarah Foster to the microphone for a tribute, but Mrs. Foster wasn't in the house. There was a minute of silence for Rube Foster and General John Pershing who had died a few days earlier. It was somewhat confusing as to why Pershing was included in the tribute to black baseball while there was no mention of the late skipper Candy Jim Taylor who had died only three months earlier. Simmons concluded by introducing some of the old time Chicago American Giants to the crowd, but forgot to introduce Jimmy Lyons, George Harney, and James Bray who were standing proudly by the Giants dugout in uniform. One of the legends of early Chicago black baseball, Joe Green, was in the stands and was not introduced. The American Giants had been accused previously of using so called "benefit games" and "tributes" merely to fill seats—this was another unfortunate example.[13]

The American Giants held their own in Negro American League—such as it was. Prior to the inroads of integration of major league baseball, Negro League baseball was essentially the black major league. Once major league baseball opened the doors (even a smidge), the mission of the Negro Leagues became unclear. Few really cared who won the pennant, the championship or who was selected to the All-Star game. Negro League owners who had survived the Great Depression and World War II adapted quickly to the new state of affairs. Doctor J.B. Martin watched his bottom line like a hawk; after the 1948 season he sold James Pendleton's contract to Branch Rickey for a tidy sum of $7,500. Martin thanked Quincy Trouppe, who had brought Pendleton to the team, by asking him to take a pay cut. Quincy waved goodbye to the Windy City and joined the New York Cubans in 1949.

1949

Doc Martin came to terms with Winfield Welch, a manager with an impressive résumé who got his start in New Orleans. Welch was an outfielder with the New Orleans Crescents, the Black Pelicans and the Monroe (Louisiana) Monarchs in the twenties, but discovered his true calling as a manager. Welch managed the Shreveport Giants, before becoming the skipper of the Cincinnati Buckeyes of the NAL in 1941 and then the Birmingham Black Barons. Welch led the Black Barons to pennants in 1944 and 1945. Along the way Welch took credit for discovering a number of star players including Piper Davis, Willard Brown and Art Wilson.

Welch counted as his close personal friend promoter Abe Saperstein. Welch managed the Birmingham Black Barons in the forties when Abe promoted the team. Welch had also worked as manager of the famous Harlem Globetrotters. Like Quincy Trouppe and Candy Taylor before him, Welch was well connected and put his own personal touch on the team by signing players with whom he had worked previously. Clyde McNeal was moved from second back to shortstop to replace James Pendleton. Tommy Sampson, who had spent his whole career with the Birmingham Black Barons, was brought in to play second. Lloyd "Ducky" Davenport, who had drawn the ire of Doc Martin when he jumped to Mexico in 1945, was an old friend of Welch's from the bayous of Louisiana and was brought in to play outfield. Lyman Bostock, who also had connections with the Birmingham franchise, returned to the American Giants to hold down first base. Lonnie Summers, who had served in World War II and played ball in the Mexican Leagues, took over as the starting catcher now that Trouppe was gone. Welch used other players along the way for short periods including Harlem Globetrotter (and later New York Knick) Nat "Sweetwater" Clifton, who held down first base for a few games with the American Giants before signing a minor league contract.

Gentry Jessup, in his eighth season with the American Giants, was again the ace on the staff. Doc Martin could not afford to keep lefthander Roberto Vargas on the payroll, but Winfield Welch coaxed Alvin Gipson (a Shreveport native who had spent most of his career with the Birmingham Black Barons) to sign on as the number two starter. Harry Rhodes, Eugene Smith, Gready McKinnis, Othello Strong and Theolic Smith were among others who saw action on the mound for the American Giants.

The long drought for the American Giants ended in 1949 when they finished in first place in the second half of the season in the Negro American League western division. The last time the American Giants could claim even a piece of the flag had been during the war torn 1943 season. The Kansas City Monarchs piloted by Buck O'Neil took first place honors for the first half of the season. Under league rules the Monarchs and the American Giants were to meet for a divisional playoff, but the legendary Monarchs — who had sold off a number of players to organized baseball — simply withdrew from the playoffs, unwilling to spend money on renting a stadium. The Monarchs' lack of interest in the playoffs demonstrated that the outcome of the baseball games in the Negro Leagues had become an afterthought.[14]

The Negro Leagues had become a marketplace for organized baseball. No one took notice when the American Giants claimed the NAL western division championship. Few took notice when the Baltimore Elite Giants, with Joe Black, Junior Gillam and Leon Day, swept the American Giants in the Negro League World Series. It was remarkable that there *was* a Negro League World Series. Meanwhile ten million watched on television as the Brooklyn Dodgers, with Don Newcombe, Roy Campanella and Jackie Robinson, slugged it out against the New York Yankees in the 1949 World Series.

Chicago fans continued to wonder if and when the Sox and Cubs would hire a black player. There was some progress. John Ford Smith, who had broken in with the American Giants ten years earlier in 1939 before going to the Monarchs, was signed to a minor league contract by the New York Giants. The Chicago Cubs signed a young black catcher named Charles Pope to a minor league contract. Pope was a third string catcher with a barnstorming black team known as the San Francisco Sea Lions. The Cubs were hoping to get lucky with this young player and could say that they had hired a black player — but nothing became of this signing. In June the Cubs inked K.C. Monarch pitcher Booker

T. McDaniel to a minor league contract. McDaniel's best years were behind him and he too was never brought up to the parent club. While the Cubs were paying lip service to integration, the Brooklyn Dodgers had brought up Don Newcombe, the Giants brought up Monte Irvin, Cleveland brought Orestes "Minnie" Minoso and Luke Easter on board. White Sox GM Frank Lane claimed the high road, stating the Sox "would not sign a black player merely to increase the gate ... but were actively scouting black players." The White Sox took a big step in good faith when they hired one of the old sages of Negro League baseball, John Donaldson, to be a scout. Donaldson came to fame back in the 1910's with the All-Nations Team owned by J.L. Wilkinson; he had been a peer and competitor with legend Rube Foster. The Cubs followed suit and signed Harold "Yellow Horse" Morris as a scout on the West Coast. Morris had pitched for the American Giants for two seasons and while he was not among the well-known popular American Giants his employment by the Cubs represented a thaw in intra-city race relations.[15]

Late in the season it was rumored that the White Sox had worked a trade with Branch Rickey to buy the rights to Sam Jethroe. The White Sox had sent scouts to Montreal to follow Jethroe in the International League where he set a new record for steals. According to Russell Cowan, writing for the *Chicago Defender*, negotiations to purchase Jethroe's contract went into six figures. Cowan also wrote, "While the deal has not been closed, it's almost a certainty the speedy Jethroe will be signed by the White Sox." The White Sox did not act quickly enough and Jethroe wound up with the Boston Braves the following year. Branch Rickey did command in the neighborhood of $200,000—an exorbitant sum in those days—for Sam Jethroe, who would be the rookie of the year in 1950. Had the White Sox taken a chance on Jethroe they might have saved face in the eyes of American Giants fans and could have paid his salary with increased attendance.[16]

1950

Following the 1949 season American Giants owner Doc J.B. Martin arranged to lease ownership of the team to William Little, a tailor and businessman who had been a part-owner of the team back in 1936, five years before Doc Martin came on the scene. Ted "Double Duty" Radcliffe, supposedly banned from Negro baseball by vote of overzealous team owners in 1947 for having played ball in Mexico, was back in the role of player/manager.[17]

Attendance in the Negro Leagues had fallen way down by 1949, but Negro League teams made up for the lost revenue by selling players to the major leagues. The American Giants came up with a scheme to draw a big crowd to opening day—tickets were distributed to business establishments all over the South Side which would allow any woman into the game for free after a twenty-cent tax. When opening day rolled around it was cold and wet, yet a hearty group of 4,000 fans turned out. Negro League baseball showed remarkable resiliency not only in Chicago, but in the other league cities too. The 1950 season opened with teams in ten cities: Baltimore, Birmingham, Chicago, Cleveland, Houston, Indianapolis, Kansas City, Memphis, New York and Philadelphia.[18]

Double Duty had rounded up a crew of young and veteran players to do battle. Due to competition from organized baseball, Negro League teams were increasingly offering tryouts to younger players who previously might not have been considered for the professional ranks. Some of the youngsters considered by Double Duty in 1950 were Marvin Price, Curtiss Pitts, and Phillip Holland, who were distinguished baseball players in Chicago area high schools. Duty brought two teenage pitchers from North Carolina State College into camp — Thomas Perry and Charles England; a catcher from Hampton Institute named Fred Lloyd; and signed a lanky 19-year-old infielder known for his hitting named John Brantley. None of these recruits stuck with the American Giants.

Among the more seasoned players with the American Giants in 1950 were Art Pennington and Cowan "Bubba" Hyde. Pennington had played with the minor league Portland Beavers in 1949 and Bubba Hyde was also coming off a season in organized baseball with the Bridgeport Bees of Bridgeport, Connecticut. Taking players in from the big league farm systems was a new phenomenon.

Later in the year the American Giants added four white players to the team. Doc Martin was thought to be behind the move, which was intended to boost attendance — which it did, for one game. The white players signed by the American Giants were pitcher Lou Chirban, outfielder Louis Clarizo, and infielders Frank Dyall and Stanley Marka. The white players saw limited action and their performance did not warrant attention from fans or major league scouts. The idea of bringing white players into the Negro Leagues was not as new as it seemed. *Chicago Defender* writer Al Monroe wrote way back in 1934, when commenting on the passing of John McGraw, that Rube Foster had long hoped to bring a few white players into the Negro Leagues back in the 1920's as a way of ending Jim Crow.[19]

In the end Double Duty relied primarily on a group of veterans for the 1950 campaign. Othello Strong emerged as the number one pitcher for the American Giants in 1950. Second baseman Jesse Douglass was picked as the MVP for the Negro American League by *Defender* sportswriter Russ Cowans. Art Pennington and Clyde McNeal joined Douglass to represent the Western division in the All-Star game held at Comiskey on August 20, 1950. The American Giants played well enough to have the best record in the West for the second half of the season. Due to a technicality the pennant was awarded to the Kansas City Monarchs; it seems the American Giants did not send reports of the games to the league office. League president Doc Martin, still the owner of the American Giants, was forced to deny his own team the pennant.[20]

Doc Martin had a penchant for rules. Even while the league was falling apart Martin kept busy handing down fines and suspensions, which he later had to reverse. At one time Martin had supposedly banned Double Duty Radcliffe and Ducky Davenport for breaking league rules, but later reversed himself. In the case of the 1950 pennant, Martin enforced the rule about reporting scores, when arguably he himself bore some responsibility for having the scores reported to his own office. This preoccupation with the "league rules" contributed to Doc Martin's reputation as a wealthy bureaucrat two steps removed from the game.[21]

While the American Giants toiled in the Negro American league, such as it was, the integration of major league baseball continued. Former Negro Leaguers Jackie Robinson, Roy Campanella, Don Newcombe and Larry Doby returned to Comiskey for the All-Star game — the major league All-Star game. Sam Jethroe was named rookie of the year. The New York Giants purchased Willie Mays from the Birmingham Black Barons for a cool $15,000. The White Sox and Cubs were still dragging their feet when it came to promoting a black player to the big league roster. The Cubs had a few black players in their farm system, the White Sox still did not. A committee of activists visited the office of Chuck Comiskey, the vice-president of the White Sox, to protest the club's lack of enthusiasm in hiring a black player. Given the White Sox and the Comiskey family's long relationship with the American Giants—the lack of a black player in the organization was a slap in the face. For their part the White Sox continued to maintain that they were looking for the "right player." It might have been a coincidence, but a few weeks after the meeting with Comiskey the White Sox signed Bob Boyd of the Memphis Red Sox and Sam Hairston from the Indianapolis Clowns to minor league contracts.

Despite efforts to reinvigorate the Negro American League, the opposite was happening. The lack of fan interest and the emphasis on selling players to organized baseball made it plain that Negro League baseball had undergone major changes. Negro League baseball was originally founded on high moral principles, an alternative to hatred and bigotry. Negro League baseball was never intended to be an outlaw baseball farm system. The signing of white players by the American Giants pointed out another obvious fallacy: the Negro American League was no longer a "Negro league."

The goal of Negro League baseball was to integrate the major leagues and that was beginning to happen. Negro League baseball survived Jim Crow, World War I, the Great Depression and World War II. Surviving was such a part of the Negro League way of life that no one realized when the time for surviving had ended.

1951

It was announced at the start of the 1951 season that Doctor John B. Martin had sold the American Giants, which he had controlled since 1941, to a group of businessmen fronted by Winfield Welch—the manager of the 1949 team—for $50,000. The story was that Winfield Welch had "won some money in France while touring with the Harlem Globetrotters." Welch worked for the Harlem Globetrotters and was closely associated with Trotter owner Abe Saperstein. Saperstein, who had expressed interest in buying the team 20 years earlier, was primary among the "group of businessmen" who purchased the Giants. Saperstein also partnered with Bill Veeck in buying the major league St. Louis Browns. Making Winfield Welch the front man was a calculated move to disguise Saperstein's true intentions—that of running an outlaw minor league team. Two Chicago American Giant spring training hopefuls—Jim Fishback and George "Sonny" Smith, both of Cincinnati, Ohio—went from the American Giant camp in Meridian, Mississippi, to the Dayton Indians of the AL St. Louis Browns organization.[22]

Winfield was not calling the shots from the owner's booth, but he was the field manager. While the Negro American League was never formally brought under the umbrella of organized baseball, it was functioning as a de facto part of the major league farm system. Negro League players in the early fifties were transients, jumping from organized baseball to different Negro League teams or to Latin or Canadian clubs. A number of players jumped from Negro League teams to the Manitoba-Dakota League, known as the Man-Dak League. The Negro American League went from ten teams to eight, still remarkable considering the decreased attendance and the uncertain status of Negro League baseball.

It was tougher to find players and Winfield Welch hired anyone he could find to fill spots on the roster. Don Johnson, who played second base for a brief period with the American Giants, tells the story of how he joined the American Giants in 1951:

> I went to see a game at Crosley Field between the Indianapolis Clowns and Chicago American Giants. I had paid $1.50 to get in the game. I was sitting next to the Chicago dugout when I got the attention of American Giant catcher Roy "Pat" Patterson — who recognized me from my play with the fast pitch softball Cincinnati Hottentots. Patterson told Winfield Welch about me, and the next thing I knew, Patterson told me to go to the bus and put on a uniform. Wait a minute, I told them, I paid a dollar and a half to get in here. Give me my dollar and a half back.[23]

It was tougher to find good young players with the added competition of the major leagues scouting many of the same dusty diamonds. Don Johnson was later given a chance in the Cincinnati farm system. Welch did get Larry Raines to play shortstop for part of the season — he replaced Clyde McNeal who had been signed to a minor league contract by the Brooklyn Dodgers. Raines would eventually make it to the big leagues as an infielder with the Cleveland Indians in 1957. Winfield Welch had a number of players with the team who had been to organized baseball and back: Ducky Davenport, Bubba Hyde, Art Pennington, Ted Strong and Parnell Woods. Catcher Paul Hardy, who had been in black baseball since 1931, was the veteran and team captain. The experiment with white players ended and there were a number of lesser-known players with the American Giants in 1951 who played off and on. Theolic Smith was the go-to pitcher for the American Giants — there was no need for a four-arm rotation because the American Giants were not playing every day.

In May of 1951 the Chicago White Sox pulled off a trade with the Cleveland Indians that brought Orestes "Minnie" Minoso to the White Sox. Minoso hit a two run homer in his first at-bat for the White Sox crowd of about 15,000 at Comiskey on May 1, 1950, against the New York Yankees. A crowd of about 38,000 turned out to see the Sox and Minoso face his former team, the Cleveland Indians with Larry Doby, Luke Easter and Harry "Suitcase" Simpson, for a Sunday double-header at Comiskey on May 13. Minnie did not get the fanfare that Jackie received at Wrigley in 1947 or Satchel at Comiskey in 1948, but having a black player in a Chicago White Sox uniform was equally historic. Jackie Robinson integrated baseball in America in 1947 but the South Side of Chicago was its own nation-state. Once Orestes Minoso stepped into a White Sox uniform the generations of Chicagoans who abided by a "color line" in baseball suffered a defeat. By 1951, minor-league teams all over the country were beginning to accept black players. Major league baseball in the metropolis of Chicago — long a beacon of hope for blacks escaping the South — should have been integrated years earlier.

The American Giants and NAL trudged forward. They played a limited schedule consisting mostly of Sunday double-headers; standings were kept, but with the aspirations of the league redefined as a minor league, even fewer fans followed. The parade of Negro League players entering the major leagues continued. Ray Noble, previously of the New York Cubans, was promoted to the N.Y. Giants. After being traded back and forth from different major league organizations, former Birmingham Black Baron infielder Artie Wilson also joined the New York Giants. Then the Giants brought up the "Say Hey Kid," 20-year-old Willie Mays, to join Monte Irvin and Hank Thompson as New York Giant outfielders. The New York Giants went to the World Series in 1951 but lost out to the Yankees. The Cleveland Indians promoted Harry "Suitcase" Simpson (Philly Stars) and "Sad" Sam Jones (Cleveland Buckeyes). The Chicago White Sox honored their commitment by promoting Bob Boyd and Sam Hairston. The addition of three black players to the Chicago White Sox didn't vault the team into the World Series like Brooklyn, Cleveland, and the New York Giants were shortly after they integrated, but having black players with both the White Sox and the American Giants playing at Comiskey was a victory for black Chicago.

In 1951, the American Giants had something no other Negro League team had, a major league pitcher who returned to the Negro Leagues—none other than Satchel Paige. Abe Saperstein and Bill Veeck were the prime movers in bringing Satch to the South Side. Opening day for the American Giants was declared "Bill Veeck Day," and a special award was given to Veeck by none other than Jesse Owens. Veeck was singled out for his "All-American spirit and fair play to Negro youth." Veeck graciously accepted the award. Satchel Paige pitched four innings against the Birmingham Black Barons, allowed one hit, and the American Giants went on to win 6–3. On July 17 Bill Veeck asked Satchel Paige to join the St. Louis Browns after two years out of major league baseball at the age of 45. Satchel stated in his autobiography that he actually took a pay cut to join the Browns. Paige made 23 appearances for the Browns in 1951, and in 1952 finished with his best record ever in the major leagues with 12 wins. Veeck's ability to "call up" Satchel from the American Giants to the St. Louis Browns confirmed what many suspected, "that Veeck had a stake in the American Giants and wanted to treat it like farm team."[24]

The American Giants set aside a Sunday double-header against the Indianapolis Clowns as a special Rube Foster tribute event. With the integration of major league baseball in Chicago on a sound footing, Rube could finally be honored with the knowledge that his efforts had not been in vain. In between the two games the Old Timer's Baseball Association presented a plaque to Sarah Foster. Billy Neisen, one-time owner of the Chicago semi-pro Gunthers and the Pyotts, presented the award and paid homage to Rube. There were a number of former major leaguers on hand for the presentation, including Jimmy Archer (catcher for the Cubs), Jimmy "Nixy" Callahan (pitcher/manager, White Sox), Ray Schalk (Hall of Fame White Sox catcher) and Urban "Red" Faber (Hall of Fame White Sox pitcher). There was also a short three-inning old-timer game between the two games that included Bingo DeMoss, Jelly Gardner, George Harney, Jimmy Lyons, Dave Malarcher and George Sweatt. Unlike the poorly organized Rube Foster day held in 1948, this memorial came off with respect and dignity. Rube's widow, Sarah Foster, beamed when she accepted the award on the field at Comiskey.

Mrs. Foster had always made it a point to keep her phone number listed in Andrew Foster's name—as if to remind the world who he was. The *Chicago Defender* called for a "Nation-wide Rube Foster Tribute," the idea had been discussed in previous years too, but never happened. The celebration of Rube Foster's life work was quieter than the praise heaped on Jackie Robinson. Thirty years later, in 1981, the Veterans' Committee elected Rube to the Hall of Fame.

1952

Negro League baseball had become an independent minor league, rather than an alternative major league. The league lost two more franchises in 1952, but there were still six teams in the NAL: Birmingham, Chicago, Indianapolis, Kansas City, Memphis and Philadelphia. Although Doc Martin had sold off his interest in the American Giants he remained the president of the Negro American League. Martin continued to fuel hope that the NAL would survive as an institution. Many agreed with Martin that there was a place for black baseball even after integration of organized baseball and the league continued.

The White Sox signed former New York Cuban Hector Rodriguez, who was the regular third baseman in 1952, joining shortstop Chico Carasquel and second baseman Nellie Fox in the infield. The Chicago Cubs, who had a number of promising black players in their farm system, still had not promoted any to the parent club. Other major league teams did not have the same difficulties finding qualified black players. Former American Giant Quincy Trouppe — 39 years old, who had managed the American Giants four years earlier — was brought up to play for the Cleveland Indians in 1952. Trouppe had made a special trip to Chicago to talk to Abe Saperstein following the 1951 season, because he had heard of Saperstein's connection with major league teams and thought that he might be able to help him find a job. Quincy was in a hotel in Caracas, Venezuela, when he got a call from Hank Greenberg in the Cleveland Indian front office with an offer. The signing that got the most attention was the purchase by the Boston Braves of a youngster named Henry Aaron from the Indianapolis Clowns. Hank Aaron played his last Negro League game in Chicago. After the Clowns did battle with the American Giants Henry loaded up a cardboard suitcase and headed for Eau Claire, Wisconsin, to join the Boston Braves' minor league organization.[25]

The Chicago American Giants and other NAL teams barnstormed the country often playing games on neutral fields. The American Giants met with the Clowns, Monarchs and Philadelphia Stars for a four-team round robin tournament at the end of the season and finished in second place. The Indianapolis Clowns had the upper hand in this era of black baseball, although the American Giants played surprisingly well considering their youth. The success of the American Giants was credited in part to skillful managing by Paul Hardy. Hardy never achieved the stature of some of his predecessors.[26]

1953 and Beyond

At the conclusion of the 1952 season Doc Martin sounded reassuring about the continuation of the NAL, stating: "The attendance at the games was better than in 1951 and we expect it to improve in 1953." However in April of 1953 Doc announced that both the Chicago American Giants and the Philadelphia Stars were dropping out of the league. The invisible hands behind the American Giants in the 1950's were those of Abe Saperstein and Bill Veeck. They apparently had hoped to break even on the cost of operating the American Giants while also harvesting players for the St. Louis Browns which they also owned. That plan did not work out — had the plan been deployed a decade earlier, in 1943, history might have turned out differently. Veeck did make a monumental contribution to the integration of major league baseball as the owner of the Cleveland Indians. Veeck and his partners were also forced to sell the St. Louis Browns franchise to Baltimore at the end of the 1953 season. In 1959 Veeck bought the Chicago White Sox and brought them their first pennant since the tainted 1919 season.[27]

On August 16, 1953, the Annual East-West All-Star game was held at Comiskey. Joining the Western squad was shortstop Ernie Banks. Banks had been recruited into the Kansas City Monarchs organization by "Cool Papa" Bell, who saw him playing with the San Antonio Black Sheepherders as a nineteen-year-old in 1950. Banks's early career was disrupted by a two-year stint in the army, but when he joined the Monarchs in 1953 he lit up the Negro American League. After the game Western manager John "Buck" O'Neil received a call from Monarch team owner Tom Baird, who told him to bring Ernie Banks to Wrigley Field the next morning for a meeting. The Cubs made an offer to Banks and also promised to hire Buck O'Neil as a scout when his time with the Monarchs ended. According to Buck O'Neil, White Sox scout John Donaldson also knew of Banks and tried to convince the White Sox to sign him. When the Sox ignored his advice Donaldson resigned.

A month after the Negro League All-Star game, on September 17, 1953, the Chicago Cubs put Ernie Banks in the game. Banks was 0 for 3 and made an error in his first appearance before a small crowd at Wrigley of only 2,793 as the Cubs fell 16–4 to the Phillies. A few days later, on September 20, 1953, Banks was joined by fellow Monarch Gene Baker in the Cubbie infield. On that day Banks hit the first of what would be 512 career home runs. Banks became the Cubs' regular shortstop and played in 424 consecutive games. On August 22, 1982, Ernie Banks became the first player to have his number retired by the Cubs organization. He was given the title "Mr. Cub" and a pennant with the number 14 now waves from Wrigley's left-field foul pole.

So in the year 1953, coincidental with the demise of the American Giants, both Chicago major league teams were integrated. The American Giants' dynasty had come to a successful end.[28]

The loss of the American Giants and the Philly Stars, two of the historic franchises in black baseball, signaled the demise of Negro League baseball, even though Kansas City, Memphis, the Indianapolis Clowns and Birmingham Black Barons continued to play in the NAL. The Negro American League continued its existence for a number of years and the annual All-Star game was still held in Comiskey Park up until 1960.

Jackie Robinson threw out the first pitch in the 1958 All-Star game and Charley Pride started the game for the West — Charley Pride, the country singer, who now has a star on the Hollywood Walk of Fame and continues to tour in the year 2005. Pride learned his musical craft strumming on the Memphis Red Sox team bus. The quality of play in the Negro Leagues post–1953 has been brought into question by some, but there was a group of players who were a bit too old for the major leagues in the 1950's, but who otherwise might have had the stuff. A theme repeated by players of that era was the necessity to lie about their age. Pitcher Ernest Westfield, who started the 1960 All-Star game, says with a chuckle: "the first thing we learned was how to lie about your age, a lot of us were 20 years old for many years." Today Ernest Westfield is a soft-spoken poet, educator and caretaker of Negro League legends.

The late Theodore "Double Duty" Radcliffe was the most colorful of the American Giants veterans. Duty made White House visits and national television appearances and generously shared his experiences with curious history buffs. Shortly before his death in the summer of 2005 he sat on a player panel for Negro League historians in Chicago, threw out a ceremonial first pitch at RFK Stadium for a Nationals vs. Cubs game, and celebrated his 103rd birthday at Comiskey Park. Soft-spoken former Chicago Cub coach

John "Buck" O'Neil, with his great memory and sharp wit, has presented the history of Negro League baseball in documentaries and as the head of the Negro League Baseball Museum in Kansas City. Veterans of the Negro Leagues like Buck O'Neil, Charlie Pride, Theodore Radcliffe and Ernest Westfield are just a small sample of the true gentlemen who came out of the Negro Leagues.

Several former American Giants went on to play in major league baseball after the demise of the team. James Pendleton, who had played with the American Giants in 1948 under Quincy Trouppe, was called up by the Milwaukee Braves in 1953 and put in eight seasons in the big leagues as a utility player. Roberto Vargas of Puerto Rico, who pitched for the American Giants in 1948, joined the Milwaukee Braves in 1954 and made 25 appearances for Milwaukee. Outfielder Joe Cephus "Cash" Taylor, who first appeared with the American Giants under Candy Taylor in 1946, went to the Philadelphia A's in 1954 and later played in Cincinnati, St. Louis and Baltimore. Larry Raines, who played shortstop with the American Giants in 1951, found work with the Cleveland Indians in 1957 after spending several seasons in the minor leagues.

The big guns of the American Giants never had a chance to play in the major leagues, among them players like Pete Hill, Bruce Petway, Cristobal Torriente, Bingo DeMoss, Joe Cyclone Williams, Mule Suttles, Sug Cornelius, Gentry Jessup, and Willie Foster — integration happened too late for them. The integration of baseball was accomplished by the hard work and great sacrifice of many who went to their graves in a strictly segregated American society. The main goal of Negro League baseball as embodied by the American Giants — that is, to integrate major league baseball — was finally accomplished. It wasn't everything that Rube Foster would have had hoped for — if he were here today he would be pushing for equal representation of black America in the ownership ranks.

The American Giants are a bright spot in the checkered history of professional baseball in the Windy City. The American Giants won enough championships to make up for the city's long drought on the MLB circuit. Over the last twenty or so years there have been many retrospectives on the Negro Leagues, whether it be books, television documentaries, web sites, or artwork, apparel and bobble heads. Major league baseball has recently agreed to pay a pension to surviving Negro League players. Major league baseball took the step of retiring Jackie Robinson's number 42 in perpetuity for all teams in 1997 on the fiftieth anniversary of his entry into major league baseball. In 2004 a unique theme restaurant was opened on Chicago's South Side called the "Negro League Café." In 2004 and 2005 a group of historians led by Peoria history buff Jeremy Kroc (who shared the hometown of Ardmore, Missouri, with Jimmie Crutchfield) raised money to put headstones on a number of Negro League stars buried in Chicago's Burr Oak Cemetery in unmarked graves, including legends Jimmy Crutchfield, John Donaldson, Candy Jim Taylor and Ted Trent.

There is a consensus now that players in Negro League baseball were often better than their counterparts in the major leagues. There is a consensus that there can never be a righting of the wrongs of institutional segregation in baseball. Embedded in the historical celebration of the American Giants are the more important lessons on the cost of intolerance and bigotry. As time passes and the lenses of history are given the proper amount of time to come into focus we will undoubtedly come to learn more of the American Giants and thus know better that tribe which the team represented: ourselves, *America*.

Appendix 1: Who Was Who with the Chicago American Giants

The following is a partial list and short sketch of the Chicago American Giants. While all of the key figures and many of the minor figures are mentioned here, this is not a complete list. There were men who may have played with the American Giants for a brief time, or as part of a tryout, or in exhibition games, possibly even under a pseudonym, who are not mentioned at all, or anywhere in this work. Some may have played for a significant amount of time with the team and some may have been listed on rosters but never played. Special thanks to James Riley, author of The Biographical Encyclopedia of the Negro Baseball Leagues, *for helping to fill in numerous blanks.*

Robert Sengstacke Abbott publisher *Chicago Defender*. Abbott was born in 1870 on St. Simon's Island, Georgia, the son of former slaves. He studied at Hampton Institute and received a law degree from Kent College of Law, Chicago, in 1898, but was unable to practice law due to discrimination. Instead, in 1905 he founded the *Chicago Defender*. The *Defender* eventually became the most important black newspaper in the country. The *Defender* spread the black baseball gospel nationwide via train porters and distribution to black population centers all over the country. Abbott died February 29, 1940. He is considered an important figure in African American history.

Stacy Adkins pitched in a few games in 1950.

Ted Alexander pitched for the 1941 Chicago American Giants and for the Palmer House (Hotel) team in 1940 before joining the American Giants.

Andy Anderson played outfield for the American Giants in 1951 and was named to the Western All-Star team.

Lewis Anderson was a backup catcher for the American Giants in 1930.

Louis B. Anderson was legal adviser to Frank Leland. Also was general counsel for the National Colored Men's Railway Association, circa 1910.

Alfred "Buddy" Armour outfielder 1947–48. Candy Jim Taylor traded up and coming middle infielder Clyde Nelson for Buddy Armour in 1947.

The trade was questionable on the face of it, given that Armour had already played ten years in the Negro Leagues. However Armour was named to the Western All-Star team in 1947, and it turned out that the rising young star Clyde Nelson's career came to an early end when he collapsed following a game in Philadelphia in 1949 and suddenly died. Buddy Armour extended his career into the 1950's finishing up in the Canadian Provincial League.

Rudolph Ash was a reserve outfielder in 1920.

Percy (Bill) Bailey pitched for part of the 1934 season.

Sammy Baker was listed as a pitcher with the American Giants in 1950.

Walter Ball pitcher 1915. Ball was born in Detroit, Michigan, in 1877. He became one of the great black pitchers in the early years of professional black baseball. He was the top pitcher on the early Chicago Union Giants and the Leland Giants. Ball got the nod to start the first game of the series against the Chicago Cubs in 1909 against Mordecai "Three Finger" Brown. Ball had been a teammate of Rube Foster on the Leland Giants and later Rube tapped him to pitch for the American Giants in 1915. While Ball spent most of his career in Chicago, he also played for short periods in Minneapolis, New York and Philadelphia. Walter Ball's abilities peaked before the establishment of the American Giants, but he was an icon in the annals of Chicago black baseball. According to the obituary published December 21, 1946, in the *Chicago Defender*, late in life Walter Ball worked as a coach for the Chicago Sports Association and had an interest in keeping teenagers off the streets.

Jesse Barbour (aka Barber) shortstop, outfield, first base, 1911–1919. Jesse Barbour initially played shortstop for the American Giants in 1911 after Pop Lloyd left Chicago for New York. Barbour then moved to the outfield, when Fred Hutchinson proved handy at short. He was with the original American Giants during the powerhouse years from 1911 to 1919. He was known for his base running ability and was successful wherever he was played in the field. Barbour's name is sometimes spelled Barber. Jesse Barbour and Jesse Barber are one and the same.

Tobias Barnes filled in at third base for the American Giants in 1937.

Herbert Barnhill was the regular catcher from 1944 to 1946.

Lloyd "Pepper" Basset catcher 1939; 1941. Bassett was recruited to become the regular catcher for the American Giants in 1939. It had been many years since the American Giants had a consistent and reliable backstop. Basset was named to the Western All-Star team in 1939 and 1941. In 1940 he jumped to the Mexican Leagues. Pepper Basset might be best known for his stunt of playing catcher while sitting in a rocking chair, which he performed during a stint with the Indianapolis Clowns. Bassett matured as a player with the Birmingham Black Barons where he played from 1944 to 1952.

Harry Bauchman second base, utility infielder 1915–1921. Omaha native Harry Bauchman became the regular second baseman for the American Giants after William Monroe died in 1915. Bingo DeMoss eventually took the starting role away from Bauchman, but Bauchman remained on the team until 1921 as a utility infielder. Bauchman was also a boxer and in 1912 he went four rounds with heavyweight fighter Jack Flynn.

John Beckwith utility 1922–23. Infielder John Beckwith was best known for his powerful bat. He goes down in history as the first person to hit a ball completely out of Redland Field in Cincinnati while playing for Joe Green's Chicago Giants. Beckwith played some 22 years in Negro League baseball, many of them with the cross-town Chicago Giants. Rube Foster hired Beckwith to play third base in 1922 after Dave Malarcher went down with a serious injury and he stayed with the team through 1923. Beckwith had a bad temper and repeatedly got in trouble with the law. In 1925 while playing and managing the Baltimore Black Sox he severely beat an umpire and left town to avoid prosecution. Beckwith's career spanned from 1916 to 1938, he was considered a great but unpolished talent. The second half of his career was spent with several Eastern teams—Harrisburg Giants, Homestead Grays, New York Black Yankees and Brooklyn Royal Giants. His half-brother Ameal Brooks also played with the American Giants.

James "Cool Papa" Bell, the Hall of Fame speedster, played outfield for the American Giants in 1942. Cool Papa Bell and manager Candy Jim Taylor went to the Homestead Grays the following season.

Julius Benvenuti was listed as a vice-president of the American Giants in 1939, according to a photograph caption in the March 25,1939, *Chicago Defender*.

William "Fireball" Beverly pitched the last two years of the American Giants' existence, 1951–1952. He was named to the All-Star team in 1952.

Junius "Rainey" Bibbs second base 1938; 1944. Rainey Bibbs played second base for the American Giants in 1938, he also made a brief appearance in 1944. He was a two-sport athlete in college at Indiana State University in baseball and football. Bibbs was traded to Kansas City, and played three seasons with the Monarchs. After baseball he went on to become a distinguished teacher and coach in Indianapolis, Indiana, which has named a school for him.

Charles Bidwell led the ownership group that bought the American Giants from William Trimble in 1931 after Rube Foster died. Amid dissension Bidwell was not able to run the team and quickly divested himself.

John Bissant outfielder, manager 1938–1948. Outfielder John Bissant was an anchor on the American Giants during the volatile period from 1938 to 1948. Bissant was named interim manager in 1944 by owner J. B. Martin after manager Ducky Davenport jumped the team. He also took over as manager when Candy Jim Taylor struggled with health issues in 1947. Bissant was a solid player for the American Giants during a lackluster period of time for the franchise. Prior to joining the American Giants he was a star athlete at Texas's Wiley College.

Clifford Blackman pitched briefly in 1937.

Timothy Bond was the regular shortstop in 1937, and returned to the team as the third baseman in 1940.

James "Pete" Booker catcher, first base, 1907–1910; 1915. Catcher Pete Booker came to Chicago along with Rube Foster from Philadelphia in 1906. Booker was an outstanding catcher but was beat out for the starting job by legend Bruce Petway in 1910, and moved to first base. Booker played for Rube on the Leland Giants from 1907 to 1910, then returned to the American Giants in 1915 after Petway suffered an injury.

Oscar Boone was a reserve catcher in 1941.

Lyman Bostock Sr. first base 1947; 1949. Bostock started his career playing for his native Birmingham Black Barons. Bostock was an All-Star in 1941, then his career was interrupted by a tour of duty in World War II. He won the starting first base job in Chicago in 1947. Later in his career he played in Mexico and Canada. His son Lyman Bostock Jr. was one of major league baseball's first highly paid free agents, picked up by the Angels from the Twins in 1978. Tragically Bostock Jr. was cut down in his prime by a deranged gunman while driving to visit an uncle in Gary, Indiana, after a game at Comiskey on September 23, 1978.

Randolph "Lefty" Bowe pitcher 1939–40. A left-handed pitcher from Burkesville, Kentucky, Bowe was with the American Giants in 1939 and 1940. He was a regular in the rotation in 1940, but jumped the team and joined the Indianapolis Clowns.

Robert Boyd never played for the American Giants, however he was the first black player to sign with the Chicago White Sox organization in 1951. Boyd, who had played with the Memphis Red Sox in the Negro Leagues, eventually went on to a major league career that extended to 1961. He played first base and outfield and pinch hit; his best years were with the Baltimore Orioles where he led the team in batting in 1957 and 1958. His signing caused some controversy when Red Sox co-owner W. S. Martin filed a lawsuit claiming that the signing had taken place without his permission. News of the litigation lingered for some time in the Chicago black press, but the suit was eventually dropped. When his illustrious baseball career ended he became a bus driver in Wichita, Kansas; he died Sept. 7, 2004, at age 84.

John Bray was a backup catcher who put in several stints with the American Giants beginning in 1925 under Rube Foster. Bray appeared again sporadically in 1927, 1930 and 1931. In 1934 John Bray was killed in a violent altercation with teammate John Hines; the two men were said to have been drinking.

Clarkson Brazelton was one of several catchers brought in after Bruce Petway was injured. He shared catching duties from 1916 to 1917.

Chet Brewer pitcher 1946. The famed Kansas City Monarch pitcher, who was better known for his work against the American Giants in the twenties and thirties, pitched a few games for the American Giants in 1946.

George Britt (aka Britton) was a Negro League legend who could pitch, field and hit, all with great skill. He grew up near Cincinnati, Ohio, and was with the original 1920 Dayton Marcos NNL franchise. He became a legend playing with Baltimore and the Homestead Grays in the NNL. Britt caught a few games for the American Giants in 1942.

Ameal Brooks caught a few games in 1929 and 1932. He was a solid player who spent his best years with the Homestead Grays and New York Cubans. He was a half-brother of slugger John Beckwith.

Dave Brown pitcher 1918–1922. Rube Foster went out of his way to hire fellow Texas pitcher left hander Dave Brown. According to reports, Rube Foster put up a $20,000 bond to get Dave Brown paroled on a highway robbery conviction in 1918. Brown came to the American Giants with catcher James Brown to form the Brown & Brown battery. He was a regular in the starting rotation, and by the time the NNL was formed in 1920 he was the ace on the staff. Following the 1922 season Brown jumped the team for the ECL Lincoln Giants; Rube responded by blowing Dave Brown's cover and letting people know he was an ex-con. In 1925, the talented pitcher became a fugitive when he was fingered for a murder. He played baseball under a false name and disappeared.

Ed Brown pitched in a few games for the American Giants in 1921.

Jim Brown catcher, manager 1918–31; 1935. Jim Brown came to the American Giants in 1918 at the same time as fellow Texan pitcher Dave Brown. Brown proved to be the next great catcher for the American Giants after Bruce Petway left the team. He was a switch hitter who had power. The American Giants enjoyed their greatest years in the NNL while Brown was behind the plate. He gradually moved to first base in 1926 to make room for a fresh young catcher, Pythias Russ. Brown remained with the American Giants even as many of his teammates jumped to different teams. He was looked to as one of the senior members of the team, and when Dave Malarcher got fed up with the moves of owner William Trimble in 1929, Jim Brown was named player/manager, a job he kept through the half-way point of the 1930 season. When the American Giants unraveled following Rube's death, promoter Abe Saperstein tried to get Jim Brown to manage a team known as the Rube Foster Memorial Giants. The Memorial Giants fell apart during spring training, but Brown went on to pilot the "Jim Brown Cleveland Cubs." Brown continued to barnstorm and played with the House of David team in 1934. Brown returned to the American Giants in 1935 to help manage the team with Larry Brown. Jim Brown reportedly had a superstition about eating peanuts—if a teammate struck out, he would holler and blame a nearby sportswriter or fan for eating peanuts and bringing on the curse.

Larry Brown catcher, manager 1927; 1933–1935. Larry Brown was considered one of the best catchers in black baseball in the hey-day of Negro League baseball: the nineteen twenties and thirties. He earned his credentials with the Indianapolis

ABCs and Memphis Red Sox. Dave Malarcher, who took over as manager in 1927, orchestrated a controversial transaction to bring Larry Brown and Nat Rogers to the team from the struggling Memphis Red Sox team. The American Giants went on to win the Negro League World Series in 1927 with Larry Brown's assistance. Brown came back to the American Giants under the Bob Cole regime in 1933 and became co-player/manager of the team with Jim Brown in 1935.

Ossie Brown was picked up by the American Giants during spring training in Houston in 1935 and saw limited action. He pitched behind Willie Foster, Willie Cornelius and Ted Trent in the starting rotation.

Earl Bumpus pitcher 1947–48. Earl Bumpus, from Uniontown, Kentucky, was signed in 1947 to bolster the pitching staff. Previous to joining the American Giants he had pitched for Kansas City and Birmingham. He was a regular in the rotation along with Gentry Jessup and Walter McCoy in 1947, but saw less playing time in 1948 and ended his Negro League career. He went on to play for Carman, Manitoba, of the Man-Dak (Manitoba-Dakota) League.

Herbert Buster played infield in 1943. He was recruited from Hot Springs, Arkansas, and was graduate of Piney Woods College, Mississippi.

Richard "Subby" Byas catcher, first base 1935–1939. Subby Byas was a local product, having been a star athlete at Wendell Phillips High. Byas was a regular with the team through a difficult period and took whatever assignment was handed to him. He was named to the All-Star team in 1936 and 1937.

Buddy Campbell was one of many backup catchers utilized in 1932.

Walter "Jesse" Cannady played second base for the American Giants during World War II in 1942, towards the end of his prolific Negro League career that stretched from 1921 to 1945. He is best known for his work with the New York Lincoln Giants and Black Yankees.

Carlson (first name unknown) filled in as a catcher in 1916.

Marlin Ted Carter played third base in 1948. Carter began his career in the early thirties with the Memphis Red Sox where he spent most of his career. He served in World War II and after his stint with the American Giants he played minor league ball.

Oscar Charleston, who was considered by many the greatest player of all time, played outfield in 1919, when the Indianapolis ABCs did not field a team due to restrictions caused by World War I. Charleston joined Cristobal Torriente and Jude Gans in one of the strongest American Giant outfields ever. In 1923, Rube hired Oscar as a ringer for a three game City League championship series. Charleston's strong-willed personality clashed with that of Rube Foster. Oscar picked up and left the NNL in 1924 to join the ECL when his hometown Indianapolis ABCs fell on tough times.

W. M. "Bill" Charter was a wartime player who played first base in 1943 and filled in behind the plate in 1946.

Louis Chirban was one of the white players recruited from the local industrial league to play for the American Giants in 1950 in hopes of increasing attendance. A nice crowd actually did turn out to see Chirban pitch, but he was shelled and left the team a short time later.

Louis Clarizio was a white player recruited from local industrial leagues to play for the American Giants in 1950.

Albert D. Clark (aka Clarke) played in left field for a handful of games in 1930.

Zack Clayton played first base in 1935 and 1937. It turned out that baseball was a minor part of his career. He was also an accomplished basketball player and played with the Harlem Globetrotters. When his basketball career ended he became a boxing referee. In the ring he wore a trademark striped shirt, like a basketball referee. He refereed the famous Ali-Foreman fight in Zaire in 1974 (the Rumble in the Jungle). He had also reffed the June 5, 1952, rematch between Jersey Joe Walcott and Ezzard Charles in Philadelphia.

Nat "Sweetwater" Clifton first base 1949. Sweetwater Clifton was best known as the first black player to sign an NBA contract, but this Chicago native played for the American Giants in 1949 and played minor league ball before signing with the New York Knicks in 1950. Clifton led the Knicks to the NBA finals in his first year, and became an NBA All-Star in 1957.

Robert Cole owner, league official 1932–1935. Cole was a hard working businessman who worked his way up from a Pullman porter to become the head of the Metropolitan Assurance Company. Cole bailed out black baseball after the team fell apart in the aftermath of Rube Foster's death. Cole was not as intimately familiar with baseball as Rube, but he did put up money to keep the team going. Cole was able to retain star players like Willie Foster, Turkey Stearnes, Mule Suttles, Willie Sug Cornelius, Dave Malarcher and others. Cole was instrumental in pulling off the Negro League All-Star game at Comiskey Park. Cole sold ownership of his team to his assistant Horace Hall halfway through the 1935 season, but retained his post as treasurer of the Negro National League. The first year under his ownership the home field of the American Giants was ripped out from under him by a group of hustlers who bought the American Giants' park to install a dog-racing track; Cole responded by temporarily relocating to Indianapolis. He was nicknamed King

Cole by some. Officially Cole changed the name of the team to "Cole's American Giants"— which drew criticism — but the team was still commonly referred to as the "American Giants."

Willie "Sug" Cornelius pitcher 1933–1939; 1941–46. Sug Cornelius was one of the greatest pitchers to take the mound for the American Giants. Born in Atlanta, Georgia, on September 4, 1908, he started his career with the Nashville Elite Giants in 1931 and played with the Memphis Red Sox and Birmingham Black Barons before coming to the American Giants in 1933. Sug Cornelius was known for his great curveball and overall good control. Teaming up with Willie Foster and Ted Trent in 1933 and 1934, he made the pitching staff among the best in black baseball. In 1937, after Willie Foster left the team, Sug Cornelius became the ace of the staff and the breadwinner for the team. In 1940 Cornelius jumped to the Mexican League, but was back in the Windy City in 1941. Cornelius was the bridge between the new and the old; he proved to be as effective in Comiskey as he was at the old South Side Park. In 1944 Cornelius was offered the job of team manager, but had to decline because he had joined the army. In the late thirties and forties, when the team struggled, he frequently carried the team on his shoulders. Willie Sug Cornelius makes the list of all-time great Negro League pitchers. He was named to the All-Star team in 1935, 1936 and 1938.

Towards the end of his career in 1946, Willie was approached by a man who complimented him on his pitching and asked him his age, to which Willie responded "39 years old." Willie found out the man had been a scout for the Detroit Tigers and regretted that he hadn't lied about his age. Grace Comiskey, owner of the White Sox, once told Cornelius, "Oh. If you were a white boy, what you'd be worth to my club."

Sam Crawford pitcher, coach 1913, 1915, 1918–19, 1925–28, 1931, 1936. Crawford was a prototypical lanky pitcher whose career stretched 28 years. Although he made only intermittent appearances with the club, he was well respected for his knowledge of the game and helped out in the capacity of coach under both Rube Foster and Dave Malarcher. A member of the "old school," Crawford went from New York, to Kansas City, to Havana — often without a contract — playing on a variety of top notch Negro League teams.

Norman Cross was the pitcher of last resort from 1932 to 1936. He was given a chance to prove himself in a few games, but was not able to break into the starting rotation.

Jimmie (John William) Crutchfield outfield 1941–42, 1944–45. Crutchfield's greatest seasons were spent with the Pittsburgh Crawfords, where he played alongside Cool Papa Bell, Oscar Charleston, Josh Gibson, Judy Johnson and Satchel Paige in the mid-thirties. Had he not been overshadowed by such talent in Pittsburgh we might better know Jimmie. He was, by all accounts, a great player and a wonderful person. He joined the Chicago American Giant outfield in 1941 and brought much needed veteran experience to the team. He joined the army in 1943, but returned to play two more seasons in 1944–1945. Like so many others who had just a "taste of State Street," he made Chicago his home. After his baseball career ended he worked for the postal service in Chicago.

Crutchfield died March 31, 1993. Although he had been celebrated in the national media with an interview in *Sports Illustrated* in July 1992, was a World War II vet and well liked in the community, he was laid to rest in an unmarked grave in Chicago's Burr Oak Cemetery. In 2004, an anesthesiologist named Jeremy Kroc, who shared Crutchfield's home town of Ardmore, Missouri and was touched when he learned of his hometown hero's fate, led a group of donors who placed a marker on Crutchfield's grave. That effort also led to marking the graves of other teammates laid to rest in Burr Oak in unmarked graves— including Candy Jim Taylor and Theodore "Ted" Trent. A picture of Jimmy Crutchfield hangs in the Negro League Café opened in 2004 on Chicago's South Side where he is still revered.

Rube Currie pitcher 1926–27. Before the 1926 season Rube Foster traded Cristobal Torriente to Kansas City for George Sweatt and Rube Currie. Currie was a solid pitcher and helped the American Giants to win back to back championships in 1926 and 1927. Currie threw a no-hitter against the NNL Dayton Marcos to give the team a psychological boost, after an incapacitated Rube Foster was forced to abandon his coaching duties. Currie refused to re-sign with the American Giants in 1928 and moved to Detroit.

Leon "Pepper" Daniels was a catcher with the 1931 Columbia American Giants.

William "Ducky" Davenport outfield, manager 1943–44, 1949, 1951. Outfielder Ducky Davenport came to the American Giants in 1943 from the Cincinnati Buckeyes, the result of a complicated trade that also involved the Homestead Grays and Memphis Red Sox. Davenport jumped around to a number of different teams including a flight from the American Giants to the Mexican Leagues in 1945. Ducky, who was a five-time All-Star, had the talent to demand higher pay and played his cards whenever needed. With the American Giants he teamed up with Art Pennington as the club's big offensive weapons. Doc Martin installed Ducky Davenport as the player-manager of the team in 1944, but Ducky consorted with Gus Greenlee who was attempting to resurrect the Pittsburgh Crawfords— and even accepted some advance money. Doc Martin sold Davenport to the Cleveland Buckeyes once he caught wind of the betrayal. Davenport was back with the American Giants under a different regime in 1949 — his fellow Louisianan Winfield Welch was running the team and brought him back. Davenport was supposedly banned for life from the Negro Leagues by Doc Martin following the 1949 season — for leaving the team prematurely to play winter ball in Venezuela — but he was back with the American Giants in 1951.

Lonnie Davis played first base in 1952, the last year of existence for the American Giants. He had been given a short tryout by the major league St. Louis Browns, prior to joining the team.

Saul Davis second base, shortstop 1925–26, 1929–30. Saul Davis's career began in 1918 and he played most of his career on teams in the South such as the Vapor City Tigers (Hot Springs), Houston Black Buffaloes, Birmingham Black Barons and Memphis Red Sox. Davis said that in 1925 Rube Foster drove a roadster down to Birmingham to hustle him to the American Giants. However he only played in a few games for the American Giants in 1925 and 1926. In 1929 he was utilized by manager Jim Brown to shore up the infield after a number of players jumped the team.

Walter "Steel Arm" Davis outfield, first base 1924, 1927–1933; 1935. "Steel Arm" earned his nickname while a pitcher with the Detroit Stars in 1923. Davis was also a strong hitter and when he joined the American Giants under Rube Foster in 1924 he was converted to an outfielder. Steel Arm Davis rejoined the team in 1927 — after Jelly Gardner jumped the team for the Homestead Grays. Walter Davis was a regular in the outfield in the post–Rube Foster era and a valuable contributor offensively.

After his ball playing days were over "Steel Arm" was shot and killed in a barroom fight at the Indiana Inn at 3729 State Street in December 1941. While "Steel Arm" had always maintained a tough reputation, he also had a sense of humor. In a barnstorming game against a group of major leaguers following the 1930 season, the *Chicago Defender* noted that he, along with Art Shires of the D.C. Senators, kept the crowd in an uproar with their clowning.

Rossie Dawson was one of several backup catchers brought on to replace Pepper Bassett in 1940.

Elwood "Bingo" DeMoss second base, captain, manager 1913, 1917–1925, 1936, 1944. Bingo DeMoss is one of the legends of Negro League baseball. He was born in Topeka, Kansas, September 5, 1889, and began his baseball career with the Topeka Giants in 1905. In 1912 he joined the West Baden Sprudels, a black team that played at a southern Indiana health resort. In 1913, he was hired by the sister resort team the French Lick

Plutos (French Lick is known to basketball trivia buffs as the hometown of Larry Bird). There was a convenient railroad spur to the resort and a number of top-notch ball players played in the "Springs Valley" resorts. At French Lick/West Baden Bingo played alongside C.I. Taylor, Ben Taylor, "Candy" Jim Taylor, Steel Arm Taylor and Dizzy Dismukes. Bingo actually appeared with the American Giants briefly in 1913 as a ringer for a post-season match with the Lincoln Giants. C.I. Taylor moved to Indianapolis in 1914, and in 1915 he persuaded Bingo DeMoss to join the ABCs. Bingo DeMoss was one reason the ABCs had success against the American Giants in 1915 and 1916. In 1917, DeMoss was lured away from Indianapolis and joined the American Giants.

Bingo's golden glove, steady hitting and superb bunting ability made him a perfect fit for Rube Foster's system. In 1919, Rube Foster made Bingo DeMoss the second ever team captain, replacing Pete Hill. DeMoss was team captain through the glory NNL years under Rube Foster from 1920 to 1925. Prior to the 1926 season Rube shipped Bingo to Indianapolis — in what appeared to be an effort to balance competition in the league overall. Bingo was effective as a player and manager for the ABCs in 1926, playing in every game and guiding the team to a .500 record — a vast improvement for the struggling franchise. The ABCs dropped out of the NNL the following year however and Bingo moved to the Detroit Stars. DeMoss became player-manager for the Detroit Stars, where he remained through 1931.

He was respected far and wide for his playing skill, managing skills and impressive knowledge of the game. In 1936, American Giant owner Horace Hall corralled DeMoss, who had been out of baseball, to pilot the American Giants. Horace Hall, in his first year of ownership, had gutted the team and the franchise was at something of a low point, but DeMoss did his part to make the team respectable. In 1944, when manager Double Duty jumped the team shortly before the season began, it was Doc Martin who tapped DeMoss to take over as interim skipper. DeMoss also piloted the Chicago Brown Bombers, who were a member of Gus Greenlee's marginal United States Negro League in the mid–1940's.

DeMoss died in Chicago January 26, 1965, and is buried in Chicago's Burr Oak Cemetery, not far from one of his friends and rivals whose career spanned an equal length of time: "Candy" Jim Taylor. If and when Cooperstown reconsiders Negro League players from the Dead Ball era, Elwood "Bingo" DeMoss certainly should be on the short list.

Kermit Dial filled a utility role in 1932 and again in 1936.

Lou Oland Dials outfielder 1925, 1927–1928,

1936–37. Dials played briefly for the American Giants under Rube Foster in 1925, but left baseball to attend college. In 1927, he arrived back on the scene travelling with Willie Foster and George Harney from Los Angeles following the California winter baseball season. Dials shared outfield duties along with a cast of characters in 1927 and part of 1928. He returned to the squad in 1936, this time a standout on a weaker team and was named to the 1936 All-Star team. In 1937, Dials jumped to the Mexican League and became a star. In 1943, the Los Angeles Angels of the PCL wanted to sign Dials but the idea was vetoed by owner Phil Wrigley. Later he became a major league scout.

William "Dizzy" Dismukes pitched in a few exhibition games for the American Giants over the years, but was better known for his work against the American Giants as a submariner for the Indianapolis ABCs. Dismukes was recruited by former teammate Bingo DeMoss to help coach the American Giants in 1936. Dismukes dabbled in journalism; his commentary appeared in the *Chicago Defender* and the *Pittsburgh Courier*. Truly a legend of Negro League baseball, he held many positions with different clubs. In 1953, the New York Yankees hired him as a scout.

George "Tubby" Dixon catcher 1917–1925. Great expectations were placed on George Dixon when he joined the club in 1917, as he was appointed to fill the shoes of legend Bruce Petway behind the plate. He proved to be an adequate catcher but not in the same category as Petway. Dixon was the alternate catcher behind Jim Brown from 1918 to 1925. Rube Foster moved Dixon to the Indianapolis ABCs following the 1925 season in a move to prop up the struggling ABC franchise. Dixon died in Cleveland August 4, 1940; the *Chicago Defender* reported on August 17, 1940, that the body was unclaimed at the Cleveland morgue.

Herbert "Rap" Dixon outfield 1930. Rap Dixon was a power-hitting outfielder who made a name for himself with the Harrisburg Giants in the Eastern Colored League in the twenties. He played in a handful of games for the American Giants in 1930.

Pat Dougherty pitcher 1909–1914. A great left-handed power pitcher of black baseball's Dead Ball era. He put fear into the hearts of opposing batters with his fastball. In his prime he was almost perfect. Indeed he did not lose a single game as a starter for the Leland Giants in 1910. When he did lose it was usually only by a single run. In 1909, he battled Chicago Cubs' Hall of Famer Mordecai Three Finger Brown for nine innings, but lost 1–0. Early in his career he played for teams in Indiana such as the Idaho Stars of Vincennes, the Indianapolis Unions and the West Baden Sprudels. The Leland Giants encountered

Dougherty while he was with the West Baden team and recruited him. Dougherty was also a capable hitter; while playing winter ball at San Diego's Athletic Park he hit a home run over the right field fence that was called the longest ever to clear that fence, preserving an American Giant 11–5 win over Palmer's San Diego Bears.

Jesse Douglass second base, shortstop, utility 1944–45, 1949–50. Jesse Douglass became the regular second baseman for the American Giants in 1944, he had previously barnstormed with Satchel Paige. After three seasons in Mexico, he returned to the American Giants. Sportswriter Russ Cowans named Douglass the "Most Valuable Player" in the Negro American League in 1950, as many other top players had been snatched up by the major leagues. Jesse Douglass was signed by the Chicago White Sox organization and played at their Colorado Springs farm club in 1952.

Andrew Drake pitched for a few games with the American Giants in 1932. He was on the losing end of a 17–0 shellacking delivered by the Kansas City Monarchs August 28, 1932, and left the team.

Al Dubbetts, according to one account, was a white pitcher from Havana, Illinois, listed as a pitcher in 1950.

Tommy "Dixie" Dukes catcher 1928, 1945. "Dixie" Dukes caught a few games for the American Giants in 1928 while on summer break from college. He rejoined the team as a regular in 1945. He spent the best years of his career with the Homestead Grays, he was the catcher and cleanup hitter prior to Josh Gibson joining that team.

Frank (Pete) Duncan left field 1909–1918. Pete Duncan was one of the original American Giants, coming to the Leland Giants in 1910. He often batted lead-off during the 1910's when the American Giants dominated all competition. Duncan was just one more star player on a team loaded with talent, sharing outfield duties with Pete Hill, Andrew Jap Payne, and Jesse Barbour. Duncan was shipped to Detroit along with Pete Hill and Bruce Petway in 1919 as Rube made way for younger players. There was another player named Frank Duncan, not related, who played for the American Giants years later.

Frank Duncan catcher 1938, 1940. Although he was born in Kansas City, Frank Duncan started his baseball career with Peters' Union Giants in Chicago in 1920. He later made his way back to Kansas City where he would spend most of his career. Duncan was on some great ball clubs in KC, but towards the end of his career he returned to Chicago. Duncan was among the players who toured Australia, China, Hawaii, Japan and the Philippines in 1927, drawing a fine and suspension from the NNL president William Hueston. In 1938, the American Giants desperately needed a catcher and Duncan answered the call. Duncan (with a number of other prominent players) went over to the Palmer House Stars (a semi-pro team sponsored by the Palmer House hotel) in 1939, then came back to the American Giants for part of the 1940 season.

Herman Dunlap (aka Dunlop) outfield 1936–39. A regular in the outfield in the late thirties, Herman Dunlap was named to the 1936 All-Star team. Dunlap broke his leg in 1938 and the American Giants donated part of the gate receipts for the August 9, 1940, game to help out Dunlap, who had fallen on hard times.

Vann Durham of Norfolk, Virginia, played outfield for the American Giants in 1952 and was named to the Western All-Star team.

Frank Dyll was one of the white players brought on as a gate attraction in 1950, he played shortstop.

Howard Easterling played in the infield for a few games for the American Giants in 1938 and 1939. He came to the American Giants from the Cincinnati Tigers. In 1940 he began a legendary career with the Homestead Grays. Easterling was the all-round player, he could hit, hit for power, run, field and throw. Later he played in Latin America in a career that went into the 1950's. Easterling was named to the All-Star team five times, but he was with the American Giants very briefly.

Harry Else was a backup catcher hired in 1940.

William "Buck" Ewing was a Massillon, Ohio, native who caught for the American Giants in 1920.

Luther Farrell was brought on as a ringer by Rube Foster to pitch in post season City League games in 1922. He later went on to be a top pitcher for the Atlantic City Bacharach Giants who vied with the American Giants for Negro League supremacy in the late 1920's.

John "Buck" Felder was a utility infielder in 1944.

Jose Fernandez was a legendary catcher for the New York–based Cuban teams, but came to the American Giants in 1930 (a lackluster season) and became the regular catcher for one season.

Willie "Trueheart" Ferrell pitcher 1941–1943. Willie Ferrell worked right alongside notables Willie Cornelius and Gentry Jessup in the American Giant starting rotation from 1941 to 1943. He started his career with the Birmingham Black Barons and was with the Homestead Grays before joining "Candy" Jim Taylor's American Giants in 1941.

Jim Fishback went into camp as a second baseman with the American Giants in Meridian, Mississippi, for spring training in 1951, but left to join the Class A Dayton Indians who were part of the St. Louis Browns' farm system.

Joe Fleet was given a tryout as a pitcher by Jim Brown in 1930. Fleet had been a star player with the Leavenworth federal prison "Booker T's," one of three such players to graduate from the Booker T's to the American Giants. Fleet had a rough go of it when he walked two batters, hit a batter, and gave up a single and double in the first inning to go down three-nothing. Then in the fifth inning he gave up two doubles, made an error and allowed two runs before being relieved — he walked off the mound and was dismissed from the team. (The story of the Leavenworth Booker T's was researched by Timothy Rives, an archivist with the National Archives in Kansas City, and was published in the National Archives and Records Administration's quarterly journal *Prologue*, summer 2004.)

Percy Forrest pitched a few games for the American Giants in 1938 and 1939.

Andrew "Rube" Foster owner, manager, pitcher 1907–1926. He was born in Calvert, Texas, September 17, 1879. His father was an elder in the local AME church. Andrew Foster was born with an asthma condition and playing ball was recommended as a way of getting needed exercise. Andrew did not need further encouragement; he began organizing baseball teams as a pre-teen. His father sent Andy off to study religion but junior gravitated to the school baseball team. He joined the Fort Worth Yellow Jackets, then descended on Hot Springs, Arkansas, where major league players gathered for spring training.

Andrew made an impression on everyone he interacted with, and many teams were desirous of his services. In 1902, Foster was persuaded to join Frank Leland's Union Giants of Chicago. Andy not only met expectations but exceeded them as he was nearly perfect for the Union Giants. While the Union Giants were touring western Michigan in August of 1902, Foster and teammate Dave Wyatt (feeling under-appreciated by Leland) joined an otherwise all-white baseball team in Otsego, Michigan. After a rough start, in which he is said to have lost five games in a row, Foster righted the ship and led Otsego to victory over every team in the Michigan State League.

Andrew left the Michigan club and joined the Cuban X-Giants of Philadelphia at the end of the 1902 season and stayed with the X-Giants through 1903 — continually sharpening his skills. In 1904 he switched from the Cuban X-Giants to the cross-town Philadelphia Giants and led that team to a championship. Following the 1904 season, Andrew Foster is said to have hooked up in a duel with pitcher Rube Waddell of the Philadelphia Athletics. After he defeated Waddell his teammates dubbed him "Rube." The name stuck and Andy Foster became "Rube" Foster. Rube claimed that in 1905 he sported a 51–4 record for the

Philadelphia Giants. Following the 1906 season Rube played ball in Cuba; when he returned from Cuba he decided to leave the "City of Brotherly Love" and headed for Chicago, Illinois.

Rube re-joined Frank Leland's team and it wasn't long before Foster convinced Leland to make him the team manager. Rube went to work retooling the Leland Giants—making room for some of his best teammates from Philadelphia, who came eagerly when Rube made sure they were compensated. Foster later claimed that the Lelands of 1907 had an astounding 103–1 record. In 1908, the Lelands battled to the top of the Chicago City Leagues, which included major league caliber players. Rube passed up his usual trip to Cuba in 1908 for nuptials, marrying Sarah Watts in Temple, Texas, on October 29, 1908. In 1909, the Lelands cleaned up in the City Leagues and finished off the season with an exciting series against the reigning World Champion Chicago Cubs. Were it not for a few careless errors and controversial umpiring decisions—the American Giants might have beaten the Cubbies. In 1910 Rube split off from Frank Leland. The rivals battled in the courtroom while Rube guided the Leland Giants—no longer associated with Frank Leland—to an incredible 126–3 record (by Rube's tally).

In 1911 Rube formed the American Giants. With the American Giants Rube had free rein to put into practice his own baseball theory. Rube worked out a business deal with tavern owner John Schorling to use the South Side Park, which had been previously used by the White Sox. Their inaugural year American Giants laid waste to visitors on the South Side and continued to do so on an extended road trip to the West Coast in the winter and spring of 1912. Soon professional black baseball became more competitive and the days of a .900 winning percentage ended. In 1913 the Lincoln Giants defeated the American Giants in a post-season series. By 1915 the American Giants faced a serious challenge from the Lincoln Stars, the Indianapolis ABCs and the Cuban Stars. In 1916, the Indianapolis team bested the American Giants in a post-season series although Rube insisted that the American Giants were the real champs. World War 1 beset baseball but Rube stuck with the game, raising the American flag in parks all over the Midwest and eastern United States. In 1919, he jumped at the chance to acquire players like Cristobal Torriente and Oscar Charleston who were made available due to the war. Strife broke out on the South Side of Chicago in 1919, when a black youth was attacked by white youths at a swimming beach. Riots broke out that lasted five days and Rube was forced to temporarily vacate Chicago.

The next year, 1920, in an all-hands meeting in Kansas City, Rube unveiled the Negro National League. Rube had stopped pitching, he was proven as an ingenious manager, but founding the NNL would be his greatest achievement. For the next six years Rube ran the American Giants on and off the field. He also ran the Negro National League. There were many demands and challenges along the way, but Rube managed to keep the league going. In 1925, Rube was nearly asphyxiated by natural gas after dozing off in an Indianapolis boarding house bathroom. Rube seemed to have recovered from that incident, but in 1926 he fell victim to mental illness. Eventually he was committed to a state hospital in Kankakee, Illinois, where he died on December 9, 1930.

It wasn't until the 1970's that the Hall of Fame even considered including Negro League players. When Negro League players finally were considered by a special "Negro Leagues Committee," incredibly Rube was left out. Knowledgeable writers and historians like Robert Peterson, author of *Only the Ball Was White*, and St. Louis writer Tweed Webb were among those who took the Hall to task and finally Rube was ushered in the door in 1981. Ironically major league baseball as we know it today would not exist were it not for Foster; the Hall of Fame owed him a plaque and a whole lot more.

Rube stands out, even against the background of colorful baseball personalities. Ahead of his time, gifted, unflappable, ingenious—he was all that and more. He was one of a kind and although we know more about Andrew Foster than we do about many of his cohorts in the Negro Leagues, he remains enigmatic. Looking back at what Rube was able to accomplish, it is all too easy to forget that he was himself a victim of profound injustice.

Chicago Defender writer Cary B. Lewis shared a story about Rube Foster's venture into vaudeville in his column on March 1, 1919:

During the time when Christie Mathewson, John McGraw and Doc White were taking to the stage [which was 1912 or thereabouts] "Uncle Rube" hit it from the South Side. It was his first night at Columbus, Ohio on the Klein Circuit (vaudeville), when "Rube" came before the footlights. As he approached the middle of the stage, a voice from the audience, "Take Him Out." "Uncle Rube" mistook this occasion and thought he was on the ball field. He forgot the footlights and approached the audience in a manner similar to one when he was manning the Giants. He forthwith stepped directly into the band pit, plunged through the bass drum, doing $200 in damage to the drummer's outfit.

One of Rube's other hobbies was automobiles. He owned a snappy Apperson Jackrabbit roadster and operated a garage.

Willie Foster pitcher, manager 1922–30, 1932–35; 1937. William Hedrick Foster was Rube Foster's half-brother. He was born in Rodney, Texas, in 1904. As a young teenager Willie Foster traveled to Chicago in hopes of finding work and playing baseball for his famous brother. Rube did the only thing he could do, he sent Willie back home. Five years later, in 1923, Willie found work with the NNL Memphis Red Sox. Rube and the American Giants came through Memphis that spring and Rube saw for himself that indeed his brother possessed the talent to play in the big leagues. Exercising the long arm of his powers as NNL commissioner, Rube was able to bring Willie to the American Giants.

During his first few years with the American Giants Willie waited until classes were over before reporting to camp. He was a serious student and went on to complete his Bachelor of Science in agriculture degree at Alcorn College. Much later in life he served as a baseball coach and dean of men at Alcorn. When Foster initially joined the American Giants he was one of several top-flight pitchers on the American Giants staff that included George Harney, Juan Padrone, Huck Rile and Aubrey Owens. Rube tried to coach his half-brother on the fine points of pitching, which occasionally resulted in friction.

It was in 1926, after Rube had suffered a mental collapse, that Willie Foster came into his own as a star pitcher. Willie pitched both ends of a double-header against the Kansas City Monarchs in the NNL playoff series and won both games, clinching a World Series berth for the American Giants. He became the ace of the staff and built on his reputation; he became known as the greatest left-hander in black baseball. William Trimble, the hustler who bought the American Giants in 1927, believed that all he needed to do to run a successful franchise was to put Willie Foster on the mound. Foster was able to carry the team a few years, but management neglected the rest of the team. In 1930, Willie Foster was named player/manager, however the heart of his supporting cast had left his team. Willie followed suit in 1931, joining the Homestead Grays, and also played for the KC Monarchs in the *Denver Post* tournament.

Willie Foster returned to the American Giants under the ownership of Robert Cole in 1932. He was named to the All-Star team in 1933 and 1934. In 1935 he began to suffer with arm soreness. In 1936, Willie was with the Pittsburgh Crawfords where he joined Satchel Paige on the staff. Willie returned to Chicago in 1937 under manager Candy Jim Taylor, and teamed with Willie Cornelius and Ted Trent on the mound. The 1937 season ended for Willie Foster when he was hit in the chest by a line drive off the bat of Bullet Rogan in a playoff game. Willie went on to play some semi-pro ball for a variety of teams including

Elgin, Illinois, Jamestown, North Dakota, the Yakima (Washington) Browns and others, but his professional career ended in 1937.

Billy Francis (the Little Corporal) third base 1914–1919; 1925. The Little Corporal was lured to Chicago by his old Philadelphia Giant teammate — Rube Foster. Francis was with the New York Lincoln Giants when they upended the American Giants in a post-season series in 1913. That winter Foster organized a team to hit the West Coast and invited Francis (along with Lee Wade and Jude Gans of the Lincolns) to come along. On returning from the road trip he stayed with the American Giants and became the regular third baseman. Francis remained at the hot corner for the balance of that great decade. In 1920, after the NNL was organized, Billy jumped for the Eastern Colored League (against Rube's wishes) and joined the Hilldale Daisies. In 1925 he rejoined his old friend Rube for a swan song and played in a number of games for the American Giants.

Billy Francis, along with Candy Jim Taylor, was among the best third basemen in black baseball's early era.

Jude (Edward) Gans outfielder 1914–1920. Jude Gans was lured to the American Giants from the Lincoln Giants following the 1913 season. He left the American Giants to join the upstart Lincoln Stars in 1915, but rejoined the team after the Stars' owner Jesse McMahon had trouble meeting payroll. Gans was called to serve in the U.S. Army in World War I in 1918, but rejoined the American Giants for the 1919 campaign teaming up with legends Oscar Charleston, Cristobal Torriente and Jesse Barbour in the outfield. Gans was also occasionally called on to pitch. He returned to the Lincoln Giants in 1921 and where he became player-manager.

Gans was a floral bearer at Frank Leland's funeral in 1914, though he had not played for Leland's team. Hall of Famer Judy Johnson was nicknamed because he looked like Jude Gans.

Jelly Gardner outfielder 1920–30. Over the years Rube Foster acquired many great players from his home state of Texas. It was no secret that he favored the Lone Star breed of ball player. In 1917, Rube organized a special "Texas Day" where the American Giants battled the barnstorming "Texas All-Stars" in Chicago. One of the ball players on the Texas All-Stars was Floyd "Jelly" Gardner, Rube took note of his play and in 1920 signed him to the American Giants. Gardner was a hard hitting hustling ball player, with a tough reputation for being not shy about using his fists. Jelly scored the winning run in the American Giants' first ever official NL World Series win against the Bacharachs in 1926. In 1927, under Dave Malarcher, Jelly held out for higher pay then jumped to the Homestead Grays, but returned to the team the following year. Jelly Gardner became the anchor in the outfield after Cristobal Torriente was dealt to Kansas City in 1925. Gardner was with the team in 1930 and ironically the rebellious Jelly Gardner was the only front line player with the team who remained from the inaugural NNL season under Foster.

In 1936 Gardner played in an old-timers game on Rube Foster Day. Floyd Jelly Gardner has a following among some Negro League history buffs, who maintain he was among the best outfielders in black baseball.

"Big" Bill Gatewood pitcher 1912–1913, 1915. Bill Gatewood was one of the great arms in early black baseball. He played with a large number of teams, making his mark early with the Leland Giants where he pitched behind legends: Walter Ball, Rube Foster and Pat Dougherty. Rube convinced him to join the American Giants in 1912, after Leland finally set aside his baseball ambitions. Gatewood was used on a regular basis in 1912 and 1913. He left in 1914, to play for the Lincoln Giants, but was back in the American Giants' starting rotation in 1915. Gatewood's career with the American Giants ended there, but he went on to play in Indianapolis then eventually settled in St. Louis where he developed into a fine manager. While in St. Louis he was also known for giving James Bell his famous nickname "Cool Papa." Gatewood applied the name after Bell struck out Oscar Charleston. Later in his career he became a pitching coach of the Birmingham Black Barons and taught the finer points of pitching craft to Satchel Paige.

Herbert Gay was a pitcher for the American Giants in 1929–30, he also saw some time in the outfield.

W. Gay, brother of Herbert Gay, pitched for the American Giants in 1929.

Alphonso Gerrard played outfield for the American Giants in 1948 under Quincy Trouppe. Gerrard later went on to play minor league ball and also played in his native Puerto Rico.

Arthur "Hamp" Gillard pitched for the American Giants in 1914. Rube Foster encountered Gillard, who was a graduate of Talladega College, when Gillard pitched for C.I. Taylor's Birmingham Giants in 1909 and West Baden Sprudels in 1910. He made a few starts in 1914; he was also known as Albert Gillard and "Hamp" Gillard.

Murray Gillespie came to the American Giants in September of the 1930 season, from Memphis, and was a regular starting pitcher for the balance of the season.

Luther Gilyard first base 1937–39. Luther Gilyard joined the American Giants in 1937 as a backup first baseman and outfielder. Gilyard was a starter for about half the season in 1938, and then once again was relegated to a backup role.

Alvin "Al" Bubber Gipson pitcher 1949– 50. Alvin Gipson made a name for himself with the Birmingham Black Barons, then became a regular in the rotation for the American Giants in 1949 and 1950.

Carl Glass was well known for his work with the Memphis Red Sox in the late 1920's, he pitched briefly for the American Giants in 1930.

Clyde Golden was a starting pitcher for the American Giants in 1952, the last year of the team's existence.

Harold Gordon pitched for the American Giants in 1950.

Leroy Grant first base 1911; 1916–1925. Leroy Grant was a fixture at first base for the American Giants from 1916 to 1922 and he had a loyal following with hometown fans. Leroy Grant was the first baseman on the American Giants their inaugural year of 1911, but left the team for the Lincoln Giants the following season. He was a big man who had an imposing presence on the bag. Grant served in the armed forces for a portion of 1919 but also played part of season. He was a valuable contributor and among the best first basemen in the business. Rube Foster loaned Leroy Grant to the Indianapolis ABCs in 1923 when that team struggled in the aftermath of C.I. Taylor's death. Local fans were shocked that Rube would loan Grant to the ABCs, but he did come back to the Chicago American Giants. In 1925 Rube unconditionally released Leroy Grant to make way for younger players.

Gray (first name unknown) pitched for the American Giants in 1951.

Joe Green outfield 1912. Joe Green was a legend on the Chicago black baseball scene. He began his career at the turn of the century and played on early Chicago black baseball teams such as the Columbia Giants, the Union Giants and the Leland Giants. When Rube Foster parted ways with Frank Leland in 1910, Green sided with Leland. In 1912, however, Rube hired Green to fill in as an outfielder. Joe Green was a close associate of Frank Leland and after Leland's death in 1914, Green inherited what remained of Frank Leland's ball club. The team was known as Joe Green's Chicago Giants and was termed a semi-pro team. However in 1920 and 1921 the team competed in the Negro National League. Green continued to run the team through the 1920's. The Chicago Giants employed a lot of players who had previously played with the American Giants and offered a start for some young players who were destined for the big time.

The *Chicago Defender* said of Green, "he encouraged and developed young baseball aspirants, then gladly sent them on to higher fields of endeavor and without the dollar sign being the main feature of the transaction." His long playing career has been remembered for one base running play he made while with the Leland Giants in an exhibition game against the Chicago Cubs. Green slid hard into third base while an errant throw got well past the third baseman. Green got up and dashed for home, but his legs weren't at full strength — he was barely thrown out. When the dust settled it was obvious he had broken his leg sliding into third.

Robert Griffin was a young man when he pitched for the Columbia American Giants under Dave Malarcher in 1931. He died of illness at the young age of 27 in Chicago in 1940.

Lacy Guice of Witchita, Kansas, played outfield in 1952. He had played previously with the New Orleans Eagles in 1951 and was offered a tryout with the Pittsburgh Pirates organization in the spring of 1952.

Nap Gulley was a journeyman pitcher and outfielder who played with a number of Negro League teams in the 1940's, eventually playing minor league ball in the 1950's. He made brief appearances with the American Giants in 1941, 1946 and 1949.

James "Earl" Gurley pitched and played outfield in a few games in 1925 and 1926.

E. "Red" Hale shared shortstop duties with Joe Sparks in 1939.

Red Haley was given a shot as the second baseman by Dave Malarcher in 1928. Author Alex Haley, known for his Pulitzer Prize–winning *Roots*, suspected that he was related to Red Haley.

Horace Hall owner, business manager 1933–42. Horace Hall worked with Robert Cole at the Chicago Metropolitan Insurance Company. When Cole bought the team in 1932, he made Horace Hall the business manager of the American Giants. In 1935, after Cole had grown weary of running the American Giants, he sold the team to Hall. Hall's first move as owner in 1936 was to drop out of the struggling Negro National League. Following the 1936 season, Hall worked closely with other owners to form the Negro American League. Horace Hall rebuilt the American Giants into winners in 1937 and they played a special playoff against the Kansas City Monarchs for the Western championship. In the 1940's when black baseball experienced a surge in popularity Hall proceeded cautiously, while owners Effa Manley (Newark Eagles), Cum Posey (Homestead Grays) and Tom Wilson (Baltimore Elite Giants) went "all out" to sign top players. When the American Giants' ballpark burned down on Christmas Day 1940, Hall was not able to come up with the money to make repairs. Former Memphis Red Sox owner, pharmacist and entrepreneur Doctor J.B. Martin came to Chicago from Memphis, Tennessee, in 1941 and bought a piece of the American Giants. By 1944, Martin had completely taken over the American Giants from Horace Hall.

Hancock (first name unknown) caught one game in 1928.

Hallie Harding played second base for the Columbia American Giants in 1931. He was better known for his work with the Kansas City Monarchs from 1928 to 1930. He also played basketball for the "Savoy Big Five" — a precursor to the Harlem Globetrotters.

Arthur Hardy (a/k/a Bill Norman) born in Kansas City — pitched with the Leland Giants from 1907 to 1909.

Paul Hardy catcher, manager 1937–38, 1951–1952. Paul Hardy was a journeyman catcher who played on a number of teams from 1931 to 1952. Candy Jim Taylor hired Hardy in 1937 to replace Subby Byas behind the plate. Hardy served in World War II. Paul Hardy took over management of the team in the very last year of the team's existence, 1952 — thus he was the last ever American Giant skipper.

George Harney pitcher 1923–1931. Prior to the 1923 season Rube held open tryouts and one of those to turn out was Alabaman George Harney. Harney saw limited action in 1923, but he was given a start against Hooks Daus and the Detroit Tigers in October of 1923. Harney won the game against the heavily favored Tigers. Harney became a regular in the starting rotation beginning in 1924 and continued in the starting role through 1928. He figured in a number of important playoff and World Series games. Following the 1928 season Harney saw less action.

He was a first class pitcher, and well known for his spitball. Harney briefly took over as interim manager in 1928, when Dave Malarcher's injuries were so serious he could not manage the team. The American Giants employed Harney as a scout in 1950, he was charged with scouting potential white players for the American Giants.

Elander "Vic" Harris was part of the talented outfielding crew in 1924–25 that included Jelly Gardner, Jimmy Lyons and Cristobal Torriente. Vic Harris moved on to the Homestead Grays where he became a fixture. Harris played with many of the greats who spent time with the Grays and also managed the team for a number of years.

Rufus Hatten of Jacksonville, Florida, appeared as a catcher in 1944.

Lem Hawkins first baseman 1928. Dave Malarcher brought Lem Hawkins, at one time a Kansas City Monarch team captain, to the American Giants in 1928 to bolster the team. While Hawkins was loaded with talent he did not fit into the team. His temperament was a world apart from Dave Malarcher's. A few years later in 1931 he was charged with murder in Kansas City, the result of a fight from a card game. He gained release from the murder charges, but a few years after that he himself was killed when he botched an armed robbery attempt.

Buddy Hayes was one of several catchers brought on in an attempt to shore up the receiving corps after Bruce Petway was seriously injured in 1916.

Burnalle "Bun" Hays pitched in a handful of games for the American Giants towards the end of the 1930 season.

Curtis Henderson played shortstop for the American Giants in 1941.

Logan "Slap" Hensley was a top pitcher with the St. Louis Stars from 1922 to 1931. He came out of retirement to pitch a few games for the American Giants in 1939.

Joe Hewitt shortstop, second base 1922, 1924. Hewitt was a backup middle infielder in 1922 and 1924. His career began in 1910 with the St. Louis Giants and he extended his career playing with a variety of different teams into the 1930's.

Wesley Hicks was recruited from the local semi-pro ranks to play outfield in 1927.

Charles "Lefty" Hill pitched a game for the American Giants in 1914 against the New York Stars—a semi-pro team.

Preston "Pete" Hill outfield, captain 1911–1918. Hill was the first captain of the American Giants, and was one of those Philadelphia Giant teammates Foster lured to the Windy City. Hill was considered by his colleagues to be one of the greatest hitters who ever lived. He could hit from both sides of the plate and had great speed. Rube put a great deal of faith in his sensibilities and made him team captain. Foster sometimes had Hill run the team on his own. Pete Hill, who had begun his baseball career in 1899, was moved to Detroit in 1919 by Rube where he took over as player/manager. If Cooperstown considers African American players from the Dead Ball era, expect to hear his name mentioned.

Samuel Hill was a regular outfielder from 1946 to 1948. He was named to the 1948 Western All-star team.

John Hines utility player 1924–1934. John Hines was recruited from the Wiley College (Marshall, Texas) baseball team in 1924. He played in a utility role for his whole career at either catcher, outfield or first base. He was a good hitter and sometimes batted in the cleanup spot. Hines had a bad temper and while drinking with former teammate James Bray he got into a fight and killed Bray. Hines was convicted of murder and sent to prison — ending his career.

Robert Hinesman from Brooklyn pitched in the 1951 season.

Elvis Holland, a native of Indianapolis, was well known for his years with Detroit and the New York Black Yankees. He was picked up by Rube as a ringer for a post-season exhibition road trip in 1921.

Robert "Frog" Holsey pitcher 1928–1931. "Frog" Holsey was one of the few fresh arms to join the team during the Depression. He held his own in a starting rotation that included Willie Foster and George Harney.

Billy Horne second base, shortstop 1938–1941. Horne anchored the middle infield for four seasons. He was named to the All-Star team in 1939 and 1941.

Dave Hoskins pitcher, outfielder 1942–43. Dave Hoskins pitched a few games for the American Giants during World War II. His career in Chicago was short and sweet, but he later went on to play for the Homestead Grays and in organized baseball, culminating with a two-year major league career with the Cleveland Indians from 1953 to 1954. He sported a 9–3 record for the Tribe in 26 appearances in 1953. Hoskins was also known for his offensive prowess in the Negro Leagues. He was one of the few American Giants to make the jump to major league baseball.

Jess Houston pitcher 1938–39. Cincinnati product Jess Houston was a regular pitcher in 1938 and 1939. He also played for the Memphis Red Sox and Cincinnati Tigers.

Herman Howard pitched in a handful of games for the American Giants in 1946 after returning from World War II service.

John Huber catcher, pitcher 1942, 1950. John Huber had two short stints with the American Giants in 1942 and 1950, playing as both a pitcher and catcher. He also played with the Birmingham Black Barons and Memphis Red Sox.

Dick Hudson pitched for Dave Malarcher's Columbia American Giants in 1931. Hudson was a former manager of the Savoy Big Five basketball team, a precursor to the Harlem Globetrotters.

Willie Hudson was vital as the number two pitcher for the American Giants in 1940 and 1941. He was named to the All-Star team in 1941, and was used as a pinch hitter.

Grover Hunt was a backup catcher in 1946.

Fred "Puggy" Hutchinson shortstop, utility 1910–1913. Puggy Hutchinson began his career with the original Indianapolis ABCs back in 1902. His talent impressed Rube Foster, who first hired him in 1908 for the Leland Giants. Hutchinson was back and forth between Chicago and Indianapolis for a couple of years, but settled in with the Leland Giants in 1910. Rube retained Puggy as a valuable utility player for the American Giants in 1911. Puggy got put to the test right away, when Rube's star shortstop John Henry Lloyd decided not to stay on with the American Giants in 1911. Hutchinson stepped into the shoes of one of the greatest shortstops ever. Hutchinson did an acceptable job at short, but did not compare with Pop Lloyd on offense. When Lloyd eventually returned to Rube's fold in 1913, Hutchinson went back to Indianapolis.

Cowan "Bubba" Hyde outfield 1950–1951. Bubba Hyde made his mark as a speedy outfielder with the Memphis Red Sox. After the color line fell in 1949, Hyde played minor league baseball in Bridgeport, Connecticut, where he was managed by Jimmy Foxx. He came to the American Giants after his stint in organized baseball, one of the few players to do so.

Ivory whose first name is unknown played briefly at first base and as a pitcher in 1936. The team was in transition and he was joined by other unknowns.

Major R.R. Jackson was involved with black baseball in Chicago off and on from the 1890's until the 1940's. He was thick with black social clubs and the infamous political machinery. Major R.R. Jackson was a city alderman, and an officer of "The Leland Giants Baseball and Amusement Association." When Rube Foster and Beauregard Mosely took issue with Frank Leland, Jackson took sides with Leland. Although he had profound differences with Rube Foster, he helped host the 1922 NNL meetings in Chicago, and supported the American Giants with lip service. Major Jackson had stopped being directly involved with baseball after Frank Leland died in 1914, but reappeared in 1937. Jackson had some sway with owner Horace Hall and was named the head of the Negro American League. In 1940, when the NAL and NNL banded into a larger organization, Jackson was put forth as a commissioner, but the teams of the Eastern based NNL refused to recognize his authority — since he had ties to the American Giants.

Major Jackson's title came from being a veteran of the Spanish-American War. He was born in Chicago, served in state as well as local politics.

Stanford Jackson utility 1926–1931. Acquired from the Memphis Red Sox by Dave Malarcher in 1926. Stanford Jackson served an important role as a utility player from 1926 to 1931. He played a variety of positions, was a decent hitter and was always available to plug a hole. He contributed to the back to back World Championships in 1926 and 1927. He was nicknamed the "Praying Churchman" and "Jambo."

Harold "Harry" Jefferies third base 1929–1931. In 1929, Harry Jefferies was tapped to play third base, when Dave Malarcher left the team. Jefferies had experience with the Chicago Giants back in 1920, and a long résumé which included playing time in Detroit, Baltimore, Cleveland and other teams.

Horace Jenkins pitcher, outfield 1914–15. Horace Jenkins pitched for the American Giants in 1914, and notched several impressive wins over the likes of Dizzy Dismukes (Brooklyn Royal Giants), Dicta Johnson (Indianapolis ABCs) and Juan Pedroso (Cuban Stars). Jenkins played in the outfield for the American Giants in 1915. He completed his career as a top player for the crosstown Chicago Giants from 1916 to 1921.

Gentry Jessup pitcher 1941–49. Gentry Jessup was the American Giants' pitching ace during the 1940's. His stature on the mound made him one of the most valuable players for the American Giants in their final decade. He appeared in the All-Star game four times in the 1940's. In 1943 he led the way for the American Giants in a 7–3 win over the Great Lakes Naval Blue Jackets who were managed by Hall of Fame catcher Mickey Cochran and led on the field by Hall of Famer Johnny Mize. Gentry Jessup was the only American Giant to play in the 1945 All-Star game where he was joined by Jackie Robinson. In 1946 Jessup turned in a remarkable performance when he pitched all 20 innings of a 3–3 tie game against the Indianapolis Clowns. Major league scouts swarmed around Jessup, and it was rumored that he would get a shot at the big leagues, but nothing came of it — probably because of his age. After leaving the American Giants he played two seasons in the Minnesota-Dakota (Man-Dak) League.

Don "Groundhog" Johnson played second base for the American Giants in 1951. According to Johnson he went to a game between the American Giants and Indianapolis Clowns at Crosley Field as a spectator when he was recruited by the American Giants, given a uniform and told to change in the bus. The following year Don Johnson was scouted by bird dog scout Stan Arnzan, the coach at Newport (Kentucky) High School, and signed by his hometown Cincinnati Reds. Don Johnson was assigned to the Reds' Ogden, Utah, farm team, but did not make it to the big leagues. Today he works for the Cincinnati recreation department and gives generously of his time to youth.

Grant "Home Run" Johnson. Known as a legend of the early days of black baseball (he started out with the primarily white Findlay, Ohio, Sluggers in 1894), he played one season with the Leland Giants in 1910 — the year before Frank Leland and Rube Foster broke off.

Louis Dicta "Spitball" Johnson pitcher, coach 1912–14; 1923–25. Spitball Johnson was a regular in the starting rotation with Rube Foster, Pat Dougherty, Bill Lindsay and Bill Gatewood. He threw a no-hitter for the American Giants in 1913, the first of back to back no-hitters for the American Giants against the Coogan Smart Sets of New York, June 8–9, 1913. Johnson spent most of his career with the Indianapolis ABCs. He had a player/manager role with the Milwaukee Bears in 1923, when that franchise failed late in the season he came back to the American Giants. Dicta Johnson pitched for the American Giants in a post-season game against the American League Detroit Tigers which finished in a 2–2 tie — only because of two errors committed by battery mate Jim Brown. Rube hired Dicta as a pitching coach the following year.

Tom Johnson pitcher 1915–1921, 1923. om Johnson was a regular in the starting rotation from 1915 to 1918, along with Frank Wickware, Cannonball Redding, Tom Williams and Dick Whitworth. Tom Johnson more than pulled his own weight on the staff. He was taken into the army in World War I, and made a lieutenant in the 365th Infantry. After the war, the lieutenant rejoined the team against a different backdrop, but was still a frontline starter. Tom Johnson was hospitalized in 1922, but recovered well enough in 1923 to try out to be an umpire in the NNL. Johnson was judged by Rube fit enough to pitch in 1923, though he saw less action. Later Tom Johnson went on to be a respected arbiter in the Negro National League.

Tommy Johnson pitcher 1938–1942. Tommy Johnson from Clayton, Missouri, was a regular in the pitching rotation from 1938 to 1940. He remained with team through 1942, but did not see as much action after 1940. He is not to be confused with the Tom Johnson who pitched in the teens and twenties.

William Fox Jones was a backup catcher in 1915.

Harry Kenyon appeared briefly as a pitcher with the American Giants early in the 1923 season. He had a ten year career in the Negro Leagues from 1919 to 1929, and played in outfield, infield and managed the Memphis Red Sox in 1929.

Keyes (first name unknown) appeared as a pitcher in 1918.

Wilbur "Dolly" King played second base for the American Giants in 1945. He later played for the Homestead Grays and played professional basketball as well as semi-pro football.

LeBeaux (first name unknown) was one of the infielders brought to the team during the transition year of 1936.

Frank Leland. Frank Leland might be called the "grandpappy of Chicago black baseball." He was from Tennessee and a graduate of Fisk University. He played baseball for a while with the Washington Capital Cities back in 1887. He came to Chicago and played with the Chicago Unions in 1888. Frank Leland soon found his true calling — not as a ball player, but as a manager, organizer and administrator. He took over as manager of the Union Giants and in 1905 changed the official name of the team to the Leland Giants. While he was taking up the reins of black baseball in Chicago, he was building a political career; the two ambitions went hand in hand. Leland prevailed in his effort to allow his team to participate in the otherwise white Chicago City Leagues, which was a major accomplishment. Leland's team overcame the race barrier and was a powerhouse in the City League. His success paved the way for the American Giants. Frank Leland had a hand in bringing Rube Foster to Chicago, and eventually that caused his own undoing. Even after Foster had formed the American Giants, Frank Leland continued in his attempts to have a team. In 1912, well after the American Giants had split off and become the dominant team, Leland gathered a team to play winter baseball in Los Angeles. In 1913 Leland raised a team with Sam Crawford as pitcher that defeated Rube's American Giants by a 10–3 count. Leland's team met the American Giants again in 1914, losing by a slim margin. Frank Leland died on November 15, 1914; a number of baseball players were the pallbearers. His political career also was successful, as he served as a deputy sheriff, a circuit court clerk and on the board of county commissioners.

Carey B. Lewis was the first sports editor of the *Chicago Defender*. Lewis came to Chicago in 1905 by way of Louisville and the *Indianapolis Freeman*. Along with other black sportswriters, Lewis helped draft the Negro League constitution in 1920.

Joe Lillard pitcher, utility 1932–34. Joe Lillard was a two-sport professional athlete. In 1932, while MLB remained closed to blacks, Lillard was a star running back with the NFL Chicago Cardinals — at that time there was no strict color line enforced in the NFL. Lillard pitched regularly in 1932 and helped the team win the Negro Southern League title that year. He also played outfield and could fill in behind the plate. The color line was drawn in the NFL in 1933, and Lillard concentrated on baseball. Robert Cole attempted to trade Lillard to Brooklyn following the 1934 season, but Lillard refused to go. Instead Lillard went to Southern California, played semi-pro football and reportedly took work as a valet for a Hollywood star. Lillard was an excellent tailback, skilled in rushing, kick returning and kicking. Lillard was one of only two black players in the NFL in 1932 and subjected to racial insults on the field.

Bill Lindsay pitcher 1911–1914. In 1910, Bill Lindsay pitched impressively for the Kansas City Giants against the Chicago Leland Giants. Rube Foster took note of the thrower nicknamed the Kansas Cyclone and signed him towards the end of the season. Lindsay was part of the original American Giant pitching rotation in 1911 and 1912. In 1913, after Frank Wickware left the team, Lindsay emerged as the ace of the staff. It appeared that the Kansas Cyclone had a stellar career ahead of him, but he fell ill in 1914. The illness was serious and he died on September 8, 1914. Services were held in Chicago and his body was taken to his birthplace of Lexington, Missouri, for burial.

William "Bill" Little part owner. Bill Little was the well connected tailor who purchased a partial interest in the American Giants in 1936 when the majority owner was Horace Hall. Little was a native of Birmingham, Alabama, and had played baseball himself as a youth. He attended Tuskegee, went on to establish the Monarch Tailoring Company in Chicago in 1910, and also became the general manager of the Porter Drug Store in Chicago. In 1950, Bill Little was given a "lease" on the American Giant club—Doc Martin was the majority owner. Little never assumed full ownership of the team, the following year Martin sold out to a group of investors headed by Abe Saperstein.

Edward R. Litzinger was a white Chicago attorney/politician who at one time played in the Chicago City Leagues and also administered the league. While running for office in 1916 Litzinger presented the American Giants team with a "World Championship" pennant and each member of the team with a solid gold emblem. His motives were not all political, he was also said to be instrumental in getting a black team into the City Leagues. The pennant and pins took on a special meaning for the American Giants—as the Indianapolis ABCs had apparently beaten them in a disputed post-season playoff.

John Henry "Pop" Lloyd shortstop 1914–1917. Pop Lloyd is considered by many to be the greatest black player of the Dead Ball era, and among the greatest players of all time. Pop Lloyd could do it all on the ball field. On and off the field he was intelligent, cultivated, funny, a conversationalist and someone you naturally wanted on your side. Rube Foster first encountered Pop Lloyd in Jacksonville, Florida, while traveling south with the Cuban X-Giants in 1905. Lloyd was persuaded to join the X-Giants of Philadelphia. Rube coaxed Lloyd to Chicago in 1910 to join the Leland Giants—at that time not connected to Frank Leland. When Rube established the American Giants he was not able to hold on to Lloyd. In 1913, after Lloyd and the New York Lincoln Giants defeated the American Giants, Foster offered John Henry a spot on his barnstorming team that traveled to the West Coast. Lloyd elected to stay with the American Giants after the road trip when the 1914 regular season rolled around. The American Giants cruised to easy championship honors with his help. He jumped to the Lincoln Stars in 1915, but rejoined the American Giants late in the season to lead the team past the Indianapolis ABCs in a post-season series. Lloyd stuck with the American Giants in 1916 and 1917. His "heads up" style of play meshed nicely with Rube's design and the American Giants dominated most teams,

though the ABCs upended the American Giants in a 1916 post-season series.

In 1918, Lloyd took a job in the Army Quartermaster Corps during WWI. After the war he returned to the New York metro area to resume his baseball career. While "Pop" Lloyd spent four seasons in the prime of his career with the American Giants, the bulk of his Hall of Fame career was spent in New York and Atlantic City. The American Giants never again produced a shortstop who could be compared to "Pop."

After baseball Lloyd worked as the Little League commissioner in Atlantic City. There is a ballpark in Atlantic City named for Pop Lloyd. He was instrumental in getting Yankee Stadium opened to Negro League teams in 1930. Pop Lloyd was elected to the National Baseball Hall of Fame in Cooperstown by the Negro Leagues Committee in 1977.

Clarence Locke pitched and played first base from 1945 to 1948.

Lester Lockett is from Princeton, Indiana, the same hometown as Gil Hodges. He played second base for the American Giants for part of 1939, again in 1942 and then again in 1950. He also played ball with the Birmingham Black Barons and Baltimore Elite Giants, in Latin America and Canada and with integrated semi-pro teams after 1950. Lester was named to the All-Star team twice with Birmingham and twice with Baltimore. Lockett is still alive as of summer 2005 and has given his time generously to Negro League researchers over the years.

George "Hubert" Lockhart pitcher 1929. Hubert Lockhart pitched a few games for the American Giants in 1929. After baseball Lockhart went on to fame as a teacher, coach and athletic director in Alabama. His teams were incredibly successful and the gymnasium at Alabama State University is named in his honor.

Bernell "Chick" Longest alternated between second base and outfield in 1946. He went on to play several years in Canada in the 1950's.

Red Longley was a backup catcher in 1950.

Lyda (first name unknown) was a starting pitcher in a handful of games on the 1932 Cole's American Giants.

John Lyles played a few games at shortstop in 1941.

Jimmy Lyons, outfield 1921–1925. Jimmy Lyons played baseball in Chicago as a youth, and was with the semi-pro Chicago Union Giants in 1909, still a teenager. He was with the St. Louis Giants in 1910, and in 1915 he went to Indianapolis where he shared the outfield with legend Oscar Charleston. Lyons was drafted into the army in 1918, and made a name for himself in the Allied Expeditionary Force League in France, where Ty Cobb's brother reportedly remarked that Lyons played better than his brother. Jimmy Lyons was considered one of the fastest players in Negro League history. They said he "could steal bases as easily as he gets on a street car." After World War I and the beginning of NNL play, Jimmie Lyons went to the Detroit Stars. Jimmy Lyons finally joined the American Giants in 1921. Rube Foster had played with Lyons in Cuba way back in 1912, but by the time he was an American Giant the popular sandlot slugger was a veteran of the Negro Leagues and World War I. In July of 1921, while on a road trip to Cincinnati to play the Cuban Stars, Jimmy Lyons fell 25 feet down an elevator shaft. The fall resulted in a serious injury that kept him on the shelf for a few weeks and seemed to affect his play for the rest of his career. In 1925, Jimmy Lyons, along with a number of other vets, was released by Rube Foster—a move some thought was a sign of Rube's impending mental impairment. In 1936, owner Horace Hall retained Jimmy Lyons in a front office advisory capacity. Lyons played in the shadow of other great outfielders like Oscar Charleston in Indianapolis and Cristobal Torriente in Chicago and for that reason Lyons did not always get the credit he deserved.

Dave Malarcher (Gentleman Dave, Cap) utility, team captain, manager, officer 1920–1934. Dave Malarcher is one of the legends of Negro League baseball. He was born in Whitehall, Louisiana; his mother was born into slavery, his father worked on a plantation. His mother saw to it that he got an education and he attended the University of New Orleans (Dillard) and Xavier University of Louisiana. He played ball for the New Orleans Eagles, where he was spotted by Indianapolis ABC manager C.I. Taylor. He started off with the Indianapolis ABCs in 1916 and thrived under C.I. Taylor while the ABCs were at their peak. Malarcher was drafted by Uncle Sam and shipped out to France where he served in the 809th Infantry in 1918–1919. The crafty Rube Foster, who would go to the ends of the earth to sign a talented player, wrote Malarcher a letter while he was in France offering a position when he returned. When Malarcher landed back in Indianapolis, he first went to C.I. Taylor to secure an advance and negotiate a contract, but C.I. hesitated and Malarcher took a train up to Chicago to take Rube up on his offer.

Malarcher seemed to be immune to many of the foibles that befell his comrades. He was happily married, well read, enjoyed clean living, commanded respect and always had a balanced temperament. While Rube was known to criticize certain "college men," he found no fault with Malarcher. Third base was his specialty, but he could truly play any position on the field including catcher and pitcher, though he took the mound only a few times in his career. He was solid offensively, a switch hitter and executed to perfection Rube's station-to-station style. After Bingo DeMoss left the team in 1925, Dave Malarcher was named team captain.

After Rube succumbed to psychosis Dave Malarcher was made the playing manager. Malarcher quickly demonstrated his skills as a skipper and guided the American Giants to back to back Negro League World Series victories in 1926 and 1927. Dave Malarcher studied under both C.I. Taylor and Rube Foster and proved to be a very skilled manager. He was an intellectual and a staunch defender of his race. The sale of the American Giants after Rube Foster's death didn't sit well with Malarcher. Owner William Trimble expected Malarcher to both manage and play without commensurate compensation, so Malarcher broke it off in 1929. In 1931, Dave Malarcher rescued black baseball in Chicago by forming the Columbia American Giants and securing a lease at South Side Park. Malarcher had enough loyalty and good will from players, who otherwise had given up on the American Giants under white ownership, to make the Columbia American Giants viable—although he elected to drop out of the Negro National League.

When businessman Robert Cole made the American Giants whole in 1932, he immediately turned to Malarcher as the brains of the baseball operation. Malarcher took the American Giants to the brink of championships in 1933 and 1934. In 1933 commissioner and Pittsburgh Crawfords owner Gus Greenlee awarded the championship to his Crawfords over the American Giants based on a technicality. In 1934, Malarcher led the American Giants to a championship playoff with the Philadelphia Stars. In one of the games Philly Star Jud Wilson slugged an umpire from behind, but there was no repercussion—because the umpire "didn't see who it was." Malarcher protested the outcome to no avail. Malarcher decided he had seen enough of the shady deals in the Negro Leagues and retired once and for all.

After baseball, Malarcher made his living as a real estate and insurance broker; he also wrote epic style poetry. Dave Malarcher died May 11, 1982. Dave's wife Mabel Malarcher was an accomplished opera singer and sometimes sang prior to American Giants games. Dave Malarcher made invaluable contributions to the history of Negro League baseball by granting interviews to curious researchers. He had an almost photographic memory and generously shared his recollections.

Everett "Ziggy" Marcelle, the son of well known Negro League star Oliver Marcelle, got behind the plate for a few games as a tryout in 1942.

John "Johnny" Markham pitched briefly in

1947, he was better known as a pitcher for the Birmingham Black Barons from 1941 to 1945.

Bobby Marshall first base (Leland Giants 1909). Bobby Marshall never played for the American Giants, however Rube Foster recruited him from the St. Paul Gophers to play first base for the Leland Giants when they met the Cubs in a storied 1909 post-season match up. Marshall made two critical errors that cost the American Giants one of the games; Rube removed him from the game and he never again played under Rube Foster.

Jack Marshall pitcher 1920–21, 1923, 1929. There were two American Giants players who went by the name Jack Marshall — one a pitcher in the twenties and the other an infielder in the thirties. The pitcher Jack Marshall quietly went about his business in the 1920's working alongside some of the American Giants' better known pitchers. Jack Marshall did not get the same press as his teammates, but pitched well enough to please the boss— Rube Foster.

Jack "Boise Jack" Marshall utility 1931–1935, 1937. Boise Jack was a spirited competitor who took a leadership role for the American Giants in the 1930's. Marshall was tapped by Dave Malarcher when he formed the Columbia American Giants in 1931 and became the starting second baseman for the American Giants in 1932. Jack Marshall was a hustler on and off the field. He played on local semi-pro teams and had barnstormed across Canada previous to joining the American Giants. Marshall was very competitive and in a game against the Kansas City Monarchs in 1937 he physically attacked an umpire who made a call with which he disagreed.

While Marshall was a notable baseball player, his best sport was bowling. Marshall set some records as a tournament bowler and had to fight the color line in that sport also. Later in life he operated a bowling alley in Chicago and ran the *Chicago Defender* baseball clinic for kids. There were two players who went by the name Jack Marshall who played for the American Giants; "Boise Jack" Marshall is not to be confused with the pitcher of the 1920's.

Dr. John B. Martin, "Doc Martin," league official, officer, owner 1941–1952. Doc Martin was one of the most pivotal figures in the history of Negro League baseball. He came to Chicago from Memphis after being drummed out by a vengeful politician. Before coming to Chicago he had co-owned the Memphis Red Sox with his brother Doctor B.B. Martin and served as president of the Negro American League. In Chicago he built an empire as a pharmacist, real estate baron and funeral home owner.

Doc Martin got involved with the American Giants a little bit at a time. He served first as secretary-treasurer, then co-owner, but by 1944 he owned and operated the team outright. This tycoon was regarded as an outsider by some, and players made jokes about "playing for the rich man." He was notoriously cheap and would let a player or manager go simply to save money. Rather than support building a new park (which he accomplished in Memphis) he continued to pay rent to the Comiskey family. Under his watch the American Giants turned in mediocre results. During the post-color-line era, while the Kansas City Monarchs, Indianapolis Clowns, Newark Eagles and Birmingham Black Barons graduated a large number of players to the major leagues, the American Giants saw only a few players move up to the bigs.

Although Doc Martin was no baseball man he shared one thing with Rube Foster, he was both team owner and league chief executive. As things played out it was Doc Martin who carried the awesome responsibility of representing the interests of black baseball when integration finally came. It was he who sat down with MLB commissioner Happy Chandler to discuss how Negro League contracts could be crafted in such a way to avoid the outright stealing of players. Doc Martin was not the most popular team owner, but it is generally acknowledged that without him the team would have been belly up in 1941. Doc Martin seemed to put more effort into running the Negro American League than the Chicago American Giants. He jumped at the chance to sell the team in 1951, but remained at the helm of the Negro American League until the league finally officially closed up shop in 1963.

William McCall was a pitcher in 1925. He made several starts throughout the season. McCall played with about ten teams in ten seasons in a career that spanned from 1922 to 1931.

Walter McCoy pitcher 1945–48. After serving in World War II, Walter McCoy, a San Diego native, came to the American Giants in 1945. McCoy proved to be much more than a war-time replacement player and stepped into the role of regular starting pitcher. He was a strong left hander and led the NAL in strikeouts in 1946 with 108 Ks. He was a friend of teammate catcher John Ritchey, who was also from San Diego, and was also a World War II vet. Thomas Turner, who played briefly with the American Giants in 1947, credits his old war buddy McCoy with helping him get a chance to play for the American Giants. McCoy went on to play in the PCL, but did play in the big leagues. In the year 2005 McCoy resides in California and, according to old friend Tommy Turner, still occasionally plays baseball.

Luther McDonald was a regular starter for Dave Malarcher's Columbia Giants in 1931. He was also listed as a pitcher in 1932 and 1935, but did not see much work.

Webster McDonald pitcher 1925–27, 1929–30. Webster McDonald was a submariner who came to the American Giants after the Washington Potomac franchise failed midway through the 1925 season. McDonald was an added element to an already very strong pitching staff, which included Willie Foster, George Harney, Willie Powell and Rube Currie. McDonald went to the Homestead Grays in 1928 and then to an otherwise white semi-pro team from Little Falls, Minnesota. He was a regular starter with the American Giants in 1930, then went back East where he became a fixture with his hometown Philadelphia Stars. He also managed teams including the Eastern squad in the 1935 All-Star game. In 1945, McDonald, along with Oscar Charleston, managed the USL Brooklyn Brown Dodgers, the second rate team used as a front for Branch Rickey's scouting operation.

Lem McDougal pitcher 1919. Lem McDougal was a World War I vet, who had previously played with the Indianapolis ABCs. C.I. Taylor did not field a team in 1919 and McDougal was one of several ABC players Rube picked up that year.

Gready McKinnis pitcher 1944–45, 1949. In 1944 left hander Gready McKinnis was received in a trade from Birmingham for the discontented Double Duty Radcliffe. He was the number two starter behind Gentry Jessup his first year with the American Giants and also earned a spot on the All-Star team. McKinnis left the team in 1946 to play for Gus Greenlee's marginal encore version of the Pittsburgh Crawfords. In 1949, he was brought back to the American Giants where he was again a regular in the rotation and named to the All-Star team in the by-then further-diminished league.

Felix McLaurin outfield 1949–1952. Felix was a regular left fielder with the American Giants the last four years of their existence. McLaurin started his career with the Jacksonville Red Caps in 1942, and played with the Birmingham Black Barons and New York Black Yankees prior to joining the American Giants. He was named to the All-Star team in 1952.

Willie McMeans pitched in a handful of games in 1945.

Hurly McNair played right field for the American Giants in 1915 and 1916. Rube spotted McNair playing with the local Chicago Giants and signed him to replace Jude Gans who returned East. McNair later went on to be a regular with the NNL Kansas City Monarchs from 1920 to 1927, for which he is best known. He also umpired in the Negro American League.

Clyde McNeal shortstop, second base 1945–1950. Clyde McNeal was a mere teenager playing with a San Antonio semi-pro team when Jim Taylor brought him on to play shortstop in 1945. Mc-

Neal proved to be a real find, in an era when scouting had become more difficult. McNeal was named to the All-Star team in 1950; in 1951 he was signed by the Brooklyn Dodger organization and played minor league ball.

Jose Mendez pitched and played shortstop in a few games for the American Giants in 1918, as Rube scrambled to fill slots for players who had been drafted into the World War I effort. Mendez was one of the great stars of the Negro Leagues, working with the Cuban Stars, All-Nations and KC Monarchs.

Henry "Speed" Merchant outfield, pitcher 1940–1942. "Speed" Merchant got his start in professional baseball with the lackluster American Giants in 1942, playing outfield and pitching a few games. In 1943 Speed joined the Indianapolis Clowns and became one of the best known players on that legendary barnstorming outfit playing from 1943 to 1954.

Jack Miles played outfield in a few games for the American Giants from 1937 to 1940.

John "Mule" Miles outfield 1946–1948. "Mule" Miles was a hard-hitting Texan who blossomed under Candy Jim Taylor's tutelage.

Zell Miles played outfield for the American Giants in 1951.

Edward "Buck" Miller pitcher, utility 1924–1931. Eddie "Buck" Miller was a native of Calvert, Texas— the same hometown as Rube Foster. Rube was impressed by Miller and he became a regular in a starting rotation that included Willie Foster, George Harney and Juan Padrone. Buck Miller pitched for the Indianapolis ABCs for most of the 1926 season, when that struggling team was propped up by Rube. Buck Miller rejoined the American Giants after Rube left, and saw more action as a utility player from 1929 through 1931.

In 1930 Buck was involved in a notable incident when Satchel Paige threw three pitches inside nearly hitting him. The near beaning was precipitated by a controversial piece of umpiring that resulted in the reversing and the re-reversing of a call. Buck responded by chasing Paige around the park with his bat and threatening to beat him.

Harvey Million (Mello) was a backup utility infielder who saw limited action in 1946 and 1947.

George Minor was a backup outfielder in 1944.

George "Big" Mitchell pitcher 1925, 1930. "Big" George Mitchell made an occasional start for the American Giants in 1925, after playing for a variety of teams for the next four seasons he landed back with the team in 1930 and pitched on a regular basis for the first half of the season.

William "Money" Monroe second base 1911–1914. Money was the original American Giants second baseman. Like so many others who had once played ball in Philadelphia with Rube, he was persuaded to join the American Giants in

1911. Monroe had actually played in Chicago years earlier with the Chicago Unions from 1896 to 1900, until he was recruited by the Cuban X-Giants— the premier team of that era. He was a showman and hammed things up with tricks and charades. Watching Monroe's play and antics was a highlight for many baseball fans. Monroe was a baseball man through and through, he memorized the baseball rulebook, engaged anyone in baseball banter and could play in all positions. Monroe was one of those players New York Giant manager John McGraw publicly coveted. Monroe was unable to make the West Coast swing with Rube following the 1914 season (winter 1915) due to illness. When the team de-trained in Los Angeles they were alerted by telegram that Monroe had died at his Chicago home on March 16, 1915. Monroe was only 38 years old when he died.

Leroy Morney shortstop 1940. Morney was a crack shortstop and one of the few bright spots in the 1940 version of the American Giants. He was named an All-Star three different times, including the 1940 season spent in Chicago. Morney followed in the tradition of the freelance ball player, jumping to whatever team would pay him the most in his career that spanned from 1930 to 1944.

Harold "Yellowhorse" Morris pitcher 1929–1930. Yellowhorse Morris was a regular starter for the American Giants in 1929–1930. In 1949, "Yellowhorse" broke new ground when he became the first black scout for the Chicago Cubs.

Beauregard Mosely. Attorney Bo' Mosely was a partner in the original Leland Giants. Mosely's legal intellect was highly respected and he led the way in the courtroom when it came to breaking up the Leland Giants. Rube Foster and Beauregard Mosely were partners in the battle against Frank Leland, but after winning in court Mosely and Foster went separate ways. Mosely wanted to keep the Leland organization together, Rube broke off and formed the American Giants. Even though Mosely was not involved with the American Giants he was an important member of the community. He became the first African American to vote in the Electoral College in the 1912 election. Mosely had attempted to form an organized Negro League in 1910, but his attempt was poorly planned and fell apart shortly after it was drawn up.

Mitch Murray catcher 1928–30. Mitch Murray of Lockland, Ohio (a Cincinnati suburb) began his career with the Dayton Marcos in 1919. He became a regular catcher with the St. Louis Stars in the mid-twenties playing alongside greats "Cool Papa" Bell and Willie Wells. Murray bailed out the depleted American Giants' receiving corps in 1928, and was the regular catcher in 1929.

Nance (first name unknown) played at shortstop in 1929.

Clyde Nelson utility infielder 1944–46. Clyde Nelson came to the American Giants in 1944 and was a regular in the infield. He was a young player with a promising future, but Candy Jim traded him to Cleveland for veteran Buddy Armour in 1947. Nelson proceeded to take on a starring role in Cleveland as that team won the NAL pennant. In 1949, while playing with the Indianapolis Clowns, Nelson collapsed following a double-header in Philadelphia at Shibe Park, he died a short time later. Were it not for his freak premature death, Nelson would have looked forward to a career somewhere in organized baseball. Nelson was born in Bradenton, Florida, on September 1, 1921, and died July 25, 1949.

Henry Newberry played shortstop for the American Giants in 1947. He went on to play minor league baseball in the fifties.

Rafaelito Ortiz was a regular pitcher in 1948 in the esteemed company of Gentry Jessup and Roberto Vargas.

Guy Ousley played shortstop under Dave Malarcher with the Columbia American Giants of 1931.

Aubrey Owens pitcher 1922–1926. Aubrey Owens was a regular in the American Giant starting rotation from 1922 to 1926. He was a fine pitcher, but baseball was Aubrey's second priority. Aubrey Owens studied dentistry and while he played for the American Giants, he waited until classes were over to report to the team. Aubrey Owens also had to forego post-season play so that he could go back to classes at Meharry College in Nashville. He later went on to practice dentistry.

Jackson Owens was listed as a pitcher with the American Giants from 1950 to 1952.

William "Bill" Owens, an Indianapolis native, was given a brief tryout at second base in 1925. He was not able to unseat Bingo DeMoss and joined the Indianapolis ABCs. Bill Owens was born November 14, 1901, and died May 5, 1999, at the age of 98. He generously shared reminiscences of his Negro League career with historians.

Juan Luis "El Mulo" Padrone pitcher 1918; 1922; 1924–25. Juan Padrone got the nickname "El Mulo" for his change-up pitch. Rube Foster first encountered Padrone in 1908 while playing in Havana. Padrone played with the American Giants during spring training in 1918 and Rube leapt at the opportunity to sign him in 1922, even though he was getting on in years. Padrone's stamina and ability to throw with little rest was almost freakish. He had played a full career in Cuba going back to 1900, yet was the workhorse for the American Giants in 1922. He learned every trick in the book and passed the knowledge on to his teammates— which was one of the reasons Rube liked him. Juan Padrone played with the Eastern Cuban Stars in 1923, but was back with the American Giants in

1924. Padrone picked up where he left off and was a regular in the rotation that included notables Willie Foster and George Harney. He stuck with the team in 1925, but was let go by Rube at the end of the season when he cleaned house. Padrone continued to play semi-pro ball into the 1930s. Juan Luis Padrone is a member of the Cuban Baseball Hall of Fame.

Leroy "Satchel" Paige pitcher 1951. While the American Giants had hoped to sign Satchel Paige earlier in his career, he didn't join the team until 1951. In 1951 the team was owned by a group that included Abe Saperstein, who was connected to Bill Veeck. Satchel had already been to major league baseball's pinnacle by that time as he had helped the Cleveland Indians to the 1948 World Championship. It seemed to some that Paige was signed as a mere gate attraction. Of course Satchel Paige was a gate attraction, but he remained a formidable pitcher. Satchel Paige pitched for the American Giants, along with Theolic Smith, for the first half of a limited NAL season in 1951. Proof that Paige still had his stuff came when he left the American Giants mid-season to join Bill Veeck's St. Louis Browns. The following year, 1952, at approximately 46 years old, Paige finished with a 12–10 record for the St. Louis Browns. Satchel was elected to the National Baseball Hall of Fame in Cooperstown by the Negro Leagues Committee in 1971.

Clarence "Spoony" Palm caught a few games in 1932.

Willie "Pat" Patterson was a catcher with the American Giants in 1952. He also helped run the team and scout players. He was named to the All-Star team in 1952 and later played with Elmwood of the Man-Dak League.

Andrew "Jap" Payne outfield 1911–1913. Jap Payne was another of Rube Foster's teammates in Philadelphia whom he lured to the Windy City when he took over management of the Leland Giants in 1907. He was one of the elite outfielders in the early days of black baseball and the original right fielder on the American Giants in 1911. Payne went back east to the New York Lincoln Stars in 1914, at that point a 12-year veteran. He later joined the New York Central Red Caps, a semi-pro railroad team, and finished his career in 1922. While Payne was born in Washington, D.C., and spent much of his life on the East Coast, when he died in New York on August 27, 1942, his body was brought back to the town where he gained fame — Chicago — for burial at Mount Glenwood Cemetery.

Frank Pearson pitched in 1950, he had previously worked in Memphis and New York.

James Pendleton shortstop 1948. When Quincy Trouppe took over management of the Chicago American Giants in 1948, he used his large sphere of influence to bring in some fresh faces, one of them was James Pendleton of Asheville, North Carolina. Pendleton was a star right away for the American Giants, and Doc Martin did not hesitate to sell his contract to Branch Rickey when an offer was made. Pendleton was one of the few American Giant players who went on to play in the major leagues. After seasoning in the minors, Pendleton played with the Milwaukee Braves from 1953 to 1956, Pittsburgh Pirates 1957–58, Cincinnati Reds 1959 and Houston Astros 1962. Pendleton switched from shortstop to outfield in the big leagues. His eight seasons in the major leagues were more than any other American Giant player who made the jump ever played.

Art "Superman" Pennington outfield, first base 1941–1945, 1950. Art Pennington was an 18-year-old kid from Memphis when he joined the American Giants in 1941. He had a humble beginning, but during the World War II years he became one of the primary offensive threats for the American Giants and earned the nickname "Superman." In 1944, the young Superman got in hot water with owner J.B. Martin because he took an advance on his salary and then refused to get in uniform for a game. That same season he was named to the All-Star squad and attempted to jump to Gus Greenlee's Crawfords. Pennington was suspended, but ended up back with the American Giants in 1945 and batted cleanup. During spring training in 1946, Pennington bolted again from the American Giants, this time for the Mexican Leagues, where continued to hit his stride. Art was in organized baseball with the PCL Portland Beavers in 1949, but in 1950 came back to the American Giants for a final season. (Some Negro League players in that era found that pay was slightly better in the Negro Leagues than in the minors.) Pennington did go back to minor league baseball after ending his career with the American Giants.

Bruce Petway, catcher 1911–1918. Bruce Petway was one of the greatest catchers in the Dead Ball era and one of the greatest catchers in the history of the Negro Leagues. He was one of the original American Giants although he had come to the Leland Giants in 1906, before Andy Foster returned to Chicago. Petway could make the throw down to second base effortlessly and with deadly accuracy. Bruce Petway etched his name into baseball history when he threw out Ty Cobb three times in three attempts during the 1910 Cuban baseball season. It was said that Cobb vowed never to play against black players again. Petway was a decent hitter and a great base runner himself. The American Giants depended heavily on Petway for insurance against base thievery, but eventually the years behind the plate took their toll. Rube had no choice but to bolster the American Giants with backup catchers to fill in for Petway due to nagging injuries. In 1919, Rube sent Petway to the Detroit Stars along with Pete Hill. Petway became the player-manager of the Detroit Stars in 1922 and continued to play until 1925. Petway died July 4, 1941, he was the best catcher of his era and made an indelible impression, for that reason Petway is considered to be a candidate for Hall of Fame consideration. Bruce Petway had attended Meharry Medical College in Nashville, Tennessee, prior to playing professional baseball. White Sox Hall of Fame catcher Ray Schalk used to come to Schorling Park on a regular basis to see Petway work.

Bill Pierce was a utility player for the American Giants in 1911–1912, the first two years of the team's existence. Like many of the original American Giants his connection to Rube went all the way back to Philadelphia.

Rogers "Perry" Pierre was listed as a pitcher in 1939.

Curtis Pitts played catcher and shortstop in 1950 and 1951.

Robert Poindexter pitcher 1926, 1929. Robert Poindexter came to the American Giants from Birmingham after a major housecleaning by Rube Foster in 1926. Poindexter's talents were expendable on the loaded American Giant staff, and he was back in Alabama the following season. Robert Poindexter was with the Memphis Red Sox in 1929 when he shot teammate J. C. McHaskell, the wounds were not fatal but did result in double amputation. Poindexter claimed the shooting was accidental and successfully avoided prosecution. The Memphis Red Sox manager had him arrested and dismissed him. The American Giants picked Poindexter back up after Memphis let him go and he pitched in a handful of games. In 1930, Poindexter got into a street fight and was stabbed to death.

Melvin Powell pitcher 1931–1937. Melvin "Putt" Powell got his start as a regular pitcher for Dave Malarcher's Columbia American Giants in 1931. He stayed with the club under the Robert Cole regime and in 1932 was a regular starter along with Willie Powell (not related) and Willie Foster. Willie was short, which accounts for his nickname. Unlike most of his colleagues, Putt Powell spent his entire career in one city. "Putt" Powell's reputation did not equal that of other American Giant starters, but he was a reliable arm for the American Giants in the 1930's.

Willie Powell ("Wee Willie," "Piggy," "Earnest," "Pigmeat") pitcher 1925–1929, 1932–33. Willie Powell was a product of the Chicago sandlots and a fan favorite. He was given the nicknames "Wee Willie," "Piggy" and "Pigmeat" because of his youthfulness when he joined the team. Despite his apparent youth he was very comfortable on the mound and an integral part of the rotation that included Willie Foster, George Harney and Webster McDonald. Willie's first full season was 1926 and he was instrumental in the American Giants' winning the World Series—including shutting out the Bacharach Giants in a crucial eighth game to send the series to the ninth game. In 1927, Willie again helped the American Giants to the World Championship. Pigmeat Powell was on the money again in 1928, as the American Giants went down to the wire with the St. Louis Stars for the NNL championship. Powell was as effective as teammate Willie Foster and appeared he might even challenge for the role of pitching ace. Following the 1928 season Willie Powell was the victim of an unfortunate hunting accident—he was shot in the face by his father-in-law. Powell was seriously injured, but slowly recuperated and pitched a few games in 1929. Powell was traded to the Detroit Stars in 1930 where he proved he still had his stuff. Powell came back to the Windy City in 1932 with Robert Cole's American Giants, fully recovered and a regular starter, his last year with the team was 1933.

Albert "Al" Preston pitched for the American Giants in their last year of existence, 1952.

Marvin Price played first base in 1950 and 1951.

Prince (first name unknown) one of three players brought on in 1936 whose first names have escaped history (LeBeaux and Ivory were the other two). Prince was the regular third baseman for most of the 1936 season.

Wes Pryor played third base for the American Giants the first year of the team's existence, 1911.

Alec Radcliffe third base 1932–1939, 1941–1944. In stark contrast to his nomadic, multi-talented brother Double Duty Radcliffe, Alec Radcliffe spent most of his career in one town playing one position. Alec took over the hot corner in 1932, coinciding approximately with the end of Dave Malarcher's playing career. Unlike his flamboyant brother, Alec Radcliffe got his job done quietly. Alec was named to the first Western All-Star team in 1933 and nine more times afterwards which is the all-time record for any player. While he was an All-Star, he was not cocky and did not have the reputation of a "game breaker." He swung a large bat, and batted in the heart of the order. His ability to stay healthy and productive at one position, for one team, was virtually unheard of in the Negro Leagues. In 1944, when Doc Martin and manager Double Duty Radcliffe reached an impasse and Duty left the team for Birmingham, Alec naturally thought he was in line for the job, given his 12 years of experience, but Doc Martin rebuffed him.

Theodore "Ted" "Double Duty" Radcliffe pitcher, catcher, manager 1934, 1941–43, 1949–50. While Rube Foster was dubbed the father of black baseball, "Double Duty" Radcliffe was the reigning King of Black Baseball for a later generation.

Double Duty lived to the age of 103 and had a special role in the telling of the history of the Negro Leagues. He was a living legend who generously shared his experiences with historians, news organizations, collectors, children and fans. He had a great memory, knew how to tell a story and often clutched a cigar in his fingers which were disfigured from years of catching. He had been to the White House and was a regular in baseball documentaries, and the Chicago White Sox annually paid tribute to him over the last decade of his life. He was dubbed "Double Duty" by sportswriter Damon Runyon who witnessed Radcliffe catch the first half of a double-header then turn around and catch the second half, which was the norm for Ted.

Radcliffe was born in Mobile, Alabama, on July 7, 1902. He came to Chicago in 1919 as a teenager and found some work playing baseball with local semi-pro teams. Ted joined the Detroit Stars of the NNL in 1928, working for Bingo DeMoss primarily as a catcher, but also filling in as a pitcher when needed. He became a regular in the rotation by 1929. Radcliffe was no novelty act, he was a top-flight pitcher and teams took notice. Radcliffe realized that he could command a higher salary. Radcliffe took advantage and played for many different teams. Even though Duty lived just a stone's throw from American Giants Park, he did not become an American Giant until 1934 when he joined the team for a post-season barnstorming trip. Radcliffe says that the American Giants had wanted him to play, but were not willing to put up enough money and he went elsewhere. He played for Neil Churchill's integrated Bismarck, North Dakota, team along with Satchel Paige. He also played for the St. Louis Stars, Homestead Grays, Pittsburgh Crawfords, Cincinnati Tigers, Birmingham Black Barons, and Kansas City Monarchs, down in Mexico, up in Canada and still more teams.

Double Duty played for part of the 1941 and 1942 seasons with his hometown American Giants and in 1943 was made the player/manager of the American Giants. Duty led the American Giants to a post-season playoff with the Birmingham Black Barons but they were defeated. Duty got into it with owner Doc Martin in 1944 and jumped the team for the Black Barons. In mid–1949, the American Giants managed by Winfield Welch brought Double Duty back and in 1950 he was again named manager of the American Giants and finished out his Negro League baseball career.

"Double Duty" played in six different East-West All-Star games: three as a catcher and three as a pitcher. Duty threw out the ceremonial first pitch for the May 13, 2005, game between the Washington Nationals and Chicago Cubs at RFK

Stadium, an early celebration of his 103rd birthday. He died in Chicago on August 11, 2005.

Larry Raines shortstop 1951. Larry Raines played shortstop in 1951 before getting into organized baseball. After several seasons in the minor leagues, he joined the Cleveland Indians as a utility player in 1957. He was one of the few American Giants to make the leap to the majors.

Ulysses Redd was a catcher and utility player with the American Giants in 1951.

Dick "Cannonball" Redding pitcher 1917. Cannonball Redding was one of the greatest pitchers in black baseball in the 1910's. He earned his reputation with the New York Lincoln Giants and other New York area teams. Smooth talking Rube Foster convinced Cannonball to join the American Giants in 1917, once more giving the American Giants an overpowering staff. Redding is one of several well known star players such as Oscar Charleston, "Cool Papa" Bell, Ben Taylor, and Satchel Paige who had a brief stay with the American Giants, but who have historically been associated with other cities/teams.

Wilson "Frog" Redus outfielder, manager 1934–1940. Wilson Redus blossomed with the St. Louis Stars in the 1920's. He was known for his heads up play, quick base running and consistent hitting. Redus came to the American Giants after the St. Louis and the Cleveland teams folded up shop during the Great Depression. Redus was part of the juggernaut that included Turkey Stearnes, Mule Suttles, and Willie Wells. He stuck with the American Giants to close out the 1930's even as his colleagues (Stearnes, Suttles, and Wells) moved on. Redus was named to the Western All-Star team in 1935 and 1936. For his hard work and loyalty, Redus was named skipper in 1940. Unfortunately the most talented American Giant players jumped ship for Mexico and even local semi-pro teams leaving Redus with little to work with. At the end of the season vandals torched the American Giants' ballpark, symbolizing the vast decline of the proud franchise and the end of an era.

John Reed was listed as backup outfielder and pitcher in 1934.

John Reese outfield 1920–1922. John Reese was a backup outfielder the first three years of the Negro National League. Reese was a Morris College graduate and had played with Hilldale before joining the team. When Reese first came on board he shared starting duties with Cristobal Torriente and Jimmy Lyons. Floyd Jelly Gardner signed with the team mid-season, consequently Reese did not see much playing time from that point on. After leaving the American Giants he became a regular with the St. Louis Stars and managed the team in 1931.

Donald "Soup" Reeves outfield 1939–41. Donald Reeves was an outstanding offensive threat for the American Giants in 1940 and 1941. According to one account he hit over 50 home runs in 1940. He was named to the All-Star team in 1940. Despite his flirtation with greatness, his baseball career ended after the 1941 season. He later taught in the Atlanta school system.

Harry "Lefty" Rhodes pitcher 1947–50. "Lefty" Rhodes was an adequate starter for the American Giants in an era when the emphasis in the Negro Leagues was to get noticed by the big league scouts.

Orville Riggins played a few games at shortstop in 1920, after leaving the American Giants he became the regular shortstop with the Detroit Stars.

Ed "Huck" Rile pitcher 1922–24. Rube acquired Huck Rile from the failed NNL Columbus Bluebirds franchise in 1922. Rile stood at 6 1/2 feet, he was a big man with stamina who could throw hard and hit hard. He worked with Dave Brown, Dick Whitworth and Juan Luis Padrone in the starting rotation in 1922. In 1923, Rile was named by the *Chicago Defender* as someone instigating the movement of players from the American Giants to the Eastern Colored League. Huck Rile and Dave Brown actually did jump to the New York Lincoln Giants prior to the 1923 season. Rube Foster came out with an announcement that anyone who jumped would be banned for life from playing in the NNL. Rube was bluffing, but it was enough to convince Rile, and he came running back to Chicago and assumed the role of ace pitcher. Rile continued as a regular in the rotation in 1924, but Willie Foster and George Harney surpassed him. He was still a good pitcher in 1925 when Rube moved him to Indianapolis, a move that was questioned by some. In subsequent years with the ABCs, Detroit Stars, Brooklyn Royal Giants and other teams Rile spent more time at first base and was known more for his hitting ability.

John Ritchey was the catcher in 1947 and was recognized as one of the top players in the Negro American League. It was announced that the Chicago Cubs were planning to sign him, but Ritchey instead signed with his hometown San Diego Padres of the Pacific Coast League. Ritchey thus became the first black player in the PCL. It is unclear whether Ritchey turned down an offer from the Cubs and went to San Diego on his own, or whether the Cubs failed to follow through. Ritchey was a close friend of fellow San Diegan Walter McCoy and they both served in World War II. He had also played semi-pro ball with Jackie Robinson in Southern California before the war.

Jacob Robinson of Little Rock, Arkansas, played on the left side of the infield in 1946 and 1947.

William "Bobby" Robinson third base, shortstop 1927. Bobby Robinson played at the hot corner in 1927. He grew up in Whistler, Alabama, the same hometown as Chicago Cub Hall of Famer Billy Williams. Robinson played for a number of teams in a career that spanned from 1925 to 1942. Bobby settled in Chicago after his baseball career and worked as a brick mason into his nineties. Bobby Robinson died in Chicago May 17, 2002, at the age of 98. In his later years Bobby had given generously of his time to those interested in the history of Negro League baseball.

Bienvenido Rodriguez played catcher and outfield in 1948. He was recruited by manager Quincy Trouppe who had played with Rodriguez in Puerto Rico.

William "Nat" Rogers outfield, utility 1927–28; 1931–34. "Nat" Rogers came to the American Giants from Memphis in a controversial trade engineered by Dave Malarcher in 1927. Rogers went on to help the American Giants win the Negro League World Series in 1927. Later NNL officials ruled that the trade that brought Nat Rogers and Larry Brown to Chicago from Memphis was invalid. Rogers stayed with the American Giants for most of 1928 despite the league ruling. Rogers did return to Memphis in 1929, but in 1931 came back to Chicago to play for Dave Malarcher's Columbia Giants. Rogers was a key member of Cole's American Giants in 1932 and 1933; he was the starting right fielder and often hit in the cleanup slot.

Harold Ross was listed as a pitcher in 1924 and 1925, he saw very limited action.

Herman "Bobby" Roth was one of many backup catchers brought on between 1923 and 1925, a period when the American Giants had trouble keeping a number one catcher healthy.

Pythias Russ catcher, shortstop 1926–1929. Pythias Russ was a natural athlete, he played baseball, basketball, and football and ran track at Sam Houston College. He was also an excellent student. Rube hired Russ away from the Memphis Red Sox in 1926 and used him as both a shortstop and catcher. Russ's natural abilities made him a key player for the American Giants under Dave Malarcher. Oddly enough, Russ usually left the squad in September prior to the post-season games in favor of studying.

In addition to playing professional baseball and going to college, Russ reportedly worked at the post office in Chicago, taught physical education at Sam Houston College, and was being scouted by the legendary New York Rens and Savoy Five basketball team shortly before he died. He was a rare individual; unfortunately his career was cut short. Russ left the world at the tender age of 26, the victim of tuberculosis—he died in his hometown of Cynthia, Kentucky, August 9, 1930.

Ormand Sampson played part of the 1938 season at third base, shortstop and catcher, but jumped to the Mexican League before the season was out.

Thomas "Tommy" Sampson second base 1948. Tommy Sampson was an Alabama native who spent most of his career with the Birmingham Black Barons. He was seriously injured in an auto accident in the middle of the 1942 Negro League World Series. Sampson recovered and resumed his career, which included a stint as Black Baron manager in 1946 and 1947. He was named to the All-Star team from 1940 to 1944. Sampson took over second base for the American Giants in 1948 towards the end of his career when Jesse Douglass jumped to Mexico. Sampson was also one of numerous people who took some credit for discovering a young Willie Mays.

Louis "Big" Santop was one of black baseball's early superstars, compared with the likes of Oscar Charleston and Cristobal Torriente. He had a career worthy of the Hall of Fame. He earned his fame with the rival eastern teams like the New York Lincoln Giants, Brooklyn Royal Giants and Hilldale. Santop was a ringer in a handful of exhibition games for the American Giants in 1915.

Abe Saperstein was born in London, England, but grew up in Chicago. He was known for founding the Savoy Big Five basketball team, which eventually became the world famous Harlem Globetrotters. Saperstein was an ingenious promoter and applied his principles to baseball as well as basketball. He tried to promote a team he intended to call "The Rube Foster Memorial Giants" in 1932, but that endeavor failed. He did succeed as a booking agent for the Indianapolis Clowns and became heavily involved with promoting the Birmingham Black Barons in the 1940's. In some cases Saperstein hired players to play both baseball and basketball for the 'Trotters. For a period of time he also owned and ran a Harlem Globetrotter semi-pro baseball team.

Abe Saperstein extended his sphere of influence to the American Giants when his friend Winfield Welch took over as manager in 1949. In 1951, the team was sold to Winfield Welch, but Abe Saperstein was presumed to be the money man behind the deal. Among Abe's other business partners was Bill Veeck. Veeck owned the St. Louis Browns and was looking to the Negro Leagues for talent.

John Schorling part-owner 1911–1927. John Schorling was a wealthy tavern owner, son-in-law of Charles Comiskey and the lessor of South Side Park at 39th Street (Pershing) and Wentworth. Schorling had a standing arrangement with Rube Foster to split the gate receipts at South Side Park. The agreement between Schorling and Foster was placed in jeopardy when Rube was incapacitated in 1926. Rube's wife Sarah was included in one or two league meetings, but Schorling essentially assumed Rube's stake in the ball club. Schorling tried to run the team on his own but failed. The friendly partnership, which had worked for 15 years, turned ugly when Schorling sold his interest in the team to a florist and gambler from Princeton, Illinois, named William Trimble.

Joe Scott played first base in 1950.

Willie Lee Scott was a back up first baseman in 1934.

Samuel Seagraves of Indianapolis was a backup catcher in 1946.

John Shackelford third base 1926. John Shackelford played third base for the American Giants in 1926. He joined the American Giants after finishing up the school year at Wiley College. Scholarship turned out to be Shackelford's true calling. He played a few years in the Negro Leagues but went on to get a law degree. When Branch Rickey took an interest in the U.S. League in 1945 Shackelford was named the president; he was also considered for the commissionership of black baseball in the 1940's.

Ted Shaw, who came to Chicago from Monrovia, California, as a young man, was given a tryout as pitcher in the spring of 1927. It was noted that he had a good drop ball. While his career in Chicago was very brief he went on to play three seasons with the Detroit Stars.

Robert Sharpe pitched in a game in 1944.

Charles Lefty Shields pitcher 1941–1943. Lefty Shields was a regular starter on the World War II era American Giants. Candy Jim put a good deal of stock in Shields' abilities. In 1942 Candy Jim named Shields to match up with Satchel Paige twice and in 1943 Candy Jim attempted to take Shields to the Homestead Grays with him when he left Chicago.

R. S. Simmons was a business manager for the American Giants under Doc Martin in the 1940's. He had served as publicity director of the Negro American League in 1942, the league secretary in 1943 and then business manager of the American Giants from 1944 to 1949. Simmons had played ball with Waco, Texas, of the Texas League and was befriended by Rube Foster who helped him establish a team in Omaha, Nebraska, in 1920.

Billy Simms center field 1938–1940. Billy Simms came from the Kansas City Monarchs in 1938 to replace an aging Turkey Stearnes. Concurrently Stearnes went to Kansas City and continued to play. Simms was the regular center fielder, but was deemed expendable by management when he insisted on an advance in his pay midway through the 1940 season and was let go. He then went back to the Kansas City Monarchs.

Owen Smaulding pitched a few games in 1928.

Ernest Smith of Rochelle, Louisiana, played outfield and occasionally catcher in 1939 and 1940.

Gene Smith was a regular in the 1949 pitching rotation.

George "Sonny" Smith went into camp as a shortstop with the American Giants in Meridian,

Mississippi, for spring training in 1951, but left to join the Dayton Indians in the St. Louis Browns' farm system.

Henry Smith was a catcher and utility infielder in 1942 and 1943.

Theolic "Fireball" Smith pitcher 1948–49; 1951. Theolic Smith was known for his fastball. He began his career with the legendary Pittsburgh Crawfords of 1936. In 1940 "Fireball" went down to Mexico, something clicked and he set the league on fire. He became a superstar in Mexico. Mexican millionaire Jorge Pasquel arranged with the U.S. government for Theolic Smith and Quincy Trouppe to be allowed to play baseball in Mexico during World War II in exchange for an arrangement allowing 80,000 Mexicans to work in U.S. defense jobs. Smith came back to the states in 1948, when Quincy Trouppe was manager of the American Giants, and joined the team. In 1951 Theolic Smith was a regular starter for the American Giants, then went on to pitch four years with the San Diego Padres of the Pacific Coast League.

Joe Sparks was a utility infielder who worked regularly for the American Giants between 1937–1940, a period of time in which players came and left frequently.

Alvin Spearman pitched for the American Giants in 1950 and 1951. He is not directly related to Clyde Spearman who appeared with the team in the 1940's.

Clyde Spearman was listed as a right fielder in 1942 and 1943.

Walter Speedy was listed as an infielder in 1914.

Zack Spencer was a pitcher recruited by Dave Malarcher for the 1931 Columbia Giants.

Otis "Lefty" Starks pitched for the American Giants in 1921. He went on to have a full career in the Negro Leagues playing mostly in New York.

Norman "Turkey" Stearnes outfield 1932–1935, 1937–38. "Turkey" Stearnes was one of the greatest home run hitters in the history of Negro League baseball. He made his mark while he was with the Detroit Stars from 1923 to 1931. Following the 1931 season the Detroit franchise had financial problems and could not afford to pay Stearnes's salary. Meanwhile Robert Cole had just invested in the American Giants and was interested in seeding the team with a salty veteran like Turkey Stearnes. So Turkey Stearnes became an American Giant in 1932. Stearnes was just a bit past his prime, but his bat helped Cole's American Giants to win the Negro Southern League championship in 1932 and finish in a dead heat for the 1933 Negro National League pennant. In 1933, Turkey Stearnes was joined by another legendary home run hitter — Mule Suttles — and the American Giants had one of their most potent offensive lineups ever. Turkey went to the Philadelphia Stars in 1936, and then was back in his adopted

home town of Detroit to start out the 1937 season. Stearnes played a few games with the American Giants at the end of the 1937 season after the Detroit Stars closed up shop. Stearnes came back to the American Giants in 1938, but manager Candy Jim Taylor decided the 18-year veteran was not his old self and let him go. Turkey Stearnes was elected to the National Baseball Hall of Fame by the Veterans Committee in 2000.

Frank Stevens pitched in a few games in 1925.

Riley Stewart pitched regularly for the American Giants in 1947 and 1948.

Leroy Stratton was a utility player in 1925 and 1926. He went on to play six seasons with the Nashville Elite Giants after leaving Chicago.

Albert Street (aka Streets) was given a tryout in 1925. Street had played infield for the Leavenworth Prison team known as the "Booker T's." He is one of three such Booker T players to join the American Giants. (The story of the Leavenworth Booker T's was researched by Timothy Rives, an archivist with the National Archives in Kansas City, and was published in the National Archives and Records Administration's quarterly journal *Prologue*, Summer 2004.)

Sam Streeter pitched for the American Giants in 1921, then went on to a prolific career spent mostly with the Birmingham Black Barons.

Fulton Strong pitched in a few games in 1923.

Othello Strong was a regular in the pitching rotation in 1950. He also played briefly with the Harlem Globetrotter basketball team.

Ted Strong of South Bend, Indiana, played in the infield for the American Giants in 1951. Strong was a great athlete and also played basketball for the Harlem Globetrotters. In baseball he was best known for his years with the Indianapolis Clowns and Kansas City Monarchs. His teammates spoke glowingly of his abilities and he was named to the All-Star team five times.

Sam Strothers was a backup catcher and first baseman in 1912. Strothers had been with the Leland Giants from 1907 to 1910, but couldn't break into Rube's American Giants. He continued to play with the cross-town Chicago Giants until 1918.

Lonnie Summers catcher, utility 1948–49; 1951. Lonnie Summers came to the American Giants after serving in World War II and spending two seasons in Mexico. Summers was solidified into the starting catcher's role when Quincy Trouppe left the team in 1949, and he was named to the All-Star team that year. Summers returned to the team in 1951, after going back to Latin America to ply his trade. Summers eventually got the attention of big league scouts and finished up his career playing in minor league baseball.

George "Mule" Suttles first base 1933–1935. Mule Suttles came to the American Giants in 1933, he had made a name for himself with the St. Louis Stars of the original Negro National League. The style of play in the 1930's changed, with more emphasis on home run hitting, and the annual East-West All-Star game, which began in 1933, became the most important event of the season. Suttles joined forces with Turkey Stearnes to return the American Giants to their traditional place as a dominating force in Negro baseball west of the Alleghenies. Suttles might have received his nickname for the stodgy manner he ran the bases. Suttles swung a 50-ounce bat and was best known for regularly hitting tape measure shots. Fans and teammates would egg him on by yelling "kick, Mule, kick!" A towering home run was known as a "Mule Kick." Owner Horace Hall could not afford to keep Mule Suttles on the payroll in 1936 and both he and Willie Wells moved to the Newark Eagles where they joined Ray Dandridge in the infield. Mule Suttles was one of the most exciting players in the Negro Leagues and his career spanned three decades. George "Mule" Suttles represented the Western squad in the first three All-Star games and played for the East twice.

Leroy Sutton of Cairo, Illinois, pitched in a few games in 1942.

George Sweatt outfield, second base 1926–1927. George Sweatt was part of a trade that sent Cristobal Torriente to Kansas City. Sweatt was a natural athlete, well educated and mild mannered; quite a contrast from Torriente. In fact Sweatt had earned his teaching credentials in college and was active in his church. While Sweatt played with the KC Monarchs he went to the World Series in 1924 and 1925; with the American Giants he went to the series in 1926 and 1927. Sweatt came away with three championships out of the four opportunities. He played a critical role for the American Giants and fit nicely into Dave Malarcher's style of management. When William Trimble bought the team he offered such meager pay that Sweatt decided to take full-time work at the post office. He continued to play semi-pro ball on the weekends.

James Talbert was a backup catcher, 1946–1948.

Ben Taylor first base 1913. The famous first baseman, who was Candy Jim's brother, was brought on to the American Giants as a ringer at the end of the 1913 season. He went on a post-season barnstorming trip with the American Giants also, but joined his brothers with the Indianapolis ABCs in 1914.

"Candy" Jim Taylor third base, manager 1912–13, 1937–1939, 1941–42; 1945–1947. Candy Jim Taylor had four stints with the American Giants, one as a player and three as manager. Candy Taylor's résumé stretches the length of Negro League baseball history. He was born in Anderson, South Carolina, on February 1, 1884, the brother of Charles Isham "C.I," John Boyce "Steel Arm," and Benjamin Harrison Taylor. The famous Taylor family of Negro League baseball was like no other. C.I. Taylor would long be remembered for his disciplinary style and dedication to Negro League baseball, though he died still a young man in 1922. Steel Arm was noted for his stamina on the mound, which made him a hot property for a few years. Ben Taylor has been called "among the greatest first basemen in Negro League history," his playing career stretched from 1909 to 1930. Candy Jim Taylor distinguished himself by staying at the top of his game from 1901 until 1947, practically the entire span of Negro League existence.

Candy Jim played at the hot corner, starting off his professional career with the Birmingham Giants in 1904 where his brother C.I. Taylor managed. In 1909, Rube Foster encountered Candy Jim and his brothers when the Leland Giants swung through the South. They met again at the end of the 1909 season when Candy Jim and Steel Arm played for the St. Paul, Minnesota, Colored Gophers and had a hand in defeating the Lelands in a late-season playoff. Candy Jim played with the Lelands in 1910, but jumped to St. Louis in 1911— the first year of existence of the American Giants. Rube was able to bring Candy Jim into the American Giant fold in 1912 and he was the regular third baseman for two seasons. Candy followed brother C.I. to Indianapolis in 1914, and stayed with the ABCs through 1918. In 1919 he took over as the player/manager of the Dayton Marcos, and managed them the first year of competition in the NNL. The Marcos were a second tier team in the NNL. Over the years he spent significant time as player/manager with a number of Ohio teams including the Cleveland Tate Stars, the Columbus Elite Giants and the Toledo Tigers. Candy took over the St. Louis Stars in 1923, where he worked with "Cool Papa" Bell and Willie Wells. He stayed with St. Louis through 1929, except for a one-year interlude in 1926. In 1928, he guided the St. Louis team to a NNL pennant.

Candy resumed his wandering ways, guiding the Memphis Red Sox in 1930 where he was remembered for signing Josh Gibson and then turning around and letting him go, stating "he'll never be a catcher." Candy Jim stayed in baseball through the 1930's. Horace Hall, who took over the American Giants in 1937, retained Candy Jim to guide the team. The American Giants went to a post-season playoff with the Kansas City Monarchs in 1937. In 1940, Candy left the American Giants for the Birmingham Black Barons. In 1941 he was right back in Chicago. While the '41 team was replenished with players who had returned from the Mexican Leagues, he did not have an answer for the Kansas City Monarchs. The old ball-park had burned down, home games were played a few times a year at Comiskey. In 1942, Candy signed "Cool Papa" Bell to the American Giants—still no answer for Satchel Paige, Hilton Smith and Connie Johnson of Kansas City. With the team firmly under the grip of Doc J.B. Martin in 1943, Candy and "Cool Papa" Bell went to the Homestead Grays—joining Josh Gibson and a cast of characters. Candy managed the legendary Homestead Grays of 1943/44 to back to back World Series championships.

In 1945, Candy Jim came back to the American Giants for his third stint as manager. The American Giants had fallen significantly in stature. Candy dealt with wartime restrictions, personal health problems and another problem he never thought he would have to deal with—competition for players from major league baseball. Candy Jim, always the professional, took it all in stride, he scouted, tutored, managed and put a professional team out on the field—even as Jackie Robinson packed the house up on the North Side. Nineteen forty-seven was Candy Jim's last year with the American Giants. He was slated to take the helm of the Baltimore Elite Giants in 1948, but shortly before the season rolled around Candy died in a Chicago hospital. All of the Taylor brothers shared a specific trait: they were unassuming soft-spoken gentlemen. The *Chicago Defender* later reported that "not a condolence was read or one word spoke from any of the 12 clubs in organized Negro baseball" at his funeral. He was buried in an unmarked grave at Chicago's Burr Oak Cemetery.

In 2004 a group of historians raised money to place a headstone on Candy Jim Taylor's grave.

Candy Jim managed the Western All-Stars three times and Eastern All-Stars once.

John "Steel Arm" Taylor was one of the famous Taylor clan. Steel Arm Taylor pitched for the American Giants in 1913. His brothers Ben and Candy Jim also played for the American Giants for part of the 1913 season. Steel Arm's career did not last nearly as long as his brother Jim's. His professional career was basically over by 1920. "Steel Arm" Taylor settled in Peoria, Illinois, where he ran a turkish bath and managed a semi-pro baseball team.

Joseph "Cephus" "Cash" Taylor catcher, outfield 1946, 1949–1950. Joseph Taylor was given a brief look by Candy Jim Taylor in 1946. He rejoined the team in 1949 under Winfield Welch and in 1950 went into organized baseball. He was a strong hitting outfielder. Eventually he played for the Philadelphia Athletics, Cincinnati Reds, St. Louis Cardinals and Baltimore Orioles—one of the few American Giants to make the jump to the big leagues.

Leroy Taylor was given a tryout as outfielder in 1925.

James Sandy Thompson outfield 1926, 1928–32. Sandy Thompson was a regular outfielder for the American Giants in the years after Rube Foster left the team. While he never got the same attention as fellow outfielder Jelly Gardner, he was a consistent player who spent most of his career in Chicago. In 1926 he hit the World Series–winning RBI in the rubber game with the Atlantic City Bacharach Giants.

Walter Thomas played outfield in 1946 and was traded to the Birmingham Black Barons for Lyman Bostock in 1947. In 1948 Thomas played minor league ball; earlier in his career he pitched.

Cristobal Torriente outfield 1918–1925. Torriente is one of the few players with the American Giants dubbed a superstar. He was a stocky center fielder with great power, often compared with Oscar Charleston and Babe Ruth. Rube Foster coveted Torriente, whom he had encountered many times on the island of Cuba and as a member of the Cuban Stars. During the upheaval of World War I, Rube was able to land Torriente in Chicago. Torriente routinely came up with big hits for the American Giants and was an indispensable part of the attack. He was accomplished with every facet of play, and like Oscar Charleston and Babe Ruth he occasionally took the mound. Over the years Rube Foster showed he had very little patience for the prima donna player, and Torriente's ego might have been his downfall. In 1925, Torriente was traded to the Kansas City Monarchs for utility player George Sweatt and pitcher Rube Currie. One of the greatest Cuban players of all time, he starred for the Chicago American Giants during the prime of his career and eventually died, destitute, of tuberculosis in New York City. His body was taken back to Cuba for burial. He was one of the original inductees into the Cuban Hall of Fame; had he played in the major leagues there is little doubt he would also be in Cooperstown.

Harold Treadwell pitcher 1924–25, 1928. Harold Treadwell joined the American Giants in 1924 he had previously been associated with the Bacharach Giants. Treadwell had impressed Rube Foster in 1920 by pitching all 20-innings in a playoff game against the American Giants losing by a 1–0 score. Rube had very high hopes for Treadwell and he did not quite meet with expectations. He ended up also playing in Detroit and Cleveland for part of the '24 season. Treadwell started the 1925 season in Chicago but was sent to Indianapolis. In 1928, Dave Malarcher recruited Harold Treadwell to come out of retirement and he was respectable as part of the regular starting rotation.

Ted "High Pockets" Trent pitcher 1934–1939. Ted Trent was a steady effective starting pitcher for the American Giants during the 1930's. When he first broke into the club in 1934 he pitched alongside Willie Foster, Willie "Sug" Cornelius and Melvin "Putt" Powell. The American Giants relied heavily on pitching in South Side Park — which was known as a pitcher's park; he fit into the scheme nicely. After Willie Foster got older and went by the wayside (about 1935) it was Willie Cornelius and Ted Trent who carried the team, both pitchers known for their curve balls. It was a toss-up as to which one's was better. Trent was named to the Western All-Star team from 1934 to 1937. He pitched through the 1939 season, but in 1940 he fell seriously ill. The American Giants actually played a benefit game for him in August 1940. Trent missed out on the Comiskey Park era and died of tuberculosis in 1944.

Quincy Trouppe catcher, manager 1933–1948. Quincy Trouppe was at the beginning of his legendary career when he joined Cole's American Giants in 1933. Robert Cole front-loaded the American Giants with talent including Turkey Stearnes, Mule Suttles, Willie Wells and Quincy Trouppe. The American Giants were forced to play home games in Indianapolis after a group of gamblers bought out the lease on South Side Park in hopes of turning it into a dog track. Trouppe was just a backup catcher at the time, but he left the squad early in the season to join the barnstorming integrated Bismarck, North Dakota, Cubs. Trouppe was intelligent, a natural athlete (he boxed and played basketball also), and a switch hitter who in a short time built his reputation as one of the best catchers in the game. He was a Missouri native and played with the St. Louis Stars and KC Monarchs. Trouppe became a star in the Mexican Leagues. Mexican millionaire Jorge Pasquel went so far as to arrange for wartime work permits for 80,000 Mexican workers in exchange for the right to sign Trouppe and pitcher Theolic Smith to his team. The seasoned veteran came back to the American Giants as a player/manager in 1948 and was able to persuade both Roberto Vargas and James Pendleton to sign with the club. (According to Trouppe he had also lined up Willie Mays for a tryout but was rebuffed by owner Doc Martin.) The following year Doc Martin eagerly sold James Pendleton to Branch Rickey and was too cheap to bring Quincy back. Quincy Trouppe himself went to the big leagues with the Cleveland Indians in 1952.

When his playing days were over Quincy scouted for the St. Louis Cardinals. His son Quincy Trouppe Jr. is a noted author and poet.

E. C. "Pop" Turner played shortstop for the Columbia American Giants in 1932, he had also played in one game in 1930. The first part of his career, 1925–28, was with the Brooklyn Royal Giants. Later he became an umpire.

Thomas "Tommy" Turner was given a chance to play first base for the American Giants in the spring of 1947. An army buddy, Walter McCoy, recommend Tommy to Candy Jim. Turner played a few games but lost the job to Lyman Bostock Sr.

Roy Tyler pitcher, outfield 1925–26. Roy Tyler played briefly for the American Giants in 1925–1926. He is better known for the route he took to the American Giants. Tyler came to the American Giants directly from Leavenworth Prison. Tyler was imprisoned because he participated in the historic 1917 "mutiny" of black soldiers in Houston who rose up against Jim Crow laws in Houston. At Leavenworth, Tyler became a friend of former Rube Foster teammate boxer Jack Johnson. Tyler proved to be a top player with the black baseball team at Leavenworth called the "Booker T's." When Tyler came up for parole in 1925, Rube Foster signed him out as his "Parole Advisor." After leaving the American Giants Tyler played in Cleveland. (The story of the Leavenworth Booker T's was researched by Timothy Rives, an archivist with the National Archives in Kansas City, and was published in the National Archives and Records Administration's quarterly journal *Prologue*, Summer 2004.)

Rube Tyree was picked up by Rube Foster in late 1916 almost as a secret weapon on the mound. Rube had high hopes for Tyree, but he ended up losing two important games against the Indianapolis ABCs in the post-season. Tyree came back to the team in 1917, but was let go still early in the season.

Roberto Vargas pitcher 1948. Quincy Trouppe met Roberto Vargas while playing winter ball in Puerto Rico. When Trouppe took over management of the American Giants he hand picked Vargas to help out on the mound. Vargas was a good weapon for the American Giants but he developed into a better player after leaving the team. Eventually in 1955 he was called up to the Milwaukee Braves and appeared in 25 games, another member of the small group of American Giants who later played in the big leagues.

Lee Wade pitcher 1914. Lee Wade was recruited from the Lincoln Giants following the 1913 season when he was instrumental in the Lincoln Giants' beating the American Giants. Lee Wade traveled with the American Giants to the West Coast and then pitched during the regular season. He was propelled to the role of the ace of the staff after promising hurler Bill Lindsay died suddenly after an illness. Wade was with the American Giants for only one season, though he spent ten years in baseball, mostly in New York.

Archie Ware started his professional career with the American Giants at first base in 1940. He was a star first baseman for ten years in the declining Negro Leagues of the forties and spent most of his years with the Cincinnati/Cleveland Buck-eyes.

Willie Ware first base 1924–1926. Willie Ware was recruited from Wiley University while the club was on spring training in Texas. Foster pegged him to replace an aging Leroy Grant, and he saw a lot of playing time the second half of the 1924 season, but did not live up to expectations and was released following the 1926 season.

Jesse Warren played second base in 1947.

Edgar "Blue" Washington pitcher 1916. Pitcher Edgar "Blue" Washington was picked up by Rube and the American Giants in the spring of 1916 when the team barnstormed through Southern California up the West Coast. Washington was an 18-year-old kid described as "a phenom." Blue put a hurt on a couple of teams in the Pacific Northwest, but did not join the club back in Chicago. A few years later, in 1920, Ed Washington played first base for the Kansas City Monarchs. While Edgar "Blue" Washington had base-ball skills, he was better known as an actor. He worked in a large number of films in the 1930's, often portraying the stereotyped African American. According to *Internet Movie Data Base.Com* (www.imdb.com) he had a small (uncredited) part in *Gone with the Wind*, as well as the role of "Sambo" in a 1933 movie called *King of the Arena*. Edgar Blue Washington was the father of Kenny Washington, the first black player in the NFL.

Jack Watts was a backup catcher in 1914 and 1915 taking over for Bruce Petway when needed. He had a similar role with the Indianapolis ABCs through that team's glory years 1915–1917.

Winfield S. Welch manager, owner 1949, 1951. Winfield Welch was a Louisiana native and his managing career began there, where he managed the Shreveport Giants. He managed in big league black baseball with the Cincinnati Buckeyes and Birmingham Black Barons—leading the Barons to championships in 1943–44. He was credited with discovering a number of players over the years in-cluding Piper Davis, Artie Wilson, Willard Brown and others. Welch became a close friend of Abe Saperstein, when Abe promoted the Black Barons and Welch worked as a manager for the Harlem Globetrotters. Welch came to the American Gi-ants in 1949. Welch did not manage the team in 1950, after ownership was optioned to William Little and Double Duty Radcliffe was made skip-per. In 1951, however, Welch was the front man in the group that bought the team outright (other key members of the ownership group were Abe Saperstein and Bill Veeck). The Negro Leagues had increasingly become more of a market place for big league teams. Welch did a great job in this environment. In 1949 the American Giants won the NAL pennant. In 1951, Welch had the luxury of handing the ball to Satchel Paige; 1951 was the last year of Welch's involvement in the dugout. Bill Veeck and Abe Saperstein's bid to dominate in the St. Louis market with the aid of Negro League players failed—and the American Giants folded a year later.

Willie Wells shortstop 1933–1935, 1944. Willie Wells was considered one of the greatest fielding shortstops in the history of the Negro Leagues. Wells was from Austin, Texas, but made a name for himself with the St. Louis Stars of the NNL from 1924 to 1931. When the St. Louis team folded during the Depression, Wells went to the Detroit Wolves, and after that team also folded he (along with Mule Suttles and Quincy Trouppe) landed with Robert Cole's American Giants. Wells (along with fellow Hall of Famers Willie Foster and Turkey Stearnes) quietly led Cole's American Gi-ants to success from 1933 to 1935. Rube Foster coveted Wells, and the two Texans had a collegial relationship. During Rube's career Wells played for St. Louis, but the pair got together to discuss baseball. Willie "the Devil" Wells played in eight All-Star games. He was also a star in Cuban and Mexican baseball. While Willie Wells was one of the greatest shortstops to play for the American Giants, he was more widely known for his play with St. Louis. Wells was elected to the National Baseball Hall of Fame by the Veterans Committee in 1997.

Edgar Wesley played first base in late 1918 when there was a lot of turnover in personnel due to the World War I draft, he later went on to have a complete career with the Detroit Stars.

Ollie West pitched in a few games in 1944 and 1945.

Frank "the Ant" Wickware pitcher 1911–1912, 1914–1918, 1920–1921. Frank Wickware was considered among the top pitchers of the Dead Ball era. He could command top dollar for his services and went from team to team during his prime. He worked for four different teams in 1914 and pitched two no-hitters. Rube appreciated Wickware's skill and loved to use him in clutch situations. Foster went to great lengths to bring Wickware back from the Schenectady, New York, Mohawk Giants in 1914, essentially convincing the whole team to jump and moving them to Louisville, Kentucky. Rube then skimmed the cream off the top and brought Wickware back to Chicago.

Frank Wickware shared the same home town of Coffeyville, Kansas, with legend Walter John-son. Wickware and Johnson met in barnstorm games three different times and Wickware won twice.

Lawrence Eugene White played a few games in the middle infield in 1950.

Burlin White one of several backup catchers used to support Bruce Petway in 1917.

Richard Whitworth pitcher 1915–1919, 1922, 1924. Dick Whitworth was a key member of the pitching staff during the teens, working alongside Frank Wickware, Cannonball Redding, Dave Brown, Tom Johnson and others. His nickname was "Big," he was very consistent for the American Giants from 1915 to 1919, some even put him into the category of greatness at the height of his career in 1917. Following the 1919 season Rube seeded the Detroit Stars with a few veteran players. Whitworth was not happy about being told where to play, and jumped the NNL arrangement for the Hilldale club of Philadelphia. Rube forgave Whitworth's transgression and signed him back in 1922. The following year Whitworth was hospitalized for a drinking problem. Rube gave him another chance in 1924, and allowed him to pitch a few games early in the season, before his brother Willie Foster and Aubrey Owens reported to the team following their semester of college. He was released thereafter.

Maurice Wiggins was a backup shortstop in 1920.

Andrew "Stringbean" Williams was used as a pitcher in 1919, he had been a star with the Indianapolis ABCs, but C.I. Taylor elected not to field a team that year due to World War I. Stringbean Williams went on to a successful career in the Eastern Colored League.

Bobby Williams shortstop 1918–1925; 1928. Bobby Williams was hand picked by Rube Foster to take the place of John Henry Lloyd at shortstop. Bobby Williams was a flashy player with a lot of hustle and became a fan favorite. He proved to be adequate at shortstop, but never lived up to the great expectation that he would compare to Pop Lloyd. Williams was an integral part of Rube Foster's 1920's teams. Rube moved Bobby Williams to Indianapolis following the 1925 season, which was a great disappointment to his local following, a move that even led some to question Rube's mental health. Williams moved on to the Homestead Grays after Indianapolis, but did come back to the American Giants briefly in 1928 when Dave Malarcher had to patch up the roster.

Charles "Cholly" Williams shortstop, second base 1926–1931. Charles Williams was an important infielder who came into his own as many of the American Giant legends like Bingo DeMoss and Bobby Williams began to age and were moved down the line by Rube Foster. Williams learned to play ball at Tuskegee, before joining the American Giants he played with Gilkerson's Giants, the Indianapolis ABCs and the Memphis Red Sox. Cholly was a member of the back to back World Series wins in 1926 and 1927. Sadly Charles Williams died in Chicago at the age of 28 of food poisoning.

Chester "Chet" Williams shortstop 1943. Chet Williams was a shortstop with the Pittsburgh Crawfords during their glory years from 1931 to 1938; he was named to the Eastern All-Star team four times during that stint. Chet finished up his career playing shortstop for Double Duty Radcliffe's 1943 American Giants. After baseball he settled in Lake Charles, Louisiana, where he managed a semi-pro team and owned a nightclub called the "Cotton Club." Chet Williams died in brawl at his nightclub on Christmas night 1952 after taking five bullets.

Henry Williams was given a tryout as a pitcher in 1939.

Smokey (aka Cyclone) Joe Williams pitcher 1914 barnstorming tour. This Hall of Fame pitcher from Texas made a barnstorming trip with Rube Foster and selected American Giants in 1914. Other than that he was best known for defeating the American Giants numerous times. He mostly played on teams based on the East Coast. His ability and record most closely compare to Satchel Paige's. He is considered one of the greatest pitchers of all time. The Veterans Committee elected him to the Baseball Hall of Fame in 1999.

John Williams quit his job as a police officer in Hot Springs, Arkansas, to play first base for the American Giants in 1948.

Johnny Williams pitched for the American Giants in 1951 and 1952. Johnny went on to play minor league ball until 1955. He currently resides on the South Side of Chicago, proudly wears his Negro League colors at Chicago White Sox games, and is known to carry custom made baseball cards which he cheerfully signs for fans.

Poindexter Williams was one of several catchers used in 1921.

Roy "Bob" Williams was listed as catcher in 1952, the last year of the team's existence.

Tom Williams pitcher 1917–1918, 1920–21, 1923–24. Tom Williams was recruited from Morris Brown College in Atlanta. His very first year with the American Giants he fit right in alongside Dick "Cannonball Reading" and Tom Johnson. He was always a solid pitcher, but in 1918 Rube booted Williams from the team for boarding a train in an "intoxicated stupor." Rube occasionally rode "college men" for their drinking and for some reason he made Williams the scapegoat. While alcohol consumption might have been a problem for Williams, he managed to stay on top of his game. After being dismissed from the American Giants he went to the Hilldale Daisies and had a good year (including a 2–0 shutout of the American Giants). Foster, not one to argue with results, brought Tom Williams back in 1920. Williams was a workhorse along with Frank Wickware, Dave Brown and Tom Johnson in 1920–21. Williams jumped to the New York Lincoln Giants in 1922. In 1923, he was back with the American

Giants when the pitching staff had changed again and he worked with Ed "Huck" Rile and Aubrey Owens. Williams was well past his prime in 1924, but still saw regular action. Fresh arms Willie Foster and George Harney came on the scene that year and Rube released Williams prior to the 1925 season.

John "Jumping Johnny" Wilson saw limited action in the outfield for the American Giants in 1948 and 1949. "Jumping Johnny" was a native of Anderson, Indiana, and was named Indiana Mr. Basketball in 1946 (an honor given to the best prep basketball player). (Another Negro League star, George Crowe, was also an Indiana Mr. Basketball.) It was said that John would have liked to play hoops for Indiana University, but the color line was still in place and he was denied the opportunity. Basketball was his main sport and he did go on to play with the Harlem Globetrotters and other black pro teams. He later coached at Wood H.S. in Indianapolis and spent 20 years as a coach and athletic director at Malcolm X College in Chicago. He is now retired and is a pillar in the Anderson, Indiana, community.

James Winston pitched for the Columbia American Giants in 1931.

Lewis Wolfolk pitcher 1923–1925. Lewis Wolfolk of Providence, Kentucky, was recruited by Rube Foster, who was impressed with his natural abilities. Wolfolk saw a lot of work the first half of the 1923 season, but his playing time was cut back dramatically later in the season coincidentally with the arrival of one Willie Foster on the team roster. Wolfolk never did live up to Rube's expectations but was kept on the roster.

Parnell Woods played third base and helped manage for part of the 1951 season. Woods was a legendary player/manager with the Cincinnati/Cleveland Buckeyes in the 1940's and became the Harlem Globetrotter business manager. Parnell Woods was one of several Abe Saperstein associates with the team in 1951.

Danny Wright was a pitcher in 1951 and 1952.

Robert Wright was a backup catcher in 1915.

Dave Wyatt was a shortstop with the Chicago Union Giants and was instrumental in getting Rube Foster to come to Chicago in 1902. Wyatt was one of black baseball's first journalists, his dispatches appeared in the *Indianapolis Freeman,* the *Chicago Whip* and other black newspapers. He was one of the co-drafters of the Negro National League constitution. Along with Frank A. Young he was one of the most important chroniclers of African American professional baseball, and probably deserves the equivalent recognition of Cooperstown's J. G. Taylor Spink Award.

Ralph Wyatt shortstop 1941–46. Ralph Wyatt came from the local lots to become the regular shortstop during the World War II years. He was much more than a replacement player and was named to the All-Star team in 1942, and he was "loaned" to the Homestead Grays for the 1943 World Series to offset the loan of "Double Duty" Radcliffe to the Birmingham Black Barons. Wyatt was also recruited by the Mexican League but remained loyal to the American Giants. Wyatt was scolded in the local press for not running out a ground ball that might have won a game in 1946, later in the season he refused to accompany the team on a road trip and was sold to the Cleveland Buckeyes.

Ed "Pep" Young first base, catcher 1936–1943, 1946. The American Giants always seemed to need a backup catcher on the squad. "Pep" Young was valuable as both a backup catcher and a power hitting first baseman. Young was relied on in a number of situations both in the field and as a cleanup hitter. In 1940, then business manager Dave Malarcher attempted to fire Young, because he had requested an advance on his pay. Malarcher was overruled by team owner Horace Hall and was reinstated. "Pep" Young left the team in 1944, but came back to the American Giants in 1946 for another season.

Frank A. "Fay" Young journalist 1907–1949. Frank Young was one of the greatest baseball writers of all time. Fay Young is also a perfect example of the unsung hero of black baseball — the type of individual he himself so often profiled in his writing. Frank A. Young, who sometimes went by Fay Young, began his career as an unpaid sportswriter for the *Chicago Defender* in 1907. It wasn't until 1915 that he took regular full time work with the *Defender*. He soon became the sports editor of the *Defender*. Frank Young's chronicle of Negro League baseball is a solid gold treasure, and while there were a number of polished baseball journalists in the black press — none really compared with Young. He wrote weekly missives on black baseball through the Negro League era, the Great Depression, World War II, and the post–Jackie Robinson era. There is really no question that Frank A. Young is deserving of the Hall of Fame's J. G. Taylor Spink Award, it is just an oversight on the part of Cooperstown waiting to be corrected. He was born in 1884 and died in Chicago on October 27, 1957.

Appendix 2: Game Log

The following is a list of scores of the games of the Chicago American Giants (and associated teams) from 1909 to 1952. While this list includes a great many scores, it is by no means complete. It is a fact that the results of many games were never published. This effort to list games relies heavily on the Chicago Defender, *the* Indianapolis Freeman, *and to a lesser degree on other papers. The American Giants were a high profile team and many other papers, both large and small, published short articles on the visit of the American Giants to their locale. This effort to gather American Giants scores did not include a thorough research of other newspapers. Readers will note that games against amateurs and semi-pros, barnstorming games, spring training, and official/ unofficial Negro League games are included without distinction. While I have done my best to record the final score, outcome and location of the games played, there are undoubtedly errors of fact and errors of transcription in this log. When location or date is uncertain I have left a blank. There have been several efforts to republish records and standings of the Negro Leagues. While all of these efforts have been noble and are certainly accurate to some degree, they all differ from each other and are inconsistent. Therefore for the final standings I have indicated only the agreed outcome, not the won-loss record. The effort to document the history of Negro League baseball is ongoing, so there are numerous gaps in the information presented.*

In the scores that follow, the information is given as follows: month/day, opponent, won or lost, score, (location).

1909 Leland Giants

Manager: Andrew "Rube" Foster. Home field: Auburn Park, 79th and Wentworth. Final standing: Winners of Chicago City League Championship (credited officially with 31–9 record in City League). Based on scores published in the *Indianapolis Freeman*.

	Memphis. w 10–1	05/25	Nashville Standard Giants. w 10–0 (Nashville)
	Memphis. w 15–6		
	Birmingham, AL. w 3–0	05/26	Nashville Standard Giants. w 9–0 (Nashville)
	Birmingham, AL. w 4–2		
04/24	Ft. Worth Wonders. w 8–5	05/27	Louisville Giants. w 7–2 (Louisville)
	Austin, TX. w 5–1	05/28	West Baden Sprudels. w 1–0 (West Baden, IN)
	San Antonio. w 5–0		
	San Antonio. w 3–2	05/29	West Baden Sprudels. w 13–1 West Baden, IN
	Prairie View College. w 6–0		
	Houston Black Buffaloes. w 5–1		West Ends. w 10–1 (Auburn Park)
	Houston Black Buffaloes. w 8–5		Gunthers. w 5–1
	Houston Black Buffaloes. w 5–0	05/31	Logans. w 4–0 (Logan Square Park)
05/02	Logans. l 7–8.		Gunthers. w 4–0 (Auburn)
	Logans. l ? ?	06/13	Senecas. w 1–0 (Seneca Park)
05/16	Anson Colts. w 8–1		Anson Colts. w 3–0 (Home)
05/?	Milwaukee White Sox. w 4–2 (Home)		West Ends. w 5–0 (Home)

221

06/27	West Ends. w 4–2 (West End Park)
	Milwaukee White Sox. w 5–0
06/??	West Ends. w 8–3 (West End Park)
	Cuban Stars. w 3–2 (Logan Square Park)
	Cuban Stars. w 7–4
07/04	Anson Colts. l 5–6
	Anson Colts. t 2–2
07/05	Gunthers. w 10–2 (Gunther Park)
	Logans. l 0–5
07/11	Milwaukee White Sox. w 8–2 (NL Park)
07/11	Milwaukee White Sox. l 6–9 (NL Park)
07/12	Cuban Stars. w 13–6 (Gunther Park)
07/26	St. Paul Gophers. l 9–10 (St. Paul)
07/27	St. Paul Gophers. w 8–1 (St. Paul)
07/28	St. Paul Gophers. w 5–1 (St. Paul)
07/29	St. Paul Gophers. l 3–4 (St. Paul)
07/30	St. Paul Gophers. l 1–3 (St. Paul)
07/31	Gunthers. w 5–3 (Gunther Park)
08/01	West Ends. w 2–1 (Auburn Park)
	Cuban Stars. l 3–6 (South Side)
	Gunthers. w 4–0 (South Side)
08/07	Logans. l 2–4
08/08	Milwaukee White Sox. w 4–0
08/12	Detroit Athletics. l 0–1 (Detroit)
08/15	Logans. w 7–0 (Auburn Park)
08/16	Philadelphia Giants. w 3–1 (Detroit)

08/17	Philadelphia Giants. l 1–5 (Detroit)
08/18	Philadelphia Giants. l 1–9 (Detroit)
08/25	Kansas City (KS) Giants. w 5–0 (KC Riverside Park)
08/26	Kansas City (KS) Giants. l 1–3 (KC Riverside Park)
08/27	Kansas City (KS) Giants. l 4–5 (KC Riverside Park)
08/28	Milwaukee. l 0–1
09/05	Gunthers. w 17–4 (Gunther Park)
	Anson Colts. w 6–5 (Home)
09/06	Anson Colts. w 2–1 (Anson's Park)
09/06	Anson Colts. w 4–2 (Anson's Park)
	Gunthers. w 2–1
	Kansas City (KS) All-Stars. w 6–1 (West End Park)
09/20	Louisville Cubs. w 15–3 (Louisville, KY)
09/20	Louisville Cubs. w 13–11 (Louisville, KY)
09/22	Louisville Cubs. l 5–6 (Louisville, KY)
09/23	West Baden Sprudels. w 6–1 (French Lick, IN)
09/24	French Lick Plutos. l 1–2 (French Lick, IN)
10/20	Chicago Cubs. l 1–4 (Gunther Park)
10/21	Chicago Cubs. l 5–6 (Gunther Park)
10/22	Chicago Cubs. l0–1 (Gunther Park)
	Total: 54-18-1

1910 Leland Giants

Manager: Rube Foster. Final standing: Second place in Chicago City Leagues. (Rube claimed a 126–3 record for 1910). Based on scores published in the *Indianapolis Freeman* and *Chicago Defender*

	Royal Giants. w 4–1 (Palm Beach)
	Royal Giants. w 1–0 (Palm Beach)
	Royal Giants. t 1–1 (Palm Beach)
	Royal Giants. l 0–1 (Palm Beach)
	Royal Giants. w 9–6 (Palm Beach)
	Royal Giants. w 6–4 (Palm Beach)
	Royal Giants. t 5–5 (Palm Beach)
	Royal Giants. l 2–5 (Palm Beach)
	Royal Giants. l 2–10 (Palm Beach)
	Royal Giants. l 4–5 (Palm Beach)
	Royal Giants. w 3–2 (Palm Beach)
	Royal Giants. w 1–0 (Palm Beach)
	Royal Giants. w 3–2 (Palm Beach)
	Royal Giants. l 0–6 (Palm Beach)
	Houston Black Buffaloes. l 2–3
	Prairie View (TX) College. w 10–1
	Dallas Black Giants. w 5–2
04/24	Oklahoma City Monarchs. w 12–0
04/25	Oklahoma City Monarchs. w 3–1
04/26	Oklahoma City Monarchs. w 6–1
07/28	Cuban Stars. t 4–4
07/29	Cuban Stars. w 7–0 (South Side Park)
08/02	Cuban Stars. w 5–2 (Gunther Park)
07/31	Roseland. l 1–3 (Roseland)

	Cuban Stars. w 8–6 (Normal)
08/10	Logan Squares. w 6–2 (Fennimore, WI)
	Logan Squares. w 3–2 (Fennimore, WI)
08/18	Gunthers. w 9–4 (Comiskey)
08/19	McNichols All-Stars. w 7–0 (Comiskey)
08/25	Gunthers. l 5–6 (North Side)
08/26	Athletics. w 4–1 (Normal Park)
	Oklahoma Giants. w 3–1 (Normal Park)
	Oklahoma Giants. w 5–0 (Gunther Park)
	Gunthers. w 6–4 (Gunther Park)
	Cuban Stars. w 4–1 (Normal Park)
09/19	Lancaster. w 7–0 (Atlantic City)
09/19	Waterbury of CT. League. w (Atlantic City)
09/19	Manhattan of CT League. w (Atlantic City)
09/22	Lancaster. w 11–7 (Atlantic City)
09/27	Trenton of Tri-State League. w 9–3 (Atlantic City)
09/27	Trenton of Tri-State League. w 5–3 (Atlantic City)
10/09	Havana. w 5–4 (Havana)
	Total: 31-8-3

1911 American Giants

Manager: Rube Foster. Home field: South Side Park (aka Schorling Field), 39th (Pershing) and Wentworth. Final Standing: American Giants won 7 of 11 games played against Frank Leland's "Giants." Based on scores published in the *Indianapolis Freeman* and *Chicago Defender*

	Poincianas. w 7–6
	Poincianas. w 9–0 (*forfeit*)
3/28	West Baden. w 4–1 (West Baden)
	French Lick Plutos. w 9–1 (French Lick)
	Gunthers. w 3–2 (Gunther Park)
6/4	West Ends. w 10–9
7/2	Frank Leland. w 8–0 (Home)
7/3	Frank Leland. l ? ?
7/4	Frank Leland. l 0–7 (Home)
7/4	Frank Leland. w 7–5 (Home)
7/5	Frank Leland. l 3–7 (Home)

7/6	Frank Leland. w 4–3 (Home)
7/7	Frank Leland. w 7–6 (Home)
7/11	Auroras. w 5–4 (Aurora)
7/29	Frank Leland. w 1–0 (Home)
7/30	Frank Leland. w 6–3 (Home)
8/6	Artesians. w 12–0
8/10	Gunthers. w 5–1 (Comiskey)
	Frank Leland. l 1–5 (Home)
9/17	Frank Leland. w 6–1
	Frank Leland. l 5–7 (Home)
	Total: 16-5

1912 American Giants

Manager: Rube Foster. Home field: South Side Park (aka Schorling Field), 39th (Pershing) and Wentworth. Final Standing: California Winter League Champions. Based on scores published in the *Indianapolis Freeman* and *Chicago Defender*.

04/21	Rogers Park. w 5–1 (Home)
06/03	ABCs. w 7–5
06/04	ABCs. w 15–3
06/05	West Baden. w 7–0
06/06	West Baden. w 5–1
06/07	West Baden. w 8–3
06/08	West Baden. l 0–1
06/09	Gunthers. w 10–4 (Home)
06/23	ABCs. w 8–1 (Home)
	Pitt. U.S. League. w 9–1 (Home)
07/01	Spaldings. w 5–3 (Home)
07/02	Cubans. l 2–7
07/03	Cubans. w 7–6
07/04	Cubans. l 0–5
07/09	West Baden. w 4–2 (Home)
07/09	West Baden. w 9–3 (Home)
07/12	Cubans. l 0–2 (Home)
07/14	St. Louis. w 8–7 (Home)
07/14	St. Louis. l 2–5 (Home)
07/16	St. Louis. w 1–0 (Home)
07/20	Uncle Sams . w 8–3 (Home)
07/21	St. Louis. l 3–4 (Home)
07/22	St. Louis. l 2–5 (Home)
07/24	St. Louis. w 14–3 (Home)
07/28	West Baden. l 6–7
07/28	West Baden. w 7–1
	Cuban Stars. w 3–1 (Home)
	Cuban Stars. w 4–3 (Home)
	Cuban Stars. w 4–1 (Home)

	Cuban Stars. w 6–4 (Home)
08/27	U.S. Leaguers. w 7–0 (Home)
	Chicago Giants. w 6–4
	Indianapolis ABCs. w 11–6 (Indianapolis)
	Indianapolis ABCs. l 3–4 (Indianapolis)
	Indpls. Abram Giants. w 5–1 (Indianapolis)
	Indpls. Abram Giants. w 5–0 (Indianapolis)
	Rogers Park. w 8–2
	Natives of California. w 7–1 (Southern California)
	H. Franks. w 14–0 (Southern California)
	L.A. Giants. w 21–0 (Southern California)
	McCormicks. l 5–8 (Southern California)
	McCormicks. w 7–3 (Southern California)
	McCormicks. w 10–4 (Southern California)
	Tufts-Lyons. w 6–0 (Southern California)
	Tufts-Lyons. l 1–5 (Southern California)
	San Diego Bears. w 11–5 (Southern California)
	McCormicks. w 7–3 (Southern California)
	McCormicks. l 6–9 (Southern California)
11/30	Tufts-Lyons. w 4–3 (Southern California)
	Tufts-Lyons. w 7–1 (Southern California)
	Tufts-Lyons. l ? (Southern California)
	Tufts-Lyons. l 1–4 (Southern California)
	Total: 38-14

1913 American Giants

Manager: Rube Foster. Home field: South Side Park (aka Schorling Field), 39th (Pershing) and Wentworth. Final Standing: Claimed Western Championship, lost to the New York Lincoln Giants in East-West Championship series. Based on scores published in the *Indianapolis Freeman*, *Chicago Defender* and *San Francisco Chronicle*.

03/13	Portland Beavers. w 8–7 (Visalia, CA)
03/14	Portland Beavers. w ? (Visalia, CA)
03/15	Portland Beavers. w 2–0 (Visalia, CA)
03/16	Portland Beavers. l 4–11 (Visalia, CA)
03/17	Portland Beavers. w 5–0 (Porterville, CA)
	San Bernardino. w 18–2
04/04	Vancouver. w 5–0 (Seattle)
04/04	Seattle. w 10–5 (Seattle)
	Seattle. w 8–3 (Seattle)

04/06	Seattle. w 17–7 (Seattle)
	Victoria. w 4–1 (Seattle)
04/10	Tacoma. w 3–2
04/12	Portland. w 2–1 (Portland)
04/27	Gary. w 6–4 (Home)
05/?	Hammond. w 13–6 (Hammond, IN)
05/04	Gunthers. w 7–2
	Roseland. w 9–3
05/17	Gunthers. w 12–11 (Gunther Park)

05/18	E. Chicago. w 6–1 (Home)	07/18	Lincoln Giants. t 11–11 (New York)
05/19	West Baden Sprudels. w 5–0 (West Baden)	07/20	Lincoln Giants. l 4–5 (New York)
05/20	West Baden Sprudels. w 4–3 (West Baden)	07/20	Lincoln Giants. w 6–5 (New York)
05/21	West Baden Sprudels. w 2–0 (West Baden)	07/30	Lincoln Giants. w 2–1
05/23	Indianapolis ABCs. l 0–2 (Indianapolis)	07/31	Lincoln Giants. w 9–5
05/24	Indianapolis ABCs. w 17–1 (Indianapolis)	08/02	Lincoln Giants. w 3–0 (Home)
	Neb. Indians. w 2–1 (Home)	08/03	Lincoln Giants. l 3–9 (Home)
05/30	Fr. Lick Plutos. w 10–2 (Home)	08/03	Cuban Stars. w 4–1 (Cincy)
05/30	Fr. Lick Plutos. w 7–1 (Home)	08/05	Cuban Stars. w 3–2(Cincy)
05/31	Fr. Lick Plutos. w 12–1 (Gunther Park)		Cuban Stars. l ? (Cincy)
06/01	Fr. Lick Plutos. l 0–1 (Home)	08/07	Chicago Giants. l 3–10 (Home)
06/02	Fr. Lick Plutos. w 5–4 (Home)	08/09	Lincoln Giants l 6–11 (Home)
06/03	Fr. Lick Plutos. w 4–3 (Home)	08/09	Lincoln Giants. l 2–14 (Home)
06/04	Fr. Lick Plutos. w 4–1 (Home)	08/12	Lincoln Giants. l 2–3 (Home)
06/08	Coogan Smart Set. w 8–0 (Home)	08/20	Lincoln Giants. l 2–3 (Home)
06/09	Coogan Smart Set. w 9–0 (Home)		Lincoln Giants. w 3–0 (Home)
06/10	Coogan Smart Set. w 5–0 (Home)	08/??	Spaldings. w 6–1
06/15	Cuban Stars. w 8–4 (Home)	08/27	Spaldings. w 5–1
06/16	Cuban Stars. w 8–5 (Home)	08/31	St. Louis Giants. w 10–6
06/17	Cuban Stars. w 13–6. (Home)	09/01	St. Louis Giants. w 6–3
06/29	W. Baden Sprudels. l 5–7 (Home)	09/02	St. Louis Giants. l 7–8
06/30	W. Baden Sprudels. w 11–1 (Home)	09/07	W. Baden Sprudels. w 6–3
07/01	W. Baden Sprudels. l 1–11 (Home)	09/09	W. Baden Sprudels. w 4–3
07/04	Cuban Stars. l 0–5 (Home)	09/10	W. Baden Sprudels. w 7–1
07/04	Cuban Stars. l 1–2 (Home)	09/11	W. Baden Sprudels. w 4–3
07/05	Cuban Stars. l 3–10 (Home)	09/13	Gunthers. w 13–4
07/06	Cuban Stars. l 5–8 (Home)	09/14	Chicago Giants. l 5–9
07/07	Cuban Stars. w 8–7 (Home)	09/27	Gunthers. w 6–5
07/10	NY Royal Giants. l 7–9 (New York)	09/28	Univ. of Hawaii. w 3–2
07/11	NY Royal Giants. l 4–8 (New York)		Gunthers. l 5–6
07/12	NY Royal Giants. w 9–0 (New York)		Gunthers. t 5–5
07/13	NY Royal Giants. w 8–2 (New York)	10/12	Logan Squares. w 9–3
07/18	Lincoln Giants. l 3–8 (New York)		Total: 59-23-1

1914 American Giants

Manager: Rube Foster. Home field: South Side Park (aka Schorling Field), 39th (Pershing) and Went-worth. Final Standing: Claimed Western Championship, defeated Brooklyn Royal Giants in East-West championship in five straight games. Based on scores published in the *Chicago Defender*, *Indianapolis Freeman* and *Seattle Post Intelligencer*.

03/21/	Portland. t 9–9 (Santa Maria, CA)	06/07	Benton Harbor. w 5–4 (Home)
	Portland. l 3–5 (Santa Maria, CA)	06/14	South Bend. w 13–5 (Home)
	Portland l	06/15	Indianapolis ABCs. w 9–3 (Indianapolis)
04/03	Seattle. w 2–1	06/16	Indianapolis ABCs. w 6–5 (Indianapolis)
04/05	Seattle. w 1–0 (Seattle)	06/17	Indianapolis ABCs. w 3–11 (Indianapolis)
04/08	Victoria Bees. w 8–7 (Victoria BC)	06/18	Indianapolis ABCs. w 3–0 (Indianapolis)
04/23	Lewiston CO. w 8–1 (Lewiston CO)	06/21	West Ends. w 2–1
	WA St, College. w 4–0 (Pullman WA)	06/28	French, Lick Plutos. w 6–0 (Home)
04/26	Gunthers. w 4–0 (Home)	06/29	French, Lick Plutos. w 6–1 (Home)
05/03	St. Joe, MI. w 13–6 (Home)	06/30	French, Lick Plutos. w 7–2 (Home)
05/10	West Ends. w 2–1 (Home)	07/04	Cuban Stars. w 5–4 (Home)
	Chicago Giant. w 9–0	07/05	Cuban Stars. w 5–4 (Home)
05/23	Cuban Stars. w 3–0 (Home)	07/06	Cuban Stars. w 5–2 (Home)
05/23	Cuban Stars. w 8–0 (Home)	07/07	Cuban Stars. l 2–3 (Home)
05/24	Cuban Stars. l 2–4 (Home)	07/09	Cuban Stars. l 3–4 (Home)
05/25	Cuban Stars. l 7–8		Cuban Stars. l ? (?)
05/28	Cuban Stars. w 1–0 (Home)	07/11	Cuban Stars. l 0–8 (Home)
05/30	Indianapolis ABCs. w 7–1 (Home)	07/12	New York Stars. w 10–1 (Home)
05/30	Indianapolis ABCs. w 7–1 (Home)	07/13	New York Stars. w 7–0 (Home)
05/31	Indianapolis ABCs. l 2–7 (Home)	07/19	Mohawk Giants. w 8–2
06/01	Indianapolis ABCs. w 2–0 (Home)	07/20	Mohawk Giants. w 7–6
06/02	Indianapolis ABCs. w 2–0 (Home)		Indianapolis ABCs. l ? (?)
06/03	Indianapolis ABCs. w 13–1 (Home)	07/27	Indianapolis ABCs. w 9–5 (Indianapolis)

07/28   Indianapolis ABCs. l 8–9 (Indianapolis)
07/29   Indianapolis ABCs. l 2–5 (Indianapolis)
07/30   Chippewa Indians. w 8–2
07/31   Indianapolis ABCs. w 13–3
08/02   Benton Harbor. w 9–1
08/09   West Ends. w 5–1
08/09   Univ. of Japan. w 4–0
08/15   Cuban Stars. l 1–5
08/16   Cuban Stars. w 2–1
08/24/   Indianapolis ABCs. w 9–1 (Home)
08/25   Indianapolis ABCs. w 7–6 (Home)
08/26   Univ. of Japan. l 2–4 (Home)
08/27   Indianapolis ABCs. l 3–4 (Home)

     Indianapolis ABCs. w 1–0 (Home)
08/30   Brooklyn Royal G's. w 3–0 (Home)
08/31   Brooklyn Royal G's. w 7–0 (Home)
09/02   Brooklyn Royal G's. w 7–6 (Home)
09/03   Brooklyn Royal G's. w 3–1 (Home)
09/04   Brooklyn Royal G's. w 3–2 (Home)
09/13   Chicago Giants. w 5–3
09/19   Gunthers. w 6–2
09/20   Indianapolis ABCs. w 9–3 (Indianapolis)
09/21   Indianapolis ABCs. l 10–12 (Indianapolis)
09/22   Indianapolis ABCs. l 4–7 (Indianapolis)
09/25   Louisville Giants. w 6–3 (Home)
     Total: 52-17-1

1915 American Giants

Manager: Rube Foster. Home field: South Side Park (aka Schorling Field), 39th (Pershing) and Wentworth. Final Standing: Rube Foster claimed championship, but no clear-cut winner. Cuban Stars, Indianapolis ABCs, and Lincoln Giants all finished with a similar record. Based on scores published in the *Chicago Defender*, *Chicago Daily Herald* and *Indianapolis Ledger*.

3/6   Giovanno Specials. w 11–3 (New Orleans)
3/7   Giovanno Specials. w 9–3 (New Orleans)
3/8   Giovanno Specials. w 10–1 (New Orleans)
3/13   New Orleans. w 5–4 (New Orleans)
3/14   New Orleans. w 13–3 (New Orleans)
3/15   New Orleans. w 10–1 (New Orleans)
     L.A. Whitesox. w 11–3
3/18   Portland ? w 4–2 (Fresno)
     Portland Beavers. l 3–4 (Fresno)
     Portland Beavers. w 11–1 (Fresno)
     Portland Beavers. l 0–1 (Fresno)
     Portland Beavers. l 3–7
3/25   Portland Beavers. w 4–2
     Portland Beavers. l 3–4
     Victoria M'Leafs. l 4–5
     Victoria M'Leafs. w 5–4
4/10   Seattle. l 2–3 (Seattle)
4/11   Aberdeen. w 9–3 (Seattle)
4/11   Seattle. w 4–0 (Seattle)
4/12   Aberdeen. w 3–1 (Everett, WA)
4/13   Tacoma. w 5–4 (Everett, WA)
     Tacoma. w 5–3 (Tacoma)
     Tacoma. w 3–2 (Tacoma)
     Tacoma. l 2–6 (Tacoma)
4/24   Storz ? w 10–1 (Omaha)
4/25   Milwaukee W. Sox. w 9–0 (Home)
5/2   Gunthers. w 5–0 (Home)
5/9   Kavanaugh's . w 8–3 (Home)
5/16   Gunthers. w 3–2 (Home)
5/23   La Porte. w 7–1 (Home)
5/30   Rogers Park. w 5–3 (Home)
5/31   Roseland Eclipse. w 2–1 (Home)
5/31   West Ends. w 3–0 (Home)
6/6   Omaha Giants. w 11–2 (Home)
6/12   Butler Bros. l 6–9 (Home)
6/13   Mathiesens. w 5–2 (Home)
6/13   Louisville W. Sox. w 5–2 (Home)
6/16   Louisville W. Sox. w 5–1 (Home)
6/17   Louisville W. Sox. w 5–4 (Home)
6/20   Indianapolis ABCs. w 8–1 (Home)
6/21   Indianapolis ABCs. l 6–10 (Home)
6/22   Indianapolis ABCs. w 6–1 (Home)
6/23   Indianapolis ABCs. l 0–4 (Home)
6/24   Indianapolis ABCs. w 2–1 (Home)

6/27   Eclipse. w 7–2 (Home)
6/28   Hastings. w 5–3 (Hastings, MI)
6/29   Charlotte, MI. w 9–4 (Charlotte, MI)
7/4   Cuban Stars. l 1–6 (Home)
7/5   Cuban Stars. l 1–4 (Home)
7/6   Cuban Stars. l 3–5 (Home)
7/9   Cuban Stars. w 7–0 (Home)
7   Cuban Stars. l 4–10 (Home)
7/11   Cuban Stars. t 6–6 (Home)
7/12   Cuban Stars. l 0–6 (Home)
7/15   Indianapolis ABCs. l 2–3
7/15   Indianapolis ABCs. l 4–7
7/21   Indianapolis ABCs. l 3–5
7/22   Indianapolis ABCs. l 6–7
7/26   Cuban Stars. w 10–2 (Home)
7/27   Cuban Stars. l 1–3 (Home)
7/31   NY Lincoln Stars. w 11–3 (Home)
8/1   NY Lincoln Stars. l 3–11 (Home)
8/2   NY Lincoln Stars. w 2–1 (Home)
8/7   NY Lincoln Stars. w 4–3 (Home)
8/8   NY Lincoln Stars. l 0–13 (Home)
8/9   NY Lincoln Stars. l 4–11 (Home)
8/10   NY Lincoln Stars. w 2–1 (Home)
8/10   NY Lincoln Stars. l 0–1 (Home)
8/12   NY Lincoln Stars. w 9–4
8/15   Roseland Eclipse. w 4–1 (Northwest Side)
8/15   Cuban Stars. w 10–3 (Home)
8/17   Cuban Stars. w 3–0 (Home)
8/22   Gertenrich Stars. w 6–0 (West Side)
8/22   Cuban Stars. w 4–3
8/23   Cuban Stars. w 3–1 (Home)
8/24   Cuban Stars. w 2–1
8/29   Cuban Stars. w 7–0 (Home)
8/30   Cuban Stars. w 2–1 (Home)
8/31   Cuban Stars. w 7–3 (Home)
9/2   Cuban Stars. w 7–6
9/6   St. Louis Giants. w 6–4
9/12   Chicago Giants. l 7–9 (Home)
9/14   St. Louis Giants. l 4–5 (St. Louis)
9/19   Chicago Giants. w 4–0 (Home)
9/19   St. Louis Giants. w 8–0 (Home)
9/21   St. Louis Giants. w 4–3 (Home)
9/24   St. Louis Giants. t 4–4 (St. Louis)
10/3   Romeos . w 8–3

10/8/15?	Normals w 9–4		11/25?	Pantages of San Diego. w 4–0 (San Diego)
10/21?	West All-Pros. w 7–5			San Bernardino. l 3–8
10/22	West All-Pros. l 1–2 (Omaha)			San Bernardino
10/25	White Sox. w 10–6 (Doyle Park L.A., CA)		12/18	Pantages of San Diego. w 7–6 (San Diego)
11/12	Pantages of San Diego. l 4–7 (San Diego)		12/19	Pantages of San Diego. w 7–3 (San Diego)
11/13?	Cline-Cline. w 4–0 (San Diego)		12/25	Pantages of San Diego. w 4–3 (San Diego)
11/14	Cline-Cline. l 0–6 (San Diego)		12/26	Pantages of San Diego. w 3–2 (San Diego)
	San Bernardino. w 6–3 (San Bernardino)			Fed. All Star. w 6–3 (California)
11/21	San Bernardino. l 1–6 (San Bernardino)			Total: 60-17-2
	Pantages of San Diego. w 3–2 (San Diego)			

1916 American Giants

Manager: Rube Foster. Home field: South Side Park (aka Schorling Field), 39th (Pershing) and Wentworth. Final Standing: Lost disputed playoff for Western Championship with Indianapolis ABCs. Based on scores published in the *Chicago Defender*, and *Indianapolis Freeman*.

	Havana. w 14–3 (Havana)		7/21	St. Louis Giants. w 6–3 (Home)
	Havana. w 2–0 (Havana)			Cubans. l 0–1 (Home)
	Alemendares. w 8–1 (Havana)			Cubans. l 0–4 (Home)
3/26	Indianapolis ABCs. l 6–7 (New Orleans)		7/23	Kokomo R. Sox. l 0–5 (Home)
3/30	Portland. w 11–6 (Sacramento)		7/27	Cubans. w 5–4 (Home)
3/31	Portland. w 5–2 (Sacramento)		7/27	Cubans. l 1–2 (Home)
4/1	Portland. w 5–2 (Sacramento)		7/28	Cubans. w 6–5 (Home)
4/4	Portland. w 13–1 (Portland, OR)		7/30	Cubans. w 5–3 (Home)
4/7	Portland. l 4–8 (Sacramento)		7/30	Cubans. w 8–4 (Home)
	Seattle. w 11–3 (Rainier Valley Park)		7/31	St. Louis Giants. l 5–7 (St. Louis)
	Oregon Agriculture Coll. w 11–2		8/1	St. Louis Giants. w 10–3 (St. Louis)
	(Corvallis, OR)		8/2	Joliet Nine. w 8–5 (Joliet, IL)
	Univ. of Oregon. w 11–0 (Eugene, OR)		8/5	Gary "Works." w 8–4 (Gary, IN)
	Seattle. w 4–3 (Seattle)		8/6	NY Lincoln Stars. w 6–5 (Home)
4/9	Seattle. w 9–6 (Seattle)		8/6	NY Lincoln Stars. l 3–6 (Home)
4/11	Vancouver. l 5–8 (Bellingham, WA)			NY Lincoln Stars. l 8–10 (Home)
	Vancouver. w 14–7 (Vancouver, BC)		8/14	NY Lincoln Stars. l 0–4 (Home)
	Vancouver. w 8–1 (Vancouver, BC)			Cubans. l 1–5 (Kenosha, WI)
	Tacoma. w 10–8 (Tacoma, WA)		8/19	Cubans. l 8–9 (Home)
	Lewiston. w 16–4 (Lewiston, ID)		8/20	Cubans. w 6–5 (Home)
5/7	West Ends. w 5–2 (Home)		8/24	Premiers. w 6–0 (Comiskey)
5/14	La Porte. w 13–1 (Home)		8/25	NY Lincoln Stars. w 1 ?(Home)
5/21	Cubans. w 2–0 (Home)		8/27	Indianapolis ABCs. w 3–1 (Home)
5/23	Cubans. l 1–3 (Home)		8/28	Indianapolis ABCs. w 4–2 (Home)
5/31	Cubans. l 4–6 (Home)		8/29	Indianapolis ABCs. l 4–7 (Home)
	Beloit. w 6–2 (Home)		8/30	Indianapolis ABCs. w 5–2 (Home)
6/7	Cubans. w 2–1 (Home)		8/31	Indianapolis ABCs. t 3–3 (Home)
6/8	Cubans. w 4–? Home		9/2	Cubans. w 6–0 (Home)
6/11	Magnets. w 7–6 (Home)		9/3	Cubans. l 3–12 (Home)
6/18	Bowsers Indianapolis ABCs. w 6–3 (Home)		9/9	Jeffery Auto. w 10–3 (Kenosha, WI)
6/19	Bowsers Indianapolis ABCs. w 7–0 (Home)		9/10	Gunthers. w 6–2 (Home)
6/25	Henry Grays. l 3–4 (Home)		9/17	Henry Grays. w 10–2 (Home)
6/25	Henry Grays. w 5?–0? (Home)		9/17	Henry Grays. l 6–9 (Home)
7/1	Cubans. w 3–0 (Chi Hts.)		9/24	Magnets . w 3–2 (Home)
7/1	Chi. Hts. . w 13–3 (Chi Hts.)		10/14	All Nations. w 3–1 (Kansas City)
7/2	Cubans. l ? (Home)		10/15	All Nations. w 5–2 (Kansas City)
7/3	Cubans. w 3–0 (Home)		10/15	All Nations. l 7–8 (Kansas City)
7/4	Cubans. w 3–2 (Home)		10/18	La Porte. w 14–7 (La Porte, IN)
7/4	Cubans. t 3–3 (Home)		10/22	Indianapolis ABCs. w 5–3 (Indpls.
7/5	Cubans. w 6–4 (Home)			Fed. League)
7/8	Eclipse (white). w 6–0		10/23	Indianapolis ABCs. l 0–1 (Indpls.
7/9	St. Louis Giants. w 6–0 (Home)			Fed. League)
7/10	St. Louis Giants. l 2–6 (Home)		10	Indianapolis ABCs. l 0–9 (Indpls.
	St. Louis Giants. w 11–0 (Home)			Fed. League)
7/12	Cubans. w 5–4 (Home)		10	Indianapolis ABCs. l 2–8 (Indpls.
7/14	Cubans. w 1–0 (Home)			Fed. League)
7/16	West Ends. w 2–1 (Home)		10	Indianapolis ABCs. l 8–12 (Indpls.
7/16	West Ends. w 4–1 (Home)			Fed. League)
7/20	St. Louis Giants. w 6–3 (Home)			Total: 63-26-2

1917 American Giants

Manager: Rube Foster. Home field: South Side Park (aka Schorling Field), 39th (Pershing) and Wentworth. Final Standing: Undisputed Western Champion. Based on scores published in the *Chicago Defender*.

	Breakers. w 3–1 (Palm Beach)
02/06	Lincoln Giants. w 4–1 (Palm Beach)
	Lincoln Giants. l 1–3 (Palm Beach)
	Lincoln Giants. t 2–2 (Palm Beach)
	Lincoln Giants. l 3–7 (Palm Beach)
	Lincoln Giants. w 7–0 (Palm Beach)
	Lincoln Giants. w 9–2 (Palm Beach)
	Lincoln Giants. l 4–8 (Palm Beach)
	Lincoln Giants. w 6–0 (Palm Beach)
03/24	Mobile. w 8–0 (Mobile, AL)
03/25	Mobile. w 8–0 (Mobile, AL)
03/25	Mobile. w 5–0 (Mobile, AL)
03/26	Atlanta Univ. . w 12–1 (Atlanta, GA)
	Morris Brown. w 11–2 (Atlanta, GA)
	Morris Brown. w 5–4 (Atlanta, GA)
04/01	New Orleans. w 9–0 (New Orleans)
04/03	New Orleans. w 4–0 (New Orleans)
	New Orleans. w 6–3 (New Orleans)
	Cuban Stars. l 3–4 (New Orleans)
	New Orleans. t 2–2 (New Orleans)
04/22	Jake Stahl's. w 5–3 (Home)
04/29	West Ends. w 3–2 (Home)
05/06	Roseland Eclipse. w 4–0 (Home)
05/13	Chicago Hts. 9. w 5–0 (Home)
05/20	Chicago Giants. w 4–2 (Home)
05/27	Cuban Stars. w 1–0 (Home)
	Dayton Giants. w 9–2 (Home)
	Dayton Giants. w 5–0 (Home)
06/10	Indianapolis ABCs. l 0–2 (Home)
06/11	Indianapolis ABCs. w 3–1 (Home)
06/12	Indianapolis ABCs. w 3–2 (Home)
06/13	Indianapolis ABCs. w 1–0 (Home)
06/18	Indianapolis ABCs. w 6–4 (Home)
06/24	Chicago Giants. w 2–1 (Home)
06/24	Roseland Eclipse. w 11–1 (Home)
06/30	Cuban Stars. w 2–0 (Home)
06/29	Cuban Stars. w 1–0 (Hammond, IN)
7/15	Indianapolis ABCs. t 4–4 (Home)

7/15	Indianapolis ABCs. w 5–0 (Home)
07/16	Indianapolis ABCs. w 6–0 (Home)
07/19	Indianapolis ABCs. w 4–2 (Cincy, OH)
07/20	Indianapolis ABCs. w 2–0 (Cincy, OH)
07/21	Indianapolis ABCs. w 13–8 (Muncie, IN)
07/22	Jewel's Indianapolis ABCs. w 5–0
	Jewel's Indianapolis ABCs. w 4–0 (Home)
	Jewel's Indianapolis ABCs. l 1–4 (?)
07/29	Texas All-Stars. w 7–5 (Home)
07/30	Texas All-Stars. w 7–6 (Home)
07/31	Texas All-Stars. w 16–2 (Home)
08/03	Indianapolis ABCs. t 2–2 (Detroit)
08/04	Indianapolis ABCs. w 3–2 (Detroit)
08/05	Indianapolis ABCs. l 4–8 (Home)
	Indianapolis ABCs. w 8–2 (Home)
08/12	Cuban Stars. w 2–1 (Home)
08/14	Cuban Stars. l 2–3 (Home)
08/19	Indianapolis ABCs. w 4–1 (Indianapolis)
08/19	Indianapolis ABCs. w 8–3 (Indianapolis)
08/25	Cuban Stars. l 0–5 (Forbes Field)
08/27	Bacharach Giants. w 5–4 (Atlantic City)
	Peerless All-Stars. w 6–5 (Phil., PA)
	Peerless All-Stars. w 3–0 (Phil., PA)
09/01	Indianapolis ABCs. w 7–0 (Detroit)
09/01	Indianapolis ABCs. w 6–3 (Detroit
09/03	Cuban Stars. w 4–2 (Detroit)
09/03	Cuban Stars. w 2–0 (Detroit)
09/04	Cuban Stars. w 6?–2 (Detroit)
09/10	All-Nations. l 1–2 (Home)
09/10	All-Nations. w 7–0 (Home)
09/16	Cuban Stars. l 2–3 (Home)
09/16	Cuban Stars. l 3–4 (Home)
09/23	Cent. League Stars. w 7–0 (Home)
10/01	Ragen's Colts. l 1–2 (Home)
10/08	Ragen's Colts. l 1–2 (Home)
10/15	Ragen's Colts. w 11–2 (Home)
	Total: 57-14-3

1918 American Giants

Manager: Rube Foster. Home field: South Side Park (aka Schorling Field), 39th (Pershing) and Wentworth. Final Standing: Western Champions. Based on scores published in the *Chicago Defender*.

01/25	Breakers. w 5–3 (Palm Beach)
	Breakers. w 6–5 (Palm Beach)
02/08	Breakers. l 2–5 (Palm Beach)
02/12	Breakers. l 0–1 (Palm Beach)
	Breakers. w 4–3 (Palm Beach)
	Breakers. w 6–2 (Palm Beach)
02/16	Breakers. l 3–7 (Palm Beach)
	Breakers. l 0–1 (Palm Beach)
02/19	Breakers. w 1–0 (Palm Beach)
02/25	Breakers. w 6–0 (Palm Beach)
	Breakers. l 1–3 (Palm Beach)
03/05	Breakers. w 4–3 (Palm Beach)
03/29	Morris Brown Univ. w 11–6 (Atlanta, GA)
03/30	Montgomery, AL. w 13–2 (Montgomery, AL)
04/01	New Orleans. w ? (New Orleans)

04/01	New Orleans. l ? (New Orleans)
	New Orleans. w 9–0 (New Orleans)
04/14	West Ends. w 8–2 (Home)
05/11	Roseland Eclipse. w 2–0 (Home)
05/18	Peoria. w 5–4 (Peoria)
05/19	West Ends. l 6–8 (Home)
05/26	Cuban Stars. w 6–5 (Home)
05/27	Cuban Stars. w 5–2 (Home)
05/30	Cuban Stars. l 0–4 (Home)
05/30	Cuban Stars. w 3–0 (Home)
06/02	Gunthers. w 2–1 (Home)
06/09	Indianapolis ABCs. w 5–2 (Home)
06/16	Columbus Giants. w 4–1 (Home)
06/16	Columbus Giants. w 9–2 (Home)
	Garden City. w 9–2

06/23	Rogers Park. w 2–1 (Home)		Bacharach Giants. l 1–3 (Atlantic City)
06/30	Dayton Marcos. w 4–3 (Home)		Bacharach Giants. l 4–5 (Atlantic City)
07/04	Cuban Stars. w 8–4 (Home)	08/09	Indianapolis ABCs. w 3–2 (Detroit)
07/06	Beloit. w 2–1 (Beloit)	08/11	Indianapolis ABCs. w 3–2 (Detroit)
07/07	Cuban Stars. w 3–1 (Home)	08/17	Logan Squares. l 2–7 (Logan Park)
07/08	Cuban Stars. l 0–4 (Home)	08/18	Joliet. w 1–0 (Home)
07/13	Garden City. w 3–0	08/24	Cuban Stars. w 3–2 (Comiskey)
07/14	Indianapolis ABCs. w 3–2 (Home)	08/25	Beloit. w 5–4 (Home)
07/16	Indianapolis ABCs. l 1–3 (Home)	09/01	Cuban Stars. w 4–3 (Detroit)
07/19	Camp Grant. w 1–0 (Home)	09/08	Cuban Stars. w 1–0 (Home)
07/20	Beloit. l 0–1 (Home)	09/08	Cuban Stars. w 5–1 (Home)
07/20	Beloit. l 1–2 (Home)	09/15	Joliet. w 2–1 (Home)
	Indianapolis ABCs. l 7–8 (Pittsburgh, PA)	09/15	Joliet. l 4–8 (Home)
	Indianapolis ABCs. t 7–7 (Pittsburgh, PA)	09/22	Beloit. l 0–5 (Home)
	Indianapolis ABCs. w 6–1 (Wash., D.C.)	09/29	All-Stars ML. l 2–3 (Home)
	Indianapolis ABCs. l 11–16 (Pittsburgh, PA)		All-Stars ML. w 4–2 (Home)
	NY Penn Red Caps. w 5–2 (Wash., D.C.)	10/06	All-Stars ML. w 4–2 (Home)
08/??	Hilldale. w 9–2 (Philadelphia)	10/13	All-Stars ML. w 7–0 (Home)
08/??	Hilldale. l 7–8 (Philadelphia)		Total: 45-22-1
	Hilldale. l 8–9 (Darby, PA)		

1919 American Giants

Manager: Rube Foster. Home field: South Side Park (aka Schorling Field), 39th (Pershing) and Wentworth. Final outcome (no organized competition). Based on scores published in the *Chicago Defender* and *Chicago Whip.*

04/13	Rogers Park. w 3–0 (Home)	08/17	Treat'm Roughs. w 9–7 (NYC)
04/20	Magnets. w 4–0 (Home)	08/21	Hilldale. l 0–2 (Darby, PA)
	Aristos. w 3–0 (Home)	08/23	Hilldale. w 8–4 (Darby, PA)
	Kenoshas. w 5–0 (Home)	08/24	Treat'm Roughs. w 2–1 (NYC-Dyckman)
	Chi. Giants. w 8–6 (Home)	08/24	Treat'm Roughs. w 7–1 (NYC-Dyckman)
05/24	Gunthers. l 5–9 (Home)	08/31	Cubans. w 4–1 (Home)
	League of Nations. w 5–0 (Home)	09/01	Cubans. l 2–3 (Home)
05/31	Cubans. l 4–5	09/07	Indianapolis ABCs. w 8–7 (Home)
06/01	Cubans. w 6–0	09/14	Dayton Marcos. w 7–4 (Home)
06/02	Cubans. l 4–6 (Home)		St. Louis. w 3–2 (St. Louis)
	Detroit Stars. w 3–0 (Home)		KC Allies. w 7–6 (AA Kansas City)
	Fairbanks-Morse. l 5–8 (Beloit, WI)		KC Allies. w 6–1 (AA Kansas City)
06/22	Dayton Marcos. l 0–4		Birmingham Black Barons. w ?
06/28	Roseland Eclipse. w 3–0 (Home)		(Birmingham, AL)
06/29	Fairbanks-Morse. w 4–0 (Home)		Birmingham Black Barons. w ?
	Cubans. w 4–3 (Home)		(Birmingham, AL)
07/13	Gunthers. w 3–2 (Home)		Birmingham Black Barons. w ?
	Gunthers. w 9–5 (Away)		(Birmingham, AL)
	Detroit Stars. l 3–7 (Detroit)		Birmingham Black Barons. w ?
	Detroit Stars. l 5–6 (Detroit)		(Birmingham, AL)
	Detroit Stars. l 8–12 (Detroit)		Peoria. w 6–1 (Home)
08/03	Detroit Stars. l 6–10 (Detroit)		Cuban Stars. w 4–2 (Home)
08/03	Detroit Stars. w 5–3 (Detroit)		Total: 31-11
08/17	Treat'm Roughs. w 2–0 (NYC)		

1920 American Giants

Manager: Rube Foster. Home field: South Side Park (aka Schorling Field), 39th (Pershing) and Wentworth. Final Standing: Negro National League pennant. Based on scores published in the *Chicago Defender* and *Chicago Whip.*

04/04	Rogers Park. w 4–2 (Home)	05/23	KC Monarchs. w 6–5 (Home)
04/25	Trainer Athletic Club . l 6–9	05/24	KC Monarchs. w 8–0
05/02	Romeos. w 7–1	05/30	Cuban Stars. w 4–1 (Home)
	Chicago Giants. w 8–3 (Home)	05/30	Cuban Stars. w 3–2 (Home)
05/16	Dayton Marcos. l 5–6 (Home)		Logan Squares. w 8–3

	Magnets. w 12–1
06/13	Indianapolis ABCs. w 6–1 (Home)
06/15	Indianapolis ABCs. w 6–0 (Home)
06/15	Indianapolis ABCs. w 7–0 (Home)
06/20	Rogers Park. l 0–1 (Home)
06/23	Ft. Sheridans. w 6–2
06/27	Indianapolis ABCs. l 0–1 (Indianapolis)
06/27	Indianapolis ABCs. t 2–2 (Indianapolis)
06/29	Indianapolis ABCs. l 5–6 (Indianapolis)
06/30	Indianapolis ABCs. w 6–2 (Indianapolis)
07/04	KC Monarchs. l 2–4 (Home)
07/04	KC Monarchs. w 8–6 (Home)
	St. Louis Giants. w 5–2 (Home)
	St. Louis Giants. w 4–2 (Home)
07/18	Dayton Marcos. w 8–1 (Home)
	Melrose Park. w 6–0 (Home)
07/25	Joliet. w 6–0 (Home)
07/31	KC Monarchs. w 9–7 (Kansas City)
08/01	KC Monarchs. l ? (Kansas City)
08/02	KC Monarchs. l 4–5 (Kansas City)
08/08	Bacharach Giants. w 7–3 (Home)
08/09	Bacharach Giants. w 3–2 (Home)

08/10?	Bacharach Giants. w 5–4 (Home)
08/11	Bacharach Giants. l 4–11 (Gary, IN)
08/15	Cuban Stars. l 5–8 (Home)
08/16	Cuban Stars. w 9–2 (Home)
08/22	KC Monarchs. w 5–1 (Home)
	Rogers Park. w 5–1 (Home)
	Lincoln Life Ins. . w 8–1 (Ft. Wayne)
09/05	Detroit Stars. w 8–3 (Detroit)
09/12	Detroit Stars. w 5–2 (Detroit)
09/12	Detroit Stars. l 1–2 (Detroit)
09/19	Indianapolis ABCs. l 2–8 (Home)
	Birmingham Black Barons. w 10–2 (Rickwood)
10/02	Knoxville . w 2–1 (Knoxville, TN)
10/09	Bacharach Giants. w 8–5 (Harrison, NJ)
10/10	Bacharach Giants. l 3–7 (Ebbetts Field)
10/10	Bacharach Giants. l 3–5 (Ebbetts Field)
10/17	Bacharach Giants. w 1–0 (Ebbetts Field)
10/17	Bacharach Giants. w 2–0 (Ebbetts Field)
10/31	Normals. l 2–4 (Home)
	Total: 35-15-1

1921 American Giants

Manager: Rube Foster. Home field: South Side Park (aka Schorling Field), 39th (Pershing) and Wentworth. Final Standing: Won NNL pennant. Based on scores published in the *Chicago Defender* and *Chicago Whip*.

	Breakers. l 6–7 (Palm Beach)
	Breakers. w 7–0 (Palm Beach)
	Breakers. t 6–6 (Palm Beach)
2/??	Royal Giants. l 1–2 (Palm Beach)
	Breakers. t 1–1 (Palm Beach)
04/24	Aurora. w 5–1 (Home)
	Progressives. w 2–0
05/07	KC Monarchs. w 2–0 (Home)
05/08	KC Monarchs. l 1–3 (Home)
05/09	KC Monarchs. w 7–5 (Home)
05/15	Briscoe Motor. w 8–5 (Home)
05/22	Bacharach Giants. w 2–1 (Home)
	Cuban Stars. l. l–2 (Home)
05/23	St. Louis Giants. l. l–13 (St. Louis)
05/24	St. Louis Giants. w 16–5 (St. Louis)
05/25	St. Louis Giants. w 7–6 (St. Louis)
05/26	St. Louis Giants. l 6–7 (St. Louis)
05/27	St. Louis Giants. l 3–9 (St. Louis)
05/29	Cuban Stars. w 10–4 (Home)
05/30	Woodlawns. l 4–6
06/04	Columbus Buckeyes. w 2–0 (Home)
06/05	Columbus Buckeyes. w 2–1 (Home)
06/06	Columbus Buckeyes. w 13–3 (Home)
06/15	Indianapolis ABCs. w 1–0 (Home)
	Indianapolis ABCs. w 4–0 (Home)
06/17	Chicago Giants. w 4–1 (Home)
06/20	Chicago Giants. w 4–3 (Home)
06/26	Indianapolis ABCs. w 9–4 (Indianapolis)
06/26	Indianapolis ABCs. t 1–1 (Indianapolis)
06/30	Indianapolis ABCs. l 4–6 (Indianapolis)
07/03	KC Monarchs. w 7–4 (Home)
07/04	KC Monarchs. l 2–4 (Home)
07/04	KC Monarchs. l 1–14 (Home)
07/05	KC Monarchs. w 2–0 (Home)
07/09	St. Louis Giants. w 16–4 (Gary, IN)
07/10	St. Louis Giants. w 2–0 (Home)

07/10	St. Louis Giants . w 6–3 (Home)
07/11	St. Louis Giants. l 3–10 (St. Louis)
07/12	St. Louis Giants. l 7–10 (St. Louis)
07/13	St. Louis Giants. l 6–7 (St. Louis)
07/17	Magnets. w 11–2 (Home)
07/31	Columbus. w 7–4 (Home)
07/31	Columbus. w 11–7 (Home)
08/06	Milwaukee Red Sox. w 5–3 (Milwaukee)
08/07	Cuban Stars. w 3–2 (Home)
08/08	Pyotts. w 7–1 (Pyott Field)
	Pyotts. w 6–2 (Pyott Field)
08/13	St. Louis Giants. w 8–3 (Home)
08/14	St. Louis Giants. w 1–0 (Home)
08/20	Detroit Stars. l 0–3 (Gary, IN)
08/21	Detroit Stars. w 2–1 (Home)
08/29	St. Louis Giants. l 5–11 (St. Louis)
08/30	St. Louis Giants. w 9–6 (St. Louis)
08/31	St. Louis Giants. l 10–11 (St. Louis)
09/03	KC Monarchs. l 2–3 (Kansas City)
	KC Monarchs. l 9–12 (Kansas City)
09/11	Montgomery Grey Sox. w 1–0 (Home)
09/11	Montgomery Grey Sox. w 5–1 (Home)
09/18	St. Louis Giants. w 2–0 (Home)
09/18	St. Louis Giants. w 6–2 (Home)
09/25	Cuban Stars. l 1–2 (Home)
09/25	Cuban Stars. w 1–0 (Home)
10/01	Bacharach Giants. l 0–4 (Fl. Park, Harrison, NJ)
10/02	Bacharach Giants. w 5–1 (Dyckman Oval, NYC)
10/02	Bacharach Giants. t 1–1 (Dyckman Oval, NYC)
10/04	Hilldale. w 5–2 (Shibe Park)
10/09	Tesreau Bears. l 1–6 (NYC)
10/09	Tesreau Bears. w 7–2 (NYC)
10/14	Hilldale. l 1–7 (Darby, PA)

10/15	Hilldale. l 5–15 (Darby, PA)	10/17	Bacharach Giants. l 2–9 (Norfolk, VA)
10/16	Bacharach Giants. w 6–3 (Bronx Oval, NY)	10/23	Bacharach Giants. w 5–4 (NYC)
10/16	Bacharach Giants. l 0–1 (Bronx Oval, NY)	10/23	Bacharach Giants. l 3–5 (NYC)
			Total: 40-25-4

1922 American Giants

Manager: Rube Foster. Home field: South Side Park (aka Schorling Field), 39th (Pershing) and Wentworth. Final Standing: Negro National League pennant. (While the American Giants had the highest winning percentage, Indianapolis, Detroit and Kansas City won more NNL games). Based on scores published in the *Chicago Defender*.

03/24	New Orleans Crescents. w 3–2 (New Orleans)	06/18	KC Monarchs. l 5–19 (KC)
	New Orleans Crescents. w 13–12 (New Orleans)	06/20	KC Monarchs. w 8–5 (KC)
	New Orleans Crescents. w 5–4 (New Orleans)	06/25	Cuban Stars. l 7–8 (Home)
	New Orleans Crescents. w 6–3 (New Orleans)	06/26	Cuban Stars. l 5–6 (Home)
	New Orleans Crescents. l 6–8 (New Orleans)	06/27	Pyotts. w 4–1 (Pyott Park)
03/25	New Orleans Crescents. w 4–2 (New Orleans)	07/01	Marquette Park Manors. l 3–5
04/01	New Orleans Crescents. w 5–4 (New Orleans)	07/02	St. Louis Stars. w 6–5 (Home)
		07/02	St. Louis Stars. w 9–2 (Home)
04/02	Cuban Stars. w 7–4 (New Orleans)	07/04	Detroit Stars. w 1–0 (Home)
04/04	Cuban Stars. l 8–9 (New Orleans)	07/08	KC Monarchs. w 8–7 (Home)
04/05	Cuban Stars. l 4–6 (New Orleans)	07/08	KC Monarchs. w 7–0 (Home)
04/08	Cuban Stars. w 5–0 (New Orleans)	07/10	KC Monarchs. l 5–6 (Home)
04/09	Cuban Stars. l 2–4 (New Orleans)	07/11	KC Monarchs. w 6–5 (Home)
04/10	Cuban Stars. w 11–10 (New Orleans)	07/15	Indianapolis ABCs. w 8–5 (Home)
04/11	Cuban Stars. w 11–10 (New Orleans)	07/16	Indianapolis ABCs. w 10–8 (Home)
04/16	Rogers Park. w 6–5 (Home)	07/17	Indianapolis ABCs. w 2–1 (Home)
04/23	6th Army Corps. w 11–0 (Home)	07/18	Indianapolis ABCs. w 5–1 (Home)
04/30	Joliet. l 4–7 (Home)	07/23	Cleveland Tigers. w 7–2 (Home)
05/06	KC Monarchs. l 1–5 (Home)	07/24	Cleveland Tigers. w 4–0 (Home)
05/07	KC Monarchs. t 2–2 (Home)	07/30	Cuban Stars. w 10–3 (Home)
05/08	KC Monarchs. w 2–1 (Home)	07/30	Cuban Stars. w 8–2 (Home)
05/09	KC Monarchs. w 5–4 (Home)		Pontiac. w 6–3
05/13	St. Louis Stars. w 15–4 (Pyotts)	08/03	Chicagos ?. w 9–5 (Pyott Park)
05/14	St. Louis Stars. w 8–7 (Home)	08/04	Chicagos ?. w 10–4 (Pyott Park)
05/15	St. Louis Stars. l 2–6 (Home)	08/12	Bacharach Giants. l 4–5 (Home)
05/16	St. Louis Stars. w 7–0 (Home)	08/13	Bacharach Giants. l 2–3 (Home)
05/17	St. Louis Stars. w 3–2 (Home)	08/14	Bacharach Giants. w 3–2 (Home)
05/20	Bacharach Giants. ?. l 1–5 (Pyotts)	08/15	Bacharach Giants. w 7–3 (Home)
05/21	Bacharach Giants. w 3–2 (Home)	08/16	Bacharach Giants. w 1–0 (Home)
05/22	Bacharach Giants. l 3–7 (Home)	08/19	Hilldale. l 0–5 (Home)
05/23	Bacharach Giants. w 2–0 (Home)	08/20	Hilldale. w 4–2 (Home)
05/27	Marquette Park Manors. w 1–0 (Home)	08/21	Hilldale. w 9–1 (Home)
05/28	Cuban Stars. l 2–5 (Home)	08/26	Canton. w 1–0 (Home)
05/29	Cuban Stars. w 6–0 (Home)	09/03	Chicagos ?. l 2–3 (Home)
05/30	Cuban Stars. w 4–1 (Home)	09/04	Detroit Stars. l 6–11 (Detroit)
06/04	Indianapolis ABCs. w 11–0 (Home)		Detroit Stars. w ? (Detroit)
06/05	Indianapolis ABCs. w 7–1 (Home)		Detroit Stars. w 5–3 (Detroit)
	Chicagos ?. w 7–4 (Home)	09/10	KC Monarchs. l 3–10 (KC)
06/06	Logan Squares. l 0–4 (Logan Sq.)	09/11	KC Monarchs. l 5–11 (KC)
06/10	Chicagos ?. w 7–6 (Logan Sq.)	09/12	KC Monarchs. w 10–8 (KC)
06/12	St. Louis Stars. l 5–10 (St. Louis)	09/18	Cuban Stars. w 4–3 (Home)
06/12	House of David. w 11–4 (Home)	09/24	Indianapolis ABCs. l 5–10 (Indianapolis)
06/17	KC Monarchs. l 6–10 (KC)	09/25	Indianapolis ABCs. l 2–5 (Indianapolis)
		09/30	Detroit Stars. l 0–3
		10/01	Detroit Stars. w 2–1
			Midwest League All-Stars. w 9–2
			Pyotts. l 8–9
			Total: 57-29-1

1923 American Giants

Manager: Rube Foster. Home field: South Side Park (aka Schorling Field), 39th (Pershing) and Wentworth. Final Standing: Third place in Negro National League. Based on scores published in the *Chicago Defender.*

04/08 Pyotts. w 4–2 (Pyott Park)
04/22 Rogers Park. w 9–1 (Home)
04/28 KC Monarchs. l 0–5 (Kansas City)
04/29 KC Monarchs. w 15–13 (Kansas City)
05/05 Milwaukee Bears. w 8–3 (Home)
05/06 Milwaukee Bears. w 9–2 (Home)
05/06 Milwaukee Bears. w 8–5 (Home)
05/13 Detroit Stars. l 2–4 (Home)
05/22 St. Louis . l 10–11 (St. Louis)
05/26 KC Monarchs. w 3–2 (Home)
05/27 KC Monarchs. w 5–4 (Home)
05/31 KC Monarchs. w 3–2 (Home)
06/03 Cuban Stars. w 4–2 (Home)
06/04 Cuban Stars. l 6–11 (Home)
06/09 St. Louis Stars. w 5–4 (Home)
06/10 St. Louis Stars. w 4–0 (Home)
06/16 Indianapolis ABCs. w 1–0 (Home)
06/17 Indianapolis ABCs. w 6–5 (Home)
06/18 Indianapolis ABCs. l 1–4 (Home)
06/23 Pyotts. w 3–2 (Pyott Park)
06/24 Centralia. w 8–2 (Home)
07/08 Indianapolis ABCs. l 5–7 (Indianapolis)
07/09 Indianapolis ABCs. w 6–3 (Indianapolis)
07/10 Indianapolis ABCs. w 4–3 (Indianapolis)
07/11 Indianapolis ABCs. w 12–2 (Indianapolis)
07/12 Indianapolis ABCs. l 1–7 (Indianapolis)
07/14 Cuban Stars. w 10–8 (Pyott Park)
07/21 Detroit Stars. w 17–12 (Home)
07/22 Detroit Stars. w 7–1 (Home)
07/28 KC Monarchs. w 6–0 (Muehlebach Field)
07/29 KC Monarchs. l 2–3 (Muehlebach Field)
07/30 KC Monarchs. l 0–14 (Muehlebach Field)
08/04 Indianapolis ABCs. w 1–0 (Home)
08/05 Indianapolis ABCs. l 4–8 (Home)
08/12 Cuban Stars. w 8–5 (Home)
08/13 Cuban Stars. w 5–4 (Home)
08/14 Cuban Stars. l 0–6 (Home)
08/15 Cuban Stars. l 6–7 (Home)
08/15 Milwaukee Bears. l 4–6 (Home)

08/16 Milwaukee Bears. w 7–2 (Home)
08/18 Logan Squares. w 7–4 (Logan Sq.)
08/21 Birmingham Black Barons. w 7–4 (Rickwood)
08/21 Birmingham Black Barons. t 1–1 (Rickwood)
08/2? Birmingham Black Barons. w 7–0 (Rickwood)
08/22 Birmingham Black Barons. w 11–5 (Rickwood)
08/25 KC Monarchs. w 5–1 (Home)
08/26 KC Monarchs. w 10–2 (Home)
08/27 KC Monarchs. l 2–3 (Home)
09/01 Detroit Stars. w 6–4 (Detroit)
09/02 Detroit Stars. l 5–9 (Detroit)
09/03 Detroit Stars . w 2–1 (Detroit)
09/04 Detroit Stars. w 11–9 (Detroit)
09/06 Sturgis, MI. w 5–2 (Sturgis)
09/08 Normals. w 5–1 (Home)
09/09 Pyotts. l 2–3 (Home)
09/15 Logan Squares. w 10–0 (Logan Sq.)
09/22 Pyotts. l 5–8 (Pyott Park)
09/23 Normals. l 3–4 (Home)
09/24 Birmingham Black Barons. w 3–0 (Rickwood)
09/25 Birmingham Black Barons. w 3–0 (Rickwood)
09/25 Birmingham Black Barons. w 4–3 (Rickwood)
09/29 Logan Squares. w 6–4 (Home)
09/30 Normals. w 2–0 (Home)
09/30 Normals. w 1–0 (Home)
10/07 Pyotts. l 7–9 (Pyott Park)
10/06 Logan Squares. w 14–4 (Logan Sq.)
10/20 Detroit Tigers AL. t 5–5 (Home)
10/21 Detroit Tigers AL. l 1–7 (Home)
10/22 Detroit Tigers AL. w 8–6 (Home)
Total: 47-20-2

1924 American Giants

Manager: Rube Foster. Home field: South Side Park (aka Schorling Field), 39th (Pershing) and Wentworth. Final Standing: Second place Negro National League. Based on scores published in the *Chicago Defender.*

03/09 Houston. w 7–1 (Houston)
03/10 Houston. w 8–5 (Houston)
03/14 Calvert, TX. w 9–2 (Calvert)
03/15 Houston. w 4–0 (Houston)
03/16 Houston. w 3–1 (Houston)
03/18 Paul Quinn College. w 8–3 (Waco)
03/20 Paul Quinn College. w 12–3 (Waco)
03/23 Dallas Giants. w 2–0 (Dallas)
03/21 Dallas Giants. w 10–5 (Dallas)
03/21 Dallas Giants. w 3–1 (Dallas)
03/28 Texas College. w 14–5 (Waco)
03/29 Paul Quinn College. w 7–4 (Waco)

04/05 Dallas Giants. w 11–5 (Waxahachie, TX)
04/06 Dallas Giants. w 6–1 (Dallas)
04/06 Dallas Giants. w 3–1 (Dallas)
04/08 Wiley Univ. . w 6–4 (Marshall, TX)
04/09 Wiley Univ. . w 4–1 (Marshall, TX)
04/12 Memphis Red Sox. w 6–1 (Memphis, TN)
04/13 Memphis Red Sox. l 4–6 (Memphis, TN)
04/14 Memphis Red Sox. w 4–2 (Memphis, TN)
04/20 Chicago Blues. w 13–2 (Home)
04/26 KC Monarchs. l 3–10 (Home)
04/27 KC Monarchs. l 5–10 (Home)
04/28 KC Monarchs. l 2–3 (Home)

04/29	KC Monarchs. l 10–14 (Home)		07/21	Birmingham Black Barons. w 3–2 (Home)
04/27	KC Monarchs. w 3–2 (Home)		07/22	Birmingham Black Barons. w 6–4 (Home)
05/11	Cleveland Browns. w 12–2 (Home)		07/26	Cuban Stars. w 8–5 (Home)
05/12	Cleveland Browns. w 5–1 (Home)		07/27	Cuban Stars. w 4–1 (Home)
05/13	Cleveland Browns. w 7–1 (Home)		07/27	Cuban Stars. w 15–6 (Home)
05/13	Cleveland Browns. w 7–1 (Home)		08/02	KC Monarchs. w 5–2 (Home)
05/17	Cuban Stars. w 8–3 (Home)		08/03	KC Monarchs. l 7–8 (Home)
05/18	Cuban Stars. w 15–14 (Home)		08/04	KC Monarchs. l 5–9 (Home)
05/20	Cuban Stars. w 10–4 (Home)		08/05	KC Monarchs. w 1–0 (Home)
05/25	Ft. Wayne. w 14–1 (Home)		08/10	Detroit Stars. l 5–6 (Home)
05/30	KC Monarchs. l 1–5 (Home)		08/12	Detroit Stars. w 5–4 (Home)
05/30	KC Monarchs. w 6–2 (Home)		08/13	Detroit Stars. l 2–4 (Home)
05/31	KC Monarchs. w 7–0 (Home)		08/16	Detroit Stars. w 8–0 (Detroit)
06/01	KC Monarchs. l 2–5 (Home)		08/17	Detroit Stars. w 9–4 (Detroit)
06/07	St. Louis Stars. l 3–4 (St. Louis)		08/19	Detroit Stars. w 6–4 (Detroit)
06/08	St. Louis Stars. w 7–2 (St. Louis)		08/20	Cermacks. l 2–3 (Home)
06/09	St. Louis Stars. w 9–2 (St. Louis)		08/23	Memphis Red Sox. w 6–0 (Home)
06/10	St. Louis Stars. w 11–6 (St. Louis)		08/24	Memphis Red Sox. w 6–0 (Home)
06/14	Indianapolis ABCs. w 8–3 (Home)		08/24	Memphis Red Sox. w 1–0 (Home)
06/15	Indianapolis ABCs. w 3–0 (Home)		08/30	KC Monarchs. w 5–3 (Home)
06/16	Indianapolis ABCs. w 5–2 (Home)		08/31	KC Monarchs. l 5–9 (Home)
06/17	Indianapolis ABCs. w 12–5 (Home)		09/01	KC Monarchs. w 5–3 (Home)
06/21	Birmingham Black Barons. w 2–0 (Home)		09/02	KC Monarchs. w 9–2 (Home)
06/23	Birmingham Black Barons. w 4–0 (Home)			Cermacks. t 6–6 (Home)
06/24	Birmingham Black Barons. l 1–3 (Home)		09/06	Niesens. w 10–7 (Niesens)
06/25	Birmingham Black Barons. w 3–1 (Home)		09/13	KC Monarchs. w 3–2 (Kansas City)
06/29	Memphis Red Sox. w 3–1 (Home)		09/14	KC Monarchs. w 4–3 (Kansas City)
06/30	Memphis Red Sox. l 7–9 (Home)		09/14	KC Monarchs. l 1–8 (Kansas City)
07/01	Memphis Red Sox. w 5–2 (Home)		09/20	St. Louis Stars. l 5–8 (Home)
07/02	Memphis Red Sox. w 7–2 (Home)		09/21	St. Louis Stars. l 8–12 (Home)
07/03	KC Monarchs. l 5–7 (Kansas City)		09/21	St. Louis Stars. w 5–0 (Home)
07/04	KC Monarchs. l 6–12 (Kansas City)		09/22	St. Louis Stars. w 5–0 (Home)
07/04	KC Monarchs. w 9–7 (Kansas City)		09/27	KC Monarchs. w 8–6 (Home)
07/05	KC Monarchs. l 1–2 (Kansas City)		09/28	KC Monarchs. l 6–11 (Home)
07/06	KC Monarchs. l 13–11 (Kansas City)		10/26	Niesens. w 4–3 (Pyott)
07/12	Cuban Stars. l 3–9 (Home)		10/26	Chicago Blues. w 6–5 (Pyott)
07/13	Cuban Stars. w 11–9 (Home)		11/02	Niesens. l 1–6 (Pyott)
07/19	Birmingham Black Barons. w 3–1 (Home)		11/02	Niesens. l 2–7 (Pyott)
07/20	Birmingham Black Barons. w 6–3 (Home)			Total: 75-23-1

1925 American Giants

Manager: Rube Foster. Home field: South Side Park (aka Schorling Field), 39th (Pershing) and Wentworth. Final Standings: Fourth place first half of season, third place second half. Based on scores published in the *Chicago Defender*.

	Chicago Blues. w 5–3 (Home)		05/23	Indianapolis ABCs. l 7–8 (Indianapolis)
04/13	Birmingham Black Barons. w 13–6 (Rickwood)		05/25	Indianapolis ABCs. w 5–1 (Indianapolis)
04/14	Birmingham Black Barons. w 12–2 (Rickwood)		05/26	Indianapolis ABCs. l 4–10 (Indianapolis)
			05/29	Kansas City Monarchs. l 2–8 (Kansas City)
	Birmingham Black Barons. w Rickwood		05/30	Kansas City Monarchs. l 0–1 (Kansas City)
	Birmingham Black Barons. w Rickwood		05/30	Kansas City Monarchs. l 3–6 (Kansas City)
05/3	Memphis Red Sox. l 2–4 (Memphis)		05/31	Kansas City Monarchs. l 5–8 (Kansas City)
05/3	Memphis Red Sox. w 11–4 (Memphis)		05/31	Kansas City Monarchs. l 0–3 (Kansas City)
05/4	Memphis Red Sox. w 3–2 (Memphis)		06/3	Pyotts. l 6–8 (Home)
05/5	Memphis Red Sox. l 2–3 (Memphis)		06/6	Memphis Red Sox. w 10–3 (Home)
05/9	Kansas City Monarchs. w 1–0 (Home)		06/7	Memphis Red Sox. w 10–0 (Home)
05/10	Kansas City Monarchs. w 3–2 (Home)		06/8	Memphis Red Sox. l 9–17 (Home)
05/11	Kansas City Monarchs. l 1–2 (Home)		06/9	Memphis Red Sox. w 5–2 (Home)
05/12	Kansas City Monarchs. w 4–3 (Home)		06/13	Birmingham Black Barons. w 9–6 (Home)
05/13	Kansas City Monarchs. l 0–8 (Home)		06/14	Birmingham Black Barons. w 8–4 (Home)
05/17	Detroit Stars. l 2–6 (Home)		06/15	Birmingham Black Barons. w 7–3 (Home)
05/18	Detroit Stars. l 4–7 (Home)		06/16	Birmingham Black Barons. l 0–1 (Home)
05/19	Detroit Stars. l 7–8 (Home)		06/20	Cuban Stars. w 6–5 (Home)
			06/21	Cuban Stars. w 14–3 (Home)

06/22	Cuban Stars. l 8–9 (Home)	08/10	Memphis Red Sox. w 6–3 (Home)
06/23	Cuban Stars. w 3–2 (Home)	08/11	Memphis Red Sox. w 4–1 (Home)
06/25	St. Louis Stars. l 2–3 (Home)	08/15	Kansas City Monarchs. l 3–6 (Kansas City)
06/28	St. Louis Stars. w 11–4 (Home)	08/16	Kansas City Monarchs. w 14–9
06/29	St. Louis Stars. l 2–5 (Home)		(Kansas City)
06/30	St. Louis Stars. w 2–0 (Home)	08/17	Kansas City Monarchs. l 2–5 (Kansas City)
07/4	Kansas City Monarchs. l 1–2 (Home)	08/18	Kansas City Monarchs. l 2–4 (Kansas City)
07/5	Kansas City Monarchs. w 4–1 (Home)	08/22	St. Louis Stars. l 3–8 (St. Louis)
07/6	Kansas City Monarchs. l 1–7 (Home)	08/23	St. Louis Stars. l 2–4 (St. Louis)
07/7	Kansas City Monarchs. w 7–1 (Home)	08/24	St. Louis Stars. l 1–2 (St. Louis)
07/11	Birmingham Black Barons. t 1–1 (Home)	08/29	Kansas City Monarchs. w 3–1 (Home)
07/12	Birmingham Black Barons. l 0–5 (Home)	08/30	Kansas City Monarchs. l 0–17 (Home)
07/13	Birmingham Black Barons. w 6–1 (Home)	09/1	Kansas City Monarchs. l 4–5 (Home)
07/14	Birmingham Black Barons. w 7–4 (Home)	09/2	Kansas City Monarchs. w 6–5 (Home)
07/18	Detroit Stars. w 9–1 (Detroit)	09/5	Indianapolis ABCs. w 8–3 (Home)
07/19	Detroit Stars. w 7–5 (Detroit)	09/6	Indianapolis ABCs. w 5–1 (Home)
07/20	Detroit Stars. l 6–7 (Detroit)	09/7	Indianapolis ABCs. w 4–1 (Home)
07/21	Detroit Stars. l 2–9 (Detroit)	09/8	Indianapolis ABCs. l 1–2 (Home)
07/25	Detroit Stars. w 3–2 (Home)	09/13	Cuban Stars. w 3–0 (Home)
07/26	Detroit Stars. l 2–3 (Home)	09/13	Cuban Stars. w 1–0 (Home)
07/28	Detroit Stars. w 12–4 (Home)	09/19	Detroit Stars. w 3–1 (Home)
08/1	Indianapolis ABCs. w 1–0 (Home)	09/20	Detroit Stars. w 3–2 (Home)
08/2	Indianapolis ABCs. w 3–0 (Home)	09/21	Detroit Stars. l 0–4 (Home)
08/3	Indianapolis ABCs. w 3–2 (Home)	09/26	Detroit Stars. w 7–2 (Detroit)
08/4	Indianapolis ABCs. w 11–3 (Home)	09/26	Detroit Stars. l 0–3 (Detroit)
08/8	Memphis Red Sox. l 0–2 (Home)	09/27	Detroit Stars. w 5–2 (Detroit)
08/9	Memphis Red Sox. w 4–3 (Home)		Total: 50-37-1

1926 American Giants

Managers: Rube Foster (May–June) and Dave Malarcher (July–October). Home field: South Side Park (aka Schorling Field), 39th (Pershing) and Wentworth. Final Standing: Defeated Kansas City Monarchs in a playoff to win the NNL pennant, defeated the Eastern Colored League Atlantic City Bacharach Giants in Negro League World Series. Based on scores published in the *Chicago Defender*.

4/	Chicago Blues. w 3–0 (Home)	06/13	St. Louis Stars. l 5–10 (St. Louis)
05/01	Detroit Stars. w 7–5 (Home)	06/14	St. Louis Stars. l 1–3 (St. Louis)
05/02	Detroit Stars. t 6–6 (Home)	06/15	St. Louis Stars. w 1–0 (St. Louis)
05/03	Detroit Stars. w 4–3 (Home)	06/16	St. Louis Stars. l 2–3 (St. Louis)
05/04	Detroit Stars. l 0–3 (Home)	06/20	Cuban Stars. w 5–0 (Home)
05/05	Detroit Stars. w 5–3 (Home)	06/20	Cuban Stars. w 1–0 (Home)
05/08	St. Louis Stars. w 12–10 (Home)	06/21	Cuban Stars. w 8–6 (Home)
05/09	St. Louis Stars. w 4–3 (Home)	06/22	Cuban Stars. w 10–3 (Home)
05/10	St. Louis Stars. l 2–5 (Home)	06/26	KC Monarchs. l 1–2 (Home)
05/11	St. Louis Stars. w 3–2 (Home)	06/27	KC Monarchs. w 3–1 (Home)
05/12	St. Louis Stars. l 3–8 (Home)		South Bend . w 8–6 (South Bend)
05/15	Dayton Marcos. w 3–2 (Home)	06/29	KC Monarchs. w 9–2 (Home)
05/16	Dayton Marcos. w 3–2 (Home)	06/29	KC Monarchs. w 3–2 (Home)
05/17	Dayton Marcos. w 10–4 (Home)	07/05	Indianapolis ABCs. w 4–3 (Home)
05/19	Dayton Marcos. w 4–0 (Home)	07/06	Indianapolis ABCs. w 5–1 (Home)
05/22	Cleveland Elites. w 4–2 (Home)	07/07	Indianapolis ABCs. w 3–1 (Home)
05/23	Cleveland Elites. w 13–2 (Home)	07/08	Indianapolis ABCs. l 1–4 (Home)
05/24	Cleveland Elites. w 6–1 (Home)	07/10	Dayton Marcos. w 4–1 (Home)
05/25	Cleveland Elites. w 6–5 (Home)	07/11	Dayton Marcos. w 7–4 (Home)
05/29	KC Monarchs. l 1–5 (Home)	07/12	Dayton Marcos. w 2–1 (Home)
05/30	KC Monarchs. l 2–4 (Home)	07/13	Dayton Marcos. w 3–0 (Home)
05/31	KC Monarchs. l 4–8 (Home)	07/13	Dayton Marcos. w 16–0 (Home)
06/01	KC Monarchs. w 7–0 (Home)	07/17	Cuban Stars. w 6–0 (Home)
06/02	KC Monarchs. l 3–4 (Home)	07/18	Cuban Stars. w 3–1 (Home)
06/05	KC Monarchs. l 2–4 (Kansas City)	07/19	Cuban Stars. w 11–7 (Home)
06/06	KC Monarchs. l 4–6 (Kansas City)	07/20	Cuban Stars. l 6–7 (Home)
06/07	KC Monarchs. l 2–11 (Kansas City)	07/21	Cuban Stars. w 9–3 (Home)
06/08	KC Monarchs. l 4–5 (Kansas City)	07/24	Detroit Stars. w 5–0 (Home)
06/12	St. Louis Stars. w 16–5 (St. Louis)	07/25	Detroit Stars. w 2–1 (Home)

07/26   Detroit Stars. w 2–1 (Home)
07/27   Detroit Stars. w 8–3 (Home)
07/28   Detroit Stars. w 6–2 (Home)
07/31   Indianapolis ABCs. w 3–2 (Home)
08/01   Indianapolis ABCs. w 2–1 (Home)
08/02   Indianapolis ABCs. w 8–4 (Home)
08/03   Indianapolis ABCs. w 3–0 (Home)
08/04   Indianapolis ABCs. w 6–2 (Home)
08/08   Indianapolis ABCs. w 7–2 (Indianapolis)
08/08   Indianapolis ABCs. t 2–2 (Indianapolis)
08/09   Indianapolis ABCs. w 8–5 (Indianapolis)
08/10   Indianapolis ABCs. w 4–3 (Indianapolis)
08/11   Indianapolis ABCs. l 3–5 (Indianapolis)
08/14   Detroit Stars. w 6–1 (Detroit)
08/15   Detroit Stars. l 4–15 (Detroit)
08/16   Detroit Stars. w 6–2 (Detroit)
08/18   Detroit Stars. l 4–6 (Detroit)
08/28   KC Monarchs. w 14–1 (Kansas City)
08/29   KC Monarchs. w 1–0 (Kansas City)
08/30   KC Monarchs. l 3–4 (Kansas City)
08/31   KC Monarchs. w 5–1 (Kansas City)
09/01   KC Monarchs. l 2–7 (Kansas City)
09/06   Indianapolis ABCs. w 2–1 (Home)
09/06   Indianapolis ABCs. w 9–2 (Home)
09/07   Indianapolis ABCs. l 3–9 (Home)

Negro National League Playoffs
09/18   KC Monarchs. l 3–4 (Kansas City)
09/19   KC Monarchs. l 5–6 (Kansas City)
09/20   KC Monarchs. l 0–5 (Kansas City)
09/21   KC Monarchs. w 4–3 (Kansas City)
09/25   KC Monarchs. l 5–11 (Home)
09/26   KC Monarchs. w 2–0 (Home)
09/27   KC Monarchs. w 4–3 (Home)
09/29   KC Monarchs. w 1–0 (Home)
09/29   KC Monarchs. w 5–0 (Home)
World Series
10/01   Bacharach Giants. t 3–3 (Atlantic City)
10/02   Bacharach Giants. w 7–6 (Atlantic City)
10/03   Bacharach Giants. l 0–10 (Baltimore)
10/04   Bacharach Giants. t 4–4 (Philadelphia NL)
10/05   Bacharach Giants. l 5–7 (Philadelphia NL)
10/06   Bacharach Giants. l 4–6 (Atlantic City)
10/09   Bacharach Giants. w 5–4 (Home)
10/10   Bacharach Giants. l 0–3 (Home)
10/11   Bacharach Giants. w 6–3 (Home)
10/13   Bacharach Giants. w 13–0 (Home)
10/14   Bacharach Giants. w 1–0 (Home)
10/16   St. Louis Stars. t 5–5 (St. Louis)
10/27   St. Louis Stars. w 7–6 (St. Louis)
         Total: 69-31-5

1927 American Giants

Manager: Dave Malarcher. Home field: South Side Park (aka Schorling Field), 39th (Pershing) and Wentworth. Final Standing: Defeated the Birmingham Black Barons in playoff to win the Negro National League pennant. Won the Negro League World Series against the Atlantic City Bacharach Giants. Also won Chicago "Semi-pro championship." Based on scores published in the *Chicago Defender*.

04/17   Chicago Blues. w 5–2 (Home)
04/23   Detroit Stars. w 2–1 (Detroit)
04/24   Detroit Stars. l 0–1 (Home)
04/25   Detroit Stars. l 1–12 (Home)
04/26   Detroit Stars. w 3–2 (Home)
04/27   Detroit Stars. w 4–0 (Home)
04/30   Detroit Stars. l 3–6 (Detroit)
05/01   Detroit Stars. l 6–7 (Detroit)
05/02   Detroit Stars. w 5–3 (Detroit)
05/03   Detroit Stars. w 9–4 (Detroit)
05/04   Detroit Stars. w 5–0 (Detroit)
05/07   Cleveland Hornets. l 2–4 (Cleveland)
05/08   Cleveland Hornets. w 6–3 (Cleveland)
05/09   Cleveland Hornets. w 9–5 (Cleveland)
05/10   Cleveland Hornets. w 6–0 (Cleveland)
05/15   Birmingham Black Barons. w 3–0 (Home)
05/16   Birmingham Black Barons. w 8–7 (Home)
05/17   Birmingham Black Barons. l 1–5 (Home)
05/18   Birmingham Black Barons. w 8–0 (Home)
05/21   Memphis Red Sox. w 11–2 (Home)
05/22   Memphis Red Sox. w 2–1 (Home)
05/23   Memphis Red Sox. w 12–4 (Home)
05/28   Cuban Stars. w 3–1 (Home)
05/29   Cuban Stars. w 5–0 (Home)
05/30   Cuban Stars. l 1–3 (Home)
06/01   Cuban Stars. w 7–2 (Home)
06/04   St. Louis Stars. w 14–7 (St. Louis)
06/05   St. Louis Stars. l 2–6 (St. Louis)
06/06   St. Louis Stars. l 6–8 (St. Louis)
06/07   St. Louis Stars. l 4–12 (St. Louis)

06/08   St. Louis Stars. w 6–2 (St. Louis)
06/11   Cleveland Hornets. w 3–0 (Home)
06/12   Cleveland Hornets. w 7–3 (Home)
06/14   Cleveland Hornets. l 2–3 (Home)
06/15   Cleveland Hornets. w 3–2 (Home)
06/15   Cleveland Hornets. w 3–2 (Home)
06/19   Birmingham Black Barons. w 8–6 (Home)
06/19   Birmingham Black Barons. w 9–8 (Home)
06/20   Birmingham Black Barons. w 7–6 (Home)
06/22   Birmingham Black Barons. w 6–2 (Home)
06/22   Birmingham Black Barons. w 12–4 (Home)
06/26   Beloit Fairies. w 4–3
07/02   KC Monarchs. l 1–3 (Home)
07/03   KC Monarchs. l 1–3 (Home)
07/04   KC Monarchs. w 7–6 (Home)
07/05   KC Monarchs. l 0–3 (Home)
07/06   KC Monarchs. w 4–0 (Home)
07/09   Cuban Stars. w 3–2 (Home)
07/10   Cuban Stars. w 2–0 (Home)
07/11   Cuban Stars. l 0–3 (Home)
07/12   Cuban Stars. w 3–2 (Home)
07/13   Cuban Stars. w 1–0 (Home)
07/16   St. Louis Stars. w 12–8 (Home)
07/17   St. Louis Stars. l 0–2 (Home)
07/18   St. Louis Stars. l 0–3 (Home)
07/19   St. Louis Stars. w 7–3 (Home)
07/20   St. Louis Stars. w 6–2 (Home)
07/22   KC Monarchs. l 3–5 (Kansas City)
07/23   KC Monarchs. l 1–9 (Kansas City)
07/24   KC Monarchs. l 0–18 (Kansas City)

07/24	KC Monarchs. l 3–4 (Kansas City)	09/04	Hammond. w 5–3 (Home)
07/25	Birmingham Black Barons. w 9–7 (Birmingham)	09/05	Duffy Florals. w 1–0 (Home)
		09/06	Duffy Florals. w 5–0 (Home)
07/26	Birmingham Black Barons. w 4–3 (Birmingham)	09/10	Detroit Stars. w 3–0 (Home)
		09/12	Detroit Stars. w 5–2 (Home)
07/26	Birmingham Black Barons. l 3–4 (Birmingham)	09/13	Detroit Stars. l 3–4 (Home)
		09/14	Detroit Stars. w 8–5 (Home)
07/27	Birmingham Black Barons. w 7–3 (Birmingham)	**Negro National League Playoffs**	
		09/19	Birmingham Black Barons. w 5–0 (Rickwood)
07/27	Birmingham Black Barons. t 1–1 (Birmingham)	09/20	Birmingham Black Barons. w 10–5 (Rickwood)
07/29	St. Louis Stars. l 4–5 (St. Louis)		
07/31	St. Louis Stars. w 6–4 (St. Louis)	09/21	Birmingham Black Barons. l 5–6 (Rickwood)
08/01	St. Louis Stars. l 5–13 (St. Louis)		
08/02	St. Louis Stars. w 3–1 (St. Louis)	09/24	Birmingham Black Barons. w 6–4 (Home)
08/03	St. Louis Stars. w 3–1 (St. Louis)	09/25	Birmingham Black Barons. w 6–2 (Home)
08/06	Detroit Stars. w 9–3 (Home)	**Negro League World Series**	
08/08	Detroit Stars. l 2–4 (Home)	10/01	Bacharach Giants. w 6–2 (Home)
08/09	Detroit Stars. w 9–1 (Home)	10/02	Bacharach Giants. w 11–1 (Home)
08/10	Detroit Stars. l 0–5 (Home)	10/03	Bacharach Giants. w 7–0 (Home)
08/13	Memphis Red Sox. w 8–7 (Home)	10/04	Bacharach Giants. w 9–1 (Home)
08/14	Memphis Red Sox. w 3–0 (Home)	10/08	Bacharach Giants. l 2–3 (Atlantic City)
08/15	Memphis Red Sox. l 1–2 (Home)	10/10	Bacharach Giants. t 1–1 (Atlantic City)
08/16	Memphis Red Sox. w 7–4 (Home)	10/11	Bacharach Giants. l 1–8 (Atlantic City)
08/20	KC Monarchs. w 2–0 (Home)	10/12	Bacharach Giants. l 5–6 (Atlantic City)
08/21	KC Monarchs. w 12–8 (Home)	10/13	Bacharach Giants. w 11–4 (Atlantic City)
08/22	KC Monarchs. w 6–5 (Home)	10/15	Logan Squares. w 4–3 (Home)
08/24	KC Monarchs. l 0–4 (Home)	10/16	Logan Squares. w 7–2 (Home)
08/25	KC Monarchs. w 2–0 (Home)	10/18	Duffy Florals. w 9–6 (Home)
08/27	Birmingham Black Barons. w 4–2 (Home)	10/19	Duffy Florals. l 3–4 (Home)
08/28	Birmingham Black Barons. w 4–3 (Home)	10/22	Duffy Florals. l 5–8 (Home)
08/29	Birmingham Black Barons. l 0–1 (Home)	10/23	Duffy Florals. w 7–5 (Away)
08/30	Birmingham Black Barons. w 3–1 (Home)	10/30	Duffy Florals. l 9–10 (Home)
08/31	Birmingham Black Barons. w 4–0 (Home)	10/30	Duffy Florals. w 4–1 (Home)
09/03	Mills. w 3–1 (Home)	Total: 79-38-2	

1928 Chicago American Giants

Manager: Dave Malarcher. Home field: South Side Park (aka Schorling Field), 39th (Pershing) and Wentworth. Final Standing: Negro National League runner up, lost playoff series to St. Louis Stars. Based on scores published in the *Chicago Defender*.

04/22	Litzingers. w 6–0 (Home)	05/30	KC Monarchs. w 3–2 (Home)
04/28	Mills. t 0–0	06/1	Memphis Red Sox. w 3–2 (Memphis)
04/29	Aurora. w 9–8 (Home)	06/2	Memphis Red Sox. w 5–3 (Memphis)
05/5	Birmingham Black Barons. w 3–2 (Home)	06/6	Birmingham Black Barons. l 5–6 (Birmingham)
05/6	Birmingham Black Barons. w 6–5 (Home)		
05/7	Birmingham Black Barons. w 2–1 (Home)	06/6	Birmingham Black Barons. l 3–5 (Birmingham)
05/8	Birmingham Black Barons. l 5–8 (Home)		
05/9	Birmingham Black Barons. w 10–4 (Home)	06/7	Birmingham Black Barons. l 3–6 (Birmingham)
05/12	Detroit Stars. l 3–5 (Home)		
05/13	Detroit Stars. w 8–2 (Home)	06/7	Birmingham Black Barons. w 7–1 (Birmingham)
05/13	Detroit Stars. l 0–1 (Home)		
05/14	Detroit Stars. l 0–2 (Home)	06/9	KC Monarchs. l 2–6 (Kansas City)
05/15	Detroit Stars. l 3–6 (Home)	06/10	KC Monarchs. l 2–3 (Kansas City)
05/19	Cuban Stars. l 0–3 (Home)	06/11	KC Monarchs. l 3–12 (Kansas City)
05/20	Cuban Stars. w 5–0 (Home)	06/12	KC Monarchs. l 9–10 (Kansas City)
05/20	Cuban Stars. w 12–0 (Home)	06/13	KC Monarchs. l 6–7 (Kansas City)
05/21	Cuban Stars. w 2–1 (Home)	06/14	Memphis Red Sox. w 1–0 (Home)
05/22	Cuban Stars. l 3–5 (Home)	06/14	Memphis Red Sox. w 3–0 (Home)
05/23	Duffys. w 7–2	06/16	St. Louis Stars. l 1–8 (Home)
05/27	KC Monarchs. w 6–4 (Home)	06/17	St. Louis Stars. l 3–6 (Home)
05/28	KC Monarchs. l 3–6 (Home)	06/18	St. Louis Stars. l 0–2 (Home)
05/30	KC Monarchs. w 2–0 (Home)	06/19	St. Louis Stars. w 11–1 (Home)

06/23	Birmingham Black Barons. w 4–3 (Home)	08/12	St. Louis Stars. l 2–3 (St. Louis)
06/24	Birmingham Black Barons. w 9–1 (Home)	08/13	St. Louis Stars. l 4–7 (St. Louis)
06/26	Birmingham Black Barons. w 10–0 (Home)	08/14	St. Louis Stars. l 3–8 (St. Louis)
06/26	Birmingham Black Barons. l 0–2 (Home)	08/14	St. Louis Stars. w 9–4 (St. Louis)
06/27	Birmingham Black Barons. w 3–2 (Home)	08/18	Bacharach Giants. l 0–13 (Home)
06/27	Birmingham Black Barons. l 0–6 (Home)	08/19	Bacharach Giants. w 4–2 (Home)
06/28	Mills. w 4–3 (Home)	08/21	Bacharach Giants. w 5–0 (Home)
06/30	Cleveland Tigers. w 3–1 (Home)	08/23	Bacharach Giants. l 2–3 (Home)
07/1	Cleveland Tigers. w 4–0 (Home)	08/26	Detroit Stars. w 5–4 (Home)
07/1	Cleveland Tigers. l 0–1 (Home)	08/27	Detroit Stars. w 6–3 (Home)
07/2	Cleveland Tigers. w 7–6 (Home)	08/28	Detroit Stars. w 9–3 (Home)
07/3	Cleveland Tigers. w 9–1 (Home)	09/1	Birmingham Black Barons. l 1–2 (Home)
07/4	Cleveland Tigers. w 1–0 (Home)	09/2	Birmingham Black Barons. w 3–0 (Home)
07/4	Cleveland Tigers. w 8–5 (Home)	09/3	Birmingham Black Barons. w 2–0 (Home)
07/7	Cuban Stars. w 8–6 (Home)	09/3	Birmingham Black Barons. l 1–5 (Home)
07/8	Cuban Stars. w 8–2 (Home)	09/4	Birmingham Black Barons. w 3–0 (Home)
07/8	Cuban Stars. w 4–0 (Home)	09/8	KC Monarchs. w 8–4 (Kansas City)
07/9	Cuban Stars. w 11–0 (Home)	09/9	KC Monarchs. w 5–4 (Kansas City)
07/10	Cuban Stars. w 6–2 (Home)	09/9	KC Monarchs. l 2–17 (Kansas City)
07/14	Detroit Stars. l 4–5 (Detroit)	09/11	KC Monarchs. l 3–4 (Kansas City)
07/15	Detroit Stars. w 15–2 (Detroit)	09/15	Mills. w 8–2
07/16	Detroit Stars. l 12–15 (Detroit)	09/16	Mills. l 4–8
07/17	Detroit Stars. w 5–4 (Detroit)	09/16	Mills. l 4–6
07/21	Cleveland Tigers. w 2–0 (Cleveland)	09/18	Lavenders of Hammond. w 6–2 (Home)
07/21	Cleveland Tigers. w 16–3 (Cleveland)	09/19	Lavenders of Hammond. l 5–7 (Home)
07/22	Cleveland Tigers. w 10–3 (Cleveland)	**Negro National League Playoff**	
07/23	Cleveland Tigers. l 3–5 (Cleveland)	09/22	St. Louis Stars. w 7–3 (Home)
07/24	Cleveland Tigers. w 8–5 (Cleveland)	09/23	St. Louis Stars. w 3–0 (Home)
	St. Louis Stars. l 4–11	09/24	St. Louis Stars. l 4–6 (Home)
07/28	Birmingham Black Barons. l 2–3 (Home)	09/25	St. Louis Stars. l 4–5 (Home)
07/29	Birmingham Black Barons. w 12–4 (Home)	09/29	St. Louis Stars. w 5–3 (St. Louis)
07/29	Birmingham Black Barons. w 7–2 (Home)	09/30	St. Louis Stars. l 7–12 (St. Louis)
07/30	Birmingham Black Barons. w 3–2 (Home)	10/2	St. Louis Stars. w 9–7 (St. Louis)
07/31	Birmingham Black Barons. l 4–6 (Home)	10/4	St. Louis Stars. l 4–19 (St. Louis)
08/4	Memphis Red Sox. w 7–2 (Home)	10/5	St. Louis Stars. l 2–9 (St. Louis)
08/5	Memphis Red Sox. w 4–1 (Home)	10/14	Duffy Florals. w 2–1
08/5	Memphis Red Sox. w 1–0 (Home)	10/14	Duffy Florals. w 7–0
08/6	Memphis Red Sox. w 4–0 (Home)	10/28	Jimmy Hutton ML All-Stars. w 1–0 (Home)
08/7	Memphis Red Sox. w 2–1 (Home)	10/28	Jimmy Hutton ML All-Stars. w 1–0 (Home)
08/11	St. Louis Stars. w 17–4 (St. Louis)		Total: 71-46-1

1929 Chicago American Giants

Manager: Jim Brown. Home field: South Side Park (aka Schorling Field), 39th (Pershing) and Wentworth. Final Standing: Third place Negro National League. Based on scores published in the *Chicago Defender.*

4/14	Duffy Florals. w 10–9	5/21	Memphis Red Sox. w 4–3 (Home)
4/20	Famous Chicagos. w 6–?	5/25	Cuban Stars. w 11–9 (Home)
4/27	KC Monarchs. l 5–7 (Home)	5/26	Cuban Stars. l 3–5 (Home)
4/28	KC Monarchs. l 2–5 (Home)	5/26	Cuban Stars. w 2–1 (Home)
4/28	KC Monarchs. l 1–3 (Home)	5/27	Cuban Stars. w 10–4 (Home)
4/29	KC Monarchs. l 2–5 (Home)	5/28	Cuban Stars. w 7–2 (Home)
4/30	KC Monarchs. w 6–5 (Home)	5/30	Detroit Stars. w 3–0 (Home)
5/5	St. Louis Stars. l. l 3 St. Louis	5/30	Detroit Stars. w 2–0 (Home)
5/11	Birmingham Black Barons. l 3–4 (Home)	5/31	Detroit Stars. l 4–8 (Home)
5/12	Birmingham Black Barons. w 5–1 (Home)	6/1	Detroit Stars. l 0–2 (Home)
5/12	Birmingham Black Barons. l 2–4 (Home)	6/2	Detroit Stars. l 2–4 (Home)
5/13	Birmingham Black Barons. l 3–4 (Home)	6/2	Detroit Stars. l 0–3 (Home)
5/14	Birmingham Black Barons. w 6–3 (Home)	6/8	St. Louis Stars. w 1–0 (Home)
5/18	Memphis Red Sox. w 10–1 (Home)	6/9	St. Louis Stars. l 1–7 (Home)
5/18	Memphis Red Sox. l 1–3 (Home)	6/9	St. Louis Stars. l 4–6 (Home)
5/19	Memphis Red Sox. w 2–1 (Home)	6/10	St. Louis Stars. w 8–6 (Home)
5/20	Memphis Red Sox. w 4–3 (Home)	6/15	KC Monarchs. l 1–7 (Kansas City)

6/16	KC Monarchs. w 10–7 (Kansas City)
6/16	KC Monarchs. l 3–9 (Kansas City)
6/17	KC Monarchs. l 5–16 (Kansas City)
6/18	KC Monarchs. l 6–9 (Kansas City)
6/21	Memphis Red Sox. w 3–2 (Memphis)
6/22	Memphis Red Sox. w 11–9 (Memphis)
6/23	Memphis Red Sox. w 3–2 (Memphis)
6/23	Memphis Red Sox. l 2–3 (Memphis)
6/24	Birmingham Black Barons. l 0–6 (Rickwood)
6/27	Birmingham Black Barons. w 6–3 (Rickwood)
6/27	Birmingham Black Barons. l 0–7 (Rickwood)
6/29	KC Monarchs. l 0–4 (Home)
6/30	KC Monarchs. l 2–7 (Home)
7/1	KC Monarchs. w 2–0 (Home)
7/3	KC Monarchs. l 5–10 (Home)
7/4	KC Monarchs. w 5–0 (Home)
7/4	KC Monarchs. w 3–2 (Home)
7/6	Birmingham Black Barons. w 9–4 (Home)
7/7	Birmingham Black Barons. w 5–3 (Home)
7/7	Birmingham Black Barons. w 3–2 (Home)
7/8	Birmingham Black Barons. w 12–6 (Home)
7/9	Birmingham Black Barons. w 2–0 (Home)
7/13	Cuban Stars. l 2–4 (Home)
7/14	Cuban Stars. l 2–7 (Home)
7/14	Cuban Stars. w 2–0 (Home)
7/15	Cuban Stars. w 7–0 (Home)
7/16	Cuban Stars. w 2–1 (Home)
7/20	Detroit Stars. l 6–20 (Detroit)
7/21	Detroit Stars. w 14–12 (Detroit)
7/21	Detroit Stars. w 7–6 (Detroit)
7/22	Detroit Stars. l 5–6 (Detroit)
7/22	Detroit Stars. w 6–4 (Detroit)
7/27	KC Monarchs. l 3–9 (Home)
7/28	KC Monarchs. l 3–5 (Home)
7/28	KC Monarchs. w 5–2 (Home)
7/29	KC Monarchs. l 4–6 (Home)
7/30	KC Monarchs. w 5–3 (Home)
	Hawleys All-Stars. w 4–0
8/4	Hawks. w 5–0
8/4	Joe Green's Giants. w 4–1 (Home)
8/10	Nashville Elites. w 5–3 (Home)
8/11	Nashville Elites. w 3–0 (Home)
8/11	Nashville Elites. w 9–0 (Home)
8/12	Nashville Elites. w 3–0 (Home)
8/17	Memphis Red Sox. w 8–3 (Home)
8/18	Memphis Red Sox. w 6–2 (Home)
8/18	Memphis Red Sox. w 8–2 (Home)
8/19	Memphis Red Sox. w ? (Home)
8/20	Memphis Red Sox. w 7–2 (Home)
8/24	Birmingham Black Barons. w 4–2 (Home)
8/25	Birmingham Black Barons. w 8–3 (Home)
8/25	Birmingham Black Barons. w 1–0 (Home)
8/26	Birmingham Black Barons. w 3–1 (Home)
8/26	Birmingham Black Barons. w 3–1 (Home)
9/1	City Firemen. w 11–6 (Home)
9/1	City Firemen. w 10–0 (Home)
9/2	Miami Giants. w 18–9 (Home)
9/2	Miami Giants. w 17–1 (Home)
9/3	Miami Giants. w 7–6 (Home)
9/4	Miami Giants. w 8–0 (Home)
9/7	St. Louis Stars. l 0–1 (Home)
9/8	St. Louis Stars. w 5–2 (Home)
9/8	St. Louis Stars. l 0–6 (Home)
9/9	St. Louis Stars. w 9–4 (Home)
9/10	St. Louis Stars. w 8–4 (Home)
9/21	Mills. l 1–3 (Home)
9/22	Mills. w 13–1 (Away)
9/22	Mills. w 3–2 (Away)
9/28	NNL All Stars. l 1–2 (Home)
9/29	NNL All Stars. l 1–2 (Home)
9/29	NNL All Stars. l 2–3 (Home)
10/5	Homestead Grays. w 2–0 (Home)
10/6	Homestead Grays. w 1–0 (Home)
10/6	Homestead Grays. w 6–0 (Home)
10/7	Homestead Grays. w 14–9 (Home)
10/8	Homestead Grays. w 7–0 (Home)
10/9	Homestead Grays. w 1–0 (Home)
10/12	AL All-Stars. w 12–11 (Home)
10/13	AL All-Stars. w 10–1 (Home)
10/14	AL All-Stars. l 0–1 (Home)
10/15	AL All-Stars. w 7–6 (Home)
10/19	AL All-Stars. w 7–4 (Home)
10/20	AL All-Stars. l 0–2 (Home)
	Total: 76-41

1930 Chicago American Giants

Managers: Jim Brown (April–June) and Willie Foster (July–October). Home field: South Side Park (aka American Giant Park), 39th (Pershing) and Wentworth. Final Standing: Finished seventh of eight teams in the first half, and third of eight in the second half of the Negro National League. Based on scores published in the *Chicago Defender*.

04/13	All–Stars. w 8–2 (Home)
04/26	Detroit Stars. l 0–3 (Home)
04/27	Detroit Stars. w 3–2 (Home)
04/27	Detroit Stars. w 2–0 (Home)
04/28	Detroit Stars. w 5–3 (Home)
04/28	Detroit Stars. w 2–1 (Home)
05/3	Cuban Stars. w 6–2
05/4	Cuban Stars. l 0–4
05/4	Cuban Stars. w 13–1
05/5	Cuban Stars. l 1–9 (Home)
05/10	St. Louis Stars. l 11–15 (St. Louis)
05/10	St. Louis Stars. l 6–12 (St. Louis)
05/11	St. Louis Stars. l 4–9 (St. Louis)
05/12	St. Louis Stars. l 13–17 (St. Louis)
05/17	Detroit Stars. l 3–12 (Detroit)
05/18	Detroit Stars. w 2–0 (Detroit)
05/18	Detroit Stars. w 6–2 (Detroit)
05/19	Detroit Stars. w 4–3 (Detroit)
05/19	Detroit Stars. l 2–3 (Detroit)
05/24	Nashville Elite Giants. l 4–6 (Home)
05/25	Nashville Elite Giants. w 3–2 (Home)
05/25	Nashville Elite Giants. w 5–0 (Home)
05/26	Nashville Elite Giants. w 6–3 (Home)
05/29	KC Monarchs. l 0–1 (Home)

05/30	KC Monarchs. l 0–2 (Home)	08/11	Memphis Red Sox. w 6–4 (Home)
05/30	KC Monarchs. l 0–6 (Home)	08/12	Memphis Red Sox. w 6–3 (Home)
05/31	Memphis Red Sox. w 9–1 (Home)	08/13	Memphis Red Sox. l 2–4 (Home)
06/1	Memphis Red Sox. l 4–9 (Home)	08/16	Birmingham Black Barons. l 5–6 (Home)
06/1	Memphis Red Sox. w 6–4 (Home)	08/17	Birmingham Black Barons. w 6–1 (Home)
06/2	Memphis Red Sox. l 6–10 (Home)	08/17	Birmingham Black Barons. w 3–2 (Home)
06/3	Memphis Red Sox. l 2–3 (Home)	08/18	Birmingham Black Barons. w 3–1 (Home)
06/7	Birmingham Black Barons. l 2–5 (Home)	08/19	Birmingham Black Barons. w 7–0 (Home)
06/8	Birmingham Black Barons. w 10–3 (Home)	08/23	KC Monarchs. l 1–11 (Home)
06/8	Birmingham Black Barons. l 1–2 (Home)	08/24	KC Monarchs. w 4–0 (Home)
06/9	Birmingham Black Barons. l 3–5 (Home)	08/24	KC Monarchs. w 3–0 (Home)
06/10	Birmingham Black Barons. w 7–2 (Home)	08/25	KC Monarchs. w 4–3
06/14	St. Louis Stars. l 1–13 (St. Louis)	08/26	KC Monarchs. w 12–8
06/14	St. Louis Stars. l 1–3 (St. Louis)	08/30	Memphis Red Sox. w 8–6 (Home)
06/16	St. Louis Stars. l 1–6 (St. Louis)	08/31	Memphis Red Sox. w 3–2
06/16	St. Louis Stars. l 4–5 (St. Louis)	08/31	Memphis Red Sox. w 10–9
06/17	St. Louis Stars. l 2–9 (St. Louis)	09/1	Memphis Red Sox. l 9–11
06/21	KC Monarchs. l 4–7 (Home)	09/1	Memphis Red Sox. l 1–17
06/22	KC Monarchs. l 5–9 (Home)	09/2	Memphis Red Sox. w 10–3 (Home)
06/22	KC Monarchs. w 4–1 (Home)	09/5	Homestead Grays. l 5–11
06/23	KC Monarchs. w 9–8 (Home)	09/6	Homestead Grays. l 4–10
06/24	KC Monarchs. w 2–0 (Home)	09/6	Homestead Grays. l 6–8
06/28	St. Louis Stars. l 7–15 (St. Louis)	09/7	Homestead Grays. w 4–3 (Home)
06/29	St. Louis Stars. l 1–11 (St. Louis)	09/7	Homestead Grays. l 1–3 (Home)
06/29	St. Louis Stars. l 3–9 (St. Louis)	09/8	Homestead Grays. l 3–4
06/30	St. Louis Stars. l 3–15 (St. Louis)	09/10	Detroit Stars. w 3–0
07/1	St. Louis Stars. l 1–12 (St. Louis)	09/11	Detroit Stars. w 5–4 (Home)
07/11	KC Monarchs. w 12–10 (Kansas City)	09/13	Houston Black Buffaloes. w 4–2 (Home)
07/12	KC Monarchs. l 5–7 (Kansas City)	09/14	Houston Black Buffaloes. w 9–8
07/13	KC Monarchs. l 1–5 (Kansas City)	09/14	Houston Black Buffaloes. w 5–4
07/13	KC Monarchs. l 1–3 (Kansas City)	09/15	Houston Black Buffaloes. w 3–2
07/19	Louisville Black Caps. w 9–4 (Home)	09/16	Houston Black Buffaloes. l 3–10 (Home)
07/20	Louisville Black Caps. w 6–3 (Home)	09/20	Callahan All Stars. w 8–5 (Away)
07/20	Louisville Black Caps. w 11–8 (Home)	09/20	Callahan All Stars. w 10–5 (Home)
07/21	Louisville Black Caps. w 3–1 (Home)	09/21	Callahan All Stars. w 5–4 (Away)
07/22	Louisville Black Caps. w 6–5 (Home)	09/22	Callahan All Stars. w 7–6
07/26	Cuban Stars. w 8–6 (Home)	09/23	Callahan All Stars. l ? (Away)
07/27	Cuban Stars. w 5–2 (Home)	09/24	Callahan All Stars. l ? (Away)
07/27	Cuban Stars. w 5–3 (Home)	09/25	Callahan All Stars. w 7–4 (Away)
07/28	Cuban Stars. w 8–6 (Home)	09/25	Callahan All Stars. w 9–3 (Away)
07/29	Cuban Stars. w 6–3 (Home)	10/4	Shires All-Stars. w 6–5 (Home)
08/1	Memphis Red Sox. w 3–2 (Memphis)	10/4	Shires All-Stars. l 3–14 (Home)
08/2	Memphis Red Sox. l 4–5 (Memphis)	10/5	Shires All-Stars. w 6–1 (Home)
08/3	Memphis Red Sox. w 18–2 (Memphis)	10/6	Shires All-Stars. w 7–6 (Home)
08/3	Memphis Red Sox. l 3–4 (Memphis)	10/11	NY All-Stars. w 7–0 (Home)
08/4	Birmingham Black Barons. l 4–5 (Memphis)	10/12	NY All-Stars. l 2–3 (Home)
08/5	Birmingham Black Barons. l 1–3 (Memphis)	10/12	NY All-Stars. t 3–3 (Home)
08/10	Memphis Red Sox. w 4–3 (Home)	10/13	NY All-Stars. l 5–7 (Home)
08/10	Memphis Red Sox. l 0–1 (Home)		Total: 65-55-1

1931 Independents and Columbia American Giants

1931 Independents
Manager: Dave Malarcher. No Home Field. Based on scores published in the *Chicago Defender*.

04/19	Duffy Florals. w 3–2 (Away)	05/17	Detroit Stars. w 3–6 (Away)
05/02	Indianapolis ABCs. w 12–6 (Away)	05/17	Detroit Stars. l 7–1 (Away)
05/03	Indianapolis ABCs. w 13–5 (Away)	05/18	Detroit Stars. w 5–14 (Away)
05/03	Indianapolis ABCs. w 7–4 (Away)		Total: 6-2
05/16	Detroit Stars. l 5–0 (Away)		

1931 Columbia American Giants
Manager: Dave Malarcher. Home field: South Side Park (aka American Giant Park), 39th (Pershing) and Wentworth. Based on scores published in the *Chicago Defender*.

05/31	Nashville Elite Giants. w 4–1 (Home)		06/23	Indianapolis ABCs. l 5–8 (Home)
06/01	Nashville Elite Giants. w 5–2 (Home)		06/24	Indianapolis ABCs. l 1–5 (Home)
06/07	St. Louis Stars. l 1–7		06/27	Green's Chicago Giants. w 4–1 (Home)
06/08	St. Louis Stars. l 0–5		06/28	Cincinnati Tigers. w 3–2 (Home)
06/09	St. Louis Stars. t 3–3		06/28	Cincinnati Tigers. l 2–8 (Home)
06/14	Detroit Stars. l 3–5 (Home)		06/29	Cincinnati Tigers. w 11–6 (Home)
06/15	Detroit Stars. l 4–11 (Home)			Little Rock. w 18–0 (Away)
06/16	Detroit Stars. w 2–0 (Home)			Vera Cruz M. . w 8–0 (San Antonio, TX)
06/20	Indianapolis ABCs. l 4–7 (Home)			Minonk, IL. l 11–12 (Away)
06/21	Indianapolis ABCs. w 3–1 (Home)			Total: 9-10-1
06/22	Indianapolis ABCs. l 4–9 (Home)			Total both teams: 15-12-1

Cole's American Giants

Manager: Dave Malarcher. Home field: South Side Park (aka American Giant Park), 39th (Pershing) and Wentworth. Final Standing: Won playoff with Nashville Elite Giants four games to three, to win Negro Southern League Championship. Based on scores published in the *Chicago Defender*.

04/16	Winnebago. w 6–5		07/9	KC Monarchs. w 8–4 (Home)
04/17+	Chicago Heights. w 3–0		07/10	KC Monarchs. w 9–4 (Home)
04/23	Indianapolis ABCs. l 1–2 (Home)		07/10	KC Monarchs. l 0–11 (Home)
04/24	Indianapolis ABCs. w 13–0 (Home)		07/11	KC Monarchs. w 6–2 (Home)
04/25	Indianapolis ABCs. w 3–2 (Home)		07/12	KC Monarchs. l 1–5 (Home)
04/30	Detroit Wolves. l 4–9 (Home)		07/16	Monroe (LA) Giants. w 2–1 (Home)
05/1	Detroit Wolves. w 5–3		07/17	Monroe (LA) Giants. l 4–9 (Home)
05/2	Detroit Wolves. w 2–1		07/17	Monroe (LA) Giants. w 4–2 (Home)
05/3	Detroit Wolves. l ? (?)		07/18	Monroe (LA) Giants. w 6–1 (Home)
05/7	Birmingham Black Barons. w 7–2 (Home)		07/19	Monroe (LA) Giants. w ? (Home)
05/8	Birmingham Black Barons. w 13–3 (Home)		07/23	Columbus Turf. w 2–1 (Home)
05/9	Birmingham Black Barons. w 6–0 (Home)		07/24	Columbus Turf. w 11–10 (Home)
05/14	Louisville Black Caps. w 5–0 (Home)		07/24	Columbus Turf. w 6–4 (Home)
05/15	Louisville Black Caps. w 5–4 (Home)		07/25	Columbus Turf. w 8–6 (Home)
05/16	Louisville Black Caps. w 11–7 (Home)		07/26	Columbus Turf. w 5–2 (Home)
05/17	Louisville Black Caps. w 6–0 (Home)		08/7	Kansas City. l 1–8 (Kansas City)
05/21	Pittsburgh Crawfords. w 3–0		08/7	Kansas City. l 2–4 (Kansas City)
05/22	Pittsburgh Crawfords. w 4–0		08/8	Kansas City. l 4–11 (Kansas City)
05/23	Pittsburgh Crawfords. l 3–6		08/14	Homestead Grays. l 4–7 (Home)
05/24	Pittsburgh Crawfords. w 6–3		08/14	Homestead Grays. w 4–2 (Home)
06/3	Indianapolis ABCs. w 11–5 (Indianapolis)		08/15	Homestead Grays. l 1–7 (Home)
06/4	Indianapolis ABCs. w 6–5 (Indianapolis)		08/16	Homestead Grays . w 4–2 (Home)
06/5	Indianapolis ABCs. l 1–3 (Indianapolis)		08/20	House of David. w 3–0
06/5	Indianapolis ABCs. w 5–2 (Indianapolis)		08/21	Buck Weavers. w 10–7
06/11	Memphis Red Sox. w 4–3 (Home)		08/21	Buck Weavers. w 7–2
06/12	Memphis Red Sox. w 11–0 (Home)		08/27	KC Monarchs. w 2–1 (Home)
06/13	Memphis Red Sox. w 6–2 (Home)		08/28	KC Monarchs. l 0–17 (Home)
06/14	Memphis Red Sox. l 2–3 (Home)		08/28	KC Monarchs. l 4–3 (Home)
06/18	Indianapolis ABCs. l 3–12 (Home)		08/30	KC Monarchs. w 7–6 (Home)
06/19	Indianapolis ABCs. w 1–0 (Home)			Cincinnati Excelsior. l 0–1
06/19	Indianapolis ABCs. w 2–0 (Home)		**Negro Southern League Playoff**	
	Indianapolis ABCs. w 12–3 (Home)		09/4	Nashville Elite Giants. l 5–6 (Home)
06/21	Indianapolis ABCs. l 4–5 (Home)		09/4	Nashville Elite Giants. l 2–3 (Home)
06/25	Louisville Black Caps. w 5–0 (Home)			Nashville Elite Giants. w 5–3 (Home)
06/26	Louisville Black Caps. l 3–7 (Home)			Nashville Elite Giants. l ? (Nashville)
06/26	Louisville Black Caps. w 5–4 (Home)			Nashville Elite Giants. w ? (Nashville)
06/27	Louisville Black Caps. w 3–2 (Home)			Nashville Elite Giants. w ? (Nashville)
06/28	Louisville Black Caps. w 5–2 (Home)		09/18	Nashville Elite Giants. w 10–5 (Nashville)
	Logan Squares. w 4–1 (Away)		10/1	Nashville Elite Giants. w 9–2 (Nashville)
	Logan Squares. l 7–8 (Away)			Total: 53-25

1933 Cole's American Giants

Manager: Dave Malarcher. Played most home games at Indianapolis' Perry Stadium, 1501 West 16th Street; other home venue was Mills Park at West Lake and Kilpatrick Street in Chicago. Final Standing: Cole's American Giants claimed pennant for the first half of the season. The second half of the season was inconclusive, however Commissioner Gus Greenlee declared his own team, the Pittsburgh Crawfords, the overall pennant winner. The American Giants protested. Based on scores published in the *Chicago Defender*.

04/1	Crescent Stars. l 2–4 (New Orleans)		07/22	Pittsburgh Crawfords. l 4–14 (Away)
04/2	Crescent Stars. w 4–2 (New Orleans)		07/23	Pittsburgh Crawfords. l 12–13 (Cleveland)
04/3	Crescent Stars. w 3–2 (New Orleans)		07/23	Pittsburgh Crawfords. l 1–8 (Cleveland)
	Wiley College. w 9–0 (Marshall, TX)		07/24	Pittsburgh Crawfords. w 4–3 (Away)
	Wiley College. w 9–2 (Marshall, TX)		07/31	Columbus Blue Birds. w 5–2 (Columbus)
04/29	Indianapolis ABCs. w 7–5			Columbus Blue Birds. l 2–14
	(Indpls. Perry Stadium)		08/12	Shroyers. w 10–3 (Dayton)
04/30	Indianapolis ABCs. w 16–8		08/19	Nashville Elites. w 9–1 (Nashville)
	(Indpls. Perry Stadium)		08/20	Nashville Elites. w 6–2 (Nashville)
04/30	Indianapolis ABCs. w 6–3		08/20	Nashville Elites. w 5–3 (Nashville)
	(Indpls. Perry Stadium)		08/26	Pittsburgh Crawfords. l 2–12
05/1	Indianapolis ABCs. l 6–7			(Indpls. Perry Stadium)
	(Indpls. Perry Stadium)		08/27	Pittsburgh Crawfords. w 9–8
05/7	Duffy's Florals. w 8–1 (Mills Park)			(Indpls. Perry Stadium)
05/13	Homestead Grays. w 10–4 (Mills Park)		08/27	Pittsburgh Crawfords. w 4–0
05/14	Homestead Grays. w 4–3 (Mills Park)			(Indpls. Perry Stadium)
05/15	Homestead Grays. w 12–4 (Mills Park)		09/2	Chicago Mills. w 9–8 (Mills Park)
05/28	Nashville Elite Giants. w 8–5		09/3	Chicago Mills. l 2–9 (Mills Park)
	(Indpls. Perry Stadium)		09/4	Chicago Mills. w 12–6 (Mills Park)
05/28	Nashville Elite Giants. l 4–6		09/4	Chicago Mills. w 8–4 (Mills Park)
	(Indpls. Perry Stadium)		09/9	Homestead Grays. l 2–7 (Akron)
05/29	Nashville Elite Giants. w ?–2		09/10	Homestead Grays. l 5–8 (Pittsburgh)
	(Indpls. Perry Stadium)		09/10	Homestead Grays. l 3–5 (Pittsburgh)
06/3	Pittsburgh Crawfords. w 15–10 (Pittsburgh)		09/23	New Orleans Crescents. w 6–0
06/3	Pittsburgh Crawfords. w 3–1 (Pittsburgh)			(New Orleans)
06/4	Pittsburgh Crawfords. l 3–17 (Pittsburgh)		09/24	New Orleans Crescents. w 6–1
06/5	Pittsburgh Crawfords. l 1–3 (Pittsburgh)			(New Orleans)
06/14	Pittsburgh Crawfords. w ? (McKeesport)		09/30	New Orleans Crescents. l 1–6
	Baltimore Black Sox. w 7–3			(New Orleans)
	(Indpls. Perry Stadium)		10/1	New Orleans Crescents. l 4–5
	Baltimore Black Sox. l 0–4			(New Orleans)
	(Indpls. Perry Stadium)		10/1	New Orleans Crescents. w 3–0
07/7	Pittsburgh Crawfords. l 2–3 (McKeesport)			(New Orleans)
07/8	Pittsburgh Crawfords. w 5–3		10/1	New Orleans Crescents. w 7–3
	(McKeesport)			(New Orleans)
07/15	Columbus Blue Birds. w 11–7		10/5	Shevlin's ML All-Stars. w 3–0
	(Indpls. Perry Stadium.)			(Cincy Redland Field)
07/16	Columbus Blue Birds. w 4–0		10/15	Chicago Mills. l 12–14 (Mills Park)
	(Indpls. Perry Stadium.)		10/15	Chicago Mills. w 10–3 (Mills Park)
07/16	Columbus Blue Birds. w 7–4			Total: 38-20
	(Indpls. Perry Stadium)			
07/17	Columbus Blue Birds. w 7–3			
	(Indpls. Perry Stadium)			

1934 Cole's American Giants

Manager: Dave Malarcher. Home field: South Side Park (aka American Giant Park), 39th (Pershing) and Wentworth. Final Standing: Negro National League runner-up, lost playoff to Philadelphia. Outcome was protested due to violent outburst. Based on scores published in the *Chicago Defender*.

04/1	Crescent Stars. l 10–23 (New Orleans)		04/29	Memphis Red Sox. l 4–7 (Memphis)
04/1	Crescent Stars. w 7–1 (New Orleans)		05/26	KC Monarchs. w 4–1 (Home)
04/8	Crescent Stars. w 9–6 (New Orleans)		05/27	KC Monarchs. w 2–1 (Home)
04/8	Crescent Stars. l 1–4 (New Orleans)		05/27	KC Monarchs. w 2–0 (Home)
04/21	Canfield Ads. w 14–1 (New Orleans)		05/28	KC Monarchs. l 11–12 (Home)
04/22	Canfield Ads. l 3–4 (New Orleans)		05/31	Homestead Grays. l 0–3 (Away)
04/22	Canfield Ads. w 9–5 (New Orleans)		05/31	Homestead Grays. l 2–4 (Away)
04/28	Memphis Red Sox. w 11–5 (Memphis)		06/3	Philadelphia Stars. w 11–2 (Philadelphia)
04/29	Memphis Red Sox. l 1–2 (Memphis)		06/3	Philadelphia Stars. w 6–2 (Philadelphia)

06/4	Philadelphia Stars. l 3–6 (Philadelphia)
06/9	Homestead Grays. w 5–3 (Home)
06/10	Homestead Grays. w 10–1 (Home)
06/10	Homestead Grays. w 3–2 (Home)
06/11	Homestead Grays. l 4–5 (Home)
06/16	Pittsburgh Crawfords. w 1–0 (Home)
06/16	Pittsburgh Crawfords. w 2–0 (Home)
06/17	Pittsburgh Crawfords. l 0–7 (Home)
06/24	Nashville Elite Giants. w 12–3 (Nashville)
06/24	Nashville Elite Giants. w 7–1 (Nashville)
06/25	Nashville Elite Giants. w 11–6 (Nashville)
06/26	Nashville Elite Giants. l 1–7 (Nashville)
07/1	Cleveland Red Sox. w 10–3 (Home)
07/2	Cleveland Red Sox. w ? (Home)
07/2	Cleveland Red Sox. w ? (Home)
07/3	Cleveland Red Sox. w 7–2 (Home)
07/8	Pittsburgh Crawfords. l 0–3 (Home)
07/14	Bacharach Giants. w 8–7 (Gary, IN)
07/15	Bacharach Giants. w 6–5 (Home)
07/15	Bacharach Giants. w 14–4 (Home)
07/16	Bacharach Giants. w 5–4 (Home)

07/21	Baltimore Black Sox. w 23–2 (Gary, IN)
07/22	Baltimore Black Sox. w 5–4 (Home)
07/22	Baltimore Black Sox. w 6–5 (Home)
07/23	Baltimore Black Sox. w 4–3 (Home)
07/28	Philadelphia Stars. l 2–3 (Philadelphia)
07/28	Philadelphia Stars. l 3–9 (Philadelphia)
07/29	Newark Eagles. w 8–4 (Newark)
07/29	Newark Eagles. l 14–20 (Newark)
09/2	Philadelphia Stars. l 1–2 (Philadelphia)
09/2	Philadelphia Stars. t 1–1 (Philadelphia)
09/9	NY Black Yankees. w 4–3 (Away)
Negro National League playoff	
09/12	Philadelphia Stars. w 4–3 (Philadelphia)
09/16	Philadelphia Stars. w 3–0 (Home)
09/16	Philadelphia Stars. l 3–5 (Home)
09/17	Philadelphia Stars. w 2–1 (Home)
09/27	Philadelphia Stars. l 0–1 (Philadelphia)
09/29	Philadelphia Stars. l 1–4 (Philadelphia)
09/30	NY Black Yankees. l 2–3 (Philadelphia)
10/12	Philadelphia Stars. l 0–2 (Philadelphia)
	Total: 35-22-1

1935 Cole's American Giants

Manager: Larry Brown. Home field: South Side Park (aka American Giant Park), 39th (Pershing) and Wentworth. Final standing: Finished in fifth place first half and seventh out of eight in second half of the Negro National League season. Based on scores published in the *Chicago Defender*.

04/1	Houston. w 5–3 (Houston)
04/13	Wichita Falls. w 10–2 (Wichita Falls)
04/13	Wichita Falls. w 7–1 (Wichita Falls)
04/22	KC Monarchs. l 2–4 (Muskogee, OK)
04/27	Laredo. w 6–2 (Laredo, TX)
04/27	Laredo. w 8–1 (Laredo, TX)
05/5	NY Cubans. w 4–3 (Shrewberg)
05/11	Detroit Elites. w 4–1 (Home)
05/11	Detroit Elites. w 4–3 (Home)
05/18	Pittsburgh Crawfords. w 7–4 (Pittsburgh)
05/19	Pittsburgh Crawfords. l 0–1 (Pittsburgh)
05/19	Pittsburgh Crawfords. l 1–4 (Pittsburgh)
05/20	Pittsburgh Crawfords. w 3–2 (Pittsburgh)
05/25	Brooklyn Eagles. w 8–2 (Brooklyn)
05/25	Brooklyn Eagles. w 9–5 (Brooklyn)
05/26	Brooklyn Eagles. l 5–6 (Brooklyn)
05/26	Brooklyn Eagles. l 4–14 (Brooklyn)
06/1	Homestead Grays. l 4–5 (Home)
06/2	Homestead Grays. l 2–8 (Home)
06/2	Homestead Grays. w 7–4 (Home)
06/3	Homestead Grays. w 6–0 (Home)
06/22	Philadelphia Stars. l 1–2 (Philadelphia)
06/22	Philadelphia Stars. l 11–12 (Philadelphia)
06/23	Philadelphia Stars. w 9–4 (Philadelphia)
06/23	Philadelphia Stars. w 11–1 (Philadelphia)
06/29	Brooklyn Eagles. l 3–6 (Home)
06/30	Brooklyn Eagles. l 1–2 (Home)

06/30	Brooklyn Eagles. w 5–4 (Home)
07/1	Brooklyn Eagles. l 3–5 (Home)
07/13	New York Cubans. l 1–2 (Away)
07/14	New York Cubans. l 5–11 (Away)
07/14	New York Cubans. w 10–5 (Away)
	Cincinnati Tigers. l 3–7 (Crosley Field)
07/20	Pittsburgh Crawfords. l 9–12
07/21	Pittsburgh Crawfords. l 2–17 (Cleveland, OH)
07/21	Pittsburgh Crawfords. l 8–12 (Cleveland, OH)
07/22	Pittsburgh Crawfords. w 9–7 (Greenlee Field)
07/27	New York Cubans. l 6–8 (Home)
07/28	New York Cubans. w 10–2 (Home)
07/28	New York Cubans. l 4–9 (Home)
08/20	Des Moines. w 11–1 (Away)
08/21	Des Moines. w 14–3 (Away)
08/22	Des Moines. w 3–2 (Away)
08/24	Pittsburgh Crawfords. l 8–11 (Home)
08/25	Pittsburgh Crawfords. w 10–? (Home)
08/25	Pittsburgh Crawfords. l 5–7 (Home)
09/22	KC Monarchs. w 7–1 (Comiskey Park)
09/25	KC Monarchs. t 0–0 (Kansas City)
09/27	KC Monarchs. l 3–6 (Omaha)
09/29	KC Monarchs. w 6–0 (Kansas City)
	Total: 260-23-1

1936 Chicago American Giants (Horace Hall owner)

Manager: Bingo DeMoss. Home field: South Side Park (aka American Giant Park), 39th (Pershing) and Wentworth. Final Standing: The American Giants played as an independent team in 1936. Based on scores published in the *Chicago Defender*.

04/19   Claybrook Tigers. w 8–7 (Claybrook, AR)
04/19   Claybrook Tigers. l 3–4 (Claybrook, AR)
04/26   Montgomery (AL) Grays. w 3–2
05/24   KC Monarchs. l 5–10 (Kansas City)
Rock Island, IL. w 12–2 (Away)
05/30   KC Monarchs. w 4–1 (Home)
05/31   KC Monarchs. l 0–8 (Home)
05/31   KC Monarchs. l 5–9 (Home)
06/1   Duffy Florals. w 8–3 (Home)
06/1   Duffy Florals. w 3–0 (Home)
06/14   Cincinnati Tigers. w 17–8 (Home)
06/15   Cincinnati Tigers. w 3–2 (Home)
06/15   Cincinnati Tigers. w 4–3 (Home)

06/16   Cincinnati Tigers. w 3–2 (Home)
06/29   St. Louis Stars. w 6–0 (Home)
06/29   St. Louis Stars. w 6–1 (Home)
07/5   Indianapolis ABCs. l 2–9 (Home)
07/5   Indianapolis ABCs. w 6–2 (Home)
07/11   Statesville Prison. w 18–4 (Joliet, IL)
07/19   Chicago Mills. l 1–2 (West Side)
07/19   Chicago Mills. w 3–2 (West Side)
08/9   St. Louis Stars. w 6–2 (St. Louis)
08/9   St. Louis Stars. l 3–4 (St. Louis)
09/28   Claybrook Tigers. l 4–5 (Claybrook, AR)
        Total: 16-8

1937 Chicago American Giants

Manager: Candy Jim Taylor. Home field: South Side Park (aka American Giant Park), 39th (Pershing) and Wentworth. Final Standing: Negro American League runner up to Kansas City. Based on scores published in the *Chicago Defender*.

04/4   Laurel, MS. w 14–4 (Laurel, MS)
04/11   Piney Woods Col. . w 12–2
04/22   Pittsburgh Crawfords. w 7–6
        (Birmingham)
04/24   Birmingham Black Barons. w 8–7
        (Birmingham)
04/25   Birmingham Black Barons. l 1–3
        (Birmingham)
05/9   Memphis Red Sox. l 6–7 (Memphis)
05/9   Memphis Red Sox. w 5–3 (Memphis)
05/10   Memphis Red Sox. w 5–3 (Memphis)
05/16   KC Monarchs. l 0–4 (Kansas City)
05/16   KC Monarchs. w 2–0 (Kansas City)
05/22   Birmingham Black Barons. w 2–0 (home)
05/23   Birmingham Black Barons. l 4–11 (home)
05/23   Birmingham Black Barons. w 7–1 (home)
05/24   Birmingham Black Barons. w 8–6 (home)
05/29   Memphis Red Sox. w ? (home)
05/29   Memphis Red Sox. w ? (home)
05/30   Memphis Red Sox. w ? (home)
05/30   Memphis Red Sox. w 7–6 (home)
05/31   Memphis Red Sox. w 8–4 (home)
06/5   St. Louis Stars. w 9–4 (home)
06/6   St. Louis Stars. w 17–4 (home)
06/6   St. Louis Stars. w 11–0 (home)
06/20   Cincinnati Tigers. w ? (home)
06/21   Cincinnati Tigers. w 6–3 (home)
06/21   Cincinnati Tigers. l 4–5 (home)
07/3   KC Monarchs. w 2–0 (home)

07/4   KC Monarchs. l 2–5 (home)
07/4   KC Monarchs. w ? (home)
07/5   KC Monarchs. l 1–5 (home)
07/5   KC Monarchs. l 1–2 (home)
07/10   Indianapolis A's. w 8–3 (Indianapolis)
07/11   Indianapolis A's. w 13–8 (Indianapolis)
07/11   Indianapolis A's. w 7–5 (Indianapolis)
07/18   Birmingham Black Barons. w 6–0
        (Birmingham)
07/18   Birmingham Black Barons. w 11–8
        (Birmingham)
07/25   KC Monarchs. l 2–3 (Kansas City)
07/25   KC Monarchs. l 3–8 (Kansas City)
07/26   KC Monarchs. w 3–2 (Kansas City)
07/31   Detroit Stars. w 12–7 (home)
08/1   Detroit Stars. w 10–4 (home)
08/1   Detroit Stars. w 12–2 (home)
08/8   KC Monarchs. l 0–3 (Decatur, IL)
08/22   KC Monarchs. w 2–1 (home)
08/22   KC Monarchs. w 3–0 (home)
08/29   Homestead Grays. l 2–4 (home)
08/29   Homestead Grays. l 3–5 (home)
09/5   Memphis Red Sox. w 4–2 (home)
09/5   Memphis Red Sox. w 5–2 (home)
09/6   Atlanta Black Crackers. w 7–1 (home)
09/6   Atlanta Black Crackers. l 3–6 (home)
09/8   KC Monarchs. w 5–4 (Dayton, OH)
09/12   KC Monarchs. t 2–2
        Total: 36-15-1

1938 Chicago American Giants

Manager: Candy Jim Taylor. Home field: South Side Park (aka American Giant Park), 39th (Pershing) and Wentworth. Final Standing: Negro American League, fourth place out of seven teams. Based on scores published in the *Chicago Defender*.

03/27   Jacksonville Red Caps. w 5–4 (Jacksonville)
04/3   Jacksonville Red Caps. t 5–5 (Jacksonville)
04/17   Jacksonville Red Caps. w 5–4 (Jacksonville)
        KC Monarchs. w 10–4 (Texarkana)
        KC Monarchs. w 3–2 (Tyler)
        KC Monarchs. l 1–9 (Marshall)
        KC Monarchs. l 3–6 (Longview, TX)

04/24   KC Monarchs. w 9–2 (Dallas, TX)
        Birmingham Black Barons. w 5–0
        (Rickwood)
        Birmingham Black Barons. w 6–1
        (Rickwood)
05/8   Atlanta Black Crackers. w 8–2 (Atlanta)
05/8   Atlanta Black Crackers. w 4–1 (Atlanta)

Baltimore Elite Giants. l 3–9 (Jackson, TN)
Baltimore Elite Giants. l 3–4 (Jackson, TN)
Baltimore Elite Giants. w 12–9
   (Jackson, TN)
05/15 KC Monarchs. w 4–2 (Away)
05/15 KC Monarchs. l 0–3 (Away)
Memphis Red Sox. l 0–2 (Home)
Memphis Red Sox. l 0–2 (Home)
Memphis Red Sox. w 9–1 (Home)
05/28 KC Monarchs. l 1–3 (Home)
05/29 KC Monarchs. l 0–5 (Home)
05/29 KC Monarchs. l 1–6 (Home)
05/30 KC Monarchs. w 6–5 (Home)
06/?? Jacksonville Red Caps. w 7–6 (?)
06/?? Jacksonville Red Caps. w 8–4 (?)
06/11 Memphis Red Sox. t 4–4 (Memphis)
06/12 Memphis Red Sox. l 3–4 (Memphis)
06/12 Memphis Red Sox. l 3–5 (Memphis)
06/27 Indianapolis/Mound City. l 2–10 (Home)
06/28 KC Monarchs. l 4–7 (Milwaukee)
07/3 Birmingham Black Barons. w 4–3 (Home)
07/4 Birmingham Black Barons. w 12–2 (Home)
07/4 Birmingham Black Barons. l 2–6 (Home)
07/16 KC Monarchs. l 10–13 (Winnipeg)
07/16 KC Monarchs. l 4–10 (Winnipeg)

07/17 KC Monarchs. w 4–3 (Fargo, ND)
KC Monarchs. w 4–3 (Regina)
07/31 KC Monarchs. w 7–2
07/31 KC Monarchs. l 1–3
08/1 Palmer House Indians. l 2–6
08/6 Indianapolis/Mound City. l 6–10 (Home)
08/7 Indianapolis/Mound City. w 5–3 (Home)
08/7 Indianapolis/Mound City. w 4–3 (Home)
08/4 Bacharach Giants. w 16–3 (Toledo)
08/13 Atlanta Black Crackers. w 12–5 (Home)
08/14 Atlanta Black Crackers. w 6–3 (Home)
08/14 Atlanta Black Crackers. w 4–2 (Home)
08/20 Birmingham Black Barons. l 11–15
   (Leeds, AL)
08/21 Birmingham Black Barons. w 11–3
   (Birmingham)
08/21 Birmingham Black Barons. w 4–1
   (Birmingham)
08/27 Palmer House Indians. l 3–5 (Home)
Memphis Red Sox. w 12–0
Memphis Red Sox. l 1–4
Memphis Red Sox. l 5–8
Memphis Red Sox. l 1–5
Total: 29-25-2

1939 Chicago American Giants

Manager: Candy Jim Taylor. Home field: South Side Park (aka American Giant Park), 39th (Pershing) and Wentworth. Final Standing: Played in Negro American League, no final standings. Based on scores published in the *Chicago Defender*.

04/?? Jacksonville Red Caps. w 8–3 (Jacksonville)
04/8 Jacksonville Red Caps. w 6–3 (Palatka, FL)
04/16 Ethiopian Clowns. w 7–3 (Miami)
04/23 Nashville Elite Giants. l 3–5 (Nashville, TN)
04/23 Nashville Elite Giants. l 0–5 (Nashville, TN)
04/26 Atlanta Black Crackers. l 1–5 (Griffin, GA)
04/30 KC Monarchs. l 7–8 (Dallas, TX)
05/7 Memphis Red Sox. l 2–3 (Memphis)
05/7 Memphis Red Sox. l 0–9 (Memphis)
05/14 Cleveland Bears. l 3–5 (Cleveland)
05/14 Cleveland Bears. l 1–5 (Cleveland)
05/20 KC Monarchs. w 4–1 (Home)
05/21 KC Monarchs. w 4–3 (Home)
05/21 KC Monarchs. w 5–0 (Home)
05/22 KC Monarchs. l 5–6 (Home)
05/28 Memphis Red Sox. l 5–6 (Home)
05/28 Memphis Red Sox. w 5–2 (Home)
05/29 Memphis Red Sox. l 7–8 (Home)
05/31 Memphis Red Sox. w 7–6 (Home)
05/31 Memphis Red Sox. w 8–2 (Home)
06/3 Cleveland Bears. w 11–1 (Home)
06/4 Cleveland Bears. w 3–2 (Home)
06/4 Cleveland Bears. w 4–3 (Home)
06/5 Cleveland Bears. w 18–14 (Home)
06/17 St. Louis Stars. w 4–3 (Home)
06/18 St. Louis Stars. w 3–1 (Home)
06/18 St. Louis Stars. w 5–0 (Home)
06/19 St. Louis Stars. w 8–2 (Home)
06/25 Memphis Red Sox. w 5–4 (away)
06/25 Memphis Red Sox. l 3–5 (away)
06/26 Memphis Red Sox. w 7–2 (away)
06/27 Memphis Red Sox. w 3–1 (Monroe, LA)

07/2 KC Monarchs. l 3–4 (away)
07/2 KC Monarchs. l 1–3 (away)
07/4 KC Monarchs. l 5–7 (away)
07/4 KC Monarchs. w 9–5 (away)
07/7 Toledo Crawfords. l 6–14 (Milwaukee)
07/8 Toledo Crawfords. l 2–3 (Home)
07/9 Toledo Crawfords. w 9–8 (Home)
07/10 Brooklyn Royal Giants. l 3–9 (Home)
07/18 KC Monarchs. l 4–9 (Regina, Canada)
07/19 KC Monarchs. l 3–6 (Regina, Canada)
07/21 KC Monarchs. w 4–2 (Regina, Canada)
07/23 KC Monarchs. w 7–6 (Bismarck, ND)
07/29 KC Monarchs. l 0–5 (Home)
07/30 KC Monarchs. l 1–4 (Home)
07/30 KC Monarchs. l 2–6 (Home)
08/12 Cleveland Bears. w 4–2 (Home)
08/13 Cleveland Bears. l 2–4 (Home)
08/13 Cleveland Bears. l 1–3 (Home)
08/14 Cleveland Bears. l 10–14 (Home)
08/20 St. Louis Stars. w 6–4 (Home)
08/20 St. Louis Stars. l 5–10 (Home)
08/27 Memphis Red Sox. l 4–6 (away)
08/27 Memphis Red Sox. w 3–2 (away)
09/2 Memphis Red Sox. w 7–2 (Home)
09/2 Memphis Red Sox. w 13–9 (Home)
09/3 Memphis Red Sox. l 5–6 (Home)
09/3 Memphis Red Sox. w 4–2 (Home)
09/10 Spencer Coals. w 6–2 (Shrewbridge)
09/10 Spencer Coals. w 11–3 (Shrewbridge)
09/17 Satchel Paige All Stars. l 5–10 (Home)
09/17 Satchel Paige All Stars. l 0–1 (Home)
Total: 31-32

1940 Chicago American Giants

Manager: Wilson Redus. Home field: South Side Park (aka American Giant Park), 39th (Pershing) and Wentworth. Final Standing: Finished second to last in Negro American League six team race in first half of season, no published results for second half, Kansas City Monarchs were declared pennant winners. Based on scores published in the *Chicago Defender.*

04/21	NY Black Yankees. l 2–6 (Little Rock)		06/30	Memphis Red Sox. w 5–4 (Home)
04/21	NY Black Yankees. l 0–1 (Little Rock)		06/30	Memphis Red Sox. l 1–17 (Home)
04/28	NAL All-Stars. w 7–3 (Greenville, MS)		07/7	Brooklyn Royal Giants. w 4–3 (Home)
05/5	Memphis Red Sox. l 3–4 (Memphis)		07/7	Brooklyn Royal Giants. l 6–7 (Home)
05/5	Memphis Red Sox. w 5–1 (Memphis)		07/14	New Orleans/St. Louis Stars. w 4–3 (Home)
05/8	Homestead Grays. l 2–5 (Monroe, LA)		07/14	New Orleans/St. Louis Stars. w 8–7 (Home)
05/9	Homestead Grays. w 9–4 (Eldorado, AR)		07/21	Birmingham Black Barons. w 3–2 (Home)
05/18	Cleveland Bears. l 4–5 (Chicago)		07/21	Birmingham Black Barons. w 12–2 (Home)
05/19	Cleveland Bears. l 6–9 (Chicago)		07/28	KC Monarchs. l 7–12 (Home)
05/19	Cleveland Bears. w 6–4 (Chicago)		07/28	KC Monarchs. w 3–1 (Home)
05/26	Indianapolis Crawfords. l 2–8 (Indianapolis)		08/4	Cleveland Bears. w 5–3 (Home)
06/2	Ethiopian Clowns. l 2–4 (Chicago)		08/4	Cleveland Bears. w 4–3 (Home)
06/2	Ethiopian Clowns. l 3–8 (Chicago)		08/11	Indpls./Toledo Crawfords. l 1–2 (Home)
06/9	KC Monarchs. l 0–11 (Kansas City)		08/11	Indpls./Toledo Crawfords. w 7–3 (Home)
06/9	KC Monarchs. w 6–2 (Kansas City)		08/25	Memphis Red Sox. l 2–5 (Memphis)
06/16	KC Monarchs. l 2–3 (Chicago)		08/25	Memphis Red Sox. l 6–10 (Memphis)
06/16	KC Monarchs. l 4–6 (Chicago)		09/1	Memphis Red Sox. l 3–5 (Home)
06/23	Indpls./Toledo Crawfords. w 20–4 (Louisville, KY)		09/2	Memphis Red Sox. w 3–2 (Home)
06/23	Indpls./Toledo Crawfords. l 4–7 (Louisville, KY)		09/8	KC Monarchs. l 2–9 (Home)
			09/8	KC Monarchs. l 3–9 (Home)
				Total: 17-22

1941 Chicago American Giants

Manager: Candy Jim Taylor. Home Field: Comiskey Park. Final Standing: Finished in last place in the Negro American League six team race, Kansas City Monarchs were declared pennant winners.

03/29	Jacksonville Red Caps. w 4–1 (Jacksonville)		07/2	Kansas City Monarchs. l 8–9 (Terre Haute, IN)
05/11	Memphis Red Sox. l 2–7 (Memphis)		07/6	Kansas City Monarchs. w 2–0 (Kansas City)
05/11	Memphis Red Sox. w 5–2 (Memphis)		07/6	Kansas City Monarchs. l 0–3 (Kansas City)
05/18	Kansas City Monarchs. l 1–3 (Comiskey)		07/20	St. Louis Stars. l 7–11 (Crosley Field)
05/18	Kansas City Monarchs. w 7–4 (Comiskey)		07/24	Brooklyn Royal Giants. w 8–3 (Springfield, IL)
05/25	St. Louis Stars. w 9–8 (Comiskey)		08/3	Jacksonville Red Caps. w 8–3 (Terre Haute, IN)
05/25	St. Louis Stars. l 6–9 (Comiskey)			
06/14	Kansas City Monarchs. l 0–5 (Canton, OH)		08/3	Jacksonville Red Caps. l 0–3 (Terre Haute, IN)
06/17	Kansas City Monarchs. w 8–4 (Huntington, WV)		08/25	Baltimore Elite Giants. w 8–3 (Baltimore)
06/22	Memphis Red Sox. w 5–4 (Comiskey)		08/31	Kansas City Monarchs. l 3–8 (Comiskey)
06/22	Memphis Red Sox. w 3–0 (Comiskey)		09/14	Kansas City Monarchs. l 4–11 (Detroit)
06/26	New York Black Yankees. l 3–5 (Indianapolis)		09/14	Kansas City Monarchs. l 3–6 (Detroit)
06/29	Birmingham Black Barons. l 3–4 (Rickwood)		09/21	Spencer Coals. l 6–7 (away)
			09/21	Spencer Coals. w 2–0 (away)
06/29	Birmingham Black Barons. w 4–0 (Rickwood)			Total: 13-14

1942 Chicago American Giants

Manager: Candy Jim Taylor. Home Field: Comiskey Park. Final Standing: No published result, finished the season well off the pace, the Kansas City Monarchs were declared Negro American League pennant winners. Based on scores published in the *Chicago Defender.*

04/5	Helena, Arkansas. w 16–5 (Helena, AR)		06/21	St. Paul Gophers. l 3–4 (St. Paul, MN)
04/12	Memphis Red Sox. w 8–7 (Little Rock, AR)		06/21	St. Paul Gophers. l 1–5 (St. Paul, MN)
04/16	Birmingham Black Barons. l 7–3		06/24	House of David. w 10–2 (Defiance, OH)
	(Rickwood)		06/28	KC Monarchs. l 7–9 (Milwaukee)
04/19	Memphis Red Sox. w 3–1 (Memphis)		07/4	Cleveland Buckeyes. l 2–5 (Cincinnati)
04/19	Memphis Red Sox. w 7–3 (Memphis)		07/5	Cleveland Buckeyes. l 0–7 (Cleveland)
05/10	KC Monarchs. l 4–7 (Comiskey)		07/6	Cleveland Buckeyes. l 0–6 (Youngstown)
05/10	KC Monarchs. l 0–6 (Comiskey)		07/12	Baltimore Grays. l 2–3 (Louisville)
05/17	Birmingham Black Barons. w 6–4		07/12	Baltimore Grays. w 8–2 (Louisville)
	(Rickwood)		07/19	KC Monarchs. l 5–11 (Comiskey)
05/17	Birmingham Black Barons. l 0–3		07/19	KC Monarchs. l 4–5 (Comiskey)
	(Rickwood)		07/18	East Chicago. w 10–1 (East Chicago)
05/24	Memphis Red Sox. l 4–5 (Memphis, TN)		08/8	Black Yankees. l 0–8 (Yankee Stadium)
05/24	Memphis Red Sox. l 2–3 (Memphis, TN)		08/28	Homestead Grays. l 0–3 (Comiskey)
05/31	Memphis Red Sox. l 2–8 (Comiskey)		09/20	Winkler Motors . w 2–1 (Rockols Stadium)
06/11	House of David. w 7–3 (Springfield, IL)		09/20	Winkler Motors . w 10–1 (Rockols Stadium)
06/14	Birmingham Black Barons. l 4–6 (Chicago)			Total: 10-21
06/14	Birmingham Black Barons. l 3–7 (Chicago)			

1943 Chicago American Giants

Manager: Ted Double Duty Radcliffe. Home Field: Comiskey Park. Final Standing: Negro American League runner up, lost playoff to Birmingham Black Barons. Based on scores published in the *Chicago Defender*.

04/25	Memphis Red Sox. l 4–7 (Memphis)		07/4	Birmingham Black Barons. w ?
04/25	Memphis Red Sox. l 0–3 (Memphis)			(Rickwood)
05/2	Memphis Red Sox. w 10–5 (Memphis)		07/11	Cincy Clowns. w 5–2 (Crosley Field)
05/2	Memphis Red Sox. w 10–2 (Memphis)		07/11	Cincy Clowns. l 2–3 (Crosley Field)
05/8	Birmingham Black Barons. w 7–6		07/25	KC Monarchs. w 8–5 (Comiskey)
	(Montgomery, AL)		07/25	KC Monarchs. w 4–3 (Comiskey)
05/9	Birmingham Black Barons. w 4–3		08/7	Great Lakes Naval. w 7–3
	(Montgomery, AL)			(G. L. Naval Station)
05/10	Birmingham Black Barons. l 2–3		08/22	Memphis Red Sox. w 8–2
	(Birmingham)			(New Orleans)
05/10	Birmingham Black Barons. w 9–4		08/22	Memphis Red Sox. l 2–4
	(Birmingham)			(New Orleans)
05/16	KC Monarchs. l 0–2 (Kansas City)		08/29	Memphis Red Sox. w 11–7 (Memphis)
05/16	KC Monarchs. l 0–1 (Kansas City)		08/29	Memphis Red Sox. w 7–2 (Memphis)
05/23	Cincy Clowns. l 0–1 (Crosley Field)		09/2	Memphis Red Sox. l 0–2 (Comiskey)
05/23	Cincy Clowns. l 1–2 (Crosley Field)		**Negro American League Playoff**	
05/30	KC Monarchs. l 3–4 (Comiskey)		09/13	Birmingham Black Barons. w 3–2
05/31	KC Monarchs. l 3–6 (Comiskey)			(Toledo, OH)
05/31	KC Monarchs. l 1–5 (Comiskey)		09/14	Birmingham Black Barons. l 5–16
06/6	Memphis Red Sox. l 1–3 (Comiskey)			(Columbus, OH)
06/6	Memphis Red Sox. l 0–2 (Comiskey)		09/15	Birmingham Black Barons. w 5–4
06/13	Cleveland Buckeyes. w 5–2 (Comiskey)			(Dayton, OH)
06/13	Cleveland Buckeyes. w 7–3 (Comiskey)		09/17	Birmingham Black Barons. l 1–4
06/20	Cleveland Buckeyes. w 4–2 (Cleveland)			(Montgomery, AL)
06/20	Cleveland Buckeyes. w 9–0 (Cleveland)		09/19	Birmingham Black Barons. l 0–1
06/27	Cleveland Buckeyes. w 6–3 (Cleveland)			(Birmingham, AL)
07/4	Birmingham Black Barons. l 1–5			Total: 20-19
	(Rickwood)			

1944 Chicago American Giants

Manager: Bingo DeMoss (April–June), Lloyd Ducky Davenport (July), John Bissant (August–September). Home Field: Comiskey Park. Final Standing: Last place in the first half and third place in the second half of the Negro American League season six team race. Based on scores published in the *Chicago Defender*.

04/9	Memphis Red Sox. w 7–1 (Memphis)		05/7	Birmingham Black Barons. l 3–5
04/16	Memphis Red Sox. l 6–7 (Dallas)			(Comiskey)
04/16	Memphis Red Sox. l 1–3 (Dallas)		05/7	Birmingham Black Barons. l 2–7
04/29	Memphis Red Sox. l 5–6 (Little Rock)			(Comiskey)
04/29	Memphis Red Sox. l 3–4 (Little Rock)		05/14	Memphis Red Sox. l 4–5 (Comiskey)

05/14	Memphis Red Sox. w 2–1 (Comiskey)	07/14	Cleveland Buckeyes. w 3–2 (Belleville, IL)
05/28	KC Monarchs. l 5–8 (Kansas City)	07/16	Cincy-Indy Clowns. w 3–1 (Comiskey)
05/28	KC Monarchs. l 4–6 (Kansas City)	07/16	Cincy-Indy Clowns. l 9–1 (Comiskey)
06/4	Cincy-Indy Clowns. l 3–7 (Indianapolis)	07/23	Memphis Red Sox. w 4–1 (Memphis)
06/4	Cincy-Indy Clowns. l 1–3 (Indianapolis)	07/23	Memphis Red Sox. w 4–2 (Memphis)
06/11	Atlanta Black Crackers. w 11–2 (Indianapolis)	07/31	Birmingham Black Barons. l 2–3 (Rickwood Field)
06/11	Atlanta Black Crackers. l 1–4 (Indianapolis)	07/31	Birmingham Black Barons. l 1–7 (Rickwood Field)
06/18	Cleveland Buckeyes. w 5–4 (Comiskey)	08/6	KC Monarchs. l 0–2 (Detroit Briggs)
06/18	Cleveland Buckeyes. l 1–3 (Comiskey)	08/6	KC Monarchs. w 14–8 (Detroit Briggs)
06/25	Cleveland Buckeyes. l 4–5 (Cleveland)	08/20	Memphis Red Sox. l 2–3 (Comiskey)
06/25	Cleveland Buckeyes. l 1–4 (Cleveland)	08/20	Memphis Red Sox. l 2–6 (Comiskey)
07/2	Memphis Red Sox. l 5–10 (Detroit Briggs)	08/25	Cleveland Buckeyes. l 2–12 (South Bend)
07/2	Memphis Red Sox. w 5–1 (Detroit Briggs)	08/30	KC Monarchs. w 3–1 (Comiskey)
07/9	KC Monarchs. l 1–3 (Comiskey)	08/31	Cleveland Buckeyes. l 2–5 (Hammond, IN)
07/9	KC Monarchs. w 3–0 (Comiskey)	09/17	Memphis Red Sox. w 5–0 (Comiskey)
07/13	Cincy-Indy Clowns. w 12–2 (Terre Haute)		Total: 13-26

1945 Chicago American Giants

Manager: Candy Jim Taylor. Home Field: Comiskey Park. Final Standing: Fourth place in the first half and second place in the second half of the six team Negro American League; the Cleveland Buckeyes won the pennant. Based on scores published in the *Chicago Defender*.

04/8	Memphis Red Sox. l 0–8 (Memphis)	07/29	KC Monarchs. l 0–2 (Kansas City)
04/12	KC Monarchs. t 10–10 (Memphis)	08/5	Cleveland Buckeyes. l 3–7 (Detroit Briggs)
04/22	Cleveland Buckeyes. l 0–2 (Dallas)	08/5	Cleveland Buckeyes. l 2–3 (Detroit Briggs)
04/22	Cleveland Buckeyes. l 6–7 (Dallas)	08/12	Homestead Grays. w 4–3 (D.C. Griffith)
04/29	Cleveland Buckeyes. l 5–8 (New Orleans)	08/12	Homestead Grays. l 0–7 (D.C. Griffith)
04/29	Cleveland Buckeyes. l 4–8 (New Orleans)		NY Black Yankees. w 1–0 (Yankee Stadium)
05/6	KC Monarchs. l 2–6 (Kansas City)		
05/13	Cleveland Buckeyes. l 2–14 (Indianapolis)	08/24	KC Monarchs. w 6–3 (Comiskey)
07/1	Cincy Clowns. l 2–3 (Columbus, OH)	08/26	KC Monarchs. w 15–0 (Comiskey)
07/1	Cincy Clowns. w 8–4 (Columbus, OH)	08/26	KC Monarchs. w 2–1 (Comiskey)
07/8	Memphis Red Sox. l 3–4 (Memphis)	09/2	Cleveland Buckeyes. l 2–6 (Cleveland)
07/8	Memphis Red Sox. l 2–3 (Memphis)	09/2	Cleveland Buckeyes. l 0–10 (Cleveland)
07/13	Memphis Red Sox. w 6–5 (Comiskey)	09/9	Cincy Clowns. w 10–7 (Comiskey)
07/15	Memphis Red Sox. w 4–1 (Comiskey)	09/9	Cincy Clowns. w 6–5 (Comiskey)
07/15	Memphis Red Sox. w 5–1 (Comiskey)	09/16	Birmingham Black Barons. l 2–4 (Comiskey)
07/20	Memphis Red Sox. t 5–5 (Dayton, OH)		
07/22	Birmingham Black Barons. w 8–2 (Comiskey)	09/16	Birmingham Black Barons. l 0–3 (Comiskey)
07/22	Birmingham Black Barons. w 3–2 (Comiskey)	09/23	Memphis Red Sox. l 4–5 (Memphis)
07/27	Cincy Clowns. w 4–0 (Comiskey)		Total: 14-19-2

1946 Chicago American Giants

Manager: Candy Jim Taylor. Home Field: Comiskey Park. Final Standing: Finished last in Negro American League six team race in first half of season, no published results for second half, Kansas City Monarchs were declared pennant winners. Based on scores published in the *Chicago Defender*.

03/31	Birmingham Black Barons. l 3–4 (Birmingham)	05/19	KC Monarchs. l 1–2 (Kansas City)
		05/20	KC Monarchs. l 2–4 (Kansas City)
04/07	Memphis Red Sox. w 14–7 (Pine Bluff)	05/30	Cleveland Buckeyes. l 0–2 (Comiskey)
04/15	Memphis Red Sox. w 8–7 (Baton Rouge)	05/30	Cleveland Buckeyes. w 8–3 (Comiskey)
04/20	KC Monarchs. l 1–9 (Houston)	06/02	Birmingham Black Barons. w 3–2 (Comiskey)
04/20	KC Monarchs. l 3–6 (Houston)		
05/05	KC Monarchs. w 9–2 (Comiskey)	06/02	Birmingham Black Barons. l 1–2 (Comiskey)
05/05	KC Monarchs. l 3–4 (Comiskey)	06/06	Birmingham Black Barons. l 2–11 (Comiskey)
05/12	Indianapolis Clowns. t 3–3 (Comiskey)		
05/19	KC Monarchs. l 1–3 (Kansas City)	06/09	Indianapolis Clowns. l 4–6 (Comiskey)

06/09	Indianapolis Clowns. w 4–3 (Comiskey)	07/24	Memphis Red Sox. l 2–7 (Danville, IL)
06/10	Indianapolis Clowns. l 1–7 (Davenport, IA)	07/28	Memphis Red Sox. w 6–1 (Memphis)
06/11	Indianapolis Clowns. w 10–4 (Springfield, IL)	07/28	Memphis Red Sox. l 3–4 (Memphis)
		08/04	Birmingham Black Barons. w 7–4 (Birmingham)
06/16	Memphis Red Sox. l 4–8 (Memphis)	08/04	Birmingham Black Barons. l 0–2 (Birmingham)
06/16	Memphis Red Sox. w 19–5 (Memphis)	08/11	KC Monarchs. l 3–4 (Kansas City)
06/23	Birmingham Black Barons. l 4–5 (Birmingham)	08/11	KC Monarchs. w 2–0 (Kansas City)
06/23	Birmingham Black Barons. w 2–1 (Birmingham)	08/18	Cincinnati Crescents. w 5–1 (Crosley Field)
07/07	Birmingham Black Barons. w 2–1 (Comiskey)	08/18	Cincinnati Crescents. l 0–3 (Crosley Field)
07/07	Birmingham Black Barons. l 2–7 (Comiskey)	08/25	Indianapolis Clowns. l 0–8 (Comiskey)
		08/25	Indianapolis Clowns. w 4–3 (Comiskey)
07/11	Birmingham Black Barons. l 0–10 (Comiskey)	08/29	Cleveland Buckeyes. l 8–13 (Comiskey)
07/14	Memphis Red Sox. l 0–2 (Comiskey)	09/01	Cleveland Buckeyes. w 17–6 (Cleveland)
07/14	Memphis Red Sox. w 4–1 (Comiskey)	09/01	Cleveland Buckeyes. l 4–8 (Cleveland)
07/18	Memphis Red Sox. l 3–4 (Comiskey)	09/03	Cleveland Buckeyes. l 5–6 (Cleveland)
07/21	Homestead Grays. l 0–13 (Comiskey)	09/03	Cleveland Buckeyes. l 2–3 (Cleveland)
07/21	Homestead Grays. l 7–9 (Comiskey)	09/08	Birmingham Black Barons. l 4–5 (Comiskey)

Total: 17-31-1

1947 Chicago American Giants

Manager: Candy Jim Taylor. Home Field: Comiskey Park. Final Standing: No published standings. Based on scores published in the *Chicago Defender*.

03/30	Birmingham Black Barons. w 13–6 (Birmingham)	06/29	Memphis Red Sox. l 3–4 (Comiskey)
03/30	Birmingham Black Barons. l 2–4 (Birmingham)	06/29	Memphis Red Sox. l 0–3 (Comiskey)
		07/4	Memphis Red Sox. l 1–4 (Comiskey)
04/13	Baltimore Elite Giants. l 1–4 (Nashville)	07/4	Memphis Red Sox. w 2–1 (Comiskey)
	Cleveland Buckeyes. l 0–9 (Chicago)	07/13	Indianapolis Clowns. w 7–4 (Indianapolis)
	Cleveland Buckeyes. l 3–4 (Chicago)	07/20	Kansas City Monarchs. l 5–6 (Crosley Field)
	Kansas City Monarchs. l 3–13 (Kansas City)		
	Kansas City Monarchs. w 8–7 (Kansas City)	07/20	Kansas City Monarchs. l 1–7 (Crosley Field)
05/11	Memphis Red Sox. l 3–11 (Memphis)	08/3	NY Black Yankees. l 5–10 (Comiskey)
05/11	Memphis Red Sox. w 14–1 (Memphis)	08/3	NY Black Yankees. w 2–0 (Comiskey)
05/18	Kansas City Monarchs. l 6–10 (Comiskey)	08/7	NY Black Yankees. w 9–4 (Comiskey)
05/18	Kansas City Monarchs. w 7–2 (Comiskey)	08/9	East Chicago Giants. w 2–1 (East Chicago)
05/25	Cleveland Buckeyes. l 4–6 (Comiskey)		
05/25	Cleveland Buckeyes. w 3–2 (Comiskey)	08/10	Cleveland Buckeyes. l 0–16 (Comiskey)
05/30	Cleveland Buckeyes. l 3–6 (Cleveland)	08/10	Cleveland Buckeyes. l 2–7 (Comiskey)
05/31	Cleveland Buckeyes. l 0–2 (Cleveland)	08/17	Cubans. l Polo Grounds
05/31	Birmingham Black Barons. l 0–3 (Birmingham)	08/15	Brooklyn Bushwicks. l 1–6 (Dexter Park)
		08/28	Homestead Grays. w 3–2 (Griffith Stadium)
06/1	Birmingham Black Barons. l 0–2 (Birmingham)	08/31	Indianapolis Clowns. w 10–2 (Indianapolis)
06/8	Memphis Red Sox. l 5–13 (Memphis)	08/31	Indianapolis Clowns. w 7–5 (Indianapolis)
06/8	Memphis Red Sox. l 5–6 (Memphis)		Globetrotter Baseball. l 2–7 (Indianapolis)
06/15	Indianapolis Clowns. w 9–0 (Comiskey)		Indianapolis Clowns. w 10–1 (Indianapolis)
06/15	Indianapolis Clowns. l 0–5 (Comiskey)		Indianapolis Clowns. w 2–1 (Indianapolis)
06/22	Birmingham Black Barons. l 2–4 (Comiskey)		Birmingham Black Barons. w 10–9 (Comiskey)
06/22	Birmingham Black Barons. w 2–1 (Comiskey)		Birmingham Black Barons. l 0–5 (Comiskey)
06/26	Birmingham Black Barons. l 3–4 (Comiskey)		Total: 28-29

1948 Chicago American Giants

Manager: Quincy Trouppe. Home Field: Comiskey Park. Final Standing: Finished in last place in the six team Negro American League for the second half of the season, no results for the first half of the season. Based on scores published in the *Chicago Defender*.

04/11	Baltimore Elite Giants. l 1–2 (Nashville)
04/18	Cleveland Buckeyes. w 5–4 (Little Rock)
04/25	Cleveland Buckeyes. w 8–1 (Comiskey)
05/2	Indianapolis Clowns. w 4–1 (New Orleans)
05/2	Indianapolis Clowns. l 1–4 (New Orleans)
05/11	KC Monarchs. w 4–3 (Kansas City)
05/12	KC Monarchs. l 0–1 (Muscogee, OK)
05/16	Memphis Red Sox. l 0–8 (Comiskey)
05/16	Memphis Red Sox. l 3–5 (Comiskey)
05/23	Birmingham Black Barons. w 7–5 (Crosley Field)
05/23	Birmingham Black Barons. w 5–2 (Crosley Field)
06/4	Cleveland Buckeyes. l 1–2 (Comiskey)
06/6	Indianapolis Clowns. l 2–4 (Comiskey)
06/6	Indianapolis Clowns. w 5–4 (Comiskey)
06/11	Kansas City Monarchs. l 0–1 (Comiskey)
06/13	Birmingham Black Barons. w 4–3 (Comiskey)
06/13	Birmingham Black Barons. l 1–3 (Comiskey)
06/20	Birmingham Black Barons. l 12–13 (Rickwood)

06/23	Birmingham Black Barons. w 7–4 (New Orleans)
06/29	Memphis Red Sox. l 3–7 (Houston, TX)
07/9	Cole Lenzis semi-pro. l
07/11	KC Monarchs. l 6–10 (Comiskey)
07/11	KC Monarchs. l 2–5 (Comiskey)
07/18	Indianapolis Clowns. w 1–0 (Comiskey)
07/18	Indianapolis Clowns. l 2–5 (Comiskey)
07/22	Memphis Red Sox. l 6–13 (Decatur, IL)
07/23	Indianapolis Clowns. w 4–0 (Comiskey)
07/25	Memphis Red Sox. l 2–4 (Comiskey)
07/25	Memphis Red Sox. w 16–5 (Comiskey)
07/29	Memphis Red Sox. l 5–7 (Comiskey)
08/15	Memphis Red Sox. w 5–3 (Martin Park)
08/15	Memphis Red Sox. w 1–0 (Martin Park)
08/28	Birmingham Black Barons. l 4–5 (Comiskey)
08/28	Birmingham Black Barons. l 4–6 (Comiskey)
09/3	Birmingham Black Barons. l 8–9 (Comiskey)
09/12	Indianapolis Clowns. w 10–2 (Comiskey)
09/12	Indianapolis Clowns. w 8–7 (Comiskey)
	Total: 16-21

1949 Chicago American Giants

Manager: Winfield Welch. Home Field: Comiskey Park. Final Standing: Finished first in second half of Negro American League, awarded Negro American League pennant (Kansas City declined playing), lost World Series against the Negro National League Baltimore Elite Giants. Based on scores published in the *Chicago Defender*.

04/14	KC Monarchs. w 8–7
05/2	Memphis Red Sox. l 5–6 (W. Frankfort, IL)
05/3	Memphis Red Sox. l 2–9 (Memphis)
05/4	Memphis Red Sox. w 9–4
05/5	Memphis Red Sox. l 4–13 (Greenwood, MS)
05/6	Memphis Red Sox. l 3–4 (Greenwood, MS)
05/8	Birmingham Black Barons. l 2–6 (Rickwood)
05/8	Birmingham Black Barons. l 1–4 (Rickwood)
05/9	Louisville Buckeyes. w 5–4 (Atlanta)
05/15	Memphis Red Sox. w 5–0 (Memphis)
05/15	Memphis Red Sox. t 2–2 (Memphis)
05/20	Indianapolis Clowns. l 4–9 (Comiskey)
05/29	Louisville Buckeyes. w 7–5 (Buffalo, NY)
05/29	Louisville Buckeyes. w 8–3 (Buffalo, NY)
06/12	Baltimore Elite Giants. l 3–4 (Baltimore)
06/12	Baltimore Elite Giants. l 4–5 (Baltimore)
06/19	Philadelphia Stars. w 11–5 (Comiskey)
06/19	Philadelphia Stars. w 7–2 (Comiskey)
06/26	Houston Eagles. w 8–7 (Comiskey)
06/26	Houston Eagles. w 7–3 (Comiskey)

07/1	South Bend Studebakers. w 4–1
07/3	KC Monarchs. w 5–3 (Comiskey)
07/3	KC Monarchs. w 5–1 (Comiskey)
07/4	KC Monarchs. l 8–11 (Comiskey)
07/24	KC Monarchs. w 8–2 (Kansas City)
07/24	KC Monarchs. w 9–5 (Kansas City)
07/31	Philadelphia Stars. l 2–6 (Comiskey)
07/31	Philadelphia Stars. w 5–2 (Comiskey)
08/14	Birmingham Black Barons. l 7–8 (Rickwood)
08/14	Birmingham Black Barons. w 7–0 (Rickwood)
09/4	Indianapolis Clowns. l 6–9 (Comiskey)
09/5	Indianapolis Clowns. w 1–0 (Comiskey)
09/5	Indianapolis Clowns. w 2–0 (Comiskey)
World Series	
09/16	Baltimore Elite Giants. l 1–9 (Baltimore)
09/18	Baltimore Elite Giants. l 4–5 (Baltimore)
09/19	Baltimore Elite Giants. l 4–8 (Norfolk, VA)
09/22	Baltimore Elite Giants. l 2–4 (Comiskey)
	Total: 19-17-1

1950 American Giants

Manager: Ted "Double Duty" Radcliffe. Home Field: Comiskey Park. Final Standing: No official results, the American Giants claimed to have the best record in the second half of the Negro American League season, but did not report scores. Based on scores published in the *Chicago Defender*.

04/30	Cleveland Buckeyes. w 12–8 (Atlanta)
	Houston Eagles . w 13–10 (Comiskey)

05/14	Memphis Red Sox. l 3–16 (Comiskey)
05/14	Memphis Red Sox. w 5–1 (Comiskey)

05/21	Memphis Red Sox. w 9–3 (Memphis)
05/21	Memphis Red Sox. l 3–4 (Memphis)
05/28	Memphis Red Sox. l 3–15 (Comiskey)
05/28	Memphis Red Sox. w 5–1 (Comiskey)
06/4	NY Cubans. l 3–6 (Comiskey)
06/4	NY Cubans. l 4–6 (Comiskey)
06/18	KC Monarchs. l 4–6 (Kansas City)
06/18	KC Monarchs. l 5–11 (Kansas City)
07/9	Indianapolis Clowns. l 2–7 (Comiskey)
07/9	Indianapolis Clowns. l 0–10 (Comiskey)
07/16	KC Monarchs. l 1–13 (Comiskey)
07/16	KC Monarchs. l 0–3 (Comiskey)
07/23	Memphis Red Sox. w 14–7 (Comiskey)
07/23	Memphis Red Sox. l 0–5 (Comiskey)
08/6	Birmingham Black Barons. l 11–12 (Rickwood)
08/6	Birmingham Black Barons. l 1–5 (Rickwood)
08/13	Baltimore Elite Giants. l 5–13 (Baltimore)
08/13	Baltimore Elite Giants. l 5–9 (Baltimore)
	Total: 6-16

1951 Chicago American Giants

Manager: Winfield Welch. Home Field: Comiskey Park. Final Standing: No official results. Based on scores published in the *Chicago Defender*.

05/20	Birmingham Black Barons. w 6–3 (Comiskey)
	Birmingham Black Barons. w 6–2
05/23	Birmingham Black Barons. l 1–2 (Birmingham)
06/3	Baltimore Elite Giants. w 6–5 (Atlanta)
06/3	Baltimore Elite Giants. l 3–5 (Atlanta)
06/10	Memphis Red Sox. w 4–1 (Memphis)
	Memphis Red Sox. l 5–7 (Memphis)
06/17	Baltimore Elite Giants. w 7–4 (Comiskey)
06/17	Baltimore Elite Giants. l 1–2 (Comiskey)
06/24	New Orleans Eagles . w 9–0 (Comiskey)
06/24	New Orleans Eagles . l 1–3 (Comiskey)
07/15	KC Monarchs. l 5–6
07/15	KC Monarchs. l 2–3
	Indianapolis Clowns. w 6–5 (Comiskey)
	Indianapolis Clowns. l 3–4 (Comiskey)
	Total: 7-8

1952 Chicago American Giants

Manager: Paul Hardy. Home Field: Comiskey Park. Final Standing: No official results. Based on scores published in the *Chicago Defender*.

05/11	KC Monarchs. w 6–1 (Comiskey)
05/11	KC Monarchs. l 1–6 (Comiskey)
05/25	Birmingham Black Barons. l 3–11 (Nashville)
05/25	Birmingham Black Barons. w 5–0 (Nashville)
06/8	Indianapolis Clowns. l 0–6 (Comiskey)
06/8	Indianapolis Clowns. w 5–1 (Comiskey)
	Philadelphia Stars. l 6–8 (Central City, IL)
	Philadelphia Stars. l 0–4 (Louisville)
	Philadelphia Stars. w 6–5 (Nashville)
	Philadelphia Stars. w 7–2 (Knoxville)
06/21	Birmingham Black Barons. l 3–4 (Cullman, AL)
06/22	Birmingham Black Barons. w 7–3 (Rickwood)
06/22	Birmingham Black Barons. w 12–1 (Rickwood)
06/29	KC Monarchs. w 6–0 (Kansas City)
06/29	KC Monarchs. w 4–2 (Kansas City)
07/19	KC Monarchs. w 4–1 (Buffalo, NY)
07/20	Indianapolis Clowns. l 2–5 (Buffalo, NY)
	Total: 10-7

Chapter Notes

Chapter 1

1. Nettie G. Speedy, "The Story of Rube Foster," *Chicago Defender*, October 10, 1920.
2. Andrew Rube Foster, " Rube Foster Relives the World Series and Tells a Little Baseball History," *Chicago Defender*, November 15, 1924; "The Story of Marvelous Rube Foster," *Afro-Magazine*, September 5, 1953 (unsourced article states that his father sent him off to Tillotson College to study for the ministry).

Chapter 2

1. Stefan Fatsis, *Wall Street Journal*, Jan. 30, 2004 (describes the research of SABR member Peter Morris on William E. "Bill" White).
2. Adrian Anson, *A Ball Player's Career*, pp. 219–220 (Anson refers to African American Clarence Duvall, a White Stockings assistant and "mascot," as a "coon" and "chocolate covered mascot" repeatedly in this autobiography, demonstrative of his bigoted attitude).
3. Sol White, *History of Colored Baseball*, p. 76.
4. Albert G Spalding, *Chicago Amateur Baseball Guide of 1904*.
5. Ray Schmidt, "The Golden Age of Chicago Baseball," *Chicago History* (Winter 2000).
6. James A. Riley, *The Biographical History of the Negro Baseball Leagues*, pp. 595–596; Sol White, *History of Colored Baseball*, p. 28.
7. Sol White, *History of Colored Baseball*, pp. 26, 28. As a player with the Page Fence Giants, the Cuban X-Giants, and the Columbia Giants, Sol White writes considerably on these teams.

8. David Pietrusza, *Major Leagues*, pp. 224–27, 145–182.

Chapter 3

1. Robert Peterson, Only the Ball Was White, p. 105.
2. *Sporting News*, March 30, 1901.
3. David Pietrusza, *Major Leagues*, p. 166.
4. Robert Peterson, *Only the Ball Was White*, p. 105
5. James Riley, *The Biographical Encyclopedia of the Negro Baseball Leagues*, p. 290. (Riley states that Rube lost only one game in three months in 1902 and was 54–1 in 1903. Only a handful of games can be documented.)
6. *Indianapolis Freeman,* March 10, 1917.
7. *Otsego Union*, August 14, 1902.
8. Robert Peterson, *Only the Ball Was White*, p 105; *Otsego Union*, September 4, 1902 (reports that Otsego defeated the Columbia Giants of Big Rapids by a 5–2 score, with Foster pitching. Several previous sketches of Rube Foster have overlooked the fact that he did in fact avenge the Columbia Giants.)
9. Sol White, *History of Colored Baseball*, p 151; John Holway, *Blackball Stars*, p. 11.
10. Robert C. Cottrell, *The Best Pitcher in Baseball*, p. 14.
11. *Chatham Daily Planet*, June 3, 1898.
12. Frederick North Shorey, "How Rube Foster Cleaned Up with One of the Best Teams in the Country," *Indianapolis Freeman*, September 14, 1907. (Shorey uses direct quotes from Rube Foster.)
13. Roberto Gonzalez Echevarria, *The Pride of Havana: A History of Cuban Baseball*, p. 126.

Chapter 4

1. Frank Leland, "Frank Leland's Chicago Giants Base Ball Club" pamphlet — part of the biography capsule for Frank Leland states the club had a 122–10 record; *Indianapolis* Freeman, January 1, 1910 — Leland shortstop James Smith stated the record was 93–25–3.
2. Sol White, *History of Colored Baseball*, p 99.
3. Robert Peterson, *Only the Ball Was White*, p. 107.
4. *Indianapolis Freeman*, August 8, 1907.
5. *Indianapolis Freeman*, September 7, 1907.
6. Cook County Circuit Court Case# 296934, 8218, filed March 21, 1910 — "Lelands Giants Baseball Club vs. Frank Leland." (In the amended complaint Rube claims a 103–1 record and 32 shutouts.)
7. Sol White, *History of Colored Baseball*, p 119.
8. *The Broad Ax*, September 28, 1907.
9. *Indianapolis Freeman*, November 23, 1907.
10. "Sporting Gossip of the Week," *Indianapolis Freeman*, February 15, 1908.
11. *Indianapolis Freeman*, August 1, 1908.
12. Ray Schmidt, "The Golden Age of Baseball," *Chicago History Magazine* 28:2 (Winter 2000), p. 55.
13. A. G. Spalding, *Spalding's Official Baseball Guide, 1909*, p. 7.
14. *Indianapolis Freeman*, March 20, 1909.
15. Ibid., February 20, 1909.
16. "Leland's Giants Complete a Successful Southern Trip," *Indianapolis Freeman*, May 15, 1909; article gives a summary of the spring tour through the South.

17. *Indianapolis Freeman*, July17, 1909 (account of game against Cuban Stars in which Rube broke leg); A.G. Spalding, *Spaulding's Official Baseball Guide 1910*, p. 9 (discusses success of City Leagues and American Giants as well as multiple injuries to American Giants).

18. *Indianapolis Freeman*, August 7, 1909 (account of series vs. St. Paul Colored Gophers); August 21, 1909 (the Lelands also dropped a game to a rag-tag black team from Detroit known as the Detroit Athletics.)

19. *Indianapolis Freeman*, November 13, 1909.

20. Ibid.

21. *Indianapolis Freeman*, September 11, 1909.

22. *Indianapolis Freeman*, October 2, 1909 (Leland's published letter states "if the Philadelphia Giants, Kansas City, KS, Giants, and St. Paul Gophers still think well of themselves, I will play any one of those teams a series of games for a side bet of $5,000"— Leland does not acknowledge Rube Foster's true role as team manager in this letter); Cook County Circuit Court Case# 296934, 8218, "Lelands Giants Baseball Club vs. Frank Leland," filed March 21, 1910; "Chicago to Have New Baseball Club," *Indianapolis Freeman*, October 30, 1909 (summarizes Leland's announcement to break off and form a new team); "Leland Giants Club in Court," *Indianapolis Freeman*, March 12, 1910 (summarizes facts of suit brought against Beauregard Mosely by Leland and cohorts, including claims going back to 1907 of exorbitant expenses— Mosely billed the Leland Giants $10,000); Andrew "Rube" Foster, "Negro Baseball," *Indianapolis Freeman*, December 23, 1911 (Rube recalls the struggle with Frank Leland and deal-making with Schorling as well as other subjects).

23. *Indianapolis Freeman*, January 8, 1910 — David Wyatt reports "it is said that the baseball clubs of Cuba have drawn the color line"; January 15,1910 — C. Dana Marshall relates the rumor of the color line in Cuba to rumored application of Cuban baseball teams for inclusion in Major League organized agreement; January 20, 1912 — Juli Jones Jr. elaborates further on drawing of the color line in Cuba, stating that Ban Johnson, John McGraw and Frank Bancroft negotiated a clause with the Cuban baseball clubs that "Cuban teams must be made of native-sons," because of the common

knowledge that the black stars from the U.S. gave the Cuban teams a distinct advantage.

24. *Indianapolis Freeman*, April 30, 1910; *Chicago Defender*, December 13, 1919.

25. Roberto Gonzalez Echevarria, *The Pride of Havana*, p 137; *Indianapolis Freeman*, October 10, 1910 (the *Freeman* reports the outcome of game one of a sixteen game series against the Havanas; Lelands won 5–4, but no other games are reported); "Pitfalls of Baseball," *Chicago Defender*, December 13, 1919 (Rube claims to have won six games in Cuba in 1910 and discloses $2,100 loss).

Chapter 5

1. Harold McGath, "In the Field of Sport," *Indianapolis Freeman*, Jan. 14, 1911 (McGath gives a blow-by-blow account of the meeting).

2. *Indianapolis Freeman*, June 24, 1911; July 15, 1911 (published scores show Mosely's Leland Giants losing 22–9 against the Louisville Cubs and 19–4 against the Kansas City Giants—for example).

3. Harold McGath, "In the Field of Sport," *Indianapolis Freeman*, Jan. 28, 1911.

4. Cary B. Lewis, "Opening of the Ball Park," *Indianapolis Freeman*, May 13, 1911; May 20, 1911.

5. *Indianapolis Freeman*, July 8, 1911.

6. *Indianapolis Freeman*, July 15, 1911; *Chicago Defender*, August 5, 1911; September 23, 1911.

7. *Indianapolis Freeman*, June 24, 1911.

8. *Chicago Defender*, August 12, 1911.

9. Andrew Rube Foster, "Negro Baseball," *Indianapolis Freeman*, December 23, 1911.

10. Roberto Gonzalez Echevarria, *The Pride of Havana*, p. 142; *Indianapolis Freeman*, February 17, 1912; "Blacks to Appear against McCormicks ... this is a colored team of players of the Leland Giants of Chicago and the Occidentals of this city," *Los Angeles Times*, November 10, 1911.

11. *Indianapolis Freeman*, April 27, 1912; Jules Tygiel, *Baseball's Great Experiment: Jackie Robinson and His Legacy*, p. 69. Benjamin Davis's son by the same name went on to be a Communist city councilman in New York City, and in the 1945 campaign he distributed a graphic flyer depicting two blacks— one a dead soldier, the other a

baseball player—captioned "Good enough to die for his country but not good enough for organized baseball."

12. American Giants Rally at Finish," *Indianapolis Freeman*, July 20, 1912.

13. David Pietrusza, *Major Leagues*, p 194.

14. *Indianapolis Freeman*, August 10, 1912.

15. "The American Giants, Champions in Los Angeles, Cal.," *Indianapolis Freeman*, November 9, 1912 (dispatch written by Rube Foster); *Los Angeles Times*, November 11, 1912; November 2, 1912; November 3, 1912.

16. *Indianapolis Freeman*, April 5, 1913 (published the full text of a speech given at the Good Fellows Club banquet at Los Angeles).

17. *Indianapolis Freeman*, April 26, 1913; William McNeil, *The California Winter League: America's First Integrated Professional Baseball League.*

18. *Indianapolis Freeman*, May 17, 1913; *Chicago Defender*, November 9, 1912.

19. *Indianapolis Freeman*, November 23, 1912; Thomas R Heitala,. *The Fight of the Century; Jack Johnson, Joe Louis, and the Struggle for Racial Equality*, pp. 93–95.

20. *Indianapolis Freeman*, August 16, 1913.

21. *Chicago Defender*, August 23, 1913; September 20, 1913.

22. *Chicago Defender*, July 5, 1913.

23. *New York Age*, July 24, 1913.

24. Rube Foster, "Review of the Past Season — Incidents and Future of Colored Baseball," *Indianapolis Freeman*, December 20, 1913.

25. "Rube Foster Challenges Cubs," *Chicago Defender*, October 18, 1913.

Chapter 6

1. *Chicago Defender*, March 21, 1914.

2. *Chicago Defender*, March 28, 1914 ("Portland team secretary Lewis Hubbard has sent his regards to the team [the American Giants] ... he expects to entertain the American Giants while they are in Portland.")

3. *Chicago Defender*, April 11, 1914.

4. Portus Baxter, "Seattle Loses a Great Game to a Great Team" (full account and box score of game between American Giants and Seat-

tle), *Seattle Post-Intelligencer*, April 4, 1914.

5. *Seattle Post-Intelligencer*, April 6, 1914.

6. "Baxter's Sporting Gossip: 'Shadow Practice' as Produced by Rube Foster's Comedy Company, With Monroe in the Lead, Proves a Scream," *Seattle Post-Intelligencer*, April 6, 1914. (This is an early reference to what would become known as "Shadowball," normally associated with the Indianapolis Clowns of the 1940's–'50's.)

7. *Seattle Post-Intelligencer*, April 5, 1914 (Rube is quoted directly by writer Royal Brougham).

8. *Indianapolis Freeman*, May 2, 1914.

9. *Chicago Defender*, May 23, 1914.

10. Frank Keetz, *The Mohawk Colored Giants of Schenectady*, p 19.

11. Frank A. Young, "Rube Foster Triumphs," *Chicago Defender*, June 6, 1914.

12. *Chicago Defender*, September, 12 1914.

13. *Indianapolis Freeman*, November 21, 1914. The *Freeman* published a detailed account of Leland's funeral.

14. "McCredle Kicks on Color Line Baseball," *Chicago Defender*, January 16, 1915.

15. *Chicago Defender*, July 10, 1915.

16. *Chicago Defender*, July 24, 1915.

17. *Indianapolis Ledge*, August 14, 1915.

18. *Chicago Defender*, July 31, 1915.

19. "Colored Giants Have Most Bricks and Win Close Game," *Indianapolis Ledger*, August 28, 1915.

20. *Chicago Defender*, August 28, 1915.

21. *Chicago Defender*, October 9, 1915.

22. *Chicago Defender*, October 16, 1915.

23. John Holway, *Complete Book of Baseball's Negro League*, p. 109. (Holway credits the American Giants/San Francisco, Cuba, with a 5–9 record in the Cuban League); *Chicago Defender*, March 11, 1916, has an account of a victory of the American Giants over Havana who had Emilio Palmero of the New York Giants on the mound.

24. *Chicago Defender*, August 5, 1916.

25. *Indianapolis Freeman*, February 12, 1916.

26. *Indianapolis Freeman*, July 15, 1916.

27. *Chicago Defender*, August 26, 1916.

28. *Chicago Defender*, September 2, 1916.

29. *Chicago Defender*, September 16, 1916.

30. *Indianapolis Freeman*, October 14, 1916; Robert Cotterell, *The Best Pitcher in Baseball*, p.3.

31. *Chicago Defender*, September 2, 1916; September 16, 1916.

32. *Chicago Defender*, April 21, 1917 (New Orleans undertaker Joe Geddes took the club to the ballpark in his autos and then entertained the entire club with dinner, after which they danced).

33. *Indianapolis Freeman*, February 17, 1917.

34. *Chicago Defender*, October 16, 1917.

35. Neil Lanctot, *Fair Dealing and Clean Playing: The Hilldale Club*, p.49.

36. *Indianapolis Freeman*, August 4, 1917.

37. *Indianapolis Freeman*, August 4, 1917; *Chicago Defender*, August 4, 1917.

38. *Chicago Defender*, July 17, 1917; September 15, 1917.

39. *Chicago Defender*, September 8, 1917.

40. "Tom Williams Starts Season with a Win over Padron," *Chicago Defender*, February 9, 1918 (article states: "A band furnished music during the intervals between innings, playing 'Over There'").

41. *Chicago Defender*, April 13, 1918; March 2, 1918.

42. *Chicago Defender*, April 6, 1918.

43. *Chicago Defender*, May 25, 1918.

44. *Chicago Defender*, July 27, 1927.

45. *Chicago Defender*, March 30, 1918; June 1, 1918; Dave Wyatt, "Andrew Foster Gets Offer for War Services," *Indianapolis Freeman*, October 12, 1918 (Wyatt writes: "Andrew Rube Foster, it is reported, has been asked to become the organizer of baseball among the French and American troops....")

46. *Chicago Defender*, November 2, 1918.

47. *Chicago Defender*, November 9, 1918.

48. Richard Bak, *Turkey Stearnes and the Detroit Stars: The Negro Leagues in Detroit*, pp 55–58.

49. James Riley, *The Biographical Encyclopedia of the Negro Baseball Leagues*, p. 117.

50. *Chicago Defender*, April 12, 1919.

51. *Chicago Defender*, April 19,1919; June 7, 1919.

52. Adam Cohen and Elizabeth Taylor, *American Pharaoh; Mayor Richard Daley, His Battle for Chicago and the Nation*, pp. 35–36; William Tuttle, *Race Riot in Chicago in the Red Summer of 1919*.

53. *Indianapolis Freeman*, August 16, 1919.

54. *Chicago Defender*, August 30, 1919.

Chapter 7

1. *Chicago Defender*, October 4, 1919.

2. *Chicago Defender*, February 14, 1920.

3. *Chicago Defender*, February 21, 1920.

4. *Chicago Defender*, April 30, 1920.

5. *Chicago Whip*, March 20, 1920; Roberto Gonzalez Echevarria, *The Pride of Havana*, p 157.

6. *Indianapolis Freeman*, April 20, 1920.

7. Neil Lanctot, *Fair Dealing and Clean Playing*, 85–86; *Chicago Defender*, May 8, 1920.

8. *Chicago Defender*, May 15, 1920; May 22, 1920; June 5, 1920.

9. *Chicago Defender*, August 14 1920.

10. *Chicago Defender*, October 23, 1920.

11. Stanley Dance, *The World of Earl Hines*, p 52.

12. Dave Wyatt, "League Meeting Assures Success in Baseball," *Chicago Whip*, December 11 1920; "Hilldale's Answer to Rube Foster," *Philadelphia Tribune*, August 21 1920.

13. *Chicago Whip*, January 8, 1921; Roberto Gonzalez Echevarria, *The Pride of Havana*, p. 161. (Echevarria dispels a popular myth about Torriente.)

14. *Chicago Whip*, April 9, 1921. ("[R]eports have Grant in the greatest catch of his life in Jacksonville, FL ... March 23, Leroy Grant and Miss Emma Sanford of Jacksonville were united in wedlock. Tom Johnson, Bobby Williams and Otis Starks stood with Grant during the ceremony.")

15. David Pietrusza, *Major Leagues*, p 256; *New York Times*, January 9, 1921.

16. *Chicago Defender*, May 14, 1921.

17. "Jimmy Lyons Falls Down Elevator Shaft," *Chicago Defender*, July 30, 1921.

18. Ibid.

19. *Chicago Defender*, November 12, 1921.

20. *Chicago Defender*, November 19, 1921.

21. Andrew "Rube" Foster, "Future of Race Umpires Depends on Men of Today," *Chicago Defender*, December 31, 1921.

22. *Chicago Defender*, February 4, 1922.

23. Neil Lanctot, *Fair Dealing and Clean Playing*, p. 92.

24. *Chicago Defender*, February 22, 1922; March 4, 1922.

25. *Chicago Defender*, March 18, 1922.

26. Neil Lancot, *Fair Dealing and Clean Playing*, p. 92.

27. *Chicago Defender*, May 13, 1922.

28. Ibid., June 10, 1922.

29. Ibid., July 22, 1922.

30. *Chicago Defender*, December 2, 1922; December 16, 1992; *Chicago Whip*, December 16, 1922; *Baltimore Afro-American*, December 15, 1922. (All three papers carried accounts of the league meetings.)

31. *Baltimore Afro-American*, December 22, 1922; January 12, 1923.

32. *Chicago Defender*, February 17, 1923; March 10, 1923.

33. *Chicago Defender*, March 10, 1923.

34. *Chicago Defender*, March 17, 1923; August 11, 1923.

35. *Chicago Defender*, January 12, 1923.

36. *Baltimore Afro-American*, February 2, 1923.

37. *Baltimore Afro-American*, February 16, 1923.

38. *Chicago Defender*, April 7, 1923.

39. *Baltimore Afro-American*, March 9, 1923.

40. *Chicago Defender*, August 11, 1923; September 1, 1923.

41. *Chicago Defender*, August 18, 1923.

42. *Chicago Defender*, November 24, 1923.

43. *Chicago Defender*, October 13, 1923. (The *Defender* states: "Rogan, the premier pitcher of the Kansas City Monarchs, is due here next week and will work out daily at the Giants park for the coming two-game series with the Detroiters"—but Rogan did not appear in the series).

44. Frank Young, "The American Giants–Detroit Tigers Games," *Chicago Defender*, October 27, 1923 (Young gives a complete account of all three games); Frank Young, "Fay Says" column, February, 2 1924 (recounting last season's game, Young says: "Monday's game drew only a handful of people. Each player's share was $5. Foster dug down in his pockets and gave Harney $20").

45. *Chicago Defender*, March 8, 1924 ("the players ... went through a hard work out despite the rain"); March 22, 1924 ("After defeating Calvert on the coldest day of the year…"); April 5, 1924 ("Down in sunny Texas hindered now and then by the rains which have caused them to cancel several games…").

46. *Chicago Defender*, April 5, 1924.

47. *Chicago Defender*, April 19, 1924; May 21, 1924.

48. *Chicago Defender*, September 13, 1924.

49. *Chicago Defender*, November 1, 1924. (The *Defender* published a complete financial report for the World Series—indicating total attendance for 10 games was 45,857, and the winning team's total purse was $4,927.32—to be split among the Monarchs.)

Chapter 8

1. "Negro National League in Harmonious Meeting; Plan Two Fifty-Game Schedules," *Chicago Defender*, February 27, 1925.

2. *Chicago Defender*, March 7, 1925.

3. Frank Young, "Drastic Action Needed," *Chicago Defender*, May 16, 1925.

4. "Gas Nearly Kills Rube Foster," *Chicago Defender*, June 6, 1925. (Article states that Rube was treated by Dr. Batiste of 2116 Boulevard Place in Indianapolis and Dr. Homer Wales of 54_ Indiana Avenue. DeMoss called Mrs. Sarah Foster. Rube insisted on joining the club in Kansas City.)

5. Robert Cottrell, *The Best Pitcher in Baseball*, pp. 168–169.

6. *Chicago Defender*, February 13, 1926.

7. *Chicago Defender*, May 15, 1926.

8. Timothy Rives, "The Booker T Four's Unlikely Journey," pp. 25–27.

9. *Chicago Defender*, July 10, 1926. ("The first half of the season ended with the Giants in fourth place"—some reference sources (Robert Peterson and Clark & Lester) show the Americans as finishing in second; however, the running standings in the *Defender* and the above quote point to the lower finish.)

10. Robert Peterson, *Only the Ball Was White*, p 114.

11. *Indianapolis Recorder*, September 11, 1926; John Holway, *Blackball Stars*, pp 33–34; Robert

Cottrell, *The Best Pitcher in Baseball*, pp 170–171.

12. "Gilmore Seeks to be Head of National League; Takes Rap at Weekly Papers," and Frank Young, "Directors of National League Hold Future…,"*Chicago Defender*, September 11, 1926.

13. "Am. Giants Win Championship and Head East," *Chicago Defender*, October 2, 1926; National Baseball Hall of Fame Museum questionnaire—Willie Foster, Cooperstown, N.Y., February 29, 1972.

14. "Fay Says," *Chicago Defender*, October 9, 1926.

15. Ibid.

16. Ibid., October 16, 1926

17. *Chicago Defender*, October 12, 1926; October 23, 1926.

18. "Chicago May Not Have Ball Club When League Season Gets Under Way," *Chicago Defender*, February 5, 1927; "Birmingham and Memphis Back; Indianapolis is Out; Gilmore Made Treasurer," February 5, 1927; "Magnates to Deal Severely with Players: Owners Frown on Trip to Japan," March 5, 1927.

19. *Indianapolis Recorder*, April 23, 1927.

20. "American Giants Get Ready for Coming Season…," *Chicago Defender*, March 12, 1927.

21. *Chicago Defender*, July 9, 1927.

22. *Chicago Defender*, July 23, 1927.

23. *Chicago Defender*, August 20, 1927; April 7, 1928 (*Defender* states "Judge Hueston has ruled that according to contract that Memphis holds Larry Brown and [Nat] Rogers are still the property of Memphis." The issue was contentious).

24. *Chicago Defender*, September 24, 1927 (*Defender* column states: "Chicago's race population is about 200,000, eight of every ten either come from the Southland or their parents were from south of Mason Dixon…. Naturally, these folks pull for the boys from their section of the country").

25. "May Call Off World's Series Play between East and West," *Chicago Defender*, November 5, 1927; October 22, 1927. (Referring to the 1927 World Series participants, the *Defender* column states: "Players have refused to keep in shape. Some would be seen on the streets in the early hours of the morning with a hard game to be played later in the day. Whisky such as it is, white mule and riotous living have shortened the life of a good

many men who might have had their names stretched across the top of newspapers, like Babe Ruth.")

26. *Chicago Defender*, February 18, 1928.

27. *Chicago Defender*, April 7, 1928; March 3, 1928 ("American Giants may train in Shreveport").

28. "…Start Season: Gardner, Currie Still Holding Out," *Chicago Defender*, March 24, 1928; "Snow, Cold Balk Spring Practice Here," March 31, 1928; "Rube Curry Awarded to the Detroit Stars by League," June 24, 1928; "McDonald Jumps American Giants for White Club," May 19, 1928.

29. "Malarcher Hurt and P. Williams Gets Leg Broke," *Chicago Defender*, May 19, 1928; "Jim Brown Operated On at Douglass Hospital," June 30, 1928; "Am. Giants Lose Three to B. Barons: Davis Injured," June 9, 1928.

30. *Chicago Defender*, May 28, 1928 (debut of Red Haley); June 9, 1928; Jim Riley, *Biographical Encyclopedia of the Negro Leagues*, p. 347 (cites possible relationship to Alex Haley).

31. "Poindexter, Satchel Sent Home, Russ Fined," *Chicago Defender*, August 4, 1928; Neil Lanctot, *Fair Dealing and Clean Playing*, p 162; *Chicago Defender*, April 7, 1928.

32. *Chicago Defender*, October 13, 1928.

33. "Am. Giants Players Join New Indoor Ball Club," *Chicago Defender*, January 19, 1929; "The Sun Shines; Chicago Fans Wonder About American Giants," March 16, 1929. (*Defender* states: "Owner W. E. Trimble who with his brother has been sojourning in Florida during the winter months, stayed over for the races and the Stribling-Sharkey bout, are expected back next week.")

34. "Dave Malarcher Threatens to Quit Giants," *Chicago Defender*, April 6, 1929; "Opening Game Sunday against Duffy Floral Nine," April 13, 1929.

35. "American Gives Out Reserve List of Players," *Chicago Defender*, March 2, 1929.

36. *Chicago Defender*, March 16, 1929, April 6, 1929.

37. "Curry Hurls All-Stars to 12–3 victory," *Chicago Defender*, May 25, 1929; "American Eagles and Evanston meet May 12," May 11, 1929.

38. "Poindexter Claims Shooting Accidental," *Chicago Defender*, June 8, 1929.

39. *Chicago Defender*, March 23, 1929.

40. "Fay Says," *Chicago Defender*, July 27, 1929.

41. "Easterners Drop All Five Games to National Leaguers Who Win Four by Shutouts," *Chicago Defender*, October 12, 1929.

42. "Wells' Two Thefts of Home, Foster's Pitching and Timely Hitting Wins; Series Continues," *Chicago Defender*, October 19, 1929.

43. John Holway, *Blackball Stars*, p. 34. (Holway quotes Willie Powell as saying that Governor Horner tried to get Foster released — however Henry Horner was not serving as governor during that time period.)

44. "Owners Unite in Plea for Better Ball," *Chicago Defender*, January 25, 1930.

45. "Taylor Tells What's Wrong in Baseball," *Chicago Defender*, February 1. 1930.

46. "Am. Giants Head Rushes Plans for Night Baseball," *Chicago Defender*, July 19, 1930.

47. "New Faces to be Seen in American Giants Line-up as Result of Drastic Shake-up," *Chicago Defender*, August 23, 1930.

48. Ibid.

49. "Willie Foster to Manage Giants," *Chicago Defender*, July 5, 1930; August 23, 1930 (new owners Bidwell and Kelly introduced); Frank A. Young, "Rube Foster the Mastermind of Baseball," *Abbotts Monthly*, November 1930 (provides some detail on the transaction from Trimble to Bidwell); Frank Young, "Rube Foster — A Name That All Baseball Fans Revere," *Chicago Defender*, August 7, 1948 (retrospective, describes Charles Bidwell as interested in dog racing — "In 1931 the late Charles E. Bidwell came into the picture bringing the late French Lane, sportswriter for the Tribune…. It was said that Bidwell had an eye out for the fine sport of dog racing and southside was the place … Bidwell claimed he discovered Satchel Paige…").

50. "Am. Giants Ready to Play Leaguers," *Chicago Defender*, September 27, 1930; "Earl Mack Brings Strong Club to Play Am. Giants in Big Series Starting Oct. 3," October 4, 1930.

51. "Shires and Co. Are No Match for Local Nine," *Chicago Defender*, October 11, 1930; "Giants Fire Holsey, Mitchell, Williams," September 6, 1930.

52. "Russ Passes after Long Illness," *Chicago Defender*, August 16, 1930; "Poindexter of Baseball Fame is Fatally Cut," June 21, 1930.

53. Joseph Mehr, *An Illustrated History of Illinois Public Mental Health Services: 1847 to 2000*, pp. 373, 97–104. (Includes a chapter on the Kankakee Asylum. The building still stands and is known today as the Shapiro Developmental Center — for developmentally disabled adults. It also houses a mental health museum.)

54. Richard Bak, *Turkey Stearnes and the Detroit Stars*, pp. 178–179. (Bak also presents speculation that Rube Foster might have suffered with syphilis, but acknowledges it is only "speculation.")

55. "Thousands Attend Last Rites for Rube Foster," *Chicago Defender*, December 20, 1930.

Chapter 9

1. Rep. William Clay (Missouri), Extension of Remarks: E3645, *U.S. Congressional Record*, July 9, 1975.

2. "Foster Resigns Managership of Am. Giants," *Chicago Defender*, January 31, 1931; "Willie Foster Goes to Pittsburgh Team," May 16, 1931.

3. *Chicago Defender*, October 31, 1931.

4. *Chicago Defender*, November 14, 1931.

5. "Pittsburgh, Cleveland and Detroit Own West's Parks," *Chicago Defender*, January 30, 1932.

6. "Local Team to Tour the South Early in March," *Chicago Defender*, February 27, 1932; January 16, 1932; Kyle McNary, *Ted "Double Duty" Radcliffe*, p 135.

7. "New Giant Boss," *Chicago Defender*, March 5, 1932; July 9 1932 ; "Win a Free Pass by Naming Local Baseball Outfit," March 19, 1932.

8. "Giants Score Trio of Wins; Eye Title," *Chicago Defender*, August 27, 1932 (article states that the series would be broadcast by the National and Columbia broadcasting systems).

9. "Cole's American Giants to Move to Indianapolis," *Chicago Defender*, May 20, 1933.

10. Quincy Trouppe, *Twenty Years Too Soon*, p. 36; Dave Ball, "Baseball Owners Make Trades but Stars Go Where They Choose," (writer points to Radcliffe as a prime example), *Chicago Defender*, January 19, 1935; James Riley, *Biographical Encyclopedia of the Negro Baseball Leagues*, pp. 648–649 (Riley lists Columbus Blue Birds, Cleveland Giants, N.Y. Black Yankees, Homestead Grays). Radcliffe

was also associated with Neil Churchill's Bismarck team, according to Trouppe.

11. Larry Lester, *Black Baseball's National Showcase: The East-West All Star Game, 1933–1953*, p. 9.

12. Al Monroe, "Those Baserunning Dogs Fail to Cash in on Baseball's Absence," *Chicago Defender*, July 22, 1933.

13. *Chicago Defender*, June 30, 1934. Captioned drawing of Grover Cleveland Alexander on a donkey ("… Alexander, famous pitcher, admits his extreme pleasure at playing 'donkey baseball.' This is a feature accompanying the House of David—Giants game at Cole's parktonight.")

14. "Greenlee, Cole in East to Plan Big Baseball Series," *Chicago Defender*, September 8, 1934. (Short article states "Dave Hawkins and R. A. Cole arrived here Tuesday by plane." This seems to be the first time that use of aircraft by league officials was mentioned.)

15. "Four Nashville Players Join Cole Crew–Game Protested," *Chicago Defender*, November 24, 1934; October 6, 1934; "Dave Malarcher Loses His Protest of Playoff Game," December 1, 1934.

16. Ibid.; Ben Lewis, "'I'll Play in Chicago or I'll Quit,' Says Star," *Chicago Defender*, February 2, 1935. (Article states: "Lillard came here to play football but after engaging in three big games went to Hollywood and found himself a job as a valet with one of movieland's major stars. He is well satisfied with his position and may after all decide to stay out of baseball in 1935. He even admitted himself his chances for returning to baseball were very, very, thin."

17. "Pair Gives Cole One of the Strongest Outfields in Loop," *Chicago Defender*, March 2, 1935; James Riley, *Biographic Encyclopedia of the Negro Baseball Leagues*, p 599.

18. "Malarcher Resigns Post as Manager of Local 9," *Chicago Defender*, February 9, 1935.

19. *Chicago Defender*, March 12, 1935; "Game Shifted to Duffy Park on West Side: Cole's Stadium Is Not Yet Ready for Action," *Chicago Defender*, May 11, 1935.

20. "Giants and the Philly Stars to Quit League," *Chicago Defender*, August 31, 1935.

21. "Sox and Cubs," *Chicago Defender*, October 26, 1935.

22. "Talk of Giant Players Going to Detroit 9," *Chicago Defender*, January 4, 1936 (reports rumor that Joe Louis is interested in rebuild-

ing Detroit Stars with American Giant players); Russ Cowans, "Louis Asked to Buy Ball Club in Detroit or Chicago," *Chicago Defender*, January 25, 1936.

23. "DeMoss to Pilot the Am. Giants," *Chicago Defender*, January 18, 1936. (Article states: "Just what additional players DeMoss will ask owner H. G. Hall to get for his 1936 Giants was not learned but advance information says Satchel Paige will very like come here.") "Giants Eye Paige, Champion Pitcher"—"The local management has wanted the stringbean hurler for years and according to H. G. Hall owner of the Giants things look bright for him finally landing here," *Chicago Defender*, March 21, 1936.

24. "Memphis Sox Here on May 16th, are Hot; Stands Are Rebuilt for Opening of Loop," *Chicago Defender*, May 2, 1936; May 16, 1936.

25. "Giants Beat Prison Nine," *Chicago Defender*, July 18, 1936; Kyle P. McNary, *Ted "Double Duty" Radcliffe*, p 31 (McNary explains that there was a barnstorming team in the thirties that called themselves the "Joliet Prison team," though none were actual prisoners.)

26. "Petway and Ball, One Time Star Battery Works Again," *Chicago Defender*, August 8, 1936.

27. Ted Benson, "'League Open to Negroes' Says Frick, League Prexy," *Chicago Defender*, August 29, 1936 (from the *Sunday Worker*).

28. "R. R. Jackson of Chicago Is Named Prexy," *Chicago Defender*, October 17, 1936; "Baseball Men Close Confab Here Smiling," December 12, 1936; "Giants Sign Jim Taylor for Season," December 26, 1936.

29. *Chicago Defender*, September 11, 1937.

30. Frank A. Young, "The Stuff is Here," *Chicago Defender*, September 25, 1937.

31. Frank A. Young, " If Our Men Could Play," *Chicago Defender*, June 18, 1938.

32. "Taylor to Lead Men to Dixie," *Chicago Defender*, March 4, 1939.

33. *Chicago Defender*, November 4, 1939.

Chapter 10

1. *Chicago Defender*, August 2, 1940 (the *Defender* called Reeves the league's home-run king); James Riley, *Biographical Encyclopedia of the Negro Baseball Leagues*, p 658 (Riley states: "In 1940 this Chicago

American Giants outfielder was credited with 36 home runs by the end of July and 50 by the end of the season).

2. *Chicago Defender*, June 2, 1940; September 14, 1940.

3. *Chicago Defender*, August 3, 1940.

4. Frank A. Young, "No Seat for Half Crowd," *Chicago Defender*, September 14, 1940.

5. "American Giants Park is Damaged by Flames," *Chicago Tribune*, December 24, 1940.

6. Fay Young, "The Stuff is Here," *Chicago Defender*, March 1, 1941 (discussion of the Ethiopian Clowns' false claim to championship).

7. Frank Young, "The Stuff is Here," *Chicago Defender*, May 17, 1941 (discussion and criticism of ball park situation).

8. *Chicago Defender*, August 16, 1941.

9. The National Baseball Hall of Fame (www.baseballhalloffame.org) posts an imaged copy of Franklin Roosevelt's so-called "green light letter" of January 15, 1942, on its website.

10. *Chicago Defender*, March 28, 1944.

11. "'Negroes in Big Leagues Soon'—Owner Wrigley," *Chicago Defender*, December 19, 1942.

12. *Chicago Defender*, March 13, 1943.

13. *Chicago Defender*, April 3, 1941.

14. Janet Bruce Campbell, *The Kansas City Monarchs*, pp. 98–100; Neil Lanctot, *Negro League Baseball*, p 134.

15. "Dedicate Rube Foster Field with 7–1 Victory," *Chicago Defender*, July 24, 1943 (Fort Huachuca defeated the 92nd Division, 5–1).

16. *Chicago Defender*, August 14, 1943; September 11, 1943.

17. *Chicago Defender*, July 31, 1943.

18. "Major Leagues Hear Plea for Negro Players," *Chicago Defender*, December 4, 1943.

19. Frank Young, "Chicago Cubs Will Scout Negro Players," *Chicago Defender*, December 25, 1943; Neil Lanctot, *Negro League Baseball*, p. 245.

20. *Chicago Defender*, February 19, 1944; "American Giants Get DeMoss as Manager," April 1, 1944; June 17, 1944.

21. *Chicago Defender*, August 28, 1944 (Frank Young exposes the disloyalty of players to Doc Martin); Frank Young, "Through the Years," September 2, 1944 (Young details the

disciplinary action taken in response by Doc. Martin); "Bad Boy Pennington Is Suspended," July 22 1944 (details of Pennington's earlier suspension for taking advance money and subsequently refusing to play).

22. *New York Times*, November 26, 1944.

23. Arnold Rampersand, *Jackie Robinson: A Biography*, p 123; William Marshall, *Baseball's Pivotal Era, 1945–1951*, p 124; Neil Lanctot, *Negro League Baseball*, p 254.

24. Albert G. Barnett, "Chandler Doesn't Believe in Barring Negro Players," *Chicago Defender*, May 12, 1945.

25. *New York Times*, May 8, 1944.

26. "No More Negro League Baseball Games at Wrigley," *Chicago Defender*, July 7, 1945.

27. Neil Lanctot, *Negro League Baseball*, p 272.

28. *Chicago Defender*, Sept. 23, 1944.

29. Frank Young, "End of Baseball's Jim Crow Seen with Signing of Jackie Robinson," *Chicago Defender*, November 3, 1945.

30. *Chicago Defender*, January 26, 1946.

31. *Chicago Defender*, April 20, 1946.

32. "Wyatt's Failure to Run Costs American Giants a Victory," *Chicago Defender*, June 8, 1946.

Chapter 11

1. *Chicago Defender*, January 25, 1947.

2. *Chicago Defender*, February 22, 1946.

3. *Chicago Defender*, September 6, 1947; August 2, 1947.

4. *Chicago Defender*, May 24, 1917; "Fay Says," *Chicago Defender*, May 17, 1947.

5. *Chicago Defender*, August 2, 1947.

6. *Chicago Defender*, September 27, 1947; James Riley, *Biographical Encyclopedia of the Negro Baseball Leagues*, p 666; *Chicago Defender*, March 16, 1948 (*Defender* states: "Dr. J. B. Martin called attention to the case of John Ritchey, Chicago catcher signed by the San Diego Padres. 'Although we could not put our hands on Richey's contract, William Starr, president of the Padres, sent me a check for a satisfactory sum'"); Amy Essington, "Ritchey in Chicago with Some Others," a presentation at the Eighth Annual Jerry Malloy Negro League Research Conference, June 16–19, 2005 (Essington states that

"inconclusive research shows the exact details of the Cubs' offer to Ritchey remain a mystery").

7. Neil Lanctot, *Negro League Baseball*, p. 359.

8. "Honor Rube Foster and Other Players," *Chicago Defender*, July 31, 1948; "Memorial Honors 3 of Negro Leagues' Best," *Chicago Tribune*, September 27, 2004.

9. Quincy Trouppe, *Twenty Years Too Soon*, p. 82.

10. Trouppe, pp. 105–106.

11. William Warren, "White Sox Needs Negro Player like Larry Doby," *Chicago Defender*, May 8, 1948.

12. *Chicago Defender*, August 14, 1948.

13. "Honor Rube Foster and Other Players," *Chicago Defender*, July 31, 1948.

14. Janet Bruce Campbell, *The Kansas City Monarchs*, p 119; *Chicago Defender*, September 17, 1949.

15. *Chicago Defender*, March 19, 1949; April 23, 1949.

16. Russ J. Cowans, *Chicago Defender*, September 17, 1949: "A few weeks ago Rickey is quoted as asking $300,000 for the fleet Montreal outfielder, who recently set a new minor league record in stolen bases. However, it is believed that the Sox could buy him for $100,000."

17. "Ban Placed on Ted Radcliffe," *Chicago Defender*, March 5, 1947.

18. *Chicago Defender*, May 6, 1950; May 13, 1950.

19. *Chicago Defender*, July 8, 1950. (The *Defender* states: "it was disclosed this week that the Giants' management had the two players, Louis Clarizio, 20, and Lou Chirban, 19, scouted for more than a year. The man doing the scouting is George Harney former ace pitcher for the Giants back in the 1930's. ... Johnny Talmo was the first to sign, but he later asked for a release from his contract."); *Chicago Defender*, July 29, 1950 — photo caption lists Lou Chirban, Frank Dyll, Stanley Marka and Lou Clarizio as the four white players with the American Giants; James Riley, *Biographical Encyclopedia of the Negro Baseball Leagues*, page 250 (Riley lists Al Dubbetts as a white prospect from Havana, Illinois, who signed with the American Giants in June — thus the total number of white players was six. The American Giants' interest in signing a white player went back to 1949, but was short lived.); "White Pitcher Fails to Last Game," *Chicago Defender*, July 15, 1950 ("A crowd of 9,568, largest attendance

of the current season, saw the Indianapolis club pound four Chicago pitchers for 22 hits.... A large number of fans were out to get a glimpse of Lou Chirban and Lou Clarizio..."); *Chicago Defender*, March 3, 1934. (Al Monroe noted at the time of John McGraw's passing, "Foster felt that one or two good white players on his American Giants would help break down baseball's one black mark; the Jim Crow. That plan did not materialize, something your author has often found time to regret. For one thing the issue never came up in league discussion. But we do know that Foster planned to sound the keynote at the meeting, illness never did permit him to attend. Al Monroe's insight has not been widely reported.)

20. Russ Cowans, "Jesse Douglass Picked as Most Valuable Player in the NAL," *Chicago Defender*, November 11, 1950.

21. "Three American Giant Players Banned by Prexy," *Chicago Defender*, October 1, 1949.

22. Neil Lanctot, *Negro League Baseball*, pp. 372–373 (Lanctot points out that Saperstein had been associated with Winfield Welch for many years, and that Saperstein was also in cahoots with Bill Veeck); "Giants Sold to Welsh for $50,000," *Chicago Defender*, January 13, 1951; Frank A. Young, "Fay Says"—recounts the implausible story that Winfield Welch won $50,000 in France with the Globetrotters, ibid.; "Speed, Hustle Stressed as New Owner-Pilot Puts Giants to Work," *Chicago Defender*, April 28, 1951.

23. *Cincinnati Enquirer*, July 4, 1999.

24. "Paige Holds Barons to One Hit," *Chicago Defender*, May 26,1951; Leroy Satchel Paige, *Maybe I'll Pitch Forever*, p. 240.

25. Hank Aaron, *I Had a Hammer*, p. 54; "Clowns Invade Am. Giants Home Park for a Pair," *Chicago Defender*, June 7, 1952; "Jim Tugerson Tosses 4-hitter in 1st game," June 14, 1952.

26. "Chicago American Giants Prove Sensations of Negro American League Loop," *Chicago Defender*, July 19,1952.

27. "Martin Predicts Better Year for NAL in 1953," *Chicago Defender*, October 18, 1952; "Philadelphia, Chicago Out of 1953 NAL Race," April 18, 1953.

28. John "Buck" O'Neil, *I Was Right on Time*, pp. 190–191.

Bibliography

Newspapers

Baltimore Afro-American
Broad Ax
Chicago Daily News
Chicago Defender
Chicago Whip
Indianapolis Freeman
Indianapolis Ledger
Indianapolis Recorder
Kansas City Call
Pittsburgh Courier
Los Angeles Times
New York Age
New York Times
Otsego Union
Saint Paul Appeal
San Francisco Chronicle
Schenectady Gazette
Seattle Post Intelligencer
Sporting News

Books, Periodicals, Journals

Aaron, Hank. *I Had a Hammer.* Edited by Lonnie Wheeler. New York: Harper Collins, 1991.

Allen, Lee. *The American League Story.* Rev. ed. New York: Hill and Wang, 1969.

Anson, Adrian. *A Ball Player's Career.* 1900. Reprint, Mattituck, NY: Amereon House, 1993.

Bak, Richard. *Turkey Stearnes and the Detroit Stars: The Negro Leagues in Detroit, 1919–1933.* Detroit: Great Lakes Book, 1994.

Bankes, James. *The Pittsburgh Crawfords: The Lives and Times of Black Baseball's Most Exciting Team.* Dubuque, IA: William C. Brown, 1991.

Benson, Michael. *Ballparks of North America; A Comprehensive Historical Reference to Baseball Grounds, Yards and Stadiums, 1845 to Present.* Jefferson, NC: McFarland, 1989.

Campbell-Bruce, Janet. *The Kansas City Monarchs; Champions of Black Baseball.* Lawrence: University Press of Kansas, 1985.

Clark, Dick, and Larry Lester, eds. *The Negro Leagues Book.* Toledo, OH: Society of American Baseball Research (SABR), 1994.

Cohen, Adam, and Elizabeth Taylor. *American Pharaoh; Mayor Richard Daley, His Battle for Chicago and the Nation.* Boston: Little, Brown, 2000.

Cottrell, Robert Charles. *The Best Pitcher in Baseball.* New York: New York University Press, 2001.

Dance, Stanley. *The World of Earl Hines.* New York: Da Capo Press, 1977.

Debono, Paul. *The Indianapolis ABCs: History of a Premier Team in the Negro Leagues.* Jefferson, NC: McFarland, 1997.

Dixon, Phil. *The Negro Baseball Leagues, 1867–1955: A Photographic History.* Mattituck, NY: Amereon House, 1992.

Echevarria, Roberto Gonzalez. *The Pride of Havana: A History of Cuban Baseball.* New York: Oxford University Press, 1999.

Fullerton, Christopher. *Every Other Sunday: The Story of the Birmingham Black Barons.* Birmingham, AL: Boozer Press, 1999.

Heaphy, Leslie. *Shadowed Diamonds: The Growth and Decline of the Negro Leagues.* Ph.D. diss., University of Toledo. Ann Arbor, MI: UMI Dissertation Services, 1998.

_____. *The Negro Leagues, 1869–1960.* Jefferson, NC: McFarland, 2002.

Hietala, Thomas R. *The Fight of the Century: Jack Johnson, Joe Louis, and the Struggle for Racial Equality.* Armonk, NY: M. E. Sharpe, 2002.

Holway, John. *Black Diamonds: Life in the Negro Leagues from the Men Who Lived It.* New York: Stadium Books, 1991.

_____. *Blackball Stars.* Westport, CT: Meckler, 1988.

_____. *The Complete Book of Baseball's Negro Leagues: The Other Half of Baseball History.* Fern Park, FL: Hastings House, 2001.

_____. *Josh and Satch: The Life and Times of Josh Gibson and Satchel Paige.* Westport, CT: Meckler, 1991.

_____. *Voices from the Great Black Baseball Leagues.* New York: Da Capo Press, 1992.

Keetz, Frank M. *The Mohawk Colored Giants of Schenectady*. Schenectady, NY: Self-published, 1999.

Kenney, William. Howland. *Chicago Jazz ; A Cultural History 1904–1930*. New York: Oxford University Press, 1993.

Kleppner, Paul. *Chicago Divided*. DeKalb: Illinois University Press, 1985.

Lanctot, Neil. *Fair Dealing and Clean Playing: The Hilldale Club and the Development of Black Professional Baseball, 1910–1932*. Jefferson, NC: McFarland, 1994.

Lanctot, Neil. *Negro Baseball: The Rise and Ruin of a Black Institution*. Philadelphia: University of Pennsylvania Press, 2004.

Leland, Frank. "Frank Lelands Chicago Giants Baseball Club" (pamphlet). Chicago: Fraternal Printing Co., Major R. R. Jackson, 1909.

Lester, Larry. *Black Baseball's National Showcase: The East-West All-Star Game, 1933–1953*. Lincoln: University of Nebraska Press, 2001.

_____, Sammy Miller, and Dick Clark. *Black Baseball in Chicago*. Chicago: Arcadia, 2000.

Lomax, Michael. "Black Entrepreneurship in the National Pastime: The Rise of Semi-Professional Baseball in Black Chicago, 1889–1915." *Journal of Sports History* 25:1 (Spring 1998).

Malloy, Jerry. "Out at Home: Baseball Draws the Color Line, 1887." *The National Pastime* (Fall 1982):14–28.

_____. "Rube Foster and Black Baseball in Chicago." In *Baseball in Chicago*. Cleveland, OH: SABR, 1986.

Marshall, William. *Baseball's Pivotal Era, 1945–1951*. Lexington: University of Kentucky Press, 1999.

McNary, Kyle. *Ted "Double Duty" Radcliffe: 36 Years of Pitching and Catching in Baseball's Negro Leagues*. Minneapolis: McNary Publishing, 1994.

McNeil, William. *The California Winter League: America's First Integrated Professional Baseball League*. Jefferson, NC: McFarland, 2002.

Mehr, Joseph J. *An Illustrated History of Illinois Public Mental Health Services: 1847 to 2000*. Victoria, BC: Trafford Publishing, 2002.

Miller, Donald. *City of the Century: The Epic of Chicago and the Making of America*. New York: Simon and Schuster, 1996.

O'Neil, John "Buck." *I Was Right on Time*. New York: Simon and Schuster, 1996.

Paige, Satchel, and David Lipman, ed. *Maybe I'll Pitch Forever*. New York: Doubleday, 1962.

Peterson, Robert. *Only the Ball Was White; A History of Legendary Black Players and All-Black Professional Teams*. Englewood Cliffs, NJ: Prentice-Hall, 1970; paperback reprint, New York: Oxford University Press 1992 (page references are to first O. U. P. paperback ed.).

Pietrusza, David. *Major Leagues: The Formation, Absorption and Mostly Inevitable Demise of 18 Professional Baseball Organizations, 1871 to Present*. Jefferson, NC: McFarland, 1991.

Rampersad, Arnold. *Jackie Robinson: A Biography*. New York: Alfred A. Knopf, 1997.

Riley, James A. *The Biographical Encyclopedia of the Negro Baseball Leagues*. NY: Carrol & Graf, 1994.

Rives, Timothy, and Robert Rives. "The Booker T Four's: Unlikely Journey from Prison to Baseball to the Negro Leagues." *Prologue* 36:2 (Summer 2004).

Robinson, Jackie. *I Never Had It Made*. Greenwich, CT: Fawcett Crest, 1972.

Rogosin, Don. *Invisible Men — Life in the Negro Leagues*. New York: Atheneum, 1987.

Schmidt, Ray. "The Golden Age of Baseball." *Chicago History Magazine* 28:2 (Winter 2000).

_____. "The Semi-Pro Team That Beat the Champ." In *Baseball in Chicago*. Cleveland: SABR, 1986.

Spalding, Albert G. *Chicago Amateur Baseball Guide of 1904*. Chicago: A. G. Spalding & Co., 1904.

_____. "Spalding's Official Baseball Guide." Chicago: A. G. Spalding & Co., 1909, 1910, 1911.

Trouppe, Quincy Sr. *Twenty Years Too Soon: Prelude to Major-League Integrated Baseball*. Reprint, Saint Louis: Missouri Historical Society Press, 1995.

Tuttle, William. *Race Riot in Chicago in the Red Summer of 1919*. New York: Atheneum, 1970.

Tygiel, Jules. *Baseball's Great Experiment: Jackie Robinson and His Legacy*. New York: Oxford University Press, 1983.

White, Sol, and Jerry Malloy. *History of Colored Baseball, With Other Documents on the Early Black Game, 1886–1936*. Lincoln: University of Nebraska Press, 1995.

Whitehead, Charles E. *A Man and His Diamonds*. New York: Vantage Press, 1980.

Public Records

Cook County, Illinois, death records.
Cook County Circuit Court Clerk, archives.
U.S. National Archives and Records Service. Draft Records of World War I (Illinois).
U.S. Congressional Record.

Index

Numbers in **bold italics** represent pages with photographs.